Growing Up Without the Goddess

This spiritual memoir is based on my life story, though some of the events have been conflated. I have retained my name, my daughters' names, and my mother and father's last names. A few human and spiritual guides have blessed this book and allowed me to use their real names. I have also used the real names of authors whose books have been important to me on my journey through wounding, depression, discovery, anger, compassion, and healing. Most other names, including place names, have been changed.

My deepest gratitude goes to Bill, who drew me back to the Fatherland this second time and provided a haven for me.

For permission, contact the author through www.growingupwithoutthegoddess.com.

Visit www.booksurge.com to order additional copies.

Growing Up Without the Goddess

A Journey through Sexual Abuse to the Sacred Embrace of Mary Magdalene

Sandra Pope

2008

Growing Up Without the Goddess

Table of Contents

Acknowledgements

In my epilogue, I have thanked those incarnations of the goddess who helped me along the way to recovering joy in my life, but I would like to thank Joan Norton again for her kind, gentle, and wise nurturing and guidance. Without her constancy, I could not have found my way out of the underworld.

Again, I thank Bill, my husband, whose unobtrusive loving presence helped me clear a sacred space to do the work to regain my center, reclaim my life, and heal myself.

To Mary Miears-Cutsinger, whose "Sophia's Dream," adorns the cover of my book, I whisper a soft "thank you" to nighttime stars, wrap that "thank you" in rainbows, and ask the angels to deliver it to her in the Otherworld where she has gone. Mary told me that during a difficult period in her life, she painted "Sophia's Dream" after she received the blessing of this image in a dream. What an affirmation of the presence of the divine feminine, as symbolized by the dove, and of Mary's connection with that presence this painting is! The painting taught me what the book teaches—*She* was always there.

To those at BookSurge who have helped bring this book into the world, I am deeply grateful. To Mabry Morrison, Maggie Hunt, Karen Miller, and especially to Lindsey Ashner, whose knowledge and calm demeanor kept me steady during endless rounds of editing and proofreading and made this book a much better book, I say thank you.

*This spiritual memoir is dedicated to
my daughters Ana and Dani, who inspired me,
and to Mary Magdalene and her daughter,
who guided me on this journey.*

Prologue

I have waited a long time to tell my family's story, waiting for the principals in it to die because my story is tied up with theirs. I supposed our family secrets had created a dark crucible that had humbled these others the way, I hoped, these secrets had humanized me. I did not wish to burden my family further.

Now that I am back in this small Southern town, where the railroad tracks run right through the middle of Main Street and divide the town between black and white neighborhoods almost the same way it did forty years ago, I see that those for whom I bridled my tongue have not died. But they have forgotten their secrets and live as though those cruel events, which warped my life, never happened. The town, too, is unchanged. Its rigidity of consciousness, reflected by its layout, pushed me away the day after I graduated from high school. But I couldn't forget it, and I carried it with me in my wounded heart across the continent to California and through the decades.

Only a few people noticed I had returned to Wisteria, and they quickly forgot that I remained. Recluse that I have become, I spend large amounts of time alone, listening to the pines whisper to the moonlight. Fortunately, my home opens to a large expanse of yard and pines in the back and on one side. Late at night when the neighborhood goes dark, I turn out my lights, too.

I open the verticals in the dining room, and nothing manmade comes into focus, just the outline of clouds and trees or a splash of moonlight on the lawn. I take comfort in knowing that the Milky Way and moon are above—always there even when the clouds block them or the moon is in its dark cycle. I have my dark cycles, too, but everything inside my heart and mind brightens when I look out, and I feel like I must have swallowed the moon on those lonely nights.

During the daytime, I ride around the countryside and welcome the vines that encase decaying tobacco barns and will one day soon drag them down upon the earth and return the materials of which they are made to the land. I apologize to the earth for the abuse it has endured and say a prayer for all those who have suffered and died from the tobacco the land was forced to produce. I talk to the tobacco and ask it to leave or to teach those who grow it how to use its hidden healing properties. I grieve with the land over its current misuse as hog lagoons gouge its surface and foul its water and its air. I rejoice when muscadine grapes, healing balms native to the area, are planted and harvested as nature's antidote to cancer.

Nature became my nurturer early in life, and in this small Southern town where the land is debased, I will let nature continue to nurture me as I tell my secrets to dismantle the power of the old ways over me, so the old belief structures can decay like the tobacco barns. Those old ways harbor poison for my spirit as deadly as the poison that tobacco harbors for the body.

I will tell my story to keep from choosing destructive ways to survive that hide the truth and keep the old stories alive. *I will refuse to create a home in which brothers are allowed to have at their sisters and then grow up to do worse. I will refuse to hold my tongue, like broken wives do, who keep their genteel silence while their husbands rape their children.*

I will tell my family's secrets as an act of survival and ultimately, of love, truth, and compassion that will heal my trust, my body, my spirit, and my family. I will tell my story straight through all my wanderings, all my dreams, visions, and nightmares, and through all my beginnings and endings that have brought me back to this moment of revelation, first given to me so many years ago by the visionary William Blake who wrote, "I must create my own mythology or be enslaved by another man's."

Book 1

Breakdown

Chapter 1

How the Mother Returns

I spent my late teens and early twenties in a rage against the South and the nation of the 1960's. I refused to be a scholarship girl and dropped out of the University of North Carolina in Greensboro after one year, relinquishing two full scholarships. I refused my generation's call to join the flower children. Instead, I aligned myself with hard-line politicos.

I organized community councils and tutorial projects in Black and Lumbee Indian communities in Greensboro and in the Black community of Fayetteville. I was on the payroll of Youth Educational Services, which was funded by Volunteers in Service to America (VISTA). I read Richard Wright, Ralph Ellison, Che Guevara, Mao, Simone de Beauvoir, Marx, Lenin, and any other text I could identify for self-styled revolutionaries of the time.

I helped organize a citywide Black poor people's organization in Fayetteville, which helped get the first Black man elected to the city council. I engaged in community organizing, Saul Alinsky style, and packed board meetings and bureaucrats' offices over concerns like sewage running in the streets in Black neighborhoods and roach-infested housing projects.

I lived in Fayetteville's Quaker House and helped organize the first anti-war demonstration, at which Grace Paley spoke, and I worked to start an anti-war coffee house for solders in that city which is the home of Fort Bragg. I considered going on a Venceremos Brigade to Cuba and almost joined the Weather Underground. Those were my credentials for being a hard-line politico, not an alternative-life-style-flower child. The closest I came to reflection was going to women's consciousness raising groups to explore how the personal is political.

When the liberal money dried up and VISTA no longer paid me, I began working in a beer hall in town. Dressed in short skirts and skimpy tops, I found I liked the work. I would intentionally bend over farther than was necessary when I had to reach to wipe a tabletop. I brought home a serviceman or two to meet my radical, political organizer husband. I ended up in the shower, fully clothed, *but in the shower,* with one of those solders. Even though my husband was home, thought it was just foolish fun, and didn't object, I knew better.

Such was the power of my conditioning to please the patriarchy, I thought, so I quit the job, left my husband, and landed in California where I continued to find the hard-liners, like Vietnam Veterans Against the War, with whom to align myself. I continued to ignore alternative life-style advocates. Even when, disillusioned, I abandoned leftist politics and returned to the mainstream by going to UCLA, got married and had children, I ignored the whole California consciousness movement.

Then, at thirty-two, I had been sure I was ready for motherhood. I had figured out that it would take only 30 degrees of the 360-degree human being I was. I would go to grad school, nurse my baby with one hand and use my other hand to take notes. My mind and my mouth would be my own. When I had twin daughters, wonderful twin daughters, and both my hands were full, those plans changed, and my world changed for the better, but that I did not know on that breeze-free summer morning when I stood behind the door, my back against the wall, hiding from my two-year-old daughters. They were quiet for the first time that morning. I could breathe. Only for a moment did I plan to linger there out of their sight.

There were invisible forces at work in my life, suddenly pulling me in directions I had not planned to go. I had begun to postulate some powerful unseen presence in my unconscious that pulled me off course, much like black holes, invisible though they are, were first known to exist by the effects they had on nearby objects—the wobble of a star's orbit, the sudden disappearance of light.

I felt that wobble within myself. I wanted to run away from everything I knew. *I had done it before.* I didn't know why I had done it other times or why I wanted to do it again. *I needed to collect myself.* I began to look around and reconstruct my world.

Yes, I had remembered to lock the screen, so my daughters couldn't get out. Through the crack in the door behind which I hid, I looked again and saw that they were still quietly playing with Strawberry Shortcake and My Little Pony. *Okay.* Their father, my husband, my second husband, *not my father*, had gone to work, not to death like my father. *Okay, again.* I was not alone. I had his family to replace the one I lost or left behind on the other side of the continent after they lost or left me.

The Past.

I had not thought of the past except to sketch it humorously in stories for my classes at UCLA, stories about the harmless antics of my remembered rustics and my mostly imagined life in the South. And for a couple of years, after these others, *yes, yes, these lovely daughters*, came, but so abundantly and so fast into my life, I had neither thought about nor written about my past, real or imagined.

Then, shattering my reverie and my attempt to reconstruct my world and my life, first Ana and then Dani screamed for her again—for *"Mommy, Mommy, Mommy,"* someone I did not know and not knowing, could not be.

From behind the door, I screamed back at them, as though they could understand the meaning of my words, "Where is *my* Mommy? Where *is* she? Where is *she?*" And then they found me.

For a few moments, we all cried together. The two of them were frightened, and each one held onto one of my pants' legs and called out for *her*. When I touched the tops of their heads and felt their fluffy dandelion-soft hair, love and pain streamed through them to me and me to them, and *I could feel them again with my heart.* My thirty degrees of sanity returned, my heart opened, and I squatted down and curled my arms around them. I pulled both of them to me and hugged them, cooing at them until their crying, and then mine, stopped.

I could call it unwitting on their part, and of course, it was not their conscious selves that called me back to my own early loss, but strange as it seems, they took on the pain of my heart and reflected it back to me. They helped me hear my own hardly audible, whispered internal cry for the *Mother.*

Then full of New Age synchronicity, in which I did not even believe at the time, the phone rang. It was Sharon Weiss, an old friend from Rexon Computers, where I worked until my daughters were born. A few sentences into the conversation, she came to the point.

"Will you go to a guided imagery demonstration with me this evening?"

"Yes, I will." I said. I thought, *guided imagery, whatever that is. But, yes, I'd go. Anywhere but home.* And my heart and mind clouded over with grief and guilt because I did not, I could not, spend every waking hour with my children.

Knowing I would be with Sharon doing something other than mothering, I made it through the afternoon with Ana and Dani. Mercifully, they slept after lunch, and so did I. Their father came home from his job as a research attorney for the municipal court of Los Angeles, and after we put the girls to bed, I told him again that I wanted to go to grad school at Cal State L.A. for a couple of nights a week to get my master's in English. Again, he said he could not take care of the girls alone for two nights a week. I went to join Sharon.

I walked through the door of an alternative medical complex into the small room in a suite where the nameplates on the doors listed psychologists or naturopaths or acupuncturists or some other non-allopathic practitioner. The room in which we gathered was brightly lit by two standing lamps, and eight people had already sat down in two rows that faced the single chair in which Joanna Elgin sat. She was doing something called guided imagery.

"Close your eyes and choose someone you want to talk with. It can be a historical or mythical person or a real person, living or dead," she said, and she began to guide us into what she described as wide-awake dreaming. She reassured us that we were safe, that what we would encounter was within us, and only that for which we were ready would be revealed.

I sought Plato, but he did not appear. I sought William Blake, and he, too, declined my invitation. Wordsworth, with whom I had spent many hours, had nothing to say though he stood with me for a while among the daffodils when I had almost given up because I could not find him at Tintern Abbey. He slipped away from me before I could engage him in conversation.

The landscape shifted. It was barren, as if it had been burned, as if someone had deliberately torched it. A hilly, brown earth stretched out before me, and through it wound a single charcoal-blackened path, the scorched ground of my psyche on which I found myself. It was not the place I wanted to be.

I looked around for trees, for I have loved them all my life. There were none alive. A single burned one appeared on the far horizon. Its trunk was black, and it had three darkened limbs that had escaped total annihilation, though each one had lost its grace. No undulation of branches there. No lovely limbs lifting themselves to heaven to pray. Just pointed, amputated stumps of limbs where branches had once webbed into tendrils and tendrils had put forth leaves.

"Have a conversation in that place you have chosen with the person you have invited in."

A moment's panic. There was no one there for me to talk with. Then on the pathway, as though discarded, a framed black-and-white photograph of my mother, taken when she was about nineteen or twenty appeared. It was a head-and-shoulders' shot, a two-dimensional image under glass that looked out at me, a smiling *Mona Lisa* of a mother.

"Ask whatever questions or for whatever guidance you desire."

There were no questions. There were too many questions. Why did you go? What did I do? Who are you? Where are you? Do you ever think of me? How can I mother my children when I was not mothered? She would not speak, my Mother the Mute.

Time passed.

"Now bring your conversation to a close, open your eyes, and find yourself back here in the room with me. You are safe, and you have brought the wisdom back with you."

I heard Joanna Elgin's words, but the photograph, one I had seen many times in my first remembered home, the Greensboro 1302 Portland Street house, sat upright in its cold metal frame in the middle of the pathway and blocked my return. *My mother.* Pretty. She was *pretty.* That word, that Southern word, described her. Not attractive, that California word that barely obscured its lustful intentions. Not big-screen, Hollywood beautiful. She was innocent. Pretty. Petite.

She wore a buttoned suit jacket that had a dark velvet collar. She wore no blouse beneath its V-neck. No cleavage to cover. A string of pearls encircled her neck, though they had to be fake, for she was a country girl who'd gone to the city of Greensboro, and pregnant though she was at seventeen, she worked in a service station. She and my daddy and my little brother Arthur and I lived in the back of that station until I was almost one. But she looked like a rich woman. Her smile was faint; her eyes, grey mist; and her hair, long and shiny. *A Breck shampoo girl for my mother!*

The sobs, choked back earlier in the day, returned. I had to come back into the room, but I managed to say to her, to my mother who appeared to me only in blacks and whites, flattened into two dimensions, "Look at this landscape. We must plant something here!"

That is how I began to look for *Her* and how she first returned. My search eventually led me to Dorothy Eugenia Morgan, the woman in the photograph and the mother who abandoned me twenty-five years earlier. But that was only the beginning, not the end of the journey.

There would be more interrogations of my personal mother and twenty-five years of unraveling before I found my true source, my true self. This is the story of that unraveling.

Chapter 2

Reunion and First Interrogation

Years before my mother's first visit, I had gleaned the facts of my birth from my birth certificate. I knew enough biology and had enough feminism and defiance, instilled in me by the Sixties, to tell the story of my beginnings my way whenever an unsuspecting person at a party asked where I came from: *"I began as a single egg, formed within one of my mother's ovaries when she was inside my grandmother's uterus. My matrilineal heritage was clearly set before my singular identity was formed when my father's sperm colonized that egg nineteen years after my mother was born. Then nine months later, Baby Girl Pope was born to Dorothy Eugenia Morgan Pope and Bernice Allen Pope. 1948. October 5. 4:20 p.m., EST. Simple. Scientific. Definite. And you?"*

But I wanted to know more than the facts recorded on my birth certificate and interpreted through my agnostic feminism. I wanted to feel the love my mother must have felt for me when I was born and for which I longed daily. I wanted to feel the wholeness such love would bring. Two years had passed since my daughters' cries for *"Mommy, mommy, mommy"* had prompted my search for my own mother. Thirty years had passed since I had lived with her, and twenty years had passed since I had seen her. Finally, I found her, and she was coming to visit me.

She was hardly settled in my home and sitting across the table from me in my house on Lafayette Park Place in the infamous Rampart Division of the Los Angeles Police Department when my hunger for love made me blurt out, "Tell me about my birth."

"Tell me first about your divorce."

"I told you already. He's gone. I asked him to go. It's been over a year. I keep the kids one week, and he does the next. It's called 'joint custody,' and I hate it except that it keeps their daddy in their lives."

I reached for the coffee pot, a hand-poured drip carafe. I held it by the wooden band that dissected the middle of the pot, a touch of elegance in my single-parent life.

"Their daddy's not dead like mine was. I always felt that if mine had lived, my life would have been much better, so I couldn't keep their daddy out of their lives. I even wrote a story about it for a magazine. God knows, maybe their daddy will be a better model of stability for them than I am."

"I bet you miss them."

"Yes-s-s." My voice broke.

Did she miss me all those years?

"When they're not here," I said, "I still leave their nightlight on, and at bedtime, I stand by each of their beds and tell them I love them. I get to see them each weekday because I pick them up from daycare, but it breaks my heart every time I have to drop them off at his house. They love him, but I think it breaks their hearts, too." I paused.

"Well, I sure know how it feels to have your children taken away, Sondra," she said.

My name is Sandra, not Sondra.

"I know, Mom." She was referring to the custody battles she faced when the courts first gave me to my Aunt Dolores and my brother Little Arthur to our grandparents and then later gave my half-sister Debbie and my half-brother Eddie to their father, Big Arthur.

"More coffee?" I asked.

She nodded. I poured our cups full. We fiddled with the creamer to get just the right burnt brown sugar color that signaled perfection.

"Your birth, huh? Well, that's some story. I told them as soon as I saw you that you weren't mine and to take you back. Gol-l-ly. I was young and ignorant maybe, but I had already given birth to your brother Arthur. He was as pretty as he could be with big brown eyes and blond hair, and his skin was a perfect tone of tan. He was all I'd known of newborns, and there you were with your big, old green eyes, way too big for your face. And you had a full head of the darkest black hair, like a grown woman."

She paused. I had to remind myself that it was my mother talking, not some stranger who didn't care about me.

"Well, you did! And your skin was red, red, red. I screamed and hollered and said you couldn't be my young'un. Uh, uh, no way!" And she laughed. "Your brother had been such a pretty baby who looked just like your daddy, but not you. Gol-l-ly! You were plum ugly." Again the pause. "I wouldn't nurse you for three whole days."

She rolled her eyes at me, green eyes like mine, and she pushed her hair back off her forehead. *There*, a widow's peak. Like mine. "She *is* my mother," I thought. Even her wrist joints had the protruding bone I used to call my "bride-of-Frankenstein" joint because it looks like the head of a round bolt lurks there beneath a thin cover of skin.

Then with her thumb and index finger only, she raised her coffee cup to her mouth. The other three fingers fanned upward in a characteristic gesture, one of few I remembered of her, and one I had mimicked unconsciously all my life.

"By then my milk had just about dried up," she added. "But it came back because you wouldn't leave me alone once you got started."

Over the years, she has told me this same story every time I have asked about my birth. It hardly varies in her telling, but its meaning has shifted for me over time. The truths hidden beneath the surface have revealed themselves to me as I have come to know who my mother was and who she wasn't. The first time I heard her tell my story, though, I was hurt only because she thought me ugly.

She sipped her coffee again. We sat at my kitchen table in a small two-bedroom, wooden frame house I rented. She was little, little like a child, not wizened yet like she would be in a couple more decades. She was only fifty-six—younger than I am now—and looked ten years younger.

"I kept asking for my baby, and they kept bringing you. I kept sending you back," she said. "My breasts hurt me so bad, I couldn't stand it. I just cried, and your daddy would rub them for me. It was him who finally made me nurse you."

And in that telling, after all those years of longing for my mother, my father became my hero.

"He brought me a bouquet of roses, yellow roses, and he begged me to nurse you. He got down on his knees like he didn't even do when he asked me to marry him. 'She's mine,' he said, 'and I can't stand to feel her or you suffer any longer.'"

Were those really the words he said? Of course, I couldn't remember hearing the words, but somehow I could see those roses, yellow ones.

"I remember a song about yellow roses. Tell me about the song, the one about the roses," I said, ready to leave this other story of first abandonment.

"Oh, he just sang that to make me mad when he was courting me in Tennessee. He was crazy about me, and he hadn't ever even been to Texas. But he showed up on my porch one night, and sang 'The Yellow Rose of Texas.' He just loved to fool around with me like that."

"How did that song go?" I asked, though I knew. It is a scrap of memory from those early eight years that I had clung to and embellished.

"I don't know if I can remember it, Sondra." (She pronounced it "Sondra" again like her daddy, my Granddaddy Morgan did.) "And there ain't no way I could sing it."

"Come on. Just say the words."

"Well, it was something like 'You can talk about your pretty Mae and sing of Rosalie, but the yellow rose of Texas beats the belles of Tennessee.'" And she did sing it and rather prettily in a voice that twined around the words and twanged, still full of the hills of Tennessee, though she had not lived there for years.

"That's it! That's what I remember."

"Now how could you remember that or anything else, Sondra? You weren't even two when he died."

I was aloft, elevated, still basking in the love of my dad for my mom and through those yellow roses, for me; both baby and bride I became in that undifferentiated love. Only a couple more years would pass before I would visit his grave and place a vase full of red roses on it. The local florist would not have yellow ones.

I finally said, "Oh, I remember lots, Mom." The moniker was new on my tongue and awkward to say and hear in my own voice.

"Well, I don't see how you could remember anything. I sure can't remember back to when I was that young, and I don't think I ever could."

"More coffee?"

As the years have passed, I have learned not to tell all I remember. I have learned not to ask if she wants coffee, too, for she has spoiled her health and now she spoils her sleep by brewing it and drinking it all night. I do believe she is afraid to sleep, and "perchance to dream," for surely her dreams would be night terrors.

I looked across the table at her. I could not see my baby-self sucking at her breasts even though I had nursed my daughters, sometimes both at once. Left to visual imagery alone, I could not believe that my mother's body ever held that bounty or that I was ever given it. But my mouth remembered. My tongue did. This same tongue, that wants to wag and wag until its truths are told, remembered what I knew from that first tug on her reluctant nipple. *My mother feared me.*

My eyes were too big for my baby face, forced open too soon by that first abandonment, searching with intelligence and memory behind them, and still too probing. She knew they sought to wrest my story from her and then to unleash my tongue like a weapon to tell my tale again and again until the telling itself contained and transformed the pain of my fall away from grace and my cruel separation from *Her.*

Chapter 3

Revelations of Memory

My daddy was gone. Dead. Before I knew him well enough, according to my mother, to love him or miss him or remember him. *But that is not how it was.*

I have two distinct memories of him that are my own, ones that no photographs recorded, so I know they are not constructed memories.

The two-story house at 1302 Portland Street in Greensboro sat back about ten feet from the blacktop street. The front of the house had a wide front porch, and a large wooden door opened into the vestibule. There was a stairway to the right and a hall to the left. Doors along the hallway opened into other worlds. *The bathroom was at the end of that wide hall.* I was rushing to reach it. *The bathroom's glass doorknob had come off in my hand.* The light of my imagination struck it, and it blazed like a diamond. Clutching it in one hand, I pushed the door open and got my panties down, so I could make it up on the commode before I wet myself. The door sprang shut in front of my face.

There was my daddy! *Somewhere.* Where? Stretched out there in the bathtub? I was not yet two. He was dead by then. I remembered little else of that event except the color of urine, the yellow bathwater, and was that Daddy in it then and me wondering across all these years why my daddy had peed in the water. And the hot, hot feeling inside me, like I had waited too long and could not hold the urine any longer.

But that's not the kind of memory you recall for your mother when you haven't lived with her for thirty years, and it's only the second time you've seen her in twenty years. I tried the other memory on her first.

"Mom?" That odd syllable again. The irony of the *"m-m-m"* did not escape my trained literary mind, nor did the *"om"* of it leave my throat unnoted.

My Ana and my Dani were asleep. I had put them to bed early because I had wanted these moments alone with my mother on the last day of her second visit, but she was already yawning.

She answered, "Yes, Sondra." It was "Sondra" again, a sound hostile to me, and she said it while she smiled. Or was she sneering? The name and the look on her face reminded me of her father, Granddaddy Morgan, with whom I was forced to live for a couple of years after my mother deserted me. He had called me "Sondra" instead of "Sandra," too, and I had disliked him intensely.

She knew how I felt. I had told her. Gently, I had told her in a phone conversation. The memory of him presented itself in her voice and in her face and in the very sound of my own name. Odd that a name that she had called me all my life brought up his presence as an obstacle that kept me from feeling close to her, but she had to know that it did. *Did she wear that look as conscious armor? Did that explain the slightly jesting tone I sensed?*

"Here's something I do remember," I said.

"What's that?" She cocked her head to one side. Her eyes dared me to speak my truths.

"I remember seeing Daddy in his coffin."

The look again. Then the jester returned. Was that how she had managed to live beyond the legion of tragedies that had been visited upon her? A sneer? A jest? *No heart on her sleeve for daws to peck at?*

She would have grown up hearing that phrase the same as I had, not knowing it was a line from Shakespeare. But she would have known that a daw is a blackbird, and she would have visualized a blackbird's repetitive peck, peck, pecking as it gleaned the fields of everything edible, for she, too, had spent long hours watching nature. She always lived in the country near big bodies of water and spent her days on their shores. This I had learned of her long years away from me, those faraway and long-ago ones in Florida and these more recent years in South Carolina near my sister Deborah. *Was I that blackbird pecking at her heart?*

"Now, Sondra, I am not even sure *I* remember all of that. It was years ago, and I have left it all alone for so long," she said before I could go on recollecting.

Clearly, she did not want to remember my father's death, so why was I bringing *him* to her when I had finally found her again? My father was simply the first of five husbands, all of whom left her by dying, and for all but one of those deaths, she was present to see, to sense, from the very first moment of their departures, the sudden absence of still another she had called *Beloved*. So, why did I speak of death to her when she was there alive and in front of me? Why did I remain in his service?

I could not help myself. I knew she remembered each one of those deaths and those funerals. *I would go easy, and she would speak of this one.* I needed her help, so I could hold onto some piece of him. No, I needed him to help me hold onto her. That first bonding! Him to her, and me to her through him. And then he was gone, and my place began to disappear, too.

"I always imagined it was in the front room of the Portland Street house," I said. "I saw the coffin, a gray metal coffin. The lid was up. And it was cold, I think. But it was August. Something was cold. I must have touched it." Or him. *I must have touched him.*

"That's it?"

She seemed astonished that I should bring up such a tiny fragment of memory, but fragments were all I had at that time. Perhaps she carried my Proustian key, and other memories would come spilling forth at some later time, and the fragments would form a whole.

That particular shard of memory, was not the only fragment I recalled, and I could, I would, eventually tell her the rest, and she would not believe me. But that evening, after decades of grieving alone, I wanted her to join me in grieving the loss of him.

Perhaps the well of her own grief was so deep that she dared not lift the lid to peep inside. Or, perhaps, she had no feelings at all. Perhaps they had died long ago—a slow death for this husband, a longer death for that one.

"No, that's not all I remember," I continued. "I remember that you and Little Arthur and I were in a separate room together for a while." Little Arthur is my older brother, older by two years, and little only in comparison to my stepfather Arthur Blair. Mom married Big Arthur when I three.

"We sat on the bed, and I remember it because we weren't supposed to be on the beds in the daytime. Over the bed was a pale yellow chenille spread that had dark yellow flowers with brown centers."

Creamy brown centers like the color of my daughters' eyes.

"You cried and cried," I said. "That's all of it, all I remember about him," I lied. I would save the bathroom memory for another time.

"Well, I don't know where that could have been. Pope died in the VA hospital in Fayetteville, and the Popes took him to Rockville and buried him there."

Pope. She called my daddy "Pope."

I shrugged.

"Maybe you are remembering when they came to Greensboro after he died and was buried. Daddy Pope came. That's what I called him. Mother Pope came. I loved them both, and when I went to live with them after Pope and I were married, I took them as my own parents. I never knew they didn't love me the way I did them until after your daddy died."

My mother sat across from me. Something quivered. Her lip? Her cheeks? Her face suddenly froze. Her right elbow, which she propped on the table, kept the cup she held steady. She was not going to cry. Her voice quavered for a single instant. Or did it? When I reached to touch her shoulder, she slouched in the opposite direction.

"I'm okay," she insisted. "That was a long time ago, and I am done with it. It took a while to get over the way they came and took Pope's tools from the service station, and Daddy Pope and Mother Pope never asked me once how I was holding up or if I wanted to go back home with them. Now your Uncle Douglas wanted to take Little Arthur away from me, and your Uncle Thomas wanted to take you, but I told them no because your daddy would have wanted me to keep you together, and Sondra, that's what I tried to do, but uh-uh, they sure got what they wanted in the end.

"Daddy Pope stood right on the back porch and didn't give me nothing but a single twenty dollar bill for the tools. They were worth hundreds, and I had nothing! No money, no job, and two kids who were hardly more than babies to raise.

"Maybe that's when you remember us sitting together and me crying. Cause I do remember gathering my children up to me—you and Little Arthur—after they drove off. I remember going inside and just sitting down and wondering what I was going to do. I really thought of them as my own mother and father, and I loved them, and then I was alone with the two of you. And there weren't no way I could go back home to my mother. Not after the way I left her and the homestead. And I wouldn't have wanted to, anyway, not even if I could have."

"How did you leave the homestead?" I asked. I knew Homestead House well because I lived there for two years after she left me when I was eight years old. She left Little Arthur there, too, and she disappeared.

"I was barely seventeen when I married your daddy. Granddaddy Morgan gave his permission—anything to get Pope off the front porch singing." She laughed. "When I left, I took an old rag with me. After the taxicab passed through the big gate at the end of the lane, I asked him to stop," she said.

"Pope thought I was going to close the gate and tried to get out ahead of me. 'Nope,' I told him. 'This is something I have to do myself.' I closed that gate, took that rag out of my purse, wiped both soles of my shoes with it, one at a time, and tossed the rag over the fence into the lane. I knew Mama was watching me from the front room window, and I did it for her to see.

"I got back into the taxi, satisfied. Pope slid in beside me and closed the door. He looked at me strangely, like he didn't know me, like he was puzzled," she said.

"'I ain't taking nothing of these hills with me, not even the dirt on the bottom of my shoes,' I told him. And then we were gone." She stopped talking for a moment. I waited.

"That's how much Mama hurt me," she said, and she looked me straight in the face with eyes that said, "Go no further." Then she spoke, "Go make me some real coffee, not that decaffeinated stuff you've been feeding me, and stop interrogating me."

My daddy died when she was twenty-two. I was almost two. August 23, 1950.

I am sure of the date for I have seen it often of late on the army-issued, small, white marble tombstone that marks his grave in the Rockville Cemetery. Twenty years after this second interrogation of my mama, I have returned to Southeastern North Carolina, the land of my father, and it is from there that I tell this story.

To get to the cemetery, I have to drive past Main Street, which consists of eight or ten buildings, mostly deserted storefronts. After I cross the railroad tracks that dissect this town, too, I go a couple of blocks and turn right onto

Pope Street. That takes me straight into the cemetery. Great Granddaddy John Pope and Great Grandmother Mary Emma E. Pope have the first lot on the left. I consider it my unofficial headquarters for my continued search for myself. I want to believe Great Granddaddy John wants to get to the bottom of the matter, too, but the last time I was there, Great Grandmother Mary Emma motioned me to join her under the mimosa tree, just out of his earshot.

Her hair was the color of a silver-plate photograph, and it was pulled back tightly from her face and wound into a bun at the back of her neck. Her clothes were hand-sewn brown plaids, and the main seam around the neckline was crooked, as though whoever made the dress was not an expert seamstress. She was not yet the matriarch, the woman of 102 she was when she died, but a younger woman, closer to my own age. Her eyes were silver, too, but they held banked fires, old anger smoldering inside them.

"Don't bother asking Daddy John what he knows because he don't know nothing. He never let himself see anything that would've made him have to speak badly of anybody. I guess he kept his innocence that way, but he turned a blind eye and deaf ear so many times, he darn near gave everybody permission to be as bad as they wanted to be."

"And you? What can you tell me?"

"Comb through your memories. And when your memories fail you, mind your dreams."

Chapter 4

Street Urchins, Garage Games, and a Mother by Any Other Name

My mother was coming to visit me again. It would be her third visit. Five years had passed since the second visit, and though we talked occasionally on the phone, we had not grown close like I imagined we might. I was busy teaching and being the best mother I could be to my daughters. I was in therapy learning to follow my dream guidance, and though I journalled some about the past, I had not found the answers my heart was looking for. As I prepared for her visit, I did more than clean the house. I gleaned the field of my memories from that other life. I wanted to be ready to ask questions, to follow the threads I knew existed that would help me unravel my past and explain my brokenness.

I remembered how the old white stucco two-story house in Greensboro had an enormous yard, large enough to hold my imagination until I was six, and we moved onto a piece of land in the country near Burlington that prepared me for the grander idylls of nature that were to come in the central Tennessee mountains. I lived in that Greensboro house before and after my daddy died, and I saw him in the bathtub and in his coffin in that house. But he had died by the time I was two, and I still lived in the 1302 Portland Street house, the one address I will always remember of the thirty-some places I have called home in my lifetime. I had found my way back to 1302 Portland Street in imagination, in dream life, and in reality many times over the years. I believed it held some secret that was mine, at last, to know.

Mine seemed like a carefree childhood, filled with games and adventures I shared with my blond-haired, brown-eyed brother Little Arthur who was two years older than I. We called ourselves Jim (that was he) and Tim (that was I) when we played in those wide yards and in the dirt-floor garage, which housed no car, and was our playhouse.

Later when Debbie and Eddie came along and became our charges during daylight hours, we called ourselves Jim and Tim and "them" because we didn't want to confuse the younger ones by giving them their own adventurer names. And there were the garage games we excluded them from, somehow knowing, even as young as we were, that we had been inducted into mysteries that children were generally excluded from. We wanted to protect them in ways we had not been protected.

The giant pecan trees were bowers at whose bases we drew floor plans in the dirt in dry weather. In rainy weather, mud puddles became moats we had to cross or oceans where hurricanes raged. We gathered our own food from among the acorns and pecans and various greenery the yard held from spring to winter, and we supplemented this occasionally with butter and sugar sandwiches when no one was looking or when the adults were away at work. I decorated the table with flowers from the mimosa tree that grew on a little strip of land outside our gate.

Late one summer we moved from foraging to planting our food when I found the seeds marked "tobacco," and located the perfect place to plant them. The garage eaves spilled extra rain into our tobacco "garden," a single row of seeds we had planted right where the water splashed and gullied the ground. Mama had laughed at us when she saw where we had put the seeds.

"Why'd you choose that place right there?" she asked and smiled. She was pregnant with Eddie, and her belly rode out in front of her, prancing beneath her flowered maternity dress. That big belly put me in mind of the hind parts of a photograph pony I'd gotten very familiar with as I chased it all over the neighborhood early that summer, begging for rides.

Mama was four feet and ten inches tall, and Eddie weighed ten pounds and eleven ounces when he was born. With him that big and strutting around inside her before he was born, she was more baby than she was mama in the late months of her pregnancy.

"The water runs right down there," Little Arthur said. He was explaining to Mama why we chose that place for our garden. That made me mad, and I stopped gazing at Mama's belly and daydreaming about the pony.

Arthur hadn't made the discovery about the rainwater! I had. One day I had slipped away from the garage where we played our secret games. It was about to rain. I had heard the thunder, and I was trying to make it to the house before the shower started, but I changed my mind. I just wanted to be out in the rain. I have always loved the fresh smell of earth after the first raindrops wash the sky clean of a city's odors and release the earth's pent-up sweet smell of soil and grass and leaves.

I didn't make it to the house before that summer cloudburst, but I didn't go back to the garage either. I stood beneath the eave with my back pressed against the garage siding, and I stayed dry except for my feet, which were barefoot all summer, anyway.

I watched the water run off the roof and drop onto the ground. Within no time, it puddled. The sun never disappeared entirely. When it came out full blast, I saw the reflection of blue sky and white clouds pooling in the long puddle at my feet. The next day the water had disappeared into the ground, taking that other world with it. In my child's mind, with sunshine and water present, that place became a realm where things would grow, so I talked Little Arthur into planting there.

Mama listened as Little Arthur explained about the water. I was silent even though it had been my discovery, that he liked so much, he took for his own. It would be that way often in my life. I would see things and say them, and the men in my life would pretend the ideas were their own. After one of my husbands made a book out of some of my insights, and it carried his name only, I learned to keep my thoughts to myself.

"Well, we'll see what happens to your garden," my mama said, and she walked off smiling to herself, one hand holding onto her prancing belly.

Hot summer days would sometimes find us inside the garage conducting our experiments with the puppy or out among the trees plotting adventures. Summer evenings found me refusing to lay aside my two-wheeled scooter. I took many a dare to ride it down the huge blacktop hill in front of our house, even after the smudge pots had been put out at night, so cars would know where the wet tar was.

I stayed out late to run among the lightning bugs and to use the bow and arrow that Barry, the boy across the street, had taught me to make out of green switches. Because my brother sponsored me and because Barry liked me, the older boys let me run with them through the twilight neighborhood, stopping now and then to knock out windowpanes.

We would lie in the hedges and wait for a lamp or light to come on in one room and illuminate a window, and then we would aim at another window that was still darkened. The crash of broken glass would send us racing through the back ways, laughing hysterically. As each summer day passed, we got bolder and wilder, and no one seemed to notice. Only fall and the return of school and shortened days checked our rush toward delinquency.

I looked for the seedlings to sprout for the first few weeks. The rains came again and again, and I saw the other worlds reflected time and again. The seeds stayed buried, and the plants never grew, but I held fast to the certainty that they were blooming in that other realm. *Even that early in life, I had begun to search the invisible worlds for my lost, my other self.*

As Mom's third trip had neared, I had gathered and sorted these and other memories. As my anxiety increased, I also sought the advice of a wise older woman. I was uneasy because I had been disappointed with Mom's previous visits. In truth, I was angry.

"Think of her as an older, interesting woman and not as 'Mother,'" the wise older woman told me. "That way you can get to know and appreciate her as a person."

I would try to take her advice. The words "Mother," "Mom," "Mamma," "Mommy," and all their derivations pitched me into pits of darkness and depression. It was the era when women's writing kept coming to the fore, and I devoured all of it, even while I felt angry that my name was not listed among the authors. I learned to accept the lives of others and their ways of making sense as guidance. They spoke for the collective, for those like me and others who could not find their voices, and I let those writers and my dreams teach me what was missing from my life and teach me to mother my daughters without wounding them.

I wrote some during those years in between my mother's visits. I even published a few articles, a single short story, a poem or two.

But mostly I taught and I mothered. I looked for models of mothers who remained with their children because I had no such mother in my life. Unconsciously, I looked for men I could afford to leave the way my father left me.

My daughters were ten years old, and I had been divorced for seven years from their father, my second husband. They were with him that night when my mother arrived, and I had not closed their door or left their light on like I usually did at night when they were not with me.

I had not left the usual Friday-night-without-my-daughters' message to myself on my answering machine to cheer me up. *She* would be with me. This older, interesting woman, who just happened to be my mother. She had come to me because I had asked her to help me. My daughter Dani was scheduled to have surgery to repair damage done to her by an inept surgeon when she was just five days old.

"I have another memory from that 1302 Portland Street house," I said after we'd settled into chairs in the living room. We each held our full, creamed cups of coffee, a regular ritual for us by that visit.

"Oh? Well, what do you think you remember this time?" she asked.

She is pretty, this little woman. And she poses more than reposes on the chair. She sits as if she is being photographed or expects to be watched by eyes that are appraising her as a woman, as a sexual being. I noticed that earlier in the day when I took her to Venice Beach, where I had lived for eight years before my babies were born. She walked out onto the sand in her aqua jogging suit, the wind in her hair until she pulled the hood up over her head. She wrapped her arms around herself, rather sensuously hugging herself.

This woman, who had never read a sonnet, and whose left leg was longer by an inch than her right one because of scoliosis, moved in iambic pentameter. She looked this way and that way. At first, I thought she was looking northward to survey the deep purples that the Santa Monica Mountains were gathering unto themselves as the sun was setting over the ocean. Then I thought she was looking southward to inspect the jetties jutting out into the water or to see what solo practitioners of Tai Chi perched on the far reaches of those jetties, or maybe she was even looking up into the sky to track the contrails of jets going hither and yon.

But as she gathered her hooded jacket about her more snugly and turned to me, she said, "We seem to be about the only ones out here this evening, Sondra."

It was neither fear nor relief at being alone that I heard in her voice. It was disappointment, disappointment that all the beauty she had put on display would go unnoticed. Perhaps she had not always been that way, but I remembered the dresses that she had hidden in the back of the closet at the Festival Lake house when I was about seven years old.

She admonished me not to tell Big Arthur about them. They were beautiful dresses that she called "sun dresses," and for years I thought she called them that because the colors were brilliant, like sun-borne rainbows caught up in the fabric of those frocks. She must have been gorgeous when she wore them.

Perhaps she had always been on display. As she lounged on her chair in my living room, her awareness of others, even when there was none other than myself, was omnipresent. How odd to see her at sixty-two, preening that way. Perhaps age, then. Perhaps like Lessing's protagonist in *The Summer Before the Dark,* that was her last hurrah. How little I knew of aging then, and how much less I knew of my mother.

"Well," I began. "Here's what I remember. I remember Aunt Shirley came to stay with us. And Annette, her daughter came, too. Did Aunt Shirley work outside of the house or did she just babysit us?"

"She stayed at home to help with you children while I worked most of the time she was with us. She was two years older than I was, and I was close to her." This older woman was letting herself be interviewed.

"But where was her husband?"

"She had already left Taylor by then. That was his last name. I don't remember his first one. He was a rough man, and she wasn't about to let him beat her anymore once Annette was born and got some years on her and knew what was happening."

I smiled, thinking of Aunt Shirley trying to protect her daughter. "Well, Mom, Aunt Shirley caught me and Arthur and Annette once, and she switched us all three. I remember that," I said.

"She'd given all of you baths and found you playing outside in the dirt. I remember it, too."

"It wasn't quite like that," I said.

"Oh?"

"Not quite. But she did spank us. I remember I thought it was so unfair," I said.

"Well, you got yourself dirty, and she had other things to do besides bathe you again. It might have been when she decided she wanted to work some, too, and she took that job at the bakery. That really beat her down because she couldn't keep up with all those cakes coming through that she had to ice by hand."

"That sounds like an episode of *I Love Lucy*," I said.

"Maybe, but it wasn't funny at the time. It was hard work, and she had to work from midnight to six in the morning and then come home and take care of you, so I could work." She stopped. She laughed. "Well, actually, it was funny to hear her talk about it *after* she quit. But while it was happening, she was a wreck."

"But, Mom—"

After my mouth opened like a baby bird's beak and formed that monosyllable, I realized I had forgot and used the "Mom" word. I rushed through the sound and to the next sentence. "It wasn't just because we got dirty that she spanked us so hard. It was because none of us was wearing any underpants. She had forgotten to put them on us."

"Well, Sondra, I never knew anything about that."

"I never knew anything about that," my mother would often say in response to one of my memories, and I would wonder how such things could occur without a mother knowing and remembering.

I remembered.

I was four. My daddy, my protector, was dead. I lay without moving in the cradle, as still as the puppy had lain when we poked and prodded at it. *How do children learn such things?*

I grumbled about being the first one to lie down in the cradle like the puppy had. I wanted to be the doctor. But once I was settled in, I lay there, without questions, without complaints, without panties, and saw—*what? Lightning bugs flitting through the dark blue dusk? The green of the grass turning indigo as nighttime came to claim it? The world by Georgia O'Keefe as the huge trunks and branches of the pecan and black walnut trees shafted toward the heavens? Or did I close my eyes and let the kaleidoscope of colors come, like I did nightly after that?*

How was such passivity possible? The twigs, the bobby pins, pushed up inside me by my six-year-old brother Arthur and my four-year-old cousin Annette must have hurt.

Why did the puppy not move?

Did Aunt Shirley call out to us? Did she turn a corner after doing the dishes—after scraping the leftover spaghetti with green pepper and meatballs in it, *the kind my mother made,* after scraping it off the plates, washing and rinsing and drying each dish, and the glasses and silverware, too, did she, tired as she was, turn a corner into the living room and see there on the couch—the stack of underwear? Did she chuckle to herself and think it would make a cute little story to tell my mother the next day?

And where was my mother that evening? She was a presser working the day shift at Blue Bell in Greensboro during those years. Was she out with Big Arthur—Debbie's father, who she wouldn't marry until after Debbie was born and looked just like him, so she could prove to Arthur's mother, Eula Blair, that she was no slut?

But let me tell the story of what Aunt Shirley did. *The story my mother didn't know* because it didn't go the way Aunt Shirley thought it might when she first picked up those three pairs of underwear, chuckled, and went to find us.

"Sandra? Arthur? Annette? Where are you? Come on in right now. It's getting dark." That's how she would have handled it. She wouldn't have called out into the neighborhood that she had forgotten to put our panties on us.

We lingered. No one had ever intruded upon Arthur and me when we conducted our experiments in the garage or played behind it in the tall weeds. We had a feeling of sanctuary when we entered those places. And Annette was a part of our adventures then. That night we were outside the garage, on the side farthest from the house, where we felt free to play our games. Perhaps, like Adam and Eve, we felt completely safe and absolutely within our rights to do what we were doing because we did not know it was wrong.

Aunt Shirley would have called to us several times, but we were transported. It must have been like later in life when I never heard the traffic roar or the children cough until after the lovemaking was over. We probably did not hear her until she was upon us.

Annette and Little Arthur must have fled. Aunt Shirley stood over me. I was still in the cradle with my thighs spread and my legs hanging over the sides of the cradle. My dress was pushed up, and she saw my nakedness. She saw, and I read her face and knew she, too, knew this secret that I thought we had invented.

In the moment after discovery, and before Aunt Shirley yanked me by one arm to my feet, her face and her voice told me she was enraged at what we knew. She seared my bare bottom when she slapped it with her bare palm. She nearly wrenched my arm from its monstrous socket with one hand while she beat my bottom repeatedly with her other hand.

What did those first few airborne steps feel like to me? How did my confusion of mind, that she should know what we invented, mix with my broken heart that she should hate us for knowing? And how did both of those terrors combine with the pain (or was it pleasure?) between my legs as she yanked me across the yard, my feet leaving the ground as I was running in the air from her?

The terror and, yes, the pain *(it was pain)* were audible. Sounds. But not words. Screams. I was screaming.

"Oh hush up! I can't be hurting you that badly."

Was she?

Would she discover bloody twigs or bobby pins later on after she had found and whipped my accomplices? I don't remember. I do remember she would come to me later when I was in bed to make sure I still had my panties on.

I did not tell my mother the whole story of that evening. Nor did I tell her how I sucked the thumb of one hand, and with the other hand I pushed this thing or that thing up inside me each night for years after that evening. I would lie in bed, full of fingers or pencils or crayons, and images would fill my mind, images I later learned to classify as pornographic. I would press my eyes shut and wait for the kaleidoscope of colors to come again to chase away my terrors and to invite in sleep.

Book 2

The Search

Chapter 5

Exotic Rides and Erotic Cards

The only birthday I remember at the Portland Street house was my fourth. I don't recall the birthday itself, but I do remember the announcement of preparations because I was riding the mimosa tree that grew at the edge of the road. The tree's trunk split and went in two directions about a foot-and-a-half off the ground, and the smaller of the two divergent trunks was limber and easy for me to climb out onto. My weight made it bow back toward the earth, and the young tree made a good rocking horse for me when I pushed off with my feet and then wrapped my legs around the branch, bouncing toward heaven.

The mimosa flowers had no fragrance, but their exotic coral blossoms spiraled outward from a spidery center into pedals that looked like frothy pink icing as they flounced back and forth beneath the fronds of ferns that were their leaves. I don't know who first discovered that ride. I only remember solitude and pleasure on the mimosa at the beginning with no line of others waiting for turns and chiding me to hurry up. It was the pleasure of any child on a rocking horse or any child who has pleaded long enough and got a grownup to give him or her a horsie ride on a knee. Innocent play, it seemed, that made the blood rush to my head, let the wind blow through my hair, and created a miracle of color and motion as the flowers and the ferns helped me play hide and seek with the world that was visible from 1302 Portland Street.

There is a little knob there on the branch where a twig has splintered off. If I position myself directly over it, it will hurt only a little. Just at first. I slip my panties away from that place between my legs and situate myself just so. My feet touch the ground. I push off with all my four-year-old might. I fly upward, but I squeeze my legs tightly around the branch, and I ride it downward toward the ground. I tell myself the pain will go. It's almost gone. The other feeling comes. I push off again. It still comes. I have almost finished when the voice calls out to me.

It comes from nowhere. I hear it. I know it. I don't want to answer it. Not yet. I am almost there. I hear it again. I look toward the dark porch, beneath its roof, see the voice coming from the dark rectangle of window. It is hers. My mother's.

"Sondra, do you hear me?"

Yes, yes, almost yes.

"What kind of cake do you want for your birthday?"

My birthday! The thought of it is news to me. I have a birthday. I remember none before this one.

"Do you want devil's food or white cake?"

I do not push off this time when my feet touch the ground. "Devil's food cake!"

"Okay."

"Is today my birthday?"

"No. It's tomorrow, but I wanted to bake the cake today."

The voice is gone. And my ride is over for the day.

Who knows why one moment lingers in memory more than other moments? Was it the voice calling out from the black rectangle that triggered the fear of discovery that seared these moments into my mind? Perhaps it was just too much stimulation all at once—the feeling of flying with the wind, the power to make the world come and go, the shivers between my legs, accompanied by the thought of chocolate—that made this wrinkle in my brain, that connected that particular path between neurons that allows me to remember *in my body* the pain and the pleasure of that day so long ago and to wonder when and how I first discovered that particular pleasure and connected it with submission to pain.

During her third visit with me in Los Angeles, I decided to see if my mother remembered that day.

"Do you remember my fourth birthday?"

"There were so many of you and so many birthdays, Sondra!"

"I know. I only remember that one from all of my childhood. I don't even recall birthdays in high school when I was with Dolores." Dolores was my father's youngest sister, and when I was eleven, the Superior Court of the State of North Carolina declared my mother unfit and awarded my custody to Dolores.

"She probably didn't do anything for you, not like *I* would have done," my mother said.

No, Mother, not like you, you who left me at the Homestead House for two years and never wrote and never called.

I ignored her complaint for the moment. I wanted to talk about me, not about her.

"When I was about to turn four, I was out front on that mimosa tree that grew near the street. You called to me from the house, from the front room window. I couldn't see you in the window, but that's where your voice came from, and you asked me what kind of cake I wanted for my birthday, and I answered you."

She laughed. Her laugh was sly. "I bet you wanted chocolate."

"Oh, yes. I do remember I chose devil's food. I don't remember my actual birthday. I don't remember you baking the cake or me eating it. I just remember you asking."

"Well, Sondra, I always celebrated my children's birthdays. Well, *when they were with me.* I couldn't do much once you were at Dolores's."

I didn't ask why she did nothing when I was at Grandmother Morgan's. Memory fails me more and more. Maybe she did.

"Do you remember anything else about that day?" I asked.

"No, but it doesn't surprise me that you wanted chocolate of some sort. I bet you still love it," She paused. Her eyes were mischief-laden. "But I bet you don't love it as much as you loved that Ex-lax the time you and Annette Taylor ate my medicine!" She laughed the sly laugh again until it became a full-blown boisterous hoot. She even snorted a little the way I do sometimes, when I suddenly find something funny. It is not a pretty habit. "Do you remember that?"

I did, but I knew she wanted to tell it anyway. It is one of her small repertoire of stories in which I star—or at least co-star—so I let her tell it, glad to have been held in memory at all.

It is a simple story, and she tells it simply—how she gave me a half-dollar and sent me to the store with Annette Taylor when we were both about five years old to buy her some Ex-lax.

"You must've eaten the whole package on the way home between the two of you."

"I think I ate most of it," I said.

"Well, I didn't punish you even when Aunt Shirley wanted to. I told her just to wait until you started going to the bathroom and that would be punishment enough!"

"Did you call a doctor to find out what to do?"

"Well, Sondra, there weren't nothing a doctor could do. You had already eaten the stuff. There was only one way for it to come out. All I had to do was wait." She snorted again. That story really entertained her. "Umm-umm-umm! You just loved chocolate, more than anything else, and I bet you still do."

I had looked at the half-dollar with awe. It filled the whole palm of my little hand. I had never held anything bigger than a nickel or worth more than a dime. I gave the clerk the paper with the word written on it. I said the word, too. "It's for excellence."

The woman laughed. "Oh, is it?" she asked. She returned with a small square blue box.

"Let's see what's in it," I urged Annette Taylor. I was jealous that my mama was going to get something that cost so much. I opened the blue box and pulled out the foil covered—chocolate! Chocolate! It looked like a miniature square Hershey's bar with lined pieces that broke off easily into tiny squares.

"Let's eat some," I urged.

"We'll get in trouble."

"Why should she have it all to herself?" I broke off two squares for me and one for Annette Taylor. I was used to eating a whole Hershey's almond bar by myself. I seldom chose the plain, lined Hershey's bar because it was made sharing too easy. I was left unsatisfied by such a petite square of this new darker chocolate. By the time we reached our front steps where my mama stood waiting for us, we had only two squares left, and I had eaten at least two squares for every one I gave Annette Taylor.

"You're right," I said to my mother. She would leave my interrogations and me the next day. Though we would talk and visit some, I wouldn't have the courage to ask her more questions for years. I would seek instead the secrecy of therapy and the privacy of dream analysis. And I would go on a search to learn more about my father, thinking to find my protector there.

"Right about what?" she asked me.

"I do love chocolate just as much now. I even steal candy out of my children's Easter baskets when they go to sleep. I keep eating whatever is around until it is all gone. That's why I don't buy it."

"Green-eyed greedy gut," she said and looked into my lime-green eyes and laughed.

At forty-three years old, five feet, six inches tall, I weighed 112. I ran, swam, worked out in a gym, and watched everything I ate to ensure I stayed that way. *Why did I starve myself?* My mother still grinned at me, pleased with her nutshell recapitulation of my character as "greedy."

"Sing that little green-eyed ditty for me," I said.

"Oh, it was nothing, Sondra."

"Come on."

"It wasn't really a song, but it went something like this: 'Brown eyes pick a pie, run home and tell a lie. Green eyes, greedy gut, eat the whole world up. Blue eyes, beauty spot, prettiest baby mama's got!'" She laughed.

I forced a smile, a higher ground kind of smile, one meant to encompass her ignorance and forgive it.

"I didn't mean nothing by it, Sondra. It was just a fun little song."

"I remember you singing it to Debbie." Debbie had clear blue eyes.

"I reckon I might have."

"She was your lucky child, right?" My mother is a small-time gambler, according to my half-sister Deborah Ann Blair, born at 7:11 a.m. on 7/11 in 52 (5+2=7). With numbers like that, plus blue eyes and blond hair and beauty that shone forth the moment she was born, she was my mama's favorite in those early years. And it was for her that my mother sang that song.

I do believe my mama is wrong about what color my eyes were when I was born. They must have been blue or gray or even brown. It was envy that turned them green, envy that began the moment Debbie was born or the moment I first heard that little ditty sung by my mother as a lullaby to this newcomer.

My daddy was dead, and now my mama was taken from me, too. With Debbie came her father, Big Arthur, a few months later when it was clear to everyone, including Eula, Big Arthur's mother, that this was a Blair baby. Eula moved into the apartment across the hall in the Portland Street house and became my Grandma Blair. Her sister Ida and her husband Will moved into the upstairs apartment and became my Aunt Ida and Uncle Will.

It was all too sudden for me. What Debbie's birth did offer me was my freedom to continue to roam the neighborhood because Debbie held my mother in thrall. I took my freedom. I clung to my brother Little Arthur, and even under the noses of all those adults, he and I became wilder and wilder.

By the time Debbie was one and walking, Mama would be back at work at Blue Bell, and Debbie would become our sometimes-charge when Grandma Blair wanted her to play outside a while. Until then, Arthur and I roamed the neighborhood and explored the belongings of our new family when they were at work and when my mama was too busy to know where we were. We also went to each other for comfort when Big Arthur beat one or the other of us. I was his target most days.

I remained jealous of Debbie for years. Once I reached into her crib to get the teddy bear. *It was not hers. It was mine.* Her cries demolished the silence and destroyed my efforts to be quiet and not wake my mama up. Mama came at me in a flash, rising from the bed instantly.

"You just wait till Big Arthur comes home, and I tell him how you have been behaving. You know I am too weak to do anything about it, but he will." She was pregnant with Eddie.

I ran out of the house and sat on the ground on the far side of the garage where I would not be visible from the house. The wall was warm against my back; the earth, cool beneath my legs. Tears were hot on my cheeks, and as they dried, my face felt tight like it had shrunk.

"Let me show you what I found." Little Arthur had materialized and stood before me. His dark brown eyes sparkled in his nut-brown, suntanned face. His blond hair was white like Mama's sheets hanging on the line to dry in the summer sun.

"No. Leave me be."

"I'll go by myself and see, and you'll be sorry."

"Go on."

"It's upstairs in the pantry."

"What?"

"Come see."

I did not speak.

"I'm going." He ran off.

I jumped up. "Wait."

He had stopped for me right around the corner, just out of my sight. I was in such a hurry to catch up, I ran past him. He laughed. "I knew you'd come."

Up the stairs we crept. I beat him to the door. I was already turning the metal knob when he reached my side. "Me first!" I said.

"Sh-h-h! Uncle Will is sleeping." Uncle Will worked nights then, and he slept during the day.

"Okay, you first."

Arthur led the way to the pantry. My bare feet felt the cool linoleum blossom into grand red roses. Arthur stood by the door to the pantry. He opened it and stepped inside.

I followed him. He reached to pull the door shut behind us.

"Don't close the door." I was already afraid of closed-in spaces.

"He'll hear us," he said, but he left the door cracked.

He moved a Bell jar of pickled peaches aside and reached behind a box of saltines. I was hungry and expected he had found some candy treats.

What he pulled out was a deck of cards.

"So what?" I said right off, disappointed. I liked cards well enough, especially the face cards with the queens and kings in profile, one eye staring straight out at you all of the time. The backs of the cards with their intricate swirls and blue or red patterns intrigued me more than the games we played with the cards. To entertain myself while we played boring card games, I'd stare at the swirls, close my eyes, and press my fingertips lightly against my eyelids. I'd lose myself in the colors and brilliance until Arthur would pinch me or punch my arm and tell me it was my turn to play. But I felt cheated. I didn't want to play cards. I turned to go.

"Wait. These are special." Arthur flipped one of them over.

I turned and looked.

Arthur was grinning at me.

Sprawled on a couch, the woman pictured on the back of the card had nothing covering the red-nippled, round breasts that spilled off her chest, one flowing one way, and the other flowing in another direction. They looked nothing like I imagined breasts would.

I had seen my mother nurse Debbie. Always she covered herself and part of Debbie's face with a baby diaper or blanket, so I couldn't see everything. I knew what was beneath the cloth, even though I didn't really know what it looked like. Once, in the garage, I had tried to get our puppy Brownie to put his mouth on my flat chest, but he licked my face and barked instead.

One full-breasted woman followed another as Arthur flipped through the deck. Something familiar was simmering inside me, *pain and pleasure together again as I felt the mimosa vibrate through my body,* and the same burning feeling, that the tears had brought earlier to my eyes, rose in my chest. It tightened.

"I can look at them whenever I want, but you can't," Arthur said.

"Cannot," I said.

"Can to. Uncle Will said so."

"Did not."

"He did, too. He was looking at them when I came up to bring him a baloney sandwich, and he showed them all to me. He even showed me where he kept them."

"Well, I get to see them, too, then."

"No, he said it was just for me and not to tell anyone."

"But you did."

"Well, yeah, but just this once cause you were crying."

I remembered Mama's threat. "Do you think I will get a whipping?"

He was looking down at one of the ladies on the card. He finished looking, put the cards back into box and then into their hiding place. He took the saltine box from my hands. I had taken out four crackers, two for him and two for me.

"I don't want to be whipped again."

He put the box in place and then the Bell jar of pickled peaches. They were not open, or I would have had me some of them, too. We heard a cough from the other room.

"Sh-sh-sh!" Arthur said.

We waited as motionlessly as the jars that lined the pantry shelves. We heard no more sounds from the other room. We crept back through the linoleum rose garden and out the door.

When we reached the bottom of the stairs, he turned to me and answered my question.

"Probably," he said. "Probably. Unless she forgets to tell him. Let's be good the rest of the day, and maybe she'll forget."

It was still early morning. Maybe he was right. I handed over his ration of two saltines and bit into one of mine. It tasted salty like my cheeks did when I stretched my tongue up until the tip of it touched them.

"You remember what tomorrow is?" he asked.

"Is it my birthday?"

He laughed. "It's your first day of school."

Chapter 6

Love and Loathing on the First Day of School

Clara J. Peck Elementary School had a wading pool with only three or four inches of water, which filled it to the brim, but to me it was infinitely deep. How else could those clouds and that faraway sky be contained in it? Scared though I was of falling into it, I stepped up onto the narrow brick retaining wall and walked the length of it behind Arthur on that first day of school. There was plenty of room for me to walk if I watched where I placed my feet. Arthur raced ahead. I looked down past my brown sandals into the water. I placed one foot in front of the other and walked cautiously.

I would begin and end most school days that first year by making the journey slowly and methodically around the pool's perimeter, rather like a religious celebrant in a walking meditation. When clouds scudded by, they dizzied me. When the summer sun struck the plane of water, it blinded me.

I would gaze at the surface of water, intrigued by the other world where clouds and trees and sky shimmered and shimmied. Only when the nearby oak trees shed their autumn leaves, and the wind blew some of them onto the water where they floated for a day or two before they sank, only then did I find bottom, only then did the two worlds collide.

I had heard church bells often on Sundays, but never a school bell before. When it rang on that first day of school, Arthur hopped off the pool wall and called to me.

"Come on or you'll be late. That's the warning bell."

Across the school yard boys and girls—who had been gathered in small groups on the ground playing marbles or lined up for turns on the merry-go-round or had reached for the sky with their feet as they swung—rose and walked or ran toward the building. I caught up with Arthur. Together we entered the hallway. The sickly smell of old wood, exposed too long to moisture, combined with the decades-old odor of bodies and spoiled milk. I felt ill.

"That's your room," he said. He pointed, turned down another hall, and was gone.

My teacher, Mrs. I. Smith—"not *Smit*, but *SmiTH*"—had long hair that curled up slightly when it reached her shoulders. Her style of dress was precise, her speech crisp, and her blue eyes enormous. We were instant zombies for her. We sat when she told us to, we rose as she directed, and we stood at the back of the room lined up behind long rectangular tables because that is what she had said to do. She stood next to a man who wore a white lab coat and was teaching us about brushing our teeth. I was ready to learn. Most of all, I was ready to please this wondrous person, this teacher, from whom I could not take my eyes.

"How many of you run water over your toothbrush after you have put the toothpaste on?" the man in the white coat asked. "Raise your hands if you do."

Well, I did run water over my toothbrush when I bothered to brush my teeth at all, so I raised my arm up fast with my hand waving, and my arm wagging like a happy dog's tail at Mrs. I. SmiTH! Many others raised and waved their hands also.

"Well, you all are wrong to do that!" he said enthusiastically.

All hands dropped instantly from the air, as if a giant eraser had removed them all at once.

I felt the excitement of finally being a first-grader and the disappointment of being wrong on the very first day of school collect there between my legs.

I saw the corner of the table in front of me as I stood there wishing I had never raised my hand. I am sure I did not have to step up to reach the table, not far anyway.

I just angled myself, one leg on one side of the table, one on the other. It was the perfect height. I didn't even have to climb up. I leaned against it. I felt relief almost instantly.

I heard him ask his second question. I was almost done.

"Now, how many of you do *not* put water on your toothbrush after you put toothpaste on it?"

Every child in the room, including me and those who had raised their hands earlier, had their arms up in the air. *We just hadn't understood the question. Now we knew what he meant. This last answer was* one. Mrs. I. SmiTH never stopped smiling at us.

"What'd you learn in school today?" my mama asked me as soon as I came into the kitchen.

"I learned about toothpaste."

"How's that?"

"You don't wet it except with your own spit," I said.

"Oh?" she said and turned her back to me to stir something in a pot on the electric range.

I learned that adults are tricky and sometimes cruel and you don't water down toothpaste, but you do the truth.

I looked at the back my mama's head.

And I learned that my mama's hair didn't bounce or flip up in a row of curls the way Mrs. I. SmiTH's did.

Chapter 7

Painting

As I recall, Gloria Steinem once wrote that if a child has just one person in her life that loves her unconditionally through time, then she can weather all the challenges that life presents and still be a whole human being. It doesn't have to be a mother or a father. It can be a grandmother or grandfather, an aunt, an uncle. It can be someone outside the family entirely.

I have searched for that one person who loved me unconditionally and consistently through time. There is none—no one person who loved me that way while I was growing up or for years after I reached adulthood, for that matter. But there was a series of people, a new one showing up just when the last had been gone long enough that my faith in myself started to falter. Many of them were teachers. Mrs. I. Smith was the first who loved me unconditionally and saw my talents and my wounds long before I knew I had either.

She was a painter, this meticulously dressed and coiffed woman who painted in oils and brought in a self-portrait one day to show us. She displayed it and several other portraits she had painted and let each of us take turns walking by them.

"Don't touch! Except with your eyes!" she encouraged. "Let your eyes sweep over the portrait like you are memorizing every color and every line. Close your eyes tightly. Now open them fast. See the painting like it was the first time you ever saw it."

She thrilled me. I screwed my eyelids shut and opened them fast to see the blues and purples and reds of nighttime swirl and clear. My gaze would fasten on the two faces of this woman I loved—the still life, melancholic face framed before me and the lively one that smiled and cajoled and encouraged. One of the faces merged inside with my own image of myself. Then she brought out the tempera colors and let us paint an extra picture every day after lunch if we fell asleep during our naps, and I became *her* when I painted.

I always slept. She always chose me. *Then came the day I was sleepless. I had placed my arms on the tabletop and crossed them just like always. I had created a circle of softness and rested my head on it just like always. I closed my eyes, but sleep did not come. Still, when Mrs. I. Smith called my name out, I did not open my eyes. I wanted to paint. I needed to paint. I stayed with the colors behind my eyelids.*

A scrappy boy across from me who never slept and never got to paint extra pictures said, "She's not sleeping! I saw her eyes move!" It was a shout. An angry tattletale shout.

The Red Wriggler Girl next to me reached over and pulled one of my eyelids up off my eyeball. We called her the Red Wriggler Girl because her daddy sold fishing worms in the neighborhood, and she sometimes helped him. My skin crawled when I thought of her touching those worms, and it hurt when she stuck her fingers in my eye to keep it open.

Yet I slept.

I slept and slept.

I slept until Mrs. I. Smith touched me on my arm. "Sandra?" she cooed. "Wake up now. I have your paints ready to go."

The colors poured out of me onto the canvas. The shapes came, too. Love, love, love flowed through me. And but for the scratched eyelid, there was no pain.

"Sandra?" Mrs. I. Smith looked over my shoulder at the picture I had made to illustrate the month of September. It was the springtime of my first grade year. I had drawn a hammock slung between two trees. One of them was a mimosa; the other was red oak tree—not a white oak tree. I knew the difference. I lived outside.

The leaves I drew had sharp points, not the round outlines of white oak leaves. Only one or two of the leaves were yellow or red among the greenness of late September. The trees rose from a narrow strip of green lawn behind which the blue sky fell like a curtain. In the hammock, a smiling boy had spikes for hair and a smiling girl had a roll of curls on the tips of her long hair. Each child held a large glass of bright red punch with a straw stuck in it. Almost as though they knew to pose for me, they presented me with camera-perfect Kool-aid pitcher grins. They looked poised to take another long pull on their cold drinks to keep them cool in the sweltering, humid heat of September.

"Yes, ma'am?" I answered back.

"Could you help with April and May?" she asked me.

We were going to present our pictures on the cafeteria stage during a class performance the next day. Each of us would hold the picture we drew and say a little poem about that month of the year. For April, I painted Easter bunnies hopping down a bunny trail that wound through rolling green hills. The bunnies carried baskets loaded with chocolate goodies and jellybeans. Fuzzy yellow baby chicks followed them.

For May, I painted robins and robins' eggs, bright blue eggs inside their brown twiggy nests. I painted a lemon sun shining in the bright, bright blue sky. I found room for a ruby-throated hummingbird feasting on an out-of-season, spidery, coral-colored mimosa blossom.

I knew the outside world because I lived in it. I could paint it because I knew it and because each brilliant stroke of paint was a gorgeous love gift for Mrs. I. Smith. I did not paint closets or pantries or bedrooms or houses or garages or pictures of large breasts like those that had disentangled themselves from the bodies of the women on the cards and joined the swirl of colors in my mind before I slept each night. I did not consciously edit them out. They did not appear because this love I felt for her did not conjure them. I do not remember finding the edge of a classroom table again, though I do remember dancing atop one during a music lesson.

Chapter 8

Hoochie-Coochie Dancing and the Red Wriggler Girl

It was the early fifties. My brother wore a Davy Crockett coonskin cap which I envied, and he played with marbles, many of which I later won from him in matches motivated by my love of beauty rather than a love of winning. Cat's eye marbles with woven swirls of iridescent blues or greens were my favorites. I would hold them up to the sky forever and fall into reveries. My bare knees grew crusty and darkened from touching the ground as I knelt to take a crack at the marbles in a circle. Grandma Blair scrubbed my knees nightly if she wasn't having one of her spells. Mama was much too busy with the baby to bathe me anymore.

"Not the way a girl should behave," Grandma Blair scolded. I remember the way the words felt. They did not feel like my mama's words. She must have said it many times. I must have tired of it, for I raised both hands to my face. I put a single finger in one side of my mouth and another finger in the other side of my mouth. I opened my mouth wide and stretched it as far as I could, and I stuck out my tongue.

She slapped me on both cheeks at the same time. I howled, and she left the bathroom, saying I could wash my own nasty self with my own hateful ways.

Freed from her watchful gaze, I splashed around for a few minutes, enjoying the water and sloshing some on the floor.

I heard him before I saw him. I looked up. Big Arthur was at the door. My punishment for insolence did not end with getting my cheeks boxed by Grandma Blair. And Big Arthur didn't use his hands. He made me stand in the slippery tub and hold onto the spigot while he used his belt on my wet, wet body. I heard the screaming.

That was my mama screaming now. Not me screaming. Her. I remember that. She stood in the doorway. She screamed at him. "Stop! Now! That's enough! You're hitting her with the buckle. Stop yourself!"

"Nobody treats my mother that way!" he growled. But he obeyed my mama that time. The belt was gone. My body knew that.

She kneeled, like I kneeled on the ground when I played marbles. She kneeled that way beside the tub. She pulled me back down into the water and she let the water drain out. My legs spouted blood, enough to color the last few streams of water red. "Stand up," she said. I stood. She rinsed the blood off my legs with cool water. Then came the Merthiolate. And someone was screaming again.

He was at the door. "You better shut up, or I'll come in there again." They were my screams, then. I shut up.

In the background I could hear my mama's radio, and sad as I was, hurt as I was, scared as I was, I watched him leave, and then I started to bounce in time with the beat.

My mama had that radio on every day of her life. If she had to hang up clothes outside or work in the yard or wanted to lie out to tan, she'd feed the radio electricity through long cords she'd plug together and stretch out the porch door. She would place the radio next to her as she lay tanning in the backyard. From early spring to late fall, she smelled like the baby oil she mixed with iodine and lavished on her body, so she would tan faster. She moved to the music even when she was lying down.

I had been too busy chasing after Little Arthur to pay music any mind. But that next day at school after that particular whipping, when Mrs. I. Smith played a record, I was entranced. I had never seen a phonograph or a record. Mrs. Smith took the black disk from its large white envelope, and she placed it on the turntable. She placed the arm that had a needle in it on the edge of this flat black wafer, and she said for us to shush.

The music entered my body in swirls the way color entered my mind at night. Then Mrs. Smith started clapping and asked us all to join in. I clapped and clapped, and I must have danced in my chair without knowing I was moving. *I was dancing sitting down. I would read those words later in life in Faulkner's* The Sound and the Fury, *and know that, like Caddy and her muddy britches, I'd lost something precious too early in life.)*

"Okay, Sandra, stand up and dance," Mrs. I. Smith said.
I did.
"Everybody stand up now, and dance the way Sandra is dancing."
She must love me, too, the way I love her, I thought.

They all stood, but nobody could dance like me. Nobody had as much pain and beauty balled up inside them waiting to get out.

Nobody had bruises and cuts beneath their long pants that wanted to grow tongues and speak like Caesar's wounds. Though I did not know Shakespeare then and could not have said it that way or this way, Mrs. I. Smith was my Mark Antony, and the music was the roar of the crowd, vindicating and elevating me.

"Look at her go! Climb on up on that table and keep on dancing," she said.

I was the original go-go girl even though I was only six years old. I was a hoochie-choochie queen come to life from a deck of dirty cards hidden in a pantry. I writhed like a grown-up woman. Two years before Elvis appeared on television, I moved my hips in ways Ed Sullivan's censors would have banned.

And Mrs. I. Smith just clapped, and laughed, and cheered me on.

There were no calls home. No social worker sent to see what was happening. And there was no judgment of me either. Just love and acceptance. *Enough for me to grow on.*

Every day after that day of dance, I stayed at school as long as I dared. I didn't hang around Mrs. Smith's classroom, but I waited most days for her to walk to her car, wave at me, and get into it before I left for home. While I waited, I would trek around the reflecting pool three or four times. Then I'd bully my way into a game of marbles and play until the scabs on my knees cracked and started to bleed. Let Grandma Blair complain all she wanted. I wasn't giving up playing marbles.

After a while, I would trudge home, sit on the front porch and pick at one or two other scabs farther down on my legs for a while. During that dark time, Little Arthur had abandoned me for the company of the gang-gone-bicycle-and-marble mad. I would sit alone, and I would take the green cat's eye out of my pocket and hold it up to the sun. It was springtime. School would be out in a few weeks. We would leave 1302 Portland Street soon, but I did not know that then. I would sink into the indigo blue of dusk. I never rode the mimosa tree again as far as I can recall, but I watched it move through its seasons, and I loved it.

That's when it began, this turning to nature for nurture, in those early years. It grew until the trees would talk to me and I would learn to listen.

On a day like that in early summer when I was left to muse alone for hours, I took the big boy's dare. I couldn't run with the boys anymore because I hadn't learned to ride my bike. It was a used bike that someone had painted a sickly green, the color of garden snakes and of my eyes. I had been delighted when the bike came through the doors into the dining area at the end of the hall. But the first time I took it out to ride it, I fell down again and again, and I put about as many bruises on myself as Big Arthur did when he beat me. My brother came along and offered to help me, but he wasn't strong enough to hold the bike with me on it.

Then Big Arthur appeared. He offered no help, only threats. "You will push that bike everywhere you go until you learn to ride it, even if it takes all year long."

Seven months had passed, and I hadn't learned yet. That's why I was on the porch when the big boy came by. His name was Chuck. I'd looked up once or twice when he rode past the house, shouting and egging the other boys on. Then on the third round, he skidded to a quick stop right in front of the steps, so that when he looked up, he looked me straight in the face. Unafraid, I met his eyes. The other boys, including Little Arthur and Barry, didn't know his plan and had overshot the front gate and steps, so I had to face him alone.

"I'll bet you're too much of a sissy to pull a trick on the Red Wriggler Girl," Chuck twanged at me.

"I reckon I'm not," I said with pride that caused me to jump straight up and fly off the steps toward him.

She lived at the corner, and she was the one we called the Red Wriggler Girl, or sometimes just "Red," because her daddy sold red wriggler worms for bait during the summer. They had a big old refrigerator they turned on its side and kept locked except when somebody was minding it. I'd seen its insides once or twice when I'd gone with my mama to buy worms, so she could go fishing. When the Red Wriggler Girl had opened the big door, inside was rich black dirt, full of worms. They were red, and they wriggled.

I didn't like the Red Wriggler Girl much because she'd pulled my eyelids up when I was faking sleep, so I could paint more pictures for Mrs. I. Smith. I was feeling like paying her back, and I was bored.

"What you want me to do?" I asked. He whispered his plan to me and took a dime out of his pocket and gave it to me. I laughed and ran ahead of the gaggle of boys on their bikes, who gathered around Chuck, clacking for answers about what was happening. It felt good to be included again, even if I couldn't ride my bike. It stood against the garage, and I remembered it as my bare feet felt the hot tar road rise up through my calluses. I knew I would be in trouble if I got caught. I did not turn back, not with the gang of boys all creeping up, their bikes abandoned, so they could hide in the bushes and watch the action.

I went up and knocked on the back door, which led into the kitchen. The Red Wriggler's mother came to the door and spoke to me through the screen, "What you want?"

"Worms," I said and held out my hand to show her I had the money.

"Edna," she called. "Edna!" That was the Red Wriggler Girl's real name. I knew that from school.

"Yes, ma'am?" she answered and appeared in the kitchen.

"Get this girl some worms."

"Yes, ma'am."

Edna came out and slid past me. She was my age, but she was smaller even than I was. Her hair was dark black and long, and her skin was white, white, white, what my mama would call "fair skinned." I followed her down the steps. I watched as she unlocked the refrigerator and opened the door. It looked odd to see a refrigerator on its side like that. I looked around and saw where some of the boys were hiding. I took the pint of worms, and I gave Edna the dime. I waited while she closed the big door and locked it. She didn't speak to me. She kept her eyes down. She knew she had done me wrong. Just as she turned to leave, and her back was to me, I called out, "Wait a minute, Edna."

She froze. She turned slightly toward me. "What?" she asked, like she was afraid to speak to me.

"You got some dirt on your back," I said. "Here. I'll brush it off."

"Oh, thank you," she said. "My mama is forever getting on me about getting dirty."

I walked over to her. She still had her back to me. She wore a loose-fitting shirt. I reached up to the neckline, moved her hair over, pulled back her collar, and dumped the whole batch of worms down her shirt!

She started screaming instantly, and the boys ran out of the bushes, laughing. She was truly wriggling! Out of the house, her mother came. She pulled Edna's shirt up, brushed the dirt away, and picked the worms off at the same time. I didn't laugh. I stood still as if I grew from the spot on the ground that my feet touched.

I saw Edna's back. Red welts rose and bloomed into a hundred circles and paths across her fair skin. She looked as though she had been switched with briars. As her mother helped her into the house, I watched.

Her mother stopped on the top step and screamed at me, "Just wait till I tell your daddy, and I will. You know I will!"

"He ain't my daddy." I said it aloud for the first time. I had said it to myself a thousand times before but never out loud.

Then I saw her. I don't know how long she had been standing there, but on the corner where the trolley stopped stood Grandma Blair, smoking. She looked me straight in the face the way Chuck had, and her eyes, too, dared me, the way his had. I did not take up her dare. Instead, I turned and walked home, knowing I'd get a beating later. Maybe two. One I knew I wouldn't deserve for leaving the bike at home. And while I grew up knowing in my heart that no kid ever deserves a beating, that day I felt I deserved the other beating I would get. I felt I deserved a lick for every Red Wriggler track that laced Edna's back.

By the time, Big Arthur finished with me, I was sure he had evened the score. I don't remember my mama even being around at the time. If she was, she must've known I'd brought that one on myself.

Chapter 9

Baby Doll and the Boulevard Queen
Take Trolley Rides

The first time I pushed the bike to the corner store, I was sent
to get a can of Carnation condensed milk for the baby, and stupidly,
I went right by Red Wriggler Edna's house. She hovered around her
back steps, watching me with her dry brown eyes. She had power
over me because she knew I was "bad to the core," like Big Arthur
said most times when he beat me.

"You still ain't learned to ride that thing, have you now?" Edna
called out.

I pushed the bike faster and tried to keep the spinning pedals
from hitting my calves.

"Can, too," I said, rushing past her.

She showered me with pebbles that she had scraped up from her
driveway.

"You cannot. All's you can do is pick on people littler than you."

"Can, too, but you ain't never gonna get to see me do it." I was at
the corner by then. The light was red, and contrite as I was for what
I'd done to her, I wasn't about to kill myself for her. I had to wait.
Red Wriggler Edna was at me again. She pelted me with handful after
handful of pebbles. I stood and took it. I had already been beat, and
I had thought that evened the score, but maybe I deserved more for
putting those wrigglers down her shirt. Those worms sure had made
a quick, hot, red mess of her back. She was out of school for days.

She screamed at me, "You're mean, you're mean, you're just plain
mean!" I knew it. She grabbed my bike out of my hands and shoved it
at me. I fell fast, scraping and bruising one side of my body as I hit the
sidewalk. The pedal gouged my left calf, and the handlebars twisted
and struck me in the jaw. The weight of the bicycle and the shock of
the fall kept me on the ground for several minutes. Somewhere in
my misery, I heard a screen door slam.

"Go inside, Edna. *Now.*" It was her mother. I saw the outline of her house, the big elm tree, and the sky beyond.

"Get yourself up and get out of here, and don't let me ever see you bothering Edna again. And don't think your daddy won't hear from me this time."

"He's not my daddy," I said, but low this time, so she wouldn't hear.

I pushed the bike to the store, got the Carnation milk, and went the opposite way home. I cleaned myself up. I put Merthiolate on my cuts and scratches, and held my screams in. To let the cuts air out, I chose a dress, and I sat on front porch like nothing had happened. I kept cuts, scrapes, and bruises on me from beatings and from my tomboy roughhousing. Nobody would notice. I refused to cry, but little hiccup sounds escaped from my lips, and I nearly got a case of the snubs.

My Grandma Blair came out and sat beside me on the porch as the boys sped by. She said, "It's just as well that bike has parked you here. You don't need to run around with them boys. And I think Little Arthur spends far too much time with them, too."

To me they were not some undifferentiated group of boy-wildness whirling through the neighborhood. They were Chuck, who said he was an Indian; Jerry, whose grandma fed us pecans and cookies from little tin dishes; Scott, Jerry's little brother; sometimes Peewee, the Wee-wee-er; always Barry, my secret boyfriend; and my brother Little Arthur, who was two years older than I.

I belonged with them more than anywhere else. In the summertime, I wore my brother's hand-me-down shirts and dungarees most of the time, and with my hair bobbed short, I looked more like a rag-tag little brother than I did a sister. The boys were barefoot and scruffy; they whooped and hollered and always made me race to keep up with them, but till I got that darn bike, they never left me behind completely or thought of me as a girl, except for Barry.

I pulled the skirt of my dress down over my legs and hugged them, but I did not draw away when Grandmother Blair put her arm around me. Usually she kept her distance, and I was glad she did, but that day I even leaned toward her a bit. I had to squeeze back tears until they found a hot resting place in the center of my chest and didn't spill out of my eyeballs to give me away.

That's how it began. From that hug on, Grandma Blair discovered I was the same sex she was, and she made it her mission to advertise my femaleness to the world by sewing me a summer wardrobe out of scraps from making this-or-that for herself or her sister Ida. Next, she insisted I accompany her wherever she went, so we spent that summer riding all over Greensboro on the trolley buses together with me dressed up "like a lady," she would say, or in a different mood, "like my baby doll." Big Arthur didn't interfere.

My most famous outfit was a pair of tight red shorts with white polka dots the size of silver dollars on them. She cut the fabric and sewed the shorts in a flash on her treadle Singer sewing machine—a few seams, and her part was done. I pinned a large diaper pin to one end of a piece of white elastic and threaded it through the waist of the shorts.

Then she made an oversized, matching halter-top, and through its wide seams at the top and bottom, I threaded more elastic. The halter-top constantly slipped down when I wore it, though, and if I didn't keep hitching it up, the gathers made me look like a buxom six-year-old.

I let her dress me any way she wanted. I was starved for trolley rides. Only stars and lightening bugs, which didn't need to be plugged in to light up, enchanted me more than the trolleys that glided nearly silently except for the occasional squealing of brakes or the opening and closing of the doors.

For me, those trolley trips were magic, powered by electricity, by something invisible just like magic carpets. Grandma Blair didn't look the part of a genie, and except in that long, lonely, tragic summer, she never brought magic into my life. But that summer, once I was on the trolley with her, she transformed into my fairy godmother.

She was in her early forties, and her square shoulders, wide hips, and full chest made her rise tall and solid like a column. Her short hair, which she dyed, was mahogany for the first few days after she "did it." Then it turned into brassy red-wire copper and set her head ablaze in the sunshine. It was amazing.

I wouldn't see those colors on a woman's head again until the Eighties when some of my high school students wore black half-slips for skirts and poured that same mahogany shade of red onto their hair, surely from dusty bottles left over from Grandma Blair's era that they found on back of the shelves at Rexall's.

She would always get off the trolley a stop early after we'd finished our errands.

"Let's walk from here," she'd say in her raspy voice. "It's a pretty day."

She smoked. They all did. My mama. Big Arthur. Aunt Ida. Uncle Will. Grandma Blair did it in private, though, or with me when we were away from the house. Her lips already had lines around them, and as she sucked on the unfiltered cigarettes, the lines would deepen.

The red lipstick stains left on the thin white paper and the gold tube with the red wand of lipstick fascinated me. Grandma Blair would take the tube from her purse, and without a mirror, she would apply the ruby-red lipstick perfectly while we walked. Most times, she'd catch me watching.

"Turn your face up," she would say.

With my head thrown back, the sun in my eyes, and my pursed lips reaching for the sky, I would stand attentively before her. She would bend down and kiss me right smack dab on the lips.

"Now rub them together," she would say.

The color always felt bright as a stoplight, and though it transformed me, it wouldn't last long enough for me to see it in the bathroom mirror when I got home. The rose-petal feel of her lips lingered, however, as did the smell of tobacco.

Adorned in this manner, into a candy store we would go, holding hands.

"Now, who is this little princess?" the man behind the counter would ask.

I would preen for him, but now that I have seen pictures from those years, I know how dissembling he was. My hair ran amok, unless my mama greased it with Vaseline. Then, stringy, it would flop into my over-sized green eyes. My red mouth popped out like a "fox's rear end," so said Big Arthur when he caught me once with my lips rouged by Grandma Blair's kiss. My outfit was styled for 1970's hot-pants nubiles or wannabe Lolita's, not for a six-year-old.

Grandma Blair would smile and say to the storeowner, "Isn't she a doll baby?" She would open her purse, which was an art object itself, so large and red, too, like her hair. She would hand me coins, fuss with my halter-top, and say, "Go on, Baby Doll. Get yourself something."

I noticed but understood neither the sneers nor leers as they crossed the faces of these candy men; nor did I enter their imaginings about what I would look like in ten years inside that same outfit. Only later would I recall and know those odd looks for what they were.

During that summer, I would run to the candy counter and take two Hershey bars, one for me and one for Little Arthur. Only occasionally, when she did not have enough coins for her cigarettes and both bars of candy, did she have me put one back. Then I could buy either a lined Hershey bar without almonds, so I could break off half for me and leave half for Little Arthur, or I could get a bar with almonds and eat it before I got home.

We would walk like queens down the block or two of boulevard before we reached the Portland Street intersection. She would puff her way along, giving in now and again to my squeals for more smoke rings. I would bite into the Hershey bar, mining it for its almonds. If Portland Street caught us by surprise before we had finished our indulgences, we would sit on the bench at the trolley stop and wave the trolleys by while we finished up. That's how we filled many a day unless it was one of Grandma Blair's bad days when she couldn't get herself out of bed. My mama said since we were partners that Grandma Blair had fewer and fewer of those bedridden days when we all crept around like we were invisible.

Grandma Blair always reminded me after that time we got caught by Big Arthur, "Don't you forget to wipe that off your face before your daddy sees it."

That's what she called Big Arthur, but I knew it wasn't so. *My real daddy was dead. My real daddy would never have beaten me like Big Arthur did.*

Late in the summer, talk of buying new school clothes mixed with talk about moving "to the country," and that put an end to the trolley rides. Most days, Grandma Blair looked after Deborah and Eddie while my mama packed. Little Arthur and I had to stay out of the way.

I went back to my long days of moping in the yard while Little Arthur rode his bike and pushed as far as he dared beyond the limits laid down by Big Arthur. My bike, which Barry had nicknamed, "The Green Demon," still rested against the side of the garage, beneath the eaves. Its front tire was flat even though I had never ridden it. Deflated, the bike rested right in the gully where I'd planted the tobacco seeds that had drowned before they could sprout.

Barry's sister Becky called to me to open the gate before I saw her coming. I couldn't rightly escape, for she was my boyfriend's sister. She was four, I would be seven in the fall, and I wasn't up for babysitting. I took my time reaching the gate. As I dragged the metal gate across the paved driveway, it sounded like a trolley's brakes, reminding me of my lost glories.

"Come on," I said. "Let's find something in the garage to fix that tire with." She followed me until we almost reached the garage. Then she tugged hard on my shirttail.

"Get off me!"

"But look!"

Her baby-girl voice was urgent, so I turned around. She pointed toward the middle window, the big one in Grandma Blair's living room.

"What's she doing?" Becky whispered. She let my shirttail go but hid behind me.

Only Grandma Blair's head was visible above the café style curtains she had sewn and pulled onto curtain rods she'd placed halfway up the window. She wasn't shouting; nor was she waving, but I felt her calling to me. As I ran toward the window, whatever I had heard, or thought I heard, ceased. I stopped. I stood four feet away from the closed glass. I stared at her. Silently she stared back, but not at me, not at anything in particular.

Her head was as bald and wrinkled as the base of a dandelion after a child, wishing for a TV, blows away all the dried-up petals. She had shaved off all her fine red hair!

My mama never asked about my trolley adventures; nor did Little Arthur. No one understood how my heart broke, when at summer's end, Grandma Blair left us and went to stay at Butler Sanitarium. No one knew how my heart broke again when I went to see her there.

We all drove out there together, but Big Arthur was about to head up the grassy hill by himself to see her in the single-story unit that looked more like a motel than a mental hospital.

"I wanna go! I wanna go!" I said.

"It'll be okay," he said. "Mother's doing so much better," he told my mama.

The sun outside was bright. The wooden room door was open. The screen door, shut. I couldn't see into the darkness. I stood outside with Big Arthur. He called to her.

"Mother? Mother? We've come to visit. Sandra's here with me."

Suddenly she was at the screen door, opening it, screaming, and trying to get at me. Her arms were flailing, and her breasts were floundering on her chest. Sunshine flooded across her body, and the shock of seeing her, enormous and naked, like the women on the deck of dirty cards in Uncle Will's pantry, made me scream, too. Big Arthur pushed her back inside with one hand and pushed me outside with his other hand. He entered the small room and shut the door.

After weeks of lockup in that hospital pantry, Grandma Blair went home. My family had moved to the country. When I visited her at Portland Street, Grandma Blair looked right past me, like we had never shared those magical summer trolley rides and like I couldn't possibly be anybody's baby doll, certainly not hers.

Chapter 10

Mama Goes to Work
and Little Arthur Runs Wild

Little Arthur's wildness grew to match the scope of the landscape when we moved to the country. Our three-room cottage housed the six of us—Mama, Big Arthur, Little Arthur, Deborah, Eddie, and me. Little Arthur had the top bunk. I slept at one end of the bottom bunk, and Deborah slept at the other end. Eddie had the crib in the same bedroom when he wasn't sleeping on the sofa-bed with Big Arthur and Mama.

The cottage had a tiny living room, a closet which opened into the living room and into the bedroom, a kitchen on the back of the house, and an outhouse for a bathroom. The cottage was small, so no wonder we continued to live outdoors more than indoors. But Little Arthur wandered farther off than I did. We moved to the country in the fall, and by the following summer, he brought the big boys back to the house with him.

We lived at the edge of a large, muddy-brown lake, and if I took the diagonal path through the tangle of weeds and undergrowth we called the backyard, I could reach its edge in a couple of minutes. For as far as I could see in the underbrush, a wire fence wound along the water's edge. A pier rode the surface of the water out to about thirty feet, and a weatherworn, picket fence gate, hardly an obstacle to anyone, stood between me and the pier. The pier was not more than three feet wide, so there was hardly room to walk more than one abreast.

The whole family spent the weekend days on the pier. My mama loved to fish, and she taught Little Arthur to catch catfish, hammer nails through their heads, and with a deft slash or two of his pocket knife, cut the skin right behind the gills without getting stung by the fish's whiskers. She showed him how to grasp the skin with his fingers and pull it back off the white, greasy flesh of the fish.

None of us children could swim. In place of lessons, we got warnings. One Saturday I sat with my legs off the pier, dangling in the water, looking at the lily pads floating atop it while Mama let Big Arthur tell us about respecting the water.

"Just 'cause you can see the bottom up around the shore, doesn't mean this lake ain't deep," Big Arthur's voice hummed across the humid air. "There's a twenty-foot drop-off as soon as you leave the shore, and it's even deeper out here where we are on the pier." He paused.

"If you fell in it, you'd probably drown, and if you didn't, the cottonmouth water moccasins would get you."

I'd studied about Thanksgiving at school already, so it took a while for me to get the image right in my mind. At first, all I could see in my mind's eye was an Indian's moccasin, but before long, Big Arthur made himself clear.

"Those snakes open their mouths and all you see is whiteness. But they have teeth hiding in their mouths that clamp onto you and chew. And every time they chew, more poison goes right into you. And every time you try to knock them off, they bite down deeper."

I heard every word he said. I was accustomed to king snakes and green snakes and knew not to fear them. I had been warned about copperheads already. Water moccasins were news to me. I wondered if they lurked beneath the surface of the pool at Clara J. Peck Elementary, but I decided they must not have, or Mrs. I. Smith would have warned me. In that moment, I realized I would never see her again.

The wind was blowing just enough to create little ripples on the lake's sun-flecked surface. It was a warm fall day, but I felt winter in the undercurrents of the breeze.

I heard Little Arthur say, "Come on, Sandra, and let's go dig some wrigglers to fish with." I didn't answer him, and I didn't budge.

Ten yards out in the lake, something was sliding through the flashing net of ripples. I watched it for a long moment as it left a trail in the water the way a king snake does in a garden. Slowly I drew my feet out of the water. I did not rush. I pulled them up and moved back onto the pier the way I always did.

Big Arthur stood beside me, looking in the same direction. He cut his cold, brown eyes toward me once, but he said nothing. I walked down the pier without a word. When I reached the path, I ran hard and caught up with my brother, who was already halfway up the path to the tree house. He'd already forgotten about the worms, but I would always remember the moccasin lurking beneath the surface of that other world.

Fall turned into winter, and Mama went back to work. When I got home each day, Big Arthur would be there with Deborah who was three and Eddie who was a year old. Big Arthur worked the second shift at Phillip Morris, and he had to leave for work by two-thirty in the afternoon. Mama didn't get back until four-thirty, so for two hours every school day, Little Arthur and I were in charge of the younger kids and the house and were supposed to do our chores.

We had a television to help keep us company. I was convinced we got it because I'd wished for it and then blown all of the petals from a dried-up dandelion. In between washing dishes and even ironing some small pieces, we'd watch *Sky King* and *Lassie* or whatever was on. I remember watching the Republican convention when Ike Eisenhower and Richard Nixon were chosen as running mates.

In between caring for the others, watching TV, and doing our chores, Little Arthur and I played games, too.

I was lying on the living room floor on my stomach. He came over to me and put his head on my fanny like it was a pillow. I rolled over.

"Stop it!"

"Just let me put my head there. It won't hurt." He was nine. I was seven.

"Don't you tickle me!" I rolled back over, and he put his head back on my fanny. We lay that way for a few minutes. Eddie lay on the couch, sucking a bottle, and Deborah sat beside him. Then it began.

When he first started rolling his head back and forth, I tried to bounce him off me. Then he was lying with his whole body over mine, pressing against me, bouncing me on the floor. I rolled over, but now he was on top of me.

"You'll be sorry," I said. "Mama said no fighting." I shoved him away and was on my feet.

"That ain't fighting. It's what Mama does with Big Arthur at night. It's that word I taught you."

"Don't say it in front of them!" He knew I meant Debbie and Eddie.

I knew the word he meant. I had even taught it to Linda Forest at Sumner School, my new school. We were both in the advanced reading book, so we got to read together. Sometimes we talked when we were supposed to be reading. The word. It became a playground taunt that was our secret code.

We would walk up to some uninitiated child and say, "If you see, Kay— tell her I want her." Then we would giggle and run off to the bars to do twirls or splits. I was never good at either, but I liked the way the round metal bars felt between my legs when I had to straddle them to try the tricks.

So I knew the word, and it excited me, but I did not know its meaning.

"But what does it mean, really?" I asked Little Arthur. "Just rolling around and fighting like this?"

"Nope. You know what I look like down there?" He pointed.

We had a chamber pot in the bedroom the three older children shared. Not only that, but I had changed Eddie's diapers, almost from the time he was born.

"Sure, I do. I see you pee with it all the time."

"Yeah, but did you know it gets hard sometimes? And then it can go inside you. Down there."

Sky King's plane was sputtering, and he was in trouble, I wanted a peanut butter sandwich, and the bottle had fallen out of Eddie's mouth, so he was crying. But I was curious. I put stuff inside myself all the time. I knew how that felt.

"Show me. In there." I pointed to the closet that was in the middle of the house.

"Okay. I will. But it doesn't always work."

I gave Eddie his bottle back. Debbie was watching television without moving. I went into the closet, but I left the door on the living room side open, so I could still see Sky King. Little Arthur pulled his pants down. It worked. He grinned.

"You better put that away now." I stood up and left the closet to make myself that peanut butter sandwich. He stayed behind a while longer. When he came out, I asked, "Who showed you how to do that?"

"A boy you never met," he said.

I knew the word was a dirty word, so I began to associate it with the dirtiest thing I had ever seen. It was the grease pit out beyond our house. Big Arthur had dug the pit for household garbage and cooking grease because we did not get garbage service in the country. He dug the pit a ways off from the house, but it stank worse than the outhouse to me.

Mama kept the outhouse scrubbed down, but there was no cleaning up the pit. It had two large pieces of aluminum roofing covering it. Nightly, I imagined that Mama and Big Arthur made their way to the grease pit, so he could put his hard thing in her. That was the only place dirty enough for such a word.

I took to riding the bars at school more than ever because, as much as the whole matter disgusted me, it aroused my little body that already knew more than some country women. I fell asleep to pornographic imagery nightly, especially after I yielded to Little Arthur's urgings and went back into the closet with him. During the daytime, I kept trying to see what was in Big Arthur's pants. By springtime, when he wore shorts and swim trunks often, I had managed to glimpse him a few times, but that only added to my misery.

By summer, I said yes when Little Arthur wanted to bring the big boys by.

Chapter 11

Dirty Secrets and Sudden Rescue

He was my brother. I loved him. *Now I had begun to love him in body ways that were way beyond my years.* I knew there was something dark—"dirty"—about our behavior. I wanted to be rescued from it, but consistent guiding adults were mostly absent from my world, or too busy to be bothered when they were present, or they were too angry or too wounded to have any help to offer.

Then began the days when Big Arthur and Mama fought with each other most of the time. More than once I sat down to eat supper with the family and hoped I'd get to eat before his temper flared. I was his target most often, though my mama and Little Arthur got their share of the beatings, too.

I loved fried chicken wings better than any other part of the chicken. I suppose it was the crisp, battered, fatty taste that I longed for. I watched eagerly as the platter went around the table. Little Arthur took two chicken wings. Two! I started to complain, but instead I watched as Big Arthur took the platter next. He also took two wings! Mama wouldn't have made more than two chickens for all of us, and so I shrieked, "Why is everybody taking all the wings? Ya'll know they're my favorites."

"Honey," my mama began, "all I made was wings." She smiled a little at me.

"But you won't be getting any at all tonight since you acted so ugly." It was Big Arthur again.

He watched as the platter went around until it came to me. I had the platter in my hands. I looked at him to see if he were watching me and to see if he would relent.

"Pass it on or put it down," he said. He sat across from me against the wall. Little Arthur sat next to him. Debbie was at the end of the table next to Eddie, who was in a high chair, and I sat on the outside of the table next to Mama.

I started to whimper and complain.

"Goddamn it! I said to put it down!"

I did, but I was too late. He turned the whole table upside down, spilling all the food onto the floor and into the laps of those too slow to get away. My mama had seen it coming. She had yanked Eddie out of his highchair and got herself and him out of the way. I moved, but not soon enough because my eyes were fastened on Big Arthur's eyes, not his hands. He had to move the table off me to get me to my feet. He did that with one hand while he unbuckled his belt with his other hand and whipped it out of his belt loops.

I heard my mama's screams. I heard Eddie and Debbie crying. I saw Little Arthur sniffling as I struggled to get out of reach of the belt. The table had bruised my legs, and I felt weak already as I started slipping and sliding in mashed potatoes that were hot to my bare feet.

All the dirty words I had learned in the last year and some others poured from his mouth. And he did not stop beating me until he ran out of words and was somehow satisfied I'd got what was coming to me. Either then or somewhere in the pain of the next few hours, I wondered if he punished me so hard, not because he loved me like he said, but because he knew that I had looked up his shorts when he sat on the slatted steps of the back porch earlier that summer.

"Now get out back and stay there until I call you."

It was dark. I was scared. My mama protested, "Arthur, you made your point. Don't scare her to death. Just send her to bed."

It was his fist, not his belt that slammed into her face. I ran out the back door. I heard the front door slam moments later. I heard the car engine and the sound of tires on gravel. I did not go back inside. I shivered even though it wasn't cold outside, and I ignored my mama's calls to me. It was Little Arthur who came to me and guided me back inside and across the kitchen floor to the couch. He wiped the food off my feet and told me to lie down.

"Mama's on your bunk bed with some ice on her face."

Eddie must have been with her. Debbie sat in the corner on the floor where she sat eating a chicken wing she must have found. Little Arthur and I saw her at the same time. We burst into laughter. He raced around and found me a wing first, and then he found one for himself.

The beating had drawn blood again, and when I had eaten until my stomach was so full of wings that it could have flown off, I went to the kitchen cabinet to get the Merthiolate. I climbed up on the sink, filled it with water, reached for the soap and washed myself off. In the meantime, Little Arthur had rescued some biscuits and some more chicken wings.

He put some on a plate for Debbie, and he made another plate that he set on the counter. I watched him while I held my breath, so I wouldn't cry when I applied the Merthiolate in red patches all over my legs. He poured four ounces of Carnation condensed milk into the baby bottle, reached over me and turned on the cold water. He added just the right amount of water to dilute the milk, screwed the bottle top on, and reached for the plate of cold food.

"Those are some pretty purple bruises," he joked. I didn't laugh. "I bet you got some marks on your back, too," he said. "I'll fix 'em for you when I get back." He disappeared around the corner into the bedroom. That was the first time I had heard her since I came back in. She was crying, but she must have stopped to try to eat.

Little Arthur was back in a few moments with the plate in his hands.

"She couldn't eat just yet. Her mouth ain't right." I saw the plate. She had taken a single bloody bite from one of the biscuits. I got up and helped Little Arthur clean the kitchen after he fixed my back. By the time we had finished, Mama came into the room.

"Eddie's sleeping. Get Debbie and yourselves ready. I'm going to borrow a car if I can."

We had done it before. Just like Big Arthur had done it before. She came back with the Murphys' 47 Buick. We were ready to go. I had Eddie, who was sleeping in my arms. Arthur picked Debbie up and carried her. Mama's face was swollen more on one side than the other, and she looked so different that I wondered if she were really my mama.

"Stop dreaming and get in the car, Sondra," she said in my mama's voice. My mama, all right, despite that alien face.

She didn't have to tell us to hunker down out of sight when we got into the area where the beer halls were. We had done it before. She must have reckoned that Big Arthur wouldn't know it was her checking up on him if he didn't see kids with her, like somehow that would make her look different. *I wonder now if she saw herself differently when she was alone and liked what she saw better than when she was with us. Is that why she left us?* I had made a pallet on the back seat floor for Eddie who was sleeping, and I stretched out on the seat. Arthur hunkered down in front with Debbie.

We'd drive around like that until she found him or she didn't. Either way, she never let him know she'd been looking. We would always end up back at home before he did, and she'd have to wake us up because we'd have fallen asleep in the car. Sleep was our way out.

"Bring the little ones on inside."

That particular time she came in to say goodnight or to check on me long after the others had fallen asleep. My body hurt, and I was still awake. Maybe the pain in my body, which kept me from sleeping, made me want to tell my mama all my sins and get forgiveness. Maybe I thought that Big Arthur kept beating me because I was bad, and I knew I was bad because of the games Little Arthur had started playing with me. So I tried to confess.

"Mama," I said to her when she came in the room. "Mama, Little Arthur made me take my panties down, and he used my fanny for a pillow." At least, I had made a start at telling the truth.

I know the door opened. I saw the light flash across the floor. I know I said it. But the door closed, and there was no answer, so I couldn't confess more. I wasn't dreaming. Perhaps I did not speak loudly enough for her to hear me and help me. Maybe it was not her. I had not heard Big Arthur come home, but maybe he had. Maybe he heard. Whoever opened that door had turned away as if I had never spoken.

The next day Little Arthur offered to bring home the big boy that he'd met while riding his bike on the country roads. I hadn't met his new friend, but I was already jealous of him because he'd stolen my brother from me.

"I can bring him after lunch," he announced to me while we sat on the porch eating pork 'n beans with little hot dogs in them. We had fixed this for ourselves. Even though Big Arthur was home until about two in the afternoon in the summertime, he started napping in the bedroom around noontime, and we took care of ourselves and the kids from then on. After a night like the one we just went through, we were especially careful about disturbing him.

"Yep, I'll bring him if you'll do *it* with him," he added.

I knew what my brother meant. He must have thought he was offering me a gift of some sort to make up for the beating I had got the night before.

I loved my brother. He was the only one who had loved me continuously from the time I was born. He always came back to me, even when he ran off to be with the boys and do things I was "too little for," as he explained. I could ride my bike by then, but that didn't matter. He still ran off and left me at times, even when we were both supposed to be taking care of the kids. He'd make it up to me by giving me a marble I wanted or bringing me some candy. Sometimes he would agree to wash the dishes for me at night if I didn't tell on him.

"I might," I said.

"How will I know?"

I thought of the darkest, dirtiest place I knew about besides the outhouse and the grease pit. It was the basement. Big Arthur had spent a lot of time in there "excavating," as he called it. It was dark and full of black dirt. It didn't have a regular door, but Big Arthur had hung a swinging door, so nobody would get trapped inside. Where the house met the ground, there were a few openings along the top of the dirt that let in some more light. Big Arthur was going to dig all the dirt out and make a room for us kids down there one day. I believed him because he had built the tree house and the go-cart, and he'd spent hours shoveling dirt into wheelbarrows that my brother and I would push outside and empty at the end of the marsh.

I didn't like going into the basement. It smelled like something had spoiled inside it, and I could never quite get my breath after I had been there for a while. But I chose it because I didn't like it. And because I knew what I was about to do was dark, dirty, and secret. I knew *it* was bad. I had tried to save myself by confessing to my mama the night before. I felt lost.

"I'll be in the basement. If the answer is 'yes,' I'll write it in the dirt at the door. And if it is 'no,' I'll write that there."

"If I bring him by, it better be 'yes'."

"It'll be what it'll be."

Debbie was with me in the basement. Eddie must have been in his crib upstairs sleeping when I heard Arthur and the big boy come up. I felt a warmth down there in my body before I heard their voices or saw their feet and legs beneath the swinging door. I felt the warmth rush up between my legs, up inside me when they stooped down to read my "yes" in the dirt. And then the door swung open. There were three of them, including Arthur. The tall one swaggered in. He must have been twelve or thirteen. I was seven.

He came over to where I stood in the dark. I pulled my shorts down. I didn't wear panties. He pulled his penis out. It was hard. He had to squat down. He pushed himself toward me. I straddled his penis. He didn't go inside. I felt the cool dank air of the basement between my legs and smelled its dead-rat odor. I pulled away.

"No. I won't do it!"

"But you wrote, 'yes!'" Arthur yelled.

"Look again," I said it as I pulled my shorts up fast and ran from the basement. I scuffed through the dirt, and wrote a quick "NO" in capital letters. I disappeared into the house and locked myself inside.

I could see them from the window when they came out of the basement a few moments later. Debbie followed them. Little Arthur picked her up. They were all laughing. I waited until the big boys had gone before I opened the doors to the house. I had the television on with the sound so low that I had to sit right next to it to hear it. When Little Arthur came inside, he didn't say a word to me. He just put Debbie on his lap and sat down on the floor next to me and started watching. He knew better than to make a commotion that would wake Big Arthur up.

I don't know where that "NO" came from. Whatever or whoever it was that prepared me to be my brother's lover had not prepared me to let others have at me that way. Not yet. Not for years. And only then when I felt love for them like I had for my brother Little Arthur.

Chapter 12

Bishop's Visit and Church Bells

My brother Arthur and I must have stopped reaching for each other in that way, or memory treats me kindly in being selective. Except for meeting Bishop, life seemed to return to normal for the rest of that summer.

The early mornings were filled with regular routines of cleaning house and helping Big Arthur hang out the clothes to dry. We didn't have to babysit until after lunch. Little Arthur still went off by himself sometimes or to run around with the big boys, but he never brought them around the house again. Of course, I was never a part of the gang again like I had been back on Portland Street. Maybe Grandma Blair had been right about that not being such a bad thing.

We had permission by then to go on the pier by ourselves or roam the woods across the dirt road where the tall pines grew and the underbrush climbed up and down hillocks. If I were left to myself, I'd wander along the edges of the pond, my bare feet feeling the smooth mat of grass transition into mud where the pussy willows grew. The first kiss of pure water, though, and I backed off fast, always aware of the water moccasin threat.

I chased butterflies and even sat out on the pier by myself. When I walked out on it, I would look into the water through the gaps made because the boards had shrunk. I was always mindful of dangers that were hidden beneath the surface of the water, but even that muddy lake caught the flecks of the sun and reflected whatever was near it. The other world beneath its surface drew me. I would sit hugging my legs and watching everything that moved on the surface of the lake, including the wind, the dragonflies, and the water-walkers.

It was a time of reverie and a time when my body felt calm in the daytime. I only remember a time or two when I sought the edge of a picnic table or walked beneath the tall wooden stairs of our back porch on which Big Arthur sat and was aware that I would see up the legs of his shorts if I lifted my eyes. I did not lift them. Still, his anger flared. Still, he beat me. Still, his mood could change in a flash.

He'd laugh one moment. The next, he'd unbuckle his belt or reach for whatever was nearby to beat me with.

One time it was the garden hose, green like the garden snakes but carrying the venom that they did not. My mama wasn't around that time, and I didn't even bother telling her. I had learned to care for the cuts, and besides, the hose made bruises mostly. Maybe Big Arthur knew he was way out of line with me. Maybe that's why he arranged the mornings, so I would be out of his view. Big Arthur disappeared at lunch, just as Little Arthur's Davy Crockett watch told us it was time to return home.

On one of those days after Big Arthur had gone off to work at Phillip Morris, somebody knocked at the door. The screen was shut, but it wasn't locked. I was the first one to get to the door.

"You must be Sondra," he said. He said it like Mama did.

I stared out at him. "I'm a friend of your mother's. Is she home?"

I still stared. I reached up and latched the screen door right in front of his face. There was something familiar about him, but I couldn't place him.

He took a step away from the door.

"Tell your mama that Bishop came by. Can you remember my name? It's Bishop."

(I have remembered that name across all these years. The odd sound of his name coupled with the unsettling sense I had that I knew him has always left me feeling a connection to him.

"Mama, tell me about Bishop." My children were grown and gone. My last marriage was over. I was on the brink of my fifth marriage, and I had come home. I had come home to this new love and to find out what happened here all those years ago. What wound did I suffer that I had carried with me and that had left me feeling unworthy and caused me to choose good men who were bad for me? Or was there no secret wound? Was it simply that in the broad light of day, I was not loved well enough and consistently enough by anyone other than my brother, who was also my abuser? Wasn't that wound enough?

"Bishop? He was one of your daddy's friends, but you were too little to remember him."

She is sitting in the front seat of the little Mercedes that her new love, Raeford, is driving. They are not well off, but they are able to take care of themselves in a South Carolina low-country sort of way. They live on a tiny

*peninsula that is surrounded by water. She always manages to find water to
live close to.*

*The pond is full of bass and brim and mud turtles that she and Raeford
feed daily, and it draws waterfowl all year long. Blue herons roost in the
trees, and emerald-green mallard drakes ski across the water's surface in the
mating season. White egrets come in such numbers to eat the fish in their
little pond that Raeford has been known to scare them off by shooting at
them. And I have heard a story or two about a crocodile or two that found a
watery grave, but he is not a bad man, this last one she has chosen. I wonder
if I have asked at a bad time, if she will speak freely with him there. Perhaps
I am not ready to hear the truth and so have chosen this time on purpose.*

*"I met Bishop once. Remember? I told you he came up to the house outside
of Greensboro when I was about eight years old. He wanted me to tell you he
had come by to see you. Who was he?"*

*"Lord, I remember he used to come up there to the service station near
High Point that your daddy and I ran. He wore those overalls like Daddy
Pope did, and he would stand outside talking with your daddy. He'd roll
those big old green eyes at me anytime I got near him. Golly, I thought he was
ugly. But he was your daddy's friend, and they would sit out in his car and
drink that white lightning he brought."*

"You ever see him since then?"

"No, but it don't surprise me he came by. He thought the world of you.")

That's as much as I could get from her, years later. That day
Bishop left me, I felt uneasy, and I was glad as the summer passed,
and his memory faded.

I loved the days Little Arthur and I chased squirrels and blue
jays together. Little Arthur was allowed to shoot blue jays—not
squirrels—with his BB gun, but he shot both. My dog Brownie, who
had acquiesced to our garage games as a puppy, usually found the kills
first, and by the time we arrived, only bloodied bits of blue feathers
or fur would be left, so I didn't have to look at dead things.

We both knew not to get too close to Old Brownie if he beat us
to the prey. Oftentimes, Little Arthur would shoot the ground near
Brownie to scare him away. Then the dog would be off and running
with his teeth clenched around whatever was left before we arrived
at the spot. Our hunting expeditions would dissolve into long chases

up and down the hillocks or up the faces of five-, six-, seven-, even ten-feet-tall road cuts. At the top, we dared one another to jump from those heights into the roadbed or gullies below us.

It was on one of those adventures when I first noticed the church bells. They must have sounded every day around noontime, but this time we were farther away from the house and closer to the church, or the wind was carrying just right for us to hear, or I was ready to differentiate them from the other sounds of the countryside.

"Did you hear that?" I asked, at the end of a long roll down a hill to the bottom where Little Arthur was already up on his feet and ready to charge to the top of the next hill.

"What?"

"The bells."

"So?"

"I'm going to that church some day."

"No, you're not."

"I bet I will."

"Well, I ain't going with you."

And he didn't. No one did. It took me almost a year to make good on my bet. But the following Easter dressed in a white nylon blouse, a sky-blue skirt that had a matching blue jacket, and wearing a hat that had little flowers on it, I pulled on my white, nylon gloves. Then I walked up the hill to the church I had seen many times when we made trips to the store across from it to get Fudgsicles or a loaf of Holsum bread, a can of condensed milk, or some candy treats for ourselves. I walked inside, unhappy that I had to go alone, but I was certain I would find the place as pretty on the inside as the sounds its bell made on the outside.

Chapter 13

Church Columns and the Troll

Easter had come in early May that year, so it was already warm and sunny. All Saturday before that Easter Sunday, the whole family went shopping. Mama bought me that blue linen ensemble, an outfit unlike any she had ever bought me before or would ever buy me thereafter. For Little Arthur, there was a suit and tie; for Debbie, a dress and hat, but not so fine as my own. Even the baby Eddie got a shirt that matched his pants and sports coat. We all got new shoes, and when we arrived back home, we dressed up and put on our own little Easter parade for Big Arthur and Mama. Nobody but me was excited about going to church, but Mama promised that we would go to the fair afterwards and get to ride on the Ferris wheel, so the others stopped complaining. Of course, there would be Easter baskets with chocolate eggs and jellybeans.

The next morning I was so excited about going to church that I hardly paid attention to my Easter basket. I pulled on most of my Easter finery before I went to my breakfast of frosted flakes and instant milk. Nobody else was getting dressed up, and I sat at the table, eating alone. Everybody was already outside looking for Easter eggs, except for Mama who was fussing around in the kitchen.

"Grandma Morgan's come to visit us. She wanted to surprise us all, so she waited until she got to the bus station in Crossville to call your aunt Ida and uncle Will. Will came over right before you got up and told us, honey. I gotta clean house before she gets to Greensboro, and I don't have much time," my mama explained.

"We're not going to the fair?"

"No."

"What about church?"

"No. You still go on if you want to, honey, but the rest of us are staying home," Mama said.

"Can't you please come with me?"

She just shook her head and turned away.

Little Arthur popped his head around the corner. He'd been eavesdropping. He cut his dark brown eyes at me as if to say, "See, I told you so. You'll never go."

"Oh, yes, I will," I blurted out to his imagined taunt. Then to my mama, "I'm going anyway."

I didn't even remember my mama's mama. She didn't mean anything to me then, so I scooted off to church without any of them. Nobody drove me because, I guess, they needed the car to get Grandma Morgan, *whoever that was.*

My mama adjusted my hat when I came out of the bedroom, and she slipped a dime into my hand.

"I don't know if they take up a collection in Sunday school or not, Sondra, but if they do, put this in the collection plate when they pass it around."

"Okay," I said, as I imagined a kitchen plate being passed around, full of coins.

I stood outside on the church steps, looking up at the bell tower. It was playing its songs, and I liked standing near it. I must have seemed lost, though, as I was looking up and then looking around at the large Easter Sunday congregation. I was simply enjoying all the finery of hats and bonnets and dresses, and feeling proud that my mama had dressed me just right. I felt like I fit right in until a tall lady bent down, so she could look me in the eyes.

"Did you lose your mommy and daddy in all this crowd?" she asked.

"No ma'am. My mama didn't come cause her mama's in the bus station, and my daddy is dead."

"Oh." Then, "Well. I mean, let's get you with someone who can take you into Sunday school." She looked around. "Laura, come here. Come here. Take—what's your name?"

"Sandra. *Sandra.* Not Sondra."

"Well, then, take Sandra to your Sunday school class with you."

Laura was pretty. Blond with blue eyes. Like Deborah. But she smiled at me, and I forgave her for being beautiful. She led me to the class, and it looked like a miniature schoolroom. I hadn't counted on that, but I liked school well enough, so I sat down. The church bells had stopped ringing, and I felt an empty cavernous ache in the air like it missed the bells the way I did.

Then a woman arrived who stood at the front of the room. She was dressed in lavender. *Everything* she wore was lavender. Her shoes, her hat, her dress, her gloves, even her lipstick was lavender, not ruby-red like Grandma Blair's. She handed out booklets to us, and she asked us to take turns reading aloud. I was a super reader, so I didn't mind that. But from the beginning, I couldn't follow along. I was scared I'd be spanked for not keeping the place or sent out to some Sunday school principal, but I couldn't understand where the others were getting the words. The things they read weren't on the page in front of me, at least not all of them.

I would start to read the words to myself, then there would be a white space, and when I continued reading the next words in the line, the story wouldn't make any sense. This church stuff was really hard to understand!

"Sandra, right? That's it, isn't it? It's your turn now."

"I can't find the place," I muttered it.

She placed a long lavender fingernail under the word on the page where I should begin reading. I started. The first few words made sense. Then when I skipped over the white space, I was just calling out words that did not add up to anything.

"Wait a minute. That's not the next line. Have you lost your place again?" Some of the kids laughed, a low, nervous, glad-it's-not-me-that-messed-up laugh of relief.

"I don't think so, ma'am, I said. I'm reading straight across the page."

"Let me see where you are. Oh!" She laughed. Then she quickly closed her mouth and pulled it into a smile. "That's why! Look," she said, "these stories are written in two *columns*. When you get to the white space, go back here." The lavender nail pointed again. More kids joined the laughter, laughter that sounded less and less like relief laughter.

I read the words silently. They made sense. Every time I got to the white space, I went back to the side instead of reading across the page. I looked up. "Okay," I said.

"These are columns," she explained. "Like in the newspaper or a magazine."

We didn't get the newspaper. We didn't take magazines. Even the *Weekly Reader* at school didn't have columns in the third grade.

"But I thought columns were what held up the roof on a porch like on our house at 1302 Portland Street."

More laughter, from her and from the other children. *The sound of ridicule in howls and guffaws: the-you-are-really-dumb-and-don't-belong-here laughter.*

"Columns are that. They are that, too, Sandra," the teacher said, still smiling wildly. She cleared her voice. "Now go on reading."

I did, but I didn't remember a thing I read. I wanted to be out of there. I hadn't intended on going to school on the weekend in the first place. I had only wanted to hear what those bells sounded like inside the church, and they had stopped ringing.

I stood up and, "I have to pee right bad." I'd learned most teachers at regular school didn't wait to see if you meant what you were saying, so it didn't surprise me when the teacher looked like I had said a bad word and let me walk out.

I pulled my hat off my head and stuffed my gloves inside it. I dawdled on the way home, and when I passed the store where I often went to get a loaf of Holsum bread for sandwiches, I went inside. I sat on the bench out front, and I ate first one, and then another Hershey bar before I went on home. I was kind of sorry I hadn't gotten to see that collection plate, but glad I had that dime to spend.

As I raced into the house, letting the screen door slam behind me, the bells were ringing at the church again. They always rang twice on Sundays about an hour apart, but I had lost my interest. I headed straight for the bedroom and pulled on shorts and a halter-top. Mama still got Grandma Blair to sew up clothes for me and then for Debbie. It wasn't like old times, though, because Grandma Blair just sent them along with Big Arthur. She didn't come herself, so she never fussed over me like she used to. But there was still something of her fragrance in the fabric, a combination of cigarette smoke and something sweet smelling I remembered from her apartment. I don't know what it was, but that indefinable odor hung in the air of her rooms and clung to her, especially around her neck in the summertime when I would hug her. By the time Mama, Big Arthur, and the kids drove up the hill with Grandma Morgan, I had eaten most of my Easter candy.

Now here into my home came this woman, whose hair was white, whose eyes were blue, and whose mouth was set against me from the first time she saw me. She came through the door, right behind my mother, and before she ever got introduced to me, she clucked— *clucked*—at me. It was something funny she did with her tongue that made that clucking sound when she looked at me and shook her head from side to side. *I imagined it was her teeth that looked too perfect to be real—false teeth, then, clacking from side to side when she wagged her head back and forth in disapproval.*

"Dorothy?" she said and turned to my mama. *Dorothy! That wasn't even my mama's name! Nobody, including Big Arthur, ever called her anything but 'Dot.' Clearly, she meant my mama, and not me, even though I knew my first name was 'Dorothy.' Let her be fooled, I thought. My mama could protect me.*

"Is that the way you're dressing your daughter up?" Grandma Morgan asked. "Well, no wonder she has no friends and has trouble fitting in. You let her dress like a hussy." Grandma Morgan stared at me and clucked again.

I had on that new set of shorts with its halter-top, the ones that had big roses all over them. I know now the print was too mature for me, but I loved it then because I felt like I was wrapped up in a rose bush without the bother of thorns. And Grandma Morgan was wrong about me not having friends. Not everybody knew all my business. I had kept Linda Forest to myself, and not just because we got into trouble over that "If-you-see-Kay" business, but mostly because I didn't want to share her.

I never went back to that church, and there was never occasion to wear that suit again. I made use of the gloves, though. I turned on my heels at the sight and sound of that white-haired woman I was supposed to call "Grandma."

She was really some kind of troll, like those I used to avoid in the culverts in the park near our 1302 Portland Street house. How could my mama's mama be such an onerous creature? I shuddered.

I went back into my bedroom, without speaking to her. When I returned, I was wearing the same rose-patterned shorts and halter-top. I had made one slight alteration, though. I had stuffed those Easter gloves in the halter-top, so it looked like I had a bosom. I poked my chest out, right at her. I knew what a hussy was, and if she wanted a hussy, I'd give her one. I stomped through the house and left the lot of them behind me for the pier and for the reflections on the lake.

I was mad at all of them, and I was mad because the beauty of the church bells had lured me inside where nothing was pretty, not even the lady in lavender. I was mad at the tall lady on the steps who met me and talked to me like she liked me, but sent me away before I was done listening to the sound of the bells and before I was done standing close to the bell tower where I could feel the peels of the bells vibrate through me. And for what? School?! On Sunday!

It was an extraordinarily bad move on my part to run off from the Troll like that because it got me off on the wrong foot with Grandma Morgan. I was to stay on that foot, rather hobbled, for a couple of years because two weeks later after school let out, my mama packed me and my brother Arthur up and took us to Crossville, Tennessee, to live with Grandma Morgan. That was an extremely bad move on my mama's part unless she meant to drive me completely into the arms of my brother and unless she meant to lose me forever.

Arthur would have at me for two years before I learned how to say, "no" to him and to the loneliness in me that sometimes reached out to him right under the noses of the adults at Homestead House where my mama grew up.

I would never live with my mother again, nor would I see her more than a half-dozen times until I was thirty-six years old. I don't know what happened to the rest of my famous Easter outfit, but I stuffed the gloves in one of my pockets on the morning I left for Tennessee to use in case the proper occasion ever arose. From what I'd seen of the Troll, I suspected those gloves would come in handy.

Chapter 14

I Am Transplanted

Before we left for Tennessee, we had another flurry of shopping, which included a dress for me that had red, blue, and yellow polka dots and elasticized bands for sleeves. The top parts of my arms showed like the dress was sleeveless, but then the straps capped my shoulder. I remember that dress well because I could still wear it two years later when I made my second debut in church. For our trip to Grandma Morgan's, my mama put me and my brother into the 1952 Mercury. Our clothes filled the trunk. Arthur sat in the front, and I sat in the back. Off we went. Our path would wind through the Appalachian Mountains, through the Blue Ridge Parkway, and into the Cumberland Mountains where Grandma Morgan lived.

Right as the sun set on the first day, my mama found a small motel that had brown wooden cabins. She must have known it was there because as soon as we got there and went into the restaurant bar, some man came up to join us. She acted like she knew him, but maybe she was just flirting around. He sat with my mama at the bar, and the two of them talked. I think he had his arm around her.

I liked him because he kept buying Little Arthur and me those skinny, salty pretzels that came in small square cellophane-covered boxes. When I finished one box and asked for another, no one reminded me that I had eaten enough. No one made jokes about how a skinny girl like me could eat so much, or was I feeding a tapeworm. I simply got what I asked for—another box! *I didn't miss Big Arthur at all.*

Mama and Arthur and I all slept together that night.

I am grateful that she did not invite her friend in, like she did years later when Debbie was about fourteen and the two of them were traveling. Debbie had lots of stories like that to tell me and more questions than I had answers and even a few accusations to hurl at me when I was thirty-six, and she was thirty-two and we met again.

But that long-ago night, when we three—my mother, my brother, and I—were on the road together and snuggled into bed together,

I felt safe and happy. I had my mother next to me, and except for Little Arthur, who seemed more like a part of me than somebody separate, I didn't have to share her. I slept hard, and I woke only once in the night when the door opened. There was a sound and a sudden shaft of brightness from the outside. I sat up as Mama came back into the room.

"What's that light?" I asked.

"The moon," she said. "Want to see?"

I slipped out of bed. She opened the door and took me outside. The full moon lay on the mountain ridge, and I stood in silent appreciation. It was warm enough to be outside in my new baby-doll pajamas, and I didn't notice any mosquitoes. I wanted to sit down on the steps and stay right there.

"There," she said and pointed. "That's what's making the night so bright. The moon seems bigger here in the mountains, doesn't it?"

I nodded and looked up at her. She looked down at me. I could see that she had a slight smile forming, but she turned away abruptly, and said, "Come on back inside, Sondra." I did as she said. She locked the door. "You go on back to sleep."

She crawled into bed next to me. I snuggled up close enough that I could feel her warmth. I stayed just far enough away to keep from touching her. I did not want her to tell me to move over. I breathed in her fragrance. There was something more than baby oil or iodine or smoke in the scent.

We spent the day gliding around mountains and through groves of trees pierced by sunlight that liquefied and pooled on forest floors. I could see the smoke on the Great Smoky Mountains, and I felt rapture as the blue mountains turned into green ones when we got up close. Mountain streams trilled along the roadside, and the air was as sweet tasting as the stream water.

We picnicked alongside a stream so clear that I couldn't see the water itself unless I squinted so that the reflections of trees and bushes on the water's surface remained visible. It was as if there were three realms here instead of the two I had found in Clara J. Peck's reflecting pool and the muddy pond behind our Burlington house. In the streams I saw the outer world, the reflected world, and the imagined one in the deep places where the sunlight did not penetrate.

I lay on the grass, put my feet in the icy water, and breathed the air. Along rocks that dotted the streamside, I danced to the music in my mother's voice even when she warned, "Watch out. Some of those rocks are slippery." I hopped and hop-scotched for the longest time. Then I napped on the blanket she had spread in the warm sun. I wanted to travel forever, making occasional stops along the way, but always returning to travel further in the company of my brother and my mother.

When the car stopped at the front gate of the homestead, it was night already. Mama got out.

"Lil' Arthur, you come with me," she said.

He jumped out of the car and was by her side.

"I'll show you how, so you can shut the gate after I drive the car through."

"All right!"

I looked down the long lane. The lights in the house were on. There was an upstairs like in the stories I read in school about princesses and castles. Rapunzel, that's who I would be!

She drove through the gate. Arthur shut it, and we drove down the lane a distance about equal to that from the 1302 Portland Street house to the bus stop. I saw the headlights sweep across the yard and then across the house. That white-haired troll I was supposed to call "Grandma" was framed in the light of the front door, and then she was out by the car.

"What took you so long, Dorothy?" she asked right off. "Supper got cold."

Dorothy got out of the car. "Come on, Sondra. Time to get out," she said.

Then Mama simply lied, "It was a longer trip than I remembered, and I didn't have anybody to help me with the driving." She didn't blame me for lingering so long by the water or for falling asleep on the blanket by the stream. *I loved my mother more than I ever had, and I really did not understand that soon I would miss her forever.*

Supper was reheated. It was strange food, but good—pan-fried potatoes, fried apples, garden peas, and ground beef and onions. But the milk was awful. It came straight from the cow to the stovetop to be heated, to the refrigerator to be cooled, and then to my glass. The cream gathered at the top in a thick layer even though, as I later learned, Grandma Morgan scooped lots of it off to churn butter. I gagged on the cream-laden milk.

"What is this?" I demanded.

"It's good food, and you better not waste it." It was Grandma Morgan.

"Mama, she's not used to it," my mama defended me.

"Well, she better get used to it. We don't waste things here."

"Just eat your supper first and save the milk for later."

"Dorothy!"

"Just eat, honey."

The milk disappeared before the meal was over. My mama saved it for me and Arthur and doctored it with chocolate syrup the next day. Grandma disapproved. After my mama left, Grandma made it clear that once that can of syrup was gone, we'd better be ready to drink that milk "the way the cow and God made it." And we did. We even came to like it.

That night, with supper and dishes done, we climbed the stairway in the middle of the house and went up to the room on the right. The pine-paneled eaves came down on both sides of the room, but in the center, the room was high enough that even adults could stand up without hitting their heads. There were two windows, one on each side of the chimney. One bed was double and the other, single.

I slept in the single bed. Arthur slept in the same room in the double bed, and Mama slept across the hall in her own room. Right away, I noticed the latched door that led to an attic space. And when I opened the closet on the other side of the room, I saw another door with the same kind of latch behind the rod on which a few clothes were hanging. Mama pushed our suitcases into the closet after she took out our pajamas.

"What's in there, Mama?" I asked and pointed to the attic.

"Don't reckon I know anymore. We used to put foods we had canned in there and store old clothes. You can explore later on. Time for bed now!"

"No baths?!" I exclaimed.

"It's late. There's no running water, and no hot water, so we'll take care of that tomorrow."

I woke even before Grandma Morgan did the next morning, and I was out the door exploring. My bare feet welcomed the cool wet dew on the overgrown grassy lawn. I heard the first birds of morning, and I looked in wonder at the two-story stone house that stood before me. No other houses were in view. The roads were unpaved, and the yard was dotted with red and white oak trees. There were flowers blooming on both sides of the driveway and all around the front of the house. I would learn the names of all those flowers—pinks and mums and tiger lilies—and all the trees, and even the weeds, like devil's bonnet and Johnny jump-ups, during the next two years. The land itself would become my mother during those first two motherless years.

Grandma Morgan came around the corner.

"You'll get the ground itch running around barefoot in that wet grass," she warned. Big-eyed, I stared at her.

"Come on up here and get your shoes," she commanded. She held them out to me, one in each of her blue-veined, wrinkled hands. She was gruff as a troll. That never changed, but she did relent and let us go barefoot eventually, and I came to mostly forgive her as I learned to love the land she knew so well and shared with me.

Chapter 15

Homestead House

The Homestead House, where my mother lived before she married my daddy, could have been a blessing for her and later for me and Arthur. Alfred Morgan, my maternal grandfather, was a carpenter who joined with a band of others during Roosevelt's WPA and built the homestead houses. Men, glad to be working, used their skilled hands to quarry the sandstone, which had oxidized into shades of pink and rose and orange and tan and was shot through with the occasional streak of marbled maroon. They cut down pine trees and milled the lumber into knotty pine paneling for the two-story homes they built on forty-acre parcels. They built hundreds of these houses, using a few different floor plans.

My grandparents' homestead house had a front porch with a cold, stone floor and wisteria winding around a trellis to keep the late afternoon sun off the porch swing. From the porch, the front door opened into the living room. Beyond that lay a master bedroom, a bathroom in the hallway that it shared with a central staircase, a dining room with a bay window that opened to the backyard and to the barnyard that had two weathered barns, one for the animals and one for hay and corn.

A kitchen that had its own drinking water well beneath the floor completed the downstairs of the house. This kitchen opened out onto its own stone-floor porch. Two bedrooms were upstairs—one for the daughters and one for the sons. There were two attics instead of a root cellar for canned foods and discarded books and clothes that I scoured for clues to my family and my world. I lived in Homestead House from the time I was almost nine until I was almost eleven.

The land outside undulated to the horizon where it rose out of the Cumberland Plateau and became the Cumberland Mountains. On the homestead when the land was cleared and the pines lined our walls as knotty pine paneling, crops were planted in the low-lying bottoms, and ponds filled the lower-lying hollows. A stream that cut across the homestead was dammed, and the pond, thus created, spawned fish and frogs whose multitudes were only somewhat aided by the trout stocking that Granddaddy Morgan engaged in.

Granddaddy Morgan was a devout poker player and fly fisherman, who drank and ran around as devoutly as he played cards and fished. My mother, Dorothy Eugenia Morgan, must have got her gambling and fishing genes from him, as well as her propensity to alter her personal reality. Like her daddy, she chose sex and gambling, but she used pills instead of alcohol.

For years, the family toiled to plant the corn and the hay for the stream of animals they raised and slaughtered and ate. They cultivated the strawberry patch, the potato patch, the summer garden, the grape arbors, the peach orchard, and the apple orchard with its many varieties.

Grandma Morgan probably made no more jams and jellies and fried no more apples nor made more apple pies or bread puddings with apples than the other farm wives in the other homestead homes that had a similar floor plan and surrounded themselves by their own forty-acre plots. But together these women fed a generation of large families on these homegrown and home-processed foods. Grandma boiled water to wash clothes by hand, she made lye soap, and she blued the sheets, fed the animals, milked the cows, churned the butter, and cooked three meals a day.

Granddaddy was somewhere in the mix, doing his carpentering, eating those three squares a day, and giving orders to all those sons and daughters who, of course, joined in the house and farm work. In the midst of it all, Grandma still had time to plant flowers, and she knew the names of every living plant or tree. In the two years I lived with her, she taught me all she could in the course of daily life before she lost control of her senses for a few years.

Eleven years after my mother had shaken the dust from her feet and left and vowed never to return, she took Little Arthur and me there to live. My time on the homestead was a time of opening to nature. Even at thirty-six when I began this quest to understand what had happened to me, when I had traveled the world and knew its tugs, I still didn't understand why all the children left. But they all did—all nine of the thirteen who survived and became adults.

The daughters left the way daughters did then and still do, sometimes: they married and moved away. The sons found their ways into various branches of the military, and those who lived beyond their active duty, returned home only briefly. Then they went off to the world again to hone the skills the army had taught them, or to find other better ones to support their lives in the cities.

So far, my story is the collective story of white, rural America during the thirties, forties, and fifties. Even where it takes on an individual face, I fear that, tragically, it will largely remain that collective tale.

That first morning on the homestead, when I was eight and Little Arthur was ten, the world was wondrous. There were paths to follow to ponds; there was Old Dan, the horse, to catch and ride; and Polk berries to smash and smear on my mouth for lipstick. There were pigs to slop, corn to husk, cows to bring up from the pasture, water to pump inside and outside the house.

Then, as the years passed and the seasons changed, there were grasshoppers and lightning bugs to catch and put in jars and June bugs onto whose legs we tied strings, so we could watch those luminescent green-winged bugs fly around in circles. There were butterflies to wonder at, porch swings to glide in and tree swings to fly up high in, corn to plant, cucumbers to harvest, potatoes to pull up and secure beneath the earth between layers of tarpaper and hay. There was clover to plant and mow and bale; there were calves and hogs to slaughter, ropes to jump, turkeys to pluck, strawberries to pick and freeze, peaches to scald and skin and can or freeze, apples to peel and core and cut and turn into jellies and butters and pies.

There were times when everything blossomed at once and all the songbirds, including the whippoorwills sang me awake in the morning and to sleep at night. There were Nancy Drew mysteries hidden in the attic, in addition to old high heels and a brassiere I filled with socks and wore on the last day of school when Grandma Morgan was away in Nashville helping Aunt Jolee have her baby, and Uncle David was in charge.

I don't know where Little Arthur disappeared to in the daytime. I recall those years as a time of solitary walks and conversations with myself. At first, he and I clung to one another in the daytime. Then I lost him, but he always came back to me at night.

Mama left us two days after she drove us to this idyllic spot. She was small, and she looked little and so alone behind the wheel of that

Chevy Impala as she backed it down the long lane. I felt an aching in my chest, and tears burned my eyes. I stood next to Grandma. Arthur was on the other side.

"Don't either one of you cry, or you'll find out what's good for you," she said. "You run play. I got things to do. Don't go far, though. I may need you."

We didn't go far, but we stayed out of sight most of the day. We talked and cried until our eyes were red. We didn't want Grandma to know. Maybe we were just trying to be brave.

"Do I look like I been crying?" I asked.

"Yeah. How about me?" Little Arthur answered.

"Yeah," I said, "but I got an idea."

"What?"

The roadbed had rocks; granite, I would later learn. Some of the rocks had been ground down to a white powder.

"We can dust this stuff over our faces." I scooped up a handful and dusted my face with it. "How's that?"

"Better."

He smoothed out a part that was too caked. Then I took more road dust and powdered his face with it, too.

We passed inspection. Or we thought we did. When we came into the house, the Troll didn't seem to notice we had puffy eyes and red noses. But later that night when we were washing our faces, hands, and feet under Grandma Morgan's supervision, she did say, "How did you get yourselves so dirty?" The water was murky brown, and the sink had a ring around it.

We looked at each other and smiled at our deception. "We just played a lot," Little Arthur said.

We were proud of ourselves for hiding the feelings that Grandma Morgan didn't want any part of anyway. We were there to help her. She needed us. Granddaddy Morgan had taken up with the Redhead in an apartment in Crossville. We learned by eavesdropping here and there that all he did was "play poker and drink and run around with that redhead." Grandma Morgan couldn't manage the homestead by herself. She needed us. *Later I would learn that we were also there because Mama needed us out of the way while she planned her escape from Big Arthur.*

We pumped water, fetched coal, lit the heater, washed dishes, fed the livestock, hoed the garden, and helped can or freeze food.

We heated water in a cauldron outside for washing clothes, and we helped hang them out on lines. Every other house on the homestead had running water and hot water, I would learn from my mama years later. Granddaddy had refused to hook ours up for over three decades. The summer I left, he fixed it.

I had no idea what it would mean to live with Grandma, to live completely without my mother. And it was complete. If she called, she did not talk with us. If she wrote, I did not get to see the letters. I imagine that she didn't write. She still misses most birthdays and holidays. Once Grandma Morgan complained that Mama was not sending the money she promised, and "I know she's getting checks from the government from your daddy's death for both of you." So I supposed there were checks, if not letters, that came.

Once, during the second year I was there, a big box of clothes came. There was a beautiful camel-colored coat with a furry collar, and two sets of flannel-lined pants and matching long-sleeve shirts. One set was red with red plaid flannel inserts and gold buttons. The other was identical, except that it was royal blue. I alternated the two outfits and wore them all winter long.

She sent me a pair of funny-looking, lace-up, brown shoes that I wore out long before summer. Grandma put cardboard in the bottom of them, so I could go up the road to a birthday party that summer. She spanked me when I got home because she had walked up to get me, and I was jumping rope. I think she was embarrassed that the holes in my shoes showed when I jumped.

What remains of those two years foremost in my memory is my loss of my mother and my nighttimes in bed with my brother, right under the noses of my grandmother and my Uncle David.

Chapter 16

Sleeping Arrangements, Secret Places, and Why My World Shrank

In the fall I turned nine that first year on the homestead. Arthur was eleven. Grandma put us in the same bed to keep us warm when we had a hard freeze in January. What may have begun again as cuddling in cold sheets to keep one another warm did not end at that. Arthur rolled on top of me. He was hard there again. We hugged. I don't believe we kissed. But I know he pushed himself up inside me. *And I wanted him to*. I was able to lose myself in school and in nature during the day, but at night, I lost myself in him. By then, it felt natural.

I was nine. He was eleven. Uncle David was twenty-one years old and just out of the navy when he came home to Grandma to run the homestead for her. For a while, he slept in the same room with us. He took the twin bed, and Arthur and I stayed in the double one. Most times, Uncle David came to bed after we were asleep, but not always.

On top of the chest-of-drawers at the other end of that small bedroom was a thirty-inch tall doll that Aunt Shirley had sent me for Christmas. The doll was a replica of a full-grown woman. She had breasts, a tiny waist, and long legs *with nothing between them*. Arthur and I checked. She wore a blue net evening gown that had shiny blue taffeta beneath the top layer of net; she had a tiara on her head and pearl earrings that had pins on the back of them to stick into the holes in her ears. She fascinated me and Arthur. He wanted her from the time I opened the box on Christmas Day. We had slipped off together and undressed the doll.

He fingered her breasts, and he put his face against them. "You'll have these one day."

I felt a tingling in my flat chest that welcomed the possibility. In my imagination, I would grow up to be as beautiful as she was, and maybe somebody would want me as much as Arthur wanted that blue-eyed, blonde doll. Whenever I played with her, I imagined

I was her, that I was desirable, and I always ended by finding the corner of a table or a bed railing to soothe my longing.

("My daddy would have killed those boys if he thought any one of them was even thinking of touching us girls," my mama told me years later. It was another of those times when I went to visit her and ended up interrogating her. No wonder she doesn't welcome my visits. But there were questions because I needed to know what story I was a part of before my remembering.

When the remembering started, I needed to know what had happened to my mother, what had happened to Grandma Morgan, what had happened between them to cause my Grandma to endanger me. I wondered why my mama didn't kill Arthur when I told her what he was doing to me. I wondered what Granddaddy Morgan would have done to him if he had known what we were doing there in the bed right beside Uncle David, and when he left, right there in the bed beside Grandma.)

As far as I remember, Uncle David did not touch me. Granddaddy's lesson must have taken root in him enough to last a lifetime. But, surely, Uncle David heard us in the bed next to him. I *remember* the first night he slept in our room, and he was already in the twin bed when Arthur reached for me.

"No, he'll hear us."

"We'll be quiet."

"He'll tell on us." Arthur was already on top of me. My body was riding the mimosa tree in my imagination. I became the elegant woman doll on the bureau, and I cannot imagine that we were very quiet.

I don't know how many nights Uncle David spent in our room before Grandma moved him to the room across the hall. I don't know why he didn't tell what he knew. Granddaddy had returned home, and he had the big bedroom downstairs. A few months later Granddaddy would move back to town, and I'd get to see the Redhead when she came to take him and his suitcase away from the homestead. I wouldn't mind seeing him go.

He chewed tobacco constantly, and I was the one chosen to empty his disgusting spittoon. And he called me "Sondra" like my mama had. My name was "Sandra." Every time he called me "Sondra," it made me miss her until one day, in my mind I lost the sound of her voice entirely. It was replaced my his harsh, gravelly, demanding command, "Sondra!"

So when Granddaddy moved out, and Uncle David moved with his new wife Toni Gayle into the big bedroom, I was delighted. Grandma started to sleep in the room with us, though, because Uncle Henry or Uncle Kevin and their wives stayed with us most of the time. Having Grandma there in the room didn't change things between me and Arthur. There was plenty of time before she came to bed because she always came late whether or not Granddaddy was there. Besides, we could hear her coming up the stairs, one creak at a time. When Granddaddy was home on one of his visits from the Redhead in town, Arthur would always wait and watch to see what Grandma Morgan did before she got in bed.

"Watch her," he told me once. "If she touches herself down there,"—he motioned—"that means she and Granddaddy *did it* before she came upstairs."

Enough light came in from the hall for me to see that, most nights, she did feel herself down there, but I didn't believe it was for the reason Arthur said. I'd watch as she took off her dress because she always slept in her slip, and right before she went to bed, right before she reached down to turn the covers back, her right hand would cradle that spot down there for just an instant. Then she'd reach up and adjust her slip strap and climb, bra-less, into the twin bed.

Once she was settled, I would sometimes slip my hand down between my own legs. Somehow it made me feel closer to her than anything else we did except planting flower bulbs. There was a secret there inside us, just like there was a secret in the earth that made things bloom. I knew that long before I ever knew the connection between sex and children.

Toward the end of my stay with Grandma Morgan, she took to sleeping across the hall again. I had the twin bed to myself, and something was happening to my body. It really was becoming like the woman-doll baby. It was the spring of the year when I would turn eleven in the fall, and my breasts were swollen, and I had one up on the woman doll because I had a few strands of pubic hair, too.

It was also the springtime when I was no longer allowed to walk down to the bottom or enter the woods by myself.

"Sandra, you and Arthur come in here right now," Grandma had said as she stood on the porch and called to me.

I was only slightly out of view. That day Arthur was with me. There was a yellow bell bush on the side of the house that was the most glorious wonder in the springtime. It grew in long separate fronds from the central trunk near the ground. It looked like a fountain of tiny yellow trumpets bursting from the ground and shooting up into the air before it arced back to touch the grass that surrounded it. I discovered I could crawl up under it and not be seen by passersby. That day I climbed beneath those fragrant branches, just the right size and flexibility for switches. Arthur was already there!

"This is my spot! Get out!" I said.

"Mine now!" he said.

"You've been spying on me. You saw me come in here, and now you are trying to take it over. But you ain't going to get it. It's mine."

"I know a secret," he said.

"What?"

"You share your hiding place?"

"For how long?"

"Always."

"No!"

"It's a big secret," Arthur taunted. "It's about Beverly Hornsby."

Beverly Hornsby was a tall, blond, pretty girl who was a couple of grades ahead of me in school. She rode on our school bus, and her father ran Hornsby's Handy Store, two or three miles down the road from us. I was jealous of her beauty and her body. She already had breasts. I hadn't seen them except beneath her clothes, but I knew they were there.

She was with Donna Ann Carlton in the girls' bathroom one day, and I heard the two of them talking. Donna Ann asked Beverly if she were wearing a bra yet.

"For a while now. Mama says she had to wear one early, too."

"I needed one for a few months, but my mama wouldn't hear of it. It took my daddy telling her that he was tired of sitting down to supper and feeling like he was at a hoochie-coochie show and for her to order me one from the Sears and Roebucks."

"Oh my." Beverly giggled. "Your daddy said that?"

"He ain't shy about anything. Just look at this," Donna Ann said. She pulled her sweater and her bra up in one motion and showed one breast to Beverly. It was the first time I had seen naked breasts since

Grandma Blair went crazy at Butler Sanitarium. Donna Ann's breast was sculpted like my baby doll's, but Donna Ann had a nipple, too. It was the raspberry color of Polk berries.

"Let me see yours," Donna Ann said.

Beverly Hornsby laughed. It was a musical sound, a low laugh, a shy one. "No," she said. She shook her head and rushed out of the bathroom.

"What about Beverly?" I asked Arthur, who was sitting up.

Then I heard Grandma's call to me and him.

"You tell me later!" I demanded, and we both scooted out and headed for the front door. When we turned the corner, Grandma was sitting on the porch swing. With the toes of her shoes, she pushed off and made the swing move gently. Behind her the wisteria vine was in full, rhythmic, fragrant, sweet, purple bloom. I sat in the swing beside her, and Arthur took the chair opposite both of us at the edge of the porch where the angel-wing begonias bloomed pink and coral, and the geraniums held up globes of tight red blossoms.

"Sandra, you can't wander off down to the bottom any more. You have to stay close enough to the house so that I can hear you if you holler, and you can hear me if I do."

I stared unbelievingly at her about this rule. From my first morning there, I had free run on the homestead. And I had used my freedom, tramping all over those forty acres, most times alone. I loved it even when I didn't love Grandma or Granddaddy or Uncle David or Aunt Toni Gayle or even Arthur.

"What'd I do wrong?" I asked, getting ready to defend myself.

"Now don't you ball up your face and cry," she said. But she didn't threaten to whip me if I did.

"But what'd I do?"

"I'm not punishing you. I'm trying to protect you."

I was astonished that I could be unsafe here, away from Big Arthur and with Granddaddy Morgan staying in town most days.

"But I ain't scared of nothing! Not bears, not snakes, not even the boogieman!" I declared.

"No backtalk! You can go east through the orchard and as far as this side of the pond." She used her arms to illustrate the direction, like I didn't know where the sun rose.

"Don't go past the gate to the big pond ever or into the woods there. You can go north as far as the front gate, but not out into the road. You can go as far as the fence to the west and not into those woods on the other side of the fence. And you can go halfway down the path to the bottom and no further. Never."

"And you." She pointed at Arthur. "You are not to play with those Stevens boys ever again."

Arthur just hung his head and looked at the stone floor of the porch. She rose to go. She was finished. Just like that, she hacked off three-fourths of my world without so much as a word of explanation.

"But why?" I asked. "I didn't do nothing wrong."

"No, but other people did."

"What? Why punish me for what others did?"

Grandma stopped at the door and turned around. She set her mouth. That usually meant she would say nothing more and neither should I. This time she surprised me.

"Beverly Hornsby was *raped* by Jerry Stevens down there in those woods beyond our bottom land." It was like she had to tell someone. She had to say it, even if it was to children. She had to get it out into the open air. She took a deep breath.

"*Raped?*" I asked. What could that possibly mean?

"Some boy hurt her real bad," Grandma said, and I saw her hand move toward herself, down there—like it did at night sometimes. I looked up at her. I was completely puzzled, but I was certain she was done with us. She had her hand on the screen door handle, and her back was to us already.

"One thing is for sure, he'll be sent to the state *penitentiary*," she told the screen door.

Penitentiary! That was a word I knew from reading Nancy Drew mysteries. Prison!

"But his brothers won't," Grandma went on. "So mind me and stay away from the woods.

I wanted to know more. "How'd—"

Arthur caught my eye and shook his head just enough for me to see he wanted me to shut up. He knew! That's what he was about to tell me beneath the yellow bell bush.

Chapter 17

Boundaries, Violets, and Violations

Chores took over the rest of the afternoon, and though I gave him several hard, knowing looks whenever we crossed paths, Arthur did not act like he knew what I meant. I was about done with my chores. I had to pump the water, and I was furiously pumping, pumping so fast that the aluminum cauldron filled before I realized it was full. Arthur came by just as it was overflowing.

"You better help me carry this water in!" I said.

"You better stop wasting water!" he shot back.

"You want to see me waste some water?" I screamed at him. With both hands, I shoved the cauldron over. "There! Now I dare you to tell on me."

He just grinned at me. He knew I'd just have to pump the cauldron full again, but I didn't care because I was mad with him because he had not told me what had happened to Beverly Hornsby and mad about something else I was just beginning to sense. That second time I pumped more slowly as the new word filled my mind.

Rape. I could not imagine something worse than murder or even as bad, bad enough for George Stevens to be sent to the penitentiary for life. Arthur had played with the Stevens boys, hunted with them, and fished with them. Now, he would be like me. Alone. That's why he was taking it real hard, but I was taking it real hard, too. I was worrying about Beverly at first, and then it changed. I began to worry about myself.

Finally, when he passed by me again on the way to slop the hogs, I called out to him.

"If you ever want to get under that yellow bell bush again, you better come talk to me."

"I don't care about no dumb yellow bell bush!" he shouted.

He disappeared around the barn to the pigsty, and I didn't see him again until suppertime. I sat across the table from him. It was just Grandma and Arthur and me that night. She sat at the head of the table. She had fried two squirrels because Granddaddy liked squirrels, and when he didn't show up in time for dinner, I saw her take the two heads that she had deep-fried and set them in the safe for him. He especially liked squirrel's brains, but she needn't have bothered to put them out of our reach. Both Arthur and I detested them.

No one talked much at suppertime. Just "pass this" or "pass that." When supper was over, Grandma said, "You better just go on and wash up, Arthur, and go to bed. Sandra will come along after she helps me with the dishes."

He was supposed to help clear the table! Grandma was favoring him again. One day she would favor me, and the next day she would favor him. One day she would either hit me or punish me in some way, no matter how good I was. The next day, no matter how bad I was, she would hit or punish Arthur. I was certain of the pattern, though Arthur and I had never talked of it. That particular day when I learned about Beverly Hornsby was supposed to be my day. Why was she giving him a break?

I did my work, washed up, and went to bed. I slipped in beside him, and he did not stir. "You better tell me what you know," I said.

Arthur didn't answer. When I shook him, he punched me once, hard in the upper arm. I turned over and cried. After that, he let me be that night.

Morning woke me with robins' songs. I saw Grandma's bed was still made. She must have slept elsewhere since no one else occupied other rooms that night. I slipped out of the house. Barefoot, I went walking through the yard, out past the orchard and the grape arbors. I passed the strawberry patch, which had just turned all its pale white blossoms into little green knots that would soon be bright, red, juicy berries. The path through the clover patch was well worn. I reached the gate. Instead of crawling onto it and jumping from its top railing, I unlatched it. I hadn't visited the pond in a while, but since new boundaries had been set for me, I wanted to test them.

I turned around, walked a few steps and looked toward the pond. *What I saw has remained in my heart and imagination all of my life. I already loved nature, but from that moment on, I have been in love with it.* The entire hollow, right up to the tree line on the opposite side, and all the way to the edge of the bowl in which the pond sat, had burst into purple bloom. The hillsides looked like they had been painted purple! I could see no green. I was standing in wild purple flowers halfway up my calves. I laughed. I breathed in their sweetness. I rolled in them. I picked more than I could carry, and I raced back to tell Grandma about them and ask her what they were called. She knew the names of everything, even weeds and bugs. She would surely know these majestic blossoms.

I raced and skipped my way back to the house, losing a purple blossom here or there. I scooted around the house to the back door. From a distance, I saw Uncle David. He had a hand on Grandma's shoulder. I slowed down. They hadn't seen me. I backed off and stood just out of eyeshot behind the corner of the house.

"I can't have these kids out here alone any longer," Grandma was saying. "It's bad enough that I can't afford them. Their mama don't help me in no way with money. I buy their clothes, their food, their birthday presents and Shirley helps out with Christmas. I am barely making it. If it wasn't for the foods we put up and the turkeys I earn when I clean them for Dale, we'd be going hungry.

"David, it is almost too late to plant, and I can't get nobody to plow the fields this year. You got to help out, or I have to sell out and move to town. That's what your daddy wants anyway." Grandma was crying softly.

"I know, Mama, but Toni Gayle loves living with her mama even though I don't care much for it myself. And after that girl was raped that way, so close by, I don't know if Toni Gayle will move back in," Uncle David said.

"They got the boy."

"I know. But there are other boys."

"Lightning ain't likely to strike in the same place twice."

"I know." Again, he paused. "I'll try. How is Sandra taking it?"

"She has no idea what is going on. But Arthur is taking it real hard. He hunted and fished with those younger Stevens boys."

"Hm-m-m. I wouldn't put it past Sandra to know more than you give her credit for," Uncle David said.

I stayed out of sight. I was afraid he was going to tell on me and Arthur. I heard Grandma ask, "What do you mean?"

He paused. "Nothing in particular, Mama, except that she is growing up, and she does live on a farm. She must have seen some of these animals when they were in heat."

"She never let on."

"Well, she wouldn't. She keeps to herself. But I bet she knows what the birds and the bees are. And I see the way she watches me and Toni Gayle when we play softball or when I hug on Toni Gayle."

"She didn't react when I told them about the rape."

"Maybe she didn't know what you meant. Maybe you need to talk to her in private, so she'll know how to protect herself."

"I'm not saying any more than I already have to her. I told her where to go and where not to go, and to stay within earshot. Lord knows, I can hardly get the picture out of my mind of that poor girl after she'd been beaten half to death and raped. I surely can't talk to Sandra about animals making babies. She'll just have to do what I say without knowing any more than I've already said."

Grandma's voice caught in her throat, and I slid around the house in the other direction. My arms were still full of the purple flowers, but I knew that I could not show them to her because she'd only be mad that I had gone beyond the new boundaries. My mind was full of confusion. I crawled under the yellow bell bush and placed my bouquet on my lap. I was trembling. *My mind was a jumble of purple blossoming squirrels hunching, their skinned, naked bodies and bloodied fur competing with images of the mature doll in an evening dress. Her skirt flew up, Arthur was on top of her, and there was smoke everywhere. I fainted.*

Arthur found me there.

I screamed when he shook me awake.

I understood what had happened to Beverly Hornsby.

"You've been raping me."

"I have not."

"You have so." He held me down. There was terror in his eyes.

"I have not! Rape is when you force someone to do that."

"Sometimes you made me. You know you did."

"Do you want me to go to the penitentiary?"

I was mad at him, but I still loved him. "No. No, I don't."

"Do *you* want to go to the penitentiary?" he asked.

"I never raped you."

"Sometimes you made me, too," he said.

Silence.

"I won't tell if you won't," I said.

"I'll never tell. Get out of here and get rid of those flowers before Grandma finds you been down to the pond."

"How'd you know?"

"I followed you."

"Why?"

"Just because," he said and slid out from under the yellow bell bush, but I knew he'd been trying to protect me.

Chapter 18

The Troll Returns, Aunt Toni Gayle
Interrogates Me, and I Outsmart Myself

Aunt Jolee, my mother's youngest sister, was PG. That's what they called it around me, but I knew they meant pregnant. Grandma Morgan had transformed back into the Troll as far as I could tell, and she could just pack up and go on to Nashville to help Aunt Jolee out when the baby came. I didn't care. Uncle David and Aunt Toni Gayle had moved back in. Nobody told me much of anything, not even Arthur, but I could figure it out, just by keeping my eyes open and my mouth shut. I knew I was about to be deserted again.

I took to sleeping in the single bed at night. In the daytime, I stayed to myself. I spent my time out tramping around the homestead, pushing up against my new boundaries, unafraid of being raped because I already had been, I reckoned, and I had lived through it. Arthur hadn't gone to the penitentiary, and neither had I.

When I tired of catching grasshoppers, or climbing trees to peek at bird nests, or singing "Que Sera, Sera" out behind the barn for hours, I raced to the front yard and jumped onto the swing and pumped my way up into the branches of the red oak tree, always looking for the sky in the openings between the leaves. Spots of sunlight on the way up with my eyes wide open were followed by rainbow colors on the way down with my eyes shut.

The Troll didn't call on me often for extra chores that spring. She was teaching Aunt Toni Gayle how to run the household. They busied themselves with cleaning and planting, and the Troll just gave me things to do if I showed up. She didn't talk to me about Beverly Hornsby or anything else really. When I grew listless, I'd sneak into one of the attics. The one inside my bedroom closet held treasures from other lives. I entered beneath the clothes, always picked up the box of Kotex my mama had left for me for when the blood came and wondered when it would and why it had to.

Then I entered the dark beyond the closet and sat with my eyes shut until the light, which came through the one small window, brightened the room through my eyelids. One particular day, I opened my eyes and saw a wooden box about the size of a footlocker that I had missed before. I thought perhaps it was one of Uncle David's he had put there since he moved back. But it wasn't.

I opened it and discovered high heel shoes, dresses my mama must have worn in the forties, and an old brassiere. I could almost smell her baby oil and iodine scent on the clothes. My breasts, which had been swollen earlier in the spring, were completely flat again, but I put that brassiere on. It fit me right well because I was average size for my age, and my mama and her sisters were petite. I lay in the darkened attic room in my underpants and that brassiere.

There was just enough light for me to read Nancy Drew mysteries in the attic, and I found *The Secret of the Twisted Candle,* a story about a young girl who was separated from her family. That story made me sad pretty fast and made me want to grow up and be Nancy Drew.

I crept back to the closet and got the Kotex box. I fidgeted with the menstruation belt until I managed to get it on with a sanitary pad strung between it. I strutted around in the attic waiting for the blood to come. One moment, I was glad my breasts had stopped swelling and my chest was flat again. In the next moment, I imagined my breasts were large and pink-tipped. Then I remembered the gloves and went to get them.

I patted the life-like evening-gowned doll that sat on the top of the bureau and peeked behind her into the narrow horizontal mirror. I looked at the doll's face. I looked at my own face. I imagined her face on my body. *There.* It was done. Then I bent over and pulled out the bottom drawer of the bureau. Beneath some socks and underwear, I found the gloves. They were sheer and perfect. I put them on my hands, like a lady would. Then I shoved some socks into the brassiere. Another glimpse of myself in the mirror, and I was strutting around the room, deliberately pausing in front of the window to expose myself when I heard voices outside. A sound behind me made me turn around fast.

There stood Aunt Toni Gayle in the doorway! Her halter-top was filled to brimming with her breasts, and her short shorts showed shapely legs. She gasped and then giggled at the sight of me. I screamed a little scream and ducked back into the attic.

"Sandra, I'm coming in there."

I slammed the small door that led to the closet. There was no latch on the inside, or I would have locked her out. Why was she coming into my room when I never invited her? She had taken my place with Grandma ever since she arrived, so why was she bothering with me?

"Sandra, I just want to talk with you."

I remembered Uncle David promising to get Aunt Toni Gayle to talk to me about the *rape*. As much as I didn't like that woman for taking my place, I decided to let her talk because I was still curious about Beverly Hornsby, and I wouldn't see her again until the fall when school began.

"Get away from the door, and I'll come out."

I didn't want her in my secret place. It was bad enough that she had seen me that way, looking almost as naked as Grandma Blair had been at the asylum. I certainly didn't want her to come inside my sanctuary. I changed quickly into my clothes. I removed the menstruation belt and Kotex and placed both in the box my mama had given me before she left.

"Sondra," My mama had said. "I want you to promise me to go to the bathroom every day, and I want to talk with you about menstruation," she said as she pulled me aside on her last night there. "When you get older, you will bleed from down there," she pointed between my legs. "I don't want you to be afraid. It is normal. It will last for a few days and go away. Then it will come again the next month."

"For how long?"

"Several days."

"No, how many months will it come back?"

"Just about forever."

She held up the Kotex box and took out the menstruation belt. "Just put this on and put one of these in it." She showed me how. "Then tell Grandma Morgan what has happened, but don't expect any help from her. She didn't even tell me what menstruation was, and neither did my older sisters. I just woke up in bed one morning with the sheets bloody and thought I was bleeding to death. When I told my mama, she just laughed and told me to drink some coffee. She was mad at me for stealing coffee when I was growing up, and that was her way of paying me back. I don't want you to wake up like that and think you are dying."

That was it. I had no questions. I was eight. She was leaving me with this woman who I did not know and did not like and who did not like me and who let my mama think she was bleeding to death. I had put the box and the belt in the back of the closet and waited for the blood to come. I had no idea why it would come, but I knew how to use the napkins to keep from bleeding to death. My mama made sure of that.

I emerged from the closet. Aunt Toni Gayle giggled about something I didn't understand.

"Hm-m-m."

She had no idea how to begin. I wasn't going to help her out by asking questions. I waited.

"Whose napkins are those?"

"Mine."

"Do you—do you need to use them?"

"Not yet. But when I do, I'll know how. My mama taught me. She didn't want me to bleed to death."

Another giggle from her.

"What do you want from me?" I glowered at her.

"I wanted to talk with you about Beverly Hornsby."

"What do you want to say about her?"

"You know she got hurt?"

"I know. And I know who did it, and I know what he did, and I know he'll pay for it in the penitentiary." I was repeating what I had heard. I didn't fully understand the words, but I knew these were the right answers. I got good at using words in my life to cover my ignorance and make myself fit in wherever I landed. *I became expert at being a chameleon later in life, and words allowed me to change my colors.*

"So, you don't have any questions about it?" Aunt Toni Gayle sat down on my bed. I still stood up by the closet door, guarding it.

"Nope," I lied.

"And you'll stay close to the house, so you will be safe?"

"Always do."

"And there's nothing I can explain or answer for you?"

"Nope."

She was trying to interrogate me like she was Nancy Drew or something, and I wasn't going to fall into her trap. She wouldn't like anything better than to get me out of the way forever, so she and Uncle David could have Grandma to themselves. I wasn't going to let that happen, even if I didn't like Grandma a whole lot. She was all

I had. Her and Arthur. I wasn't going to no penitentiary just to please her. She could stay in the best bedroom in the house, and just keep the door closed when she wanted to. I wouldn't ever bother her. I wouldn't even listen at the door anymore or peep through the crack when then door wasn't quite shut. I knew all I needed to know.

She turned to go.

I was trying so hard to become a woman, but I feared growing up because none of the women I knew were happy, not even Aunt Toni Gayle, though she pretended to be. Now I wonder how she could not have seen that my dressing up and my "performing or practicing" was different from other little girls. Was she so ignorant or so abused herself that she couldn't see what was right in front of her face? I was acting out, trying to bring to the surface the image of the slut that had somehow been seared into my soul when I was too young to defend myself. I was preoccupied in abnormal ways with sex. Perhaps she was, too, and that blinded her. Years later, my mother told me that Uncle David divorced her.

"Why?"

"He caught her in the basement trying to get your Uncle Henry to have sex with her. That's why."

"Well, if she was oversexed, Uncle David made her that way," I thought, as I recalled the times he made her take off her bra when we played softball and the times he left us outside alone and insisted she accompany him in the house. It didn't happen once in a while, or even once a day, that summer Grandma Morgan went off to help Aunt Jolee have her baby. It happened several times a day. I caught her crying afterwards a couple of times. And as much as I didn't like her, I wondered back then why she kept letting him rape her and when he would be sent to the penitentiary where he belonged.

I didn't tell my mama all I knew. Instead I asked, "What did Uncle David end up doing after he went to Detroit to live with Aunt Shirley?"

"Why, I thought you knew. He became a preacher."

On that particular late spring day when I was ten, and Aunt Toni Gayle had come to talk to me about protecting myself, she stopped at the door before she left.

"Honey," she said.

"What?"

"You might want to take that brassiere off before you come downstairs."

I looked down at my chest. It stuck out like I had breasts. Nice size breasts. I had done a good job selecting the socks.

I glared at her. "I ain't stupid," I said.

Chapter 19

The Redhead

I believe I got to see the Redhead twice. Here's where memory and dream and imagination get mixed up a bit, though.

I do know that when Grandma Morgan left me that summer to go stay with Aunt Jolee, I wasn't going to say goodbye. She had Uncle David put her suitcases on the front porch right after breakfast, and I heard her call for a taxicab. She was going to take a bus from downtown Crossville, and I was going to let her go, without crying. I was curious, though, about the taxi driver, wondering if it would be the Redhead. The only way I could get a good look was by going downstairs. And as it turned out, I actually had to go out onto the front porch before I could see clearly.

Not only was the Redhead in the front seat driving, but Granddaddy was in the back seat. I saw him open the door and get out. He walked up to the porch and picked up Grandma's suitcases. I heard him speak to Grandma, "Just didn't want you taking the bus this time. I'm going to drive you all the way to Nashville."

"You?" Grandma asked, and motioned toward the car. "Or *her*?"

The Redhead didn't get out of the car at first. I couldn't see her face well, but I thought she looked pretty enough. She wasn't smiling, but her face looked like it had something to be happy about. She certainly wasn't chewing on her tongue like Grandma did when she was mad. *But not mad at me or Arthur for once.* Granddaddy acted like it didn't bother him at all when Grandma turned and pushed by him on her way into the house. He simply followed her in. From all I'd seen, I knew he'd get his way, sooner or later, and I moved quickly to get a better look at the Redhead.

I practically had my head pushed through the wisteria vine trellis when she got out of the car and leaned back on the door. She held a pretty gold case in one hand, opened it with the other, and looked at herself in the small mirror. She patted the top of her hair, and leaned her head down to get a look at her lips. That's when she caught my reflection in the small mirror. She snapped it shut fast as she turned around. She stared at me.

I tried to yank my head back, but I had pushed it through an opening in the wisteria and had to bend down and roll my head to one side before I could back out of it. It took me several moments to figure it all out, and I must have looked ridiculous. But she didn't laugh. She still had that happy look when she strolled over to where I was after I had gotten untangled.

"Get yourself a little ruffled?" she asked.

"Naah. I didn't. I'm fine." Her eyes were green like mine, but there was something different about her voice.

"Well, tell me, whose orchard is that?" She pointed to our orchard, and the answer seemed obvious to me until I saw her looking hard at the fence.

"It's ours." I watched her. She walked over to the fence, stopped, and waited.

"Want an apple?" I asked slyly.

"Yes, I do."

"You're not from around here, are you?"

"Why, no. It's the way I talk, isn't it?"

"That, and the fact that you don't know what seasons apples grow in. Ain't one of those trees got an apple on it yet. They barely stopped blooming. Anybody around here would know that."

"So you found me out. You are quite a little detective, aren't you?"

I didn't answer.

"Why were spying on me?"

I didn't hesitate. "I wanted to see what the Redhead that took my granddaddy away from my grandma looked like up close."

"Well, how do I look up close?" She turned her head so I could see her full face, and then she smiled a little.

"Pretty," I said. "Right pretty."

She laughed. We hung on the fence for another moment. Then I said, "There might be a strawberry or two. I ain't looked for one a week or so. Want to see?"

She had raced out ahead of me, even though I was the one who knew the way. We had almost reached the strawberry patch when the horn blew. She stopped. She turned around and said, "Darn it. I have to go!"

"It ain't far. We're practically there," I pleaded.

She smiled. "Tell your granddaddy to bring you into town sometime," she said. "You could stay overnight at my place. I have a little kitten you would love."

I frowned.

"Don't want to come?"

"Grandma would never let me."

"Oh. Well, now she's going to be gone for a while, isn't she?"

"Why did you take him away from her?"

She laughed. She was ahead of me, hurrying to the car, but she stopped and waited for me to catch up. Then she said in a low voice, "I don't live with your granddaddy. He's old enough to be my granddaddy, too. He's all by himself, except for when he has his poker games. I've never even been inside his place. He just pays me to take him places."

"He doesn't like you?"

"Oh, I guess he does. I know he likes looking at me, but that's all he gets from me. Might not give him that if I could help it, but he's not blind."

"Why don't he tell grandma?"

"That's his business, not mine, but I think he just lets your grandma believe we're an item, so she will leave him alone and not come by his place."

I must have looked at her like I didn't believe it.

"Don't believe me? Okay. But don't ever tell your grandma. I am supposed to play the part of the bad woman."

"And you don't mind that?"

She smiled mysteriously, and then she turned to go.

I shrugged. I could understand anybody not wanting to be around Grandma all of the time, especially when it wasn't *their day*. I could also understand somebody wanting to be with the Redhead instead of just about anybody else. She was fun!

"I might believe you. What's your name?" I demanded.

She laughed and said, "You know. The Redhead. And yours, little girl?"

I was mad at her for teasing me, and at the same time, I wanted to be her instead of me. She was already walking away again. It was a long-legged, lilting walk that I would imitate for days. But she had made me mad because she'd stop for a moment and then go again before I could quite reach her.

"Little Girl," I yelled. "That's my name."

She beat me to the fence that separated the house and fields and made her way through the barbed wire without my help. I had just slid through the wire myself when I heard Grandma say something from inside the house. I headed for the yellow bell bush and ducked under it. I could see out down the lane well enough. I didn't like good-byes.

Out came Grandma and Granddaddy. Into the cab went the suitcases. Little Arthur, Uncle David, and Aunt Toni Gayle all gathered in the driveway for the final good-byes. I stayed under the yellow bell bush, and I watched the Redhead back the car down the long lane like my mama had nearly two years earlier. When she got almost to the gate, Granddaddy got out to open it. He had been sitting behind the Redhead in the back with Grandma. I slipped out from under the yellow bell bush, and the Redhead raised her arm and waved once to me. Grandma waved, too. I waved back to the Redhead, but not to Grandma.

Grandma called once a week after she left, and each time she did, I would not talk with her. Each time she called, it was to say she would have to stay longer. The baby had not come yet. At the homestead, things were disorganized, and the chores were falling to me and Arthur mostly. Aunt Toni Gayle's mother broke her hip right after Grandma left, so Aunt Toni Gayle went back home to stay with her. Aunt Toni Gayle had two brothers, who were younger than she was, and a father. And not one of those men was good for anything except laying up at the house and eating when they weren't out quarrying rocks or cutting school. That's what my Uncle David said. I rather liked them myself, and me and Arthur got to go over there with Uncle David whenever he went to visit his new wife, which was often.

That's when I learned how to dip snuff and smoke cigs.

Chapter 20

The Softball Game, the Broken Collarbone, the Shot in the Leg, and More on the Redhead

Uncle David always insisted Arthur and I play softball with him and Aunt Toni Gayle whenever he rescued her from her mama and brought her to the homestead that summer. I never understood why. We never got to finish a game. I do remember one game, in particular. Aunt Toni Gayle had managed to get the ball over the fence, and it should have been a foul, though nobody but me noticed. Uncle David was up next, and he was watching Aunt Toni Gayle run. He had convinced her to play in her short shorts and to take her bra off, and I knew it the moment she began running by the way she bounced beneath her shirt.

Arthur was on the pitcher's mound, and he knew it, too. All he could do was watch as she ran. I raced for the ball, but she had really blasted it, and it should have been foul. But like I said, nobody but me knew that or cared about it. I threw the ball hard to Arthur, but he didn't even know it had whizzed by him. He stood spellbound, so instead of him, I rushed for it. Uncle David caught Aunt Toni Gayle in his arms and hugged her when she made the run before I could tag her out, and then he held her at arm's length by her shoulders and eyed her breasts.

By then, I was close enough to hear him say, "They're great now, but we'll make them grow," he laughed. Embarrassed, she caught my eye as she tried to pull away from him. He continued to hold her and talk. "I once saw a woman in San Diego who could balance four beer bottles on each of hers. Yours will be like that, too."

He laughed a high, hysterical laugh, and he picked her up and carried her up the steps into the house.

From the pitcher's mound, Arthur had figured out the direction of things, and walked off toward the rabbit hutch. I didn't want to follow him, so I found my way to the swing in the red oak tree. I was angry that the game was over; I was angry that they both wanted her; I felt hungry between my legs, and I was angry about that, too.

I jumped off the swing when it was at its highest, and I fell to the ground, not quite shy of the stone front steps. I whacked myself pretty hard on the shoulder but didn't hit my face. I tried the front screen door, but it was hooked, and I knew from experience that the back door would be locked, too, so I didn't bother going around there. I scrambled up the stone chimney to my bedroom window, and popped the loosened screen off. My shoulder was humming some, but I kept ignoring it. The window was already open, and I climbed inside.

I picked up the evening-gown doll and put her into the closet. I didn't want to see another female body but my own for a while, especially not one with breasts. I stripped down to nothing. I left my room door open and lay in my bed with my hands on my bare stomach and listened to *their sounds*. I did not touch myself otherwise. *First, his loud laughs, then his shouts, and finally her soft sobs.* That was the part my body understood most. She sounded like a baby that has cried so long, it has almost lost its strength, and I cried with her until I fell asleep.

"Get yourself up, Sandra." It was Aunt Toni Gayle. "We're going to have supper at my mama's house." She called from the open door, and I awoke abruptly, leaving behind dreams of Greensboro, moments in my mama's kitchen, afternoons on the pier at the lake. I didn't want to come back, but when I did, I was glad for the promise of fried chicken and gravy. She turned the corner into my room.

I heard the gunshots ring out from the barnyard.

She screwed her face up and said, "He's out there with his gun and holster again practicing."

Uncle David had a fancy set of cowboy pistols and a red holster for them. He'd bought them somewhere on his travels in the navy. I'd watched him practice the first time or two, but it wasn't much fun because he didn't hit the Bell jars very often, though he certainly did draw his pistol fast. I knew fast. I remembered Hop-Along Cassidy from those few months of television in Greensboro before I had to come live with the Troll, who only listened to some radio station from Cincinnati, Ohio, on Saturday nights.

Aunt Toni Gayle's face had red blotches on it, the way mine did when I cried long and hard. I felt sorry for her, so I didn't grumble that she came on in talking and without knocking. I just got up and started putting on my clothes. I had to be really careful with my shoulder—or was it my neck? Somewhere in between. I figured out that even if I turned just a little the wrong way, it hurt. I made sure I looked straight ahead.

"Why'd you take your clothes off?"

"Don't you feel how hot it is up here?"

"Yeah, it's stifling." She looked around at the room like it had just been built, and she'd never laid eyes on it. She looked back at me. I was dressed and ready to go. In the distance I heard shots ring out again. I'd noticed that Uncle David got his target practice most times after his bedroom visits.

"Sandra," Aunt Toni Gayle began.

"Yeah."

"I need a favor."

"I need to borrow one of those Kotex. I can't wait till I get to Mama's."

I wondered what it felt like to bleed from down there. Maybe that's why she'd been crying.

I walked over to the closet and took out the box. "Here," I said. "You can have them. I don't think I'll ever need them. I'm starting to hope not, anyway."

Aunt Toni Gayle wasn't even twice my age. I was ten, almost eleven, that third summer with Grandma Morgan. Aunt Toni Gayle was eighteen. She seemed completely grown up to me at the time, something I couldn't ever imagine being. She giggled.

"Oh, you'll need them," she said. She reached for the box and took out a single bandage. "This will do for me." She unzipped her shorts. I watched. "Sorry, honey, but if I don't do this, I'll soil these shorts for sure by the time I get to the bathroom."

She reached into her panties and pulled out a wad of toilet paper. I saw a bright red stain on it before she folded it over. She slipped the bandage into her panties and zipped her shorts back up. She didn't ask for the belt, and I didn't offer it. Maybe she was right, and I'd need it someday. She had a bulge between her legs inside the tight shorts. She patted the bulge and giggled.

"I'll surely have to wear a skirt to supper," she said. Then she patted me on my head, and said, "Thanks."

That's when we both heard the blast that was different from the others because of the screams that followed it. I don't know which one of us screamed first or loudest in response, but we both raced down the steps at the same time, nearly falling over one another. I was certain it was Uncle David's voice, not Arthur's I had heard.

We found Uncle David out by the barn, lying on the ground and clutching his leg with both hands. Arthur had gotten there before us and was standing over him, and Uncle David was cussing like I wouldn't hear again until I grew up and met Suzie Taylor, who prided herself in cussing and taught me how to swear better than anybody but her. Big Arthur used to holler and cuss when he beat me. Granddaddy Morgan yelled at us until I jumped the minute he came in the room; my body was always ready to leap up and run. But these words were new—and old. Everything he said had the "If-you-see-Kay" word somewhere in it, and every other word came right out of the Bible stories I'd checked out from the library and read. It was the words in between the Bible story words that were new.

Uncle David's red cowboy hat had flown off his head and landed near the watering trough for the cows. He still had his pointy-toed, red-and-white cowboy boots on, and his red gun belt was buckled around his waist with the holster tied down around his thighs. He did not have on his chaps, and he was clutching his leg right where his dungarees had turned a dark slimy brown. Aunt Toni Gayle was down on both knees over him right away. She reached to touch him, to comfort him, and he hauled off and hit her, slamming her away from him. I jumped back. I ran toward the house.

"Jesus——-* *, ain't nobody here got sense enough to call for a taxi or an ambulance to get me to the doctor, or am I supposed to stay here and bleed to death?" he demanded.

The pain between my neck and my left shoulder was pulsing, so when I ran to the house, I hugged myself with my arms to keep from jiggling. I couldn't beat Arthur, who just showed up out of nowhere, and by the time I reached the house, he was already on the phone.

I started to race him back to the barnyard, but when I grabbed the door handle with my right hand and shoved my shoulder against the door to open it fast, I must have fainted. I do remember seeing Granddaddy somewhere in all of this, and I can still smell the alcohol

on him and hear him yelling at Uncle David about responsibility and
him having a wife to take care of.

I dreamed I came to, and the Redhead was standing over me.
"Am I dying?"
*"No, no, you just hurt your arm somehow." She smiled a sweet smile. "You
need to go to the doctor."*
"What's your name?"
"Brenda," she said.
"Like Brenda Starr," I said.
*In my dream, I went to sleep with her face in my mind, and when I woke
up in pain and sweating several times that night, I saw her face again and
again.*
I heard the gunshot ring out again and saw Uncle David on the ground.
*Granddaddy was drunk. I could smell it. It wasn't the first time I had
smelled it on him. Then Granddaddy did something I knew he was capable
of. That's why I always kept my distance from him.*
*Granddaddy kicked Uncle David on the leg that was shot and bleeding.
Uncle David howled.*
*The Redhead and I climbed between the barbed wires, each of us holding
the wires open for the other one. It took us several minutes to get to the
strawberry patch, but when I saw it come into view, I sped ahead and was
in it in a flash. I spied the first red strawberry, plucked it, and held it up for
her to see. It looked just perfect, and I wanted it for myself, but I waited
until she reached the spot where I was.*
"Here try this one," I said.
"Um-m-m! That's good."
*Then we were both down on our knees in the rows between the strawberry
hills. We were gently pushing the vines apart, spreading them so we could
find a bright one here, another one there. We ate them as fast as we found
them, and there were many of them ripe, enough for both of us.*
*Then she was taking me to see her kitten, and as we drove off, the
Redhead looked over at me and smiled. "Look in the glove compartment. I
got us something special back there at the house."*
*Inside the compartment was the gun that Uncle David had tossed after
he shot himself with it while it was still in his holster.*
"What'll you do with this gun?"
"I don't know. Maybe I'll become the new Annie Oakley." She laughed.

When morning came, I opened my eyes when I heard a voice, and I expected to see Brenda. But it was Grandma Morgan. Granddaddy wasn't around, and I didn't dare ask where the Redhead was.

"Well, look at you. How many times have I told you not to go running around like a tomboy all over creation? Your Aunt Jolee just had her baby, and I had to leave her to come back to this. Well, get up, and come on down to breakfast. You have already slept half the day away."

The Troll was back.

The rest of the day was spent at the doctor's office. I had a broken collarbone and had to wear a brace. After supper, I went up to bed early. Grandma had come upstairs with me, but she was already out the door when she stuck her head back in and said, "And don't you think this is going to keep you from having to do your chores. You got off easy when Toni Gayle was here, but you'll have to get back on the stick now."

Chapter 21

My Day, Your Day, and the Revelation

Grandma Morgan never really liked me. I knew it. I tried to stay away from her during those two years I spent on the homestead, but she'd call me to her, either to tell me the name of a plant or to quiz me to see if I remembered from the last time she told me. I always did. I think it pleased her. She'd ask me to get the hoe or to take a peck of apples inside, or to sit down and learn to can tomatoes or peaches or apples, or to freeze strawberries, or singe and pluck a chicken or a turkey. She didn't need to teach me to wash dishes or iron clothes because I already knew how, and she never tried to teach me to cook. Maybe that would have come later, but as it turned out, there wouldn't be a later. Arthur and I saw to that.

When Grandma Morgan came back from Nashville earlier than she'd planned, she just got meaner and meaner.

There was something inside her that had come to life, a discontent that had smoldered all her life, perhaps, and was starting to rage like wildfire as she hit the middle of her sixth decade. She seemed like Grandma Blair right before she cut her hair off. I know that now, but then, I only felt my own fear and caution increase.

Uncle David was in town with Aunt Toni Gayle and her family, Granddaddy was down in Florida with my mama, and Brenda Starr was gone from my life forever except in my imagination. During that time right after Grandma's return, I stayed away even more than usual. My "skulking around," as she called it, started one windy day when Arthur and I were helping her get the sheets off the clotheslines.

It was late June, but it felt like the dog days of August. The day was still and humid; it sat heavy upon my skin and felt thick and sticky like syrup on my body when I walked outside. A thunderstorm was coming fast upon us. Winds galloped through the skies like invisible, excited stallions, kicking up clouds and lightning that forked and flashed and clashed, making its way over the mountaintops that

ringed that high, broad Cumberland plateau. I loved the roar of the
thunder as the lightning split and peeled the skin off the hot, humid
day. The scent of earth was in the cool wind. The sheets flapped
rhythmically at first, then wildly, as the storm approached. Soon the
rain would be bathing us.

"Hurry up," Grandma yelled. "Don't bother folding them."

Grandma was at the far end of one of the clotheslines, down near
the house. Her line was stripped bare of all its laundry. I still had the
brace on to make my collarbone heal straight, so I had to reach with
my left hand mostly. It slowed me down. There was one last sheet on
the line, and Arthur and I were working together.

I reached for the clothespin at one end of the sheet and moved
methodically to take that center clothespin off, also. Arthur must
have reached for the pin at the other end at the same time. All it
took was one great gust, and the sheet wrapped itself around me,
beating me as it continued to flap.

"You look like a mummy," Arthur screamed as I giggled and
fought to stay standing while I unfurled the sheet from myself. He
didn't offer to help.

I got my head free first and just in time to see Grandma Morgan
coming at us with her jaw clenched and chewing her tongue. *I
remembered that it was my day, and that on my day she never did anything
bad to me, not even when I deserved it. There was benevolence about her that
I really believe she wanted to maintain all the time, but she did not have the
inner resources to do so. She needed a whipping boy or girl.* I figured she
was going for Arthur because he'd caused this and hadn't bothered
to help me out. *Besides it was my day for the magic.* She walked right up
to him and got in his face.

"Go get me a switch! Right now! Then get on up on the porch
before this rain starts pouring down on us. Wait! Take that basket
first," she demanded.

He didn't dally. There was no reason for her to repeat herself. He
was not in hearing distance when she said to me, "You are about to
get a whipping you'll remember all your life, young lady."

"But—but—"I stuttered. Then I tried again, "It's—it's—"

Grandma yanked the sheet off me, and I darted toward the
house.

"You wait right there on the porch for me, young lady."

Arthur was back fast with the switch. He handed it to Grandma when she arrived, and he turned his back to her. He stood right still, waiting for the switching to begin.

"You get on in the house, Arthur," she said.

He didn't move.

"Go now, unless you want one, too."

He turned around and looked me straight in the eye in disbelief. We had never spoken about Grandma choosing days, so I figured I was the only one who saw the pattern.

"But it's *her* day," he said in a near whisper.

Shocked, I looked from his face to hers. Somewhere in the background, I could still hear the storm. Either Grandma didn't hear or she didn't understand what he had said, but I knew. I also knew I'd talk with him later. I didn't mind Grandma so much when I knew that, no matter what I did right or wrong, every other day I wouldn't be hit. Now that Grandma had broken the pattern, I wouldn't know how to find safety.

The yellow bell bush switch was nothing like Big Arthur's belt or the garden hose he once beat me with. I yelled loudly anyway. The switch did sting, and my legs would wear its stripes for a couple of days; but it was the fear, the terror of not ever being able to relax around her again, that made me scream.

Decades would pass before I would understand that she switched me that day because I broke my collarbone, because she was stuck with me, because Granddaddy left her, and most of all, because I was my mother's daughter, "through and through," she would say when she whipped me like she was doing then, my mother's daughter who had gotten away from the homestead while Grandma herself was stuck there, stuck there with somebody else's children, while Granddaddy left to go to Florida where my mama was, the very day Grandma came back from Aunt Jolee's.

"The more you yell, the more you're going to get," Grandma warned.

I stepped out of the line of fire, twirled around and wrenched the switch from her hand. I felt the fire ignite in my neck from my broken collarbone, but I didn't care. She fell on me with her fists, but I was young and fast and able to move beyond her and out into the rain.

"Don't you dare run away from me," she yelled. But she didn't follow me into the storm.

I stopped. Pelted by the warm summer rain, I stood beneath the big red oak tree that held my swing. I twisted that yellow bell bush switch until its green stalk splintered and broke. I threw it on the ground. Calmly, I sat down in the swing and began to pump my feet until I was flying high enough to touch the leaves of the low-hanging branches.

She was still talking to me, but she never left the porch. I heard her last threat to lock me out until I came to my senses, but I planned never to do that. I knew that being under a tree, practically in it, during a lightning storm was dangerous. But I just kept swinging, reaching for the sky, for another dimension where there were rules and ways to protect me, and people to love me. Just there in the openings in the leaves, I believed they would come, and if they didn't, I wanted the lightning to take me away.

When the lightning didn't strike me dead and when the sun came out and pierced through the openings, I felt jubilant. I didn't even need the rainbow I saw beyond the house. I believed I had changed the world by wishing it. I left the swing, and despite my broken collarbone, I climbed the chimney to get into the house. Nothing Grandma could do would ever hurt me again.

When I swung myself into the room, Arthur was sitting on his bed.

"I'm sorry," he said. His face wouldn't change for the rest of the time he was in my life. He was simply a miniature of his future self. He'd grow taller, and his head would grow to fit his body, but his expression and his features, the pain in his eyes would always be there. He would always purse his lips that way and sniffle a little when he was uncomfortable.

I found dry clothes and stepped into the closet to put them on. I was done in a flash and back out to confront him.

"What did you say just as she was about to hit me?" I asked.

"That it was your day."

"How'd you know about that?'

"How'd you?"

"I figured it out."

"So did I," he said.

"I ain't staying here any longer. She's gone crazy."

"I know. And there's not any money left either."

"How do you know?"

"She took me into the pantry and showed me the money bag. She said Mama never sends her any money, and all she had left was what was in the bag. I counted it."

"You counted it?" I knew about the money bag. I sometimes touched it when I had to look for something in that pantry, but I never opened the bag.

"She made me do it. There were only pennies in it. Only two dollars and twenty-three cents."

"We got to get away from her."

"Where can we go? We don't even know where Mama is."

"We can write to Grandma Pope. I still remember her address."

He laughed. Then I did, too. I had gotten a snowflake bracelet from Aunt Shirley for Christmas that I loved. I wrote to everyone I could think of and described it. I probably had re-written the snowflake bracelet Christmas letter five times and sent it in separate envelopes to each of the family members who lived at RFD 1, Wisteria, North Carolina. We both laughed. Then I went for paper and pen.

I was almost eleven. Arthur was almost thirteen.

The letter read:

Dear Grandmother and Grandfather Pope,
How are you? Fine, I hope. Could you please come get us? Our grandmother is not well. We do not know where our mama is.
Love,
Sandra and Arthur Pope

Carefully, I addressed the envelope to Mr. and Mrs. M. C. Pope, RFD 1, Wisteria, North Carolina. Even more carefully, I wrote the return address: Sandra and Arthur Pope, c/o Mrs. Alfred Morgan, 310 Coon Hollow Road, Crossville, Tennessee.

We waited until early the next morning. Then together we slipped down the lane to the mailbox, put the letter inside, and put the red flag up.

Chapter 22

The Crumpled Letter and Remorse

I spent the morning in all the places I loved, crossing boundaries I had been warned not to cross. As I skipped through the apple orchard, I saw that the hard green apples had grown into knots the size of my fist. The strawberry patch stretched out in front of me, and as I surveyed it, I spied a few late berries, which I picked. The arbors had hard, green clusters of grapes that would ripen in another month. I climbed over the gate that led to the pond and raced imaginary competitors to the water's edge. I won, even though I had to go more carefully because of the broken collarbone and because of the little knot of strawberries I had rolled and tied in the bottom of my shirttail.

I sat on a rock at the pond's edge and dipped my feet into the water. Then, I hopped up and leapt over the run-off stream and ran on top of the dam, something I had never done before because I'd been told not to. The water was deep, they said. *The water was always deep.* But my footing was sure, and my angels must have been close by. I found a resting place on the far side of the pond where the sweet grass grew. That's what Grandma called it. Sweet grass. *She taught me so much about nature that I loved.*

The grass grew as high as my knees and gave way easily to my weight when I nestled down into it. I curled up there on the soft mat of grass, lay in the bright sunlight, and breathed in the sweetness of the land. I loved that place, that sanctuary, that land. I felt the thump, thump of my heartbeat as I lay there at peace, like a child on its mother's breast. I listened to the whippoorwills. I shooed away the horseflies. I gazed at the butterflies as they came tippling over the sweet grass. Then I fell asleep and dreamed, *sweet dreams I would forget the moment I awoke. I was saying good-bye without knowing it.*

My stomach growled me awake. I ate the warm strawberries, one slow bite at a time. Then I walked through the grass, back across the dam, and up the hill toward the house. I could tell by the feel of the day and the slant of the sun that I had missed lunch. A sudden thrill seized me! The mailman would have already passed. The letter would be on its way!

I didn't care how much Grandma fussed at me then. I remembered the other farm, the lazy summer weeks spent there splashing in the clear, sandy-bottom creek or making drawings in the sand beds, eating watermelons on the front porch, and playing with cousins who shared their paper dolls and comic books and their chocolate milk with me. I had another Grandma who loved me. I knew it, and I was going to be with her!

Opening the screen door wide, I let my fanny stop the door's return before it slammed shut. I had some manners after all. I heard Grandma from the front room. She was in the kitchen. I could hear Arthur in there with her. He was pulling up the metal cylinder of water from the well beneath the kitchen, and I heard the pulley whistle, the sound it always made as the rope rode over it. I started toward the hallway, so I could sneak upstairs because I knew better than to ask for lunch when I wasn't on time.

"Sandra," Grandma called. "Come on in the kitchen."

She'd heard me. I strutted in, jaunty and gleeful, thinking of the letter on its way to free me from the Troll. My mind was jittery with joy. *"Run, run, run, fast as you can, you can't catch me,"* it sang. *"I'm the—"*

Grandma stepped inside the doorway. She held up the envelope. She waved it at me. "I don't know what you thought you were doing writing a letter to the Popes without telling me, but it ain't going nowhere now," she said.

I could not react quickly enough to hide my shock, my disappointment. I felt it stalk across my face. She crumpled the envelope and threw it in the trashcan.

"Your mama is in charge of where you live, and she says you live here. Believe me, if I could change it, I would sometimes. The ungrateful way you act." She started toward the back door. She stopped and said, "I saved you back some biscuits and potatoes from lunch. They're probably cold by now." Then she was gone.

"Did you tell her? Did you chicken out?" I whispered in murderous tones to Arthur.

"No." His voice was hoarse and angry. "I did not! She saw the flag up, she said, and went to put it down so the mailman wouldn't stop if he didn't have to. But she looked in and saw the letter."

I turned to the trashcan. I pulled the letter out. She had opened it with her letter opener with one neat slash across the top. I looked. She had put the letter back inside! I took it out and read it again. Then I put it back in the envelope, found the tape, and taped the envelope shut. Arthur followed me around and even helped with the tape. Luckily, Grandma had left the stamp on it. The letter was ready to go again, except that it was crumpled. I smoothed it out as well as I could.

"She'll see the red flag again," Arthur warned.

"Nope. Because we won't raise it ahead of time. One of us will wait in the bushes, and right as the mailman comes over the hill, we'll raise the flag and fly away fast. Okay?"

"Yeah," he said. "I just wish it was Mama we were writing to."

"Do you know her address?"

"No."

"Well, neither do I."

The next day we waited in the big ditch behind the Queen Anne's lace for the mailman. Arthur found a tortoise and wanted to put it in the roadway so the car would run over it, but I told him to stay put, so Grandma wouldn't see us. I didn't want him to think I cared about the tortoise. I admired its black-and-yellow patterned shell in silence and kept my fingers away from its mouth, glad I didn't have to hear the whack of its shell cracking under the tire of a car, see the black ooze of the soft dead animal on the dirt road, or smell the hot fleshy scent of death.

The car was in sight. "You go," Arthur said. So I did. The flag was up. I was out of sight, and the mailman stopped.

As soon as I heard the mailbox door slam, I popped up from the ditch. As I watched the back of the car as it drove off, I suddenly felt sick, like I did when Arthur punched me in my stomach. I turned and looked down the long lane to the house. I was certain Grandma was looking out the window straight at me. She looked so harmless from far away.

In a less than a week, the aunts and the uncle would come and take us away. I would look one last time down the lane at a white-haired lady waving from the porch of this two-story brown limestone house. The lane would become a fairy-tale lane with tiger lilies blooming along both sides. I would visit there again in my forties, but the house would have burned down by then. I would take a stone from the rubble, a smooth, cool marble slab to use as a doorstop.

I would never see the house again except in memory, dream, and imagination. No matter how good the writer was, nor how unlike the description the homestead house was, every time I read a story that called for a stone two-story house, Grandma Morgan's would come to life. I would see the white-haired lady again when she was ninety, thirty years after my departure. I would lead her to her bedroom at Aunt Jolee's home in Nashville, where she moved shortly after Arthur and I left Homestead House. She'd turn to me and ask in her gruff way, "Well, are you going to come back this time?" I'd say I was. And I would—three years later for her funeral.

When I stood up in that ditch that day and looked back toward the house, I must have fallen out of time, and all of that future coiled up inside me must have sprung loose for an instant. I did not see the future events. I simply felt the pain of them all at once in my stomach. Then it was gone.

I took one step down the dusty lane. Arthur followed me. I leaned over and picked up a handful of dust and brushed my checks with it even though I hadn't been crying. It was my way of saying "The crying's over." He saw me and laughed and did the same. But for the rest of my life, I would have to live out the good and the bad and the necessary consequences of raising that red flag as I left that second mother, that land, that earth I loved and that loved me back, and went south, and then east, to the Fatherland.

Chapter 23

The Sudden Visit

Perhaps my certainty that the aunts and uncle would come was not so strong that day when I rose up out of the ditch as I now recall. Perhaps my recollection has been tempered by what *did* happen, and now in the future of it all, it seems certain it had to turn out the way it did. I do remember waiting, waiting for *what*, I wasn't so sure. *Would Grandma Pope write first? Would she call?* I stayed far away from Grandma Morgan and tried to avoid the long reach of her anger.

Then one day, even though I knew Grandma was in the kitchen cooking because it was close to dinnertime, I went on in. I opened the door to the "safe," a cabinet where she kept the dishes and the flour and the sugar. The cabinet was white and had glass doors and no lock. That she called it a "safe" had puzzled me before. I decided to ask her why. Her stony silence was disturbing me. Making her talk made me feel safe when I had to be around her. At least that gave me some idea what she was thinking and whether or not her mind was ruminating on wrongdoings she imagined I engaged in.

"Why do you call this old thing a safe?" I asked.

"What do you mean?" She didn't look up from the potatoes she was frying. She had peeled the potatoes, and sliced them so that the pan was filled with circular slices of raw potatoes. Beneath them was a bed of partially fried onions. As the potatoes fried, the smells began to blend and awaken my hunger.

"It's just a cabinet. It has no lock. It can't keep nobody out. So how can it be a safe?" I was drawing on my vast knowledge of safes and burglars that I had accumulated from reading Nancy Drew.

She laughed. "It's not supposed to keep people out. It's not that kind of safe. It's to keep bugs off the plates and out of the flour and sugar. To keep them safe."

I didn't mind that she laughed at me. I laughed at myself. I liked it when she explained things to me. I felt included. I had learned much about the world from her that would last me all my life. But Grandma Morgan turned quickly from me. She was at the window by the side of the safe, fast. There was a car driving up the lane. She had keen hearing.

"Now who could that be?" she asked. She took her apron off, smoothed her dress and her hair. "You look after those potatoes, so they don't burn." She went to the front door to greet the visitors.

I stood a moment longer by the window looking out. I saw the white hair of the man in the driver's seat. Startled, I turned to find Arthur right behind me. He did his fair share of skulking around those days, too!

"Get off me," I growled.

"Then let me see," he demanded.

I moved aside. I could still see the car. The doors were opening, and out came three people. I recognized them instantly. The white-haired man was Uncle Douglas, the tall skinny woman with dark brown hair and cat's eye glasses was his wife Aunt Evelyn, and the large-boned, big-breasted, tiny-waisted, and big-hipped woman with the short, red hair was Aunt Addie. I liked her best from what I could remember. In a moment, they were at the screen door. Then in another instant, they were inside the house. In our living room! Their voices burbled and gurgled from behind the closed kitchen door, and I could make out nothing of what was being said until I heard a loud, sharp command.

"Sandra, Arthur, you two come on in here and see your aunts and uncle," Grandma Morgan called.

That's when I remembered the potatoes. I jumped toward the stove, grabbed the potholder, then the handle of the skillet and shook them hard. I turned them over fast with a spatula. They were toasty, but not too toasty underneath. I chopped at them hastily with the spatula. Grandma had made enough for a family reunion. Arthur was at my elbow again.

"She'll be all over you with that yellow bell bush switch if you've burned them," he warned in a low voice.

I picked the skillet up and set it off the flame. I turned the gas down until I heard it whoop and die out.

"No, she won't. She ain't never going to whip me again. And neither is anybody else," I announced. *That inner knowledge made me feel safe. I had no idea that there were other ways, far more cruel ways, without ever hitting me, to burrow into my soul and devour me.*

I looked at the potatoes. I said to Arthur, "They ain't burned much, and it ain't my fault anyway. Nobody ever taught me to cook."

"Sandra. Arthur. Come on in here now." Grandma's voice was insistent, but it was her company voice, so it was not harsh like it sometimes was when we were alone.

Arthur pushed me ahead of him. There were more hellos and hugs and kisses than I could remember getting in my whole lifetime. Then there were good-byes and more hugs and kisses, and off they went. They were to return later in the day to take us to a state park, and Uncle Douglas said to Grandma, "Then we'll see."

"I have to call their mama. She left them with me, and I can't let them go without her permission," Grandma said to Uncle Douglas, who was the last one to leave.

"We'll be back around three o'clock to take them to the state park. We didn't mean to disturb your dinner."

"You're welcome to stay and eat with us. It ain't fancy, but it's abundant, and you're welcome to it, such as it is," Grandma Morgan said with vigor.

"No, thank you, ma'am. We ate early. So we'll go and leave you to eat in peace. And do try to reach their mother."

I was on the front porch, hanging onto the post and leaning out far over the yard. I didn't want them to go because I feared they'd never come back. And I didn't want to face Grandma. She left me there when she went inside to finish fixing dinner. I watched them and waved to them as they backed down the lane and until they were out of sight down Coon Hollow Road.

Reluctantly, I went back inside and sat down to eat my dinner.

Grandma looked up as I came in. All she said to me was, "Well, I see you've gone and done it now."

We ate in silence, cleaned up the table, and did the dishes. Her jaw was set, and she was chewing on her tongue. At any minute I expected her to send one or the other of us off to get a switch.

"Go get yourself washed up. And wear those new shorts sets Aunt Shirley sent the two of you last week. Go on. And be sure you wash your ears!"

We washed our ears and every other part of our bodies. Then Grandma skinned my hair back into a tight ponytail. In my two years there, my hair had grown out from the short, choppy cuts my mama always gave me. I had some bangs that fell down over my widow's peak and hid my cowlick. I didn't know what Uncle Douglas meant when he said, "We'll see." I didn't know what there was to see, but if he wanted to know if we cleaned up good, he was about to experience us at our best.

Right before the car came back up the drive, I heard Grandma on the telephone with my mama. I was sure it was her! My mama! I hadn't spoken to her in two years. I didn't even know Grandma had her phone number. Grandma was saying something like, "Well, all right then, Dorothy, I'll let them go." She was about to say good-bye when I burst into the room.

"Is that my mama? Is it? Can I talk to her? Let me have that phone!"

"Stop it!" Grandma yelled at me.

I was crying by then, and Arthur was in the room, too.

"Is that Mama?" he asked. "Mama?" he called into the receiver.

Mama must have said something to Grandma Morgan. I heard Grandma say, "Okay, Dorothy. Okay. But I don't think it's good for them."

Then she handed the phone to Arthur first! He listened mostly, and then he said, "Yes, ma'am. Yes, ma'am. I will. I love you, Mama. Good-bye."

I thought he was going to hang that phone up, and I screamed, "NO!" He gave it to me.

"Mama? Mama? Are you coming to get us instead of the Popes? *Please*, Mama. We much rather be with you," I cried.

Then I heard her voice. It was far away. It felt cold like the air-conditioning in the emergency room where they set my broken collarbone. "Sondra, you go on to the Popes for now. I can't come for you." I heard kids in the background. Debbie! And Eddie! I was certain of it. They had my mama!

"You'll have fun there. Remember how much fun you used to have playing there in the creek and being with your cousins?"

Another breeze swept through the room. It was a warm, humid, remembered breeze, a sea breeze that had blown inland fifty or sixty miles and become landlocked. It held the sticky heat of a hot Southern day without the coolness of the ocean evaporating into blue-sky air. I remembered the sandy bed of the creek, and how the water cooled my feet and eased my homesickness.

"Yeah," I said. "I'll have fun." I didn't say good-bye. I just handed the phone to Grandma and walked out of the room.

We must have passed the park test because the next day we began the long ride south. We twisted through the mountains, stopping by streams for picnics, the same streams I remembered from two years earlier when my mama had driven Arthur and me to Homestead House. I slept most of the way this time. I said I was carsick, but it was my heart that hurt. I felt it twist and turn the way the road did as though the land itself, which I had learned to love, was unwinding and exiting my heart until, motherless, I entered the coastal plain of North Carolina with my father's people.

Chapter 24

The Bedstead that Lightning Struck

When we arrived, a thunderstorm, complete with wild, Southern lightning and booming thunder, shocked me from my sleep just in time for me to walk on my own from the car and up the ramshackle, weathered, wood steps, across a porch of similar character, and into the front room of Grandma Pope's home. There Grandma Pope stood in the middle of the front room. Her long, gray hair was untamed around her face and billowed down her back as it wound its way to her ankles. It wasn't her daytime hair, so maybe that's why I didn't recognize her right off. In the daytime she plaited it and wrapped it several times around her head. I had no idea it was so long.

She wore a thin nightgown, no robe, and no shoes. She had drawn on a man's blue work shirt over her nightgown, and she crossed her arms over her mid-section to keep her bulbous breasts from swinging freely. I noticed things like that. She did not reach out to hug me or kiss me. Behind her was Granddaddy Pope. His white hair wisped around the sides and back of his head, and curled in one Gerber-baby lock on top. He had pulled on his overalls over an undershirt. Granddaddy Pope, too, kept his distance.

A single light bulb dangled on a wire from the rafters. There was no ceiling, just the roof through the rafters. It was after midnight, according to the big round alarm clock on the dresser top.

"Addie," he said, "you go on and help Mama put these kids to bed without waking up the rest of the household. Douglas, you take Evelyn on home and come back for Addie."

Then he turned to me and Arthur. He didn't use our names, but he looked into my eyes. His were marbled cat's-eye blue. Next, he looked directly into Arthur's eyes. "You kids are here to live. You better mind your Grandma." He turned around, walked toward his bedroom, opened the door, and disappeared.

Arthur and I stood there silently and looked at one another and then at our feet. The linoleum rug reminded me of 1302 Portland

Street in Greensboro for an instant, and that pain in my stomach returned. I looked away from the floor quickly.

"He could sleep on the couch there in the corner or she could, and the other one could have the bed," Grandma said to Aunt Addie. In the summers before, we had always slept in the back of the house. I wondered who else had taken our room. I knew it couldn't be Debbie and Eddie because I'd heard them in the background when I talked with Mama.

I looked at the bed and saw its iron bedstead. The lightning brightened the room almost more than the light bulb did. Suddenly, I remembered an old story from the summers we had spent there. Larry Pope, Uncle Douglas's boy, who was about twelve at the time he told the story, had warned us about this very iron bedstead.

We had been down playing in the creek. As I recalled, that's about all we did at Grandma Pope's during our summer visits besides eat her fried chicken, banana pudding, griddle cakes, and other sumptuous food, which we washed down with chocolate milk.

"You better come on out of that water," Larry had said. We had always been told to leave the water when the rain came. But I thought the rain was still a way's off. I must have been seven at the time, and fairly fearless. "You better come on before you get struck by lightning. It likes the water."

I was skinny and swimming in my shorts only, not the fancy bathing suits that my young cousin Betty wore, like I'd make sure my own daughters had decades later. I stuck out my tongue at him and jumped off the bridge into the water just as the lightning flashed, and then the thunder rolled. When I hit the water, my belly stung so badly, I was sure I'd been struck by lightning. I was up and out of that creek faster than I had dived into it! I started running to the house ahead of everybody else, and I was screaming. Larry and Arthur caught up with me, and Betty wasn't too far behind.

"Don't go so close to the trees!" warned Larry. "If there's anything lightning likes better than the water, it's trees," he said. As I raced away from the tree line and ran right up the middle of the sandy road, Larry nearly laughed himself hoarse. I ran into Grandma's house and headed straight under the bed, the bed with the iron bedstead that I stood facing on that first night of my arrival at Grandma Pope's.

"Oh, surely you shouldn't be under that bed. That's the bedstead that lightning struck!" Larry had squealed. And I scuttled out from under it like a sand crab making for the surf.

I jumped to my feet and started hitting him, "Leave me alone. I already been struck by lightning once," I wailed.

Grandma Pope materialized in the room. "Who says they been struck by lightning?" she asked. Larry pointed to me and laughed.

"Child, you've not been struck by lightning. You'd be knocked out if you had. Now settle down."

"But look at my belly," I cried.

She did. Sure enough, it was red from my waistline almost up to my neck. It looked redder than the Red Wriggler girl's back!

Larry laughed. Arthur laughed. Grandma laughed softly, mostly with her eyes. Even little Betty giggled, as if she knew what was going on!

"You've been jumping off that bridge again, haven't you, child? Well, I reckon you got your bellyful of it now, haven't you." She looked again at my red stomach. "It must have been quite a flop!" she said. Everybody laughed again.

"You kids can play here for a while, but go on up to Douglas's when the storm gets over. Meantime, don't aggravate one another to death. And, Larry, don't you go trying to scare them to death with your stories," she said and went out of the room, fanning herself with her apron.

Then she was at the door again. The twinkle was still in her eyes. "But let me warn you all to stay away from that iron bedstead. One time lightning struck it while Bernice (my daddy!) and your mama were in it. He screamed, and I came into the room just in time to see a ball of fire travel all the way around the bedstead. It should have killed them both, or at least knocked them out," she said.

"I know why it didn't," Larry piped up.

"What do you know about it?" Grandma Pope asked.

"Well, my daddy works with cars and batteries and electrical systems, and he says that the only thing that saved them was the rubber sheet they'd put on the mattress because Sandra was sleeping with them part of the time, and she still peed in the bed," he said.

"I did not!" I screamed, and I would have kicked him, but Grandma Pope's presence stopped me.

"Hm-m-m, imagine that. A rubber sheet saving them," she had said and walked away.

Then, three years later, I stood before that same bedstead. It was in the exact location. I had memorized the mallard duck design that was pressed in the middle bar at the bed's head. My eyes traveled over the arch of the iron at the bed's foot. I wasn't about to be the one to sleep in it.

"Arthur can have the bed. He's bigger," I said.

"No, you go on and start getting ready for bed. Arthur, go dress in the other room. Sandra, get into your pajamas here. Then climb on into that bed." It was Aunt Addie. She was no longer my favorite aunt. I didn't know who was. But it wasn't her.

Then they were gone. The light was out. Crying, I huddled in the middle of the bed. I was scared. That must have been why I let him slip into bed with me. He huddled close to me. He may have been trying to avoid touching the metal railings of the bed. He may have been trying to comfort me.

I really don't know which of us reached for the other first, in that particular way, or when comfort shifted into desire so that our bodies took over. And I don't know what sounds we made, but we must have made some that others heard and recognized. We fell asleep in one another's arms, and when we woke our world had changed again—in ways that made me wish many times over the years that lightning had struck me dead that night.

Chapter 25

The Creek Shrinks and We Lose Paradise

The roosters crowed us awake. We lay in bed, me hugging one side; and Arthur, hugging the other. We said nothing to one another, and I lay there imagining that it had all been a dream. He got up quietly and went to his couch bed. Grandma came to the door, and without a good morning, said, "Your breakfast is ready." Then she was gone to the kitchen.

The kitchen hadn't moved since our last visit. Hot grits with churned butter and fried eggs, sunny-side up, awaited us. And then there were biscuits, just coming out of the oven when we reached the table! And fatback and molasses and more biscuits. We feasted on the food and did not look into one another's eyes. *It all must have been a dream—Grandma Morgan's, the homestead, and the long journey here. And in a week or so, Mama would return to pick us up like she always had after our summertime visits to my daddy's people.*

"We're putting in tobacco today, so everybody else is already up and at the barn," Grandma said. I'm going up to the garden to pick some butterbeans. If you go wandering off, be back here in an hour to help me get dinner going. We have to feed the hands."

I looked at Arthur as she left the room, and dared him, "I bet you can't beat me to the creek."

We left our dishes sitting on the table and raced for the back door. I was barefoot. When my feet hit the dirt yard, where the chickens gathered to eat corn Grandma scattered there daily, I let out a hoot. The chickens left behind slick droppings that stuck to the bottoms of my feet. Arthur saw my predicament, laughed, turned, and ran back through the house to the front door.

I didn't even try to get the poop off my feet. I was far too intent on beating him to the water. I was halfway down the sandy lane that led to the sandy county road when he nearly caught up to me. The sand was caking onto the poop, and I felt like I had shoes soles glued on the bottoms of my feet. I almost stopped, but with one more step the poop cakes broke free of my feet, and I was on my way. I was still taller than Arthur was at that time of life, and I beat him easily, once my feet were free.

I hovered at the creek's edge, though, when I got there. My eyes were filling up with the scene, and what I saw did not match what I remembered. The location was the same, but the creek must have dried up some. It was so much smaller. And something else seemed askew. The bridge was gone! A huge metal cylinder, like the culverts in the Portland Street Park, went under the roadbed, and the creek flowed through it. Arthur had stopped at the water's edge, too.

"What happened?" he asked.

"I dunno," I said. "It shrank."

"Yeah," he said, and then before I could respond, he gave me a forceful push that landed me in the water, the cold morning water, colder because the sun wasn't hot enough yet to make escaping its heat desirable and the cold water welcome.

"You, you, you!" I could hardly get my breath at first. I stood up, and the water was only up to my knees, not my waist like I remembered. I felt warmer instantly, and I splashed him mercilessly until he jumped into the water to fight me off. Before long, it didn't matter that the creek was small, and as the sun rose in the sky, its warmth contrasted wondrously with the cold creek water.

I'd walked through culverts before in the Portland Street Park, but this one had water flowing through it, and I remembered from summers past that we never went in the water on the other side of the road. It was darker and deeper and the vegetation grew in closer, so that we feared snakes, water moccasins mostly, might be hiding there.

"Let's investigate," Arthur said.

I knew he meant the culvert, but I started downstream instead.

"Great idea! Nobody ever let us wander down the stream before."

"Not that way. This way," he jerked his head toward the culvert.

"That's not an adventure. We've been in culverts, but we've never been downstream."

"I have," he said and smiled mischievously.

"You have not!"

"Yeah, I have. Larry and I went down there once."

"I don't believe you!"

"We found an Indian burial ground." He paused. "Remember those arrowheads?"

"You said they were from Larry's collection he got from the mountains! That he gave them to you."

"I lied. We got them out of the graveyard, but he said we'd get in trouble if we said so."

"Show me."

"No."

"Then you're lying."

"It's just that it was—it was kind of spooky, really."

"Scaredy-cat!"

"I'll take you there. Later."

"Now!" I demanded, and then before he could answer I saw them coming! The cousins! Larry and Betty were running down the road. She was eight years younger than he was. He was tall and lanky, nearly fifteen years old. He was only pretending to race her, and he made sure she got to us first.

"Mama said she bet this is where we would find you!" Larry shouted. Then he splashed through the creek and greeted us with sprays of water in our faces.

Betty squealed her way into the group, and we splashed and played like water babies until the culvert idea came up again. It was an idea that would not go away until we had, one at a time, given ourselves to it. We fussed about who would go first; then we did scissors, paper, rock, and I got paper. I had to go first.

"Wait," Arthur said. "When you come back out, you'll have to get past us." He paused. "And you'll have to take your clothes off!"

"I will not," I said.

Betty giggled.

"Oh, go on," Arthur said.

"No!"

"Well, I'll do it for you," Arthur taunted. Larry's presence made him bold. "Oh, go on. You're already half way there. All's you're wearing is them shorts." He said it like he owned me. He lunged for my waistband. I hollered and entered the gaping metal mouth of the culvert and stopped just beyond his reach.

"Won't let you out, if you don't do it!" he laughed as he teased me. He stood blocking the way I had come in.

I turned to fix my eyes on the light at the other end of the culvert. That's where the dark and snaky water was. Larry's head appeared there now. He was leaning down from the roadbed. He waved his arms and made hooting sounds. Crying, I turned toward the opening where my brother Arthur stood.

"Let her keep her clothes on," Larry said. She'll have to get by us when she turns around and comes back. But if we catch her, we get to kiss her!"

Something in the way he said it made me want him to kiss me and made me hate him, both at the same time. But for the moment, he had saved me, for Arthur disappeared from view after a few more hoots that Larry joined him in.

The water reached my mid-thighs and smelled of swampy creatures to my young mind. An occasional strand of slippery vegetation would swirl past, grazing my legs as it did so. *Years later I would picture this particular walk as I read of Jean Valjean's trek through the sewers of Paris and when I read Rilke's poem about the descent of Orpheus to find Eurydice and rescue her from Hades.*

I heard some squeals, then splashes in the water, and a faraway sound of branches being brushed by someone's hurried departure. I turned around to look behind me. I saw no one blocking my way. I no longer heard anyone. My stomach knotted. Then relaxed. *A troupe of Javerts!* They are just trying to scare me, and I won't let them, I thought. They will probably pop out of the weeds when I reach the other side, I told myself.

"I know you're hiding in the bushes, but you can't scare me any more," my voice sounded fake, metallic, as it echoed off the culvert's sides.

"May as well show yourselves because here I come, and just so's you know, I ain't kissing anyone." I gritted my teeth and dashed through to the other side. I jumped out into the sunlight, and to my surprise, the water was shallow, not nearly as deep as it was on the other side where we generally played. I was standing up straight. The water barely reached my knees.

"Hey," I yelled. "Where are you guys?"

I turned and looked at the road, and gasped! A stranger, a tall, hatted man, whose face I could not see because the sun was in my eyes, stood above the culvert on the road.

I screamed.

Rape, I thought. Even though I had my shorts on, I immediately covered that hidden place that had only recently announced itself with a few silky strands of darkness. I started to dash back into the culvert when he spoke.

"Get the rest of clothes on, Sandra, and get on back up to the house."

The voice! It was Granddaddy Pope!

I was back in the culvert.

"I'll be waiting for you on up there. I saw the others scatter when I approached. There's nothing like a guilty conscience to make people hide themselves. Your grandmother has had to cook dinner for the whole work crew by herself whilst you and the others were down here playing your dirty little games," his voice bellowed the words at me. *Had he heard us arguing about me taking my clothes off?*

I cowered in the culvert.

"Get on, now!" he yelled. Let me hear the water splashing."

I raced, humped over, splashing all the way to the other side. I stuck my head out of the culvert, and I saw that he had already turned his back on me and was making his way up the sandy road. He was walking in long, slow strides, deliberately gauged to use the least effort required to get where he needed to go before the sun got to him.

Bare-chested, I went to meet my fate. It wouldn't be the belt this time, nor the yellow bell bush, and I wouldn't even recognize it as punishment until I began to live under the new conditions Granddaddy Pope laid down. I was about to learn that there were far worse things than trolls.

Chapter 26

Repentance and the Serpent

I had to pass a passel of field hands, who were waiting on the front porch for dinner. Most of them were young men. I felt naked in front of them. I didn't speak, and I crossed my arms over my bare, flat chest as I walked up the steps and over the warped wooden porch to get into the house. Little Arthur lounged among the field hands. I found a shirt and put it on before I went into the kitchen where the table was already crowded with people who'd been working in tobacco that morning. White people. The black people had to bring their own food. I remembered that from other summers. This was the first sitting. Those waiting on the porch were younger and would be fed at the second and third sittings.

Grandma Pope was at the stove stirring a big pot of fresh, cooked butterbeans to which she had added thin strips of flat-rolled dough—pastry, she called it. I walked across to her and asked, "Is there anything I can do to help, ma'am?"

"You can start on those dishes," she said.

I stood next to her as she spoke. She turned toward me, and our eyes met. Hers were brown, like Little Arthur's, like my daddy's, I was told. I was almost as tall as she was. She had some plumpness about her hips, but she was frail-boned beneath it. I felt taller and stronger than her. My heart hurt when I looked into her eyes. There was a deep sadness there that I recognized, even at ten years old. My tummy twisted in guilt as I looked at how small and old she was and knew how hard she'd worked to feed all the tobacco hands.

I scrubbed the pots and pans from the morning cooking, and as soon as someone finished eating at the table, I scooped up their plate, glass, fork and spoon and washed and dried them, readying them for the next table full of people. Grandma Pope and I worked elbow to elbow. I was washing dishes, and she was making biscuits. Then I was washing dishes, and she was taking pies out of the wood-burning oven. The temperature in the room was steadily climbing. I was washing dishes, and she was making more griddle cakes. I was still washing dishes, when Aunt Pauline, my Uncle Clifford's wife, who had worked at the barn all morning, came up.

"You're not too big to give me a hug, are you?" she asked from behind me.

I drew my hands out of the soapy dishwater, turned around quickly, and threw my arms around her neck.

"Whoa," she said. "Don't give me a bath yet, honey. I'll just get dirty again. I still got work to do." She laughed, and I knew she wasn't mad, even though her back was wet from my dishwashing hands. It didn't surprise me that she wasn't mad. I was her favorite. I was sure of it. I wouldn't even mind living with Granddaddy because she and Uncle Clifford, my daddy's brother, lived there, too. She was the one who always made sure I got chocolate milk when I visited in the summers. She was the one who always managed to smile and laugh with me and take me by the hand when we walked anywhere.

"I have to go back to the barn, but after supper tonight, I'll beat you in Chinese checkers!" She sat down and ate with the others. Before I knew it, she was touching my arm again.

"You go sit down and have your dinner," she said.

"I have to do these dishes," I said.

"You've done them all. Look."

I looked first to the table and saw that no one was sitting there anymore. Then I looked at the dishes, and they all stood, washed and dried, in endless stacks that no longer were returning to the table as fast as I could wash them.

Aunt Pauline picked up a plate for me. She filled it with a little bit of everything, including a piece of apple pie. I looked at each serving as she placed it on my plate. There were even some fried chicken wings left! There was one boiled chicken foot, too, but I had no interest in it. She winked at me as she passed right over it, and she said, "I'll bet those are your favorites, honey, but Grandma Pope would just die if I gave you the last one."

She put the plate on the table, pulled the molasses jar close to me, went to the refrigerator, and reached way behind lots of things to find the chocolate milk she'd hidden there for me! She smiled as she poured me a full glass. She put the milk away and turned to go.

"But where's Grandma?"

"She's already at the barn working. Be sure to put away the leftovers. We'll have them for supper," she said. Then she, too, was gone.

I didn't think about Arthur until I'd almost finished eating. Then I called for him. "Arthur? Arthur? Where are you?" There was no answer. I was alone in the house. He was probably at the barn, too. I looked around me. The door to the room off the kitchen where Arthur and I used to sleep looked like a second kitchen from where I sat. I turned and looked through the screen door that led to the back porch where the pump was.

Chickens were on the back porch. They sipped water from the boards around the pump. Grandma Morgan would never have let a chicken get that close to her house! I watched them for a while as they took turns sipping until a bantam rooster, with his fiery tail feathers and trembling red comb, crowed and jumped up on the railing where he flapped his wings. King of the creek like Little Arthur! The hens scattered. He jumped down and strutted around the tiny pools of water for several minutes. He eyed me with one eye while he stood in profile. Even through the screen door, I sensed his stern gaze. I turned back to my food and then to my survey of the room.

It was an unpainted room. Like the front room, it had never been finished. There were only rafters above. There was no ceiling, just the bottom side of the tin roof. Darkness gathered along the walls and traveled up to lodge in the rafters. I searched the darkness as well as my eyes could. Then something up there seemed to move, just for an instant. I froze. So did it. I shifted my weight and slid my chair out slowly. Again, I thought I saw a shadow shift in the rafters. I jumped up from the table and ran into a new, second kitchen. I realized that this second kitchen used to be the third bedroom. I couldn't understand why one house needed two kitchens. I stood in the doorway, and I strained to see into the rafters. Nothing was visible. Nothing moved.

There was no door leading out of that second kitchen, except the one I stood next to. There was a window I could try, but I didn't dare leave without putting the food away. Granddaddy Pope was mad at me already, and I couldn't risk more of his anger. He put me in mind of Arthur Blair, and that made me cower inside and out, so I had to go back into the main kitchen. I had no choice. I listened. I looked up. I lingered in the doorway for as long as I dared. I heard nothing. I saw nothing. Yet I knew it lurked there in the darkness. *I sensed it the same way all my life, I'd sense the eyes of men on my backside when I passed by years later.* Then I crossed over the threshold and went back into the old kitchen.

I did what Grandma Morgan had taught me. I covered every dish with a plate if it had no top of its own. I moved quickly, but quietly, with my ears tuned to all the new sounds and searching for anything that signaled something in the rafters. I put all the covered food in the center of the table, and I carefully took one end of the oilcloth tablecloth and pulled it up over the center of the table to cover the food. I moved to the side of the table, picked up the tablecloth, and folded it toward the middle. The oilcloth rustled as I moved it. Or was it the oilcloth? *My sense of being watched from behind hummed in the back of my head.* I stopped before moving to the head of the table. I listened. I did not move the oilcloth.

Suddenly, I heard the scratchy rustling again. I looked up into the darkness. Dangling from the rafters was a long black snake. It suddenly dropped to the floor. It lay perfectly still, its serpentine curves motionless. It had stunned itself in the fall. Instead of running, I stood petrified. The fall had stunned me, too. I memorized that snake's markings well enough to last a lifetime. It was black with inner-circling spirals of red streaming up its body to its head, which was suddenly black again.

It was not a king snake, nor a garden snake, nor a gopher snake, nor a green snake. It was not a copperhead, nor a moccasin, nor a rattlesnake. Arthur Blair and Grandma Morgan had taught me well.

The snake came to life before I did and raced straight at me. I jumped toward the door. I pushed it open with one hand. Before I could step out onto the back porch, the snake slid past me and out the open door. I let the screen door slam behind it, and I turned and ran toward the front of the house and out onto the porch. I took the steps two at a time. I watched the ground to be sure there was nothing beneath my feet, and I screamed as I fled across the front yard.

I didn't see her or the car. She suddenly appeared and reached right out and stopped me as if I had no strength at all. I screamed and fought for a moment, still thinking somehow that it was the snake that had me.

She shook me. She shook me hard. "Sandra," she said. "Sandra, what is wrong? Don't you remember me?"

I stopped screaming for a moment and looked up. It was Aunt

Dolores, my daddy's youngest sister, the baby of the family. I remembered eating pecans at her house, how she had called them "pee cans," and how odd I thought she was. I started to cry.

She pulled me close to her. Her bosom was large. I felt smothered. She squeezed me hard, so hard it hurt. "Don't worry," she said. "I'll never let anything or anybody hurt you again. I've come to take you home with me."

Almost fifty years later, I know she meant what she said, but out of her own wounding she ushered in a stage in my life so terrifying that my spirit went underground for decades. I lived twisted, stunted lives, the same pain constellating in slightly different patterns again and again until I could wrest enough of the truth from her to redeem myself and set my spirit free.

Chapter 27

Sudden Separation

I never told anyone about that snake. It wasn't meanness or fear of not being believed, not at first anyway. I was simply swept up in a flurry of activity as the aunts and uncles arrived and gathered at the kitchen table. They spread back the tablecloth to pick at this or that while they waited for the workday to end, and Granddaddy and Grandma Pope to return.

I hung around the edges of the kitchen, looking up occasionally into the rafters and wondering if there were others where that one snake had been. One by one, the aunts and uncles called me to them and gave me a hug or asked for some sugar from under my neck, like they used to when I was littler. I hugged them all, but I kept my neck to myself after my Uncle Douglas laughed at the ring of dirt that had gathered there while I sweated in the hot kitchen, washing dishes for hours.

He ran his finger along it and laughed, "You keeping all that dirt for growing sweet potatoes or black-eyed peas, sugh? Which one will it be?" All the others joined in the laughter.

They were joking around, but I had my feelings hurt. Also, I was afraid they'd eat up all of Grandma Pope's leftovers before supper, and she'd be mad with me. I scowled at all of them, one at a time.

"Sandra," Aunt Addie said, "go on out to the front room and start putting all your things back into those boxes, sugh. That way you'll be ready to go when Arthur gets back."

I turned to go as I was told. She called out, "And put Arthur's stuff back in, too."

There wasn't much to do. We'd only been there a night and day. We'd taken all we had for summer from Grandma Morgan's, but it wasn't much. I was able to fit it all in one box. I moved the box off the unmade bed when I had finished packing it. I began to make up the bed, all the while listening to see if there was distant thunder, seeking any early warning of lightning. There was none. I pulled the chenille bedspread up over the bed sheets, tucked it under the pillows, and turned to fix the sofa where Arthur should have slept. Instead, I sat down on it. Then I stretched out.

Aunt Dolores shook me awake. "Come on, Sandra, wake up now." I opened my eyes. I saw her standing over me, and I shut my eyes again. "No, no, no. You got your sleep, and you need to get up and dress. You should be all rested for church tonight. We got a revival going on with a singing quartet of preachers. Now run on down to the kitchen and eat something. Then get rid of the garden growing in that dirt beneath your neck, and come on back here and find something to wear."

"Yes ma'am." None of what she said made much sense to me at the time. Church had not been my strong suit since my solitary journey there on that Easter morning long, long ago. I rubbed my eyes open. I felt drained. "Where's Arthur?" I asked suddenly.

"He's already gone to Douglas's. I separated out all his clothes for him. He wanted to say good-bye, but you were sleeping so soundly, we didn't let him wake you up."

"So, he's spending the night there with Larry and Betty? Can I go?"

"No, sugh, he's not just spending the night there. He's to be living there from now on."

"He's not staying here with Granddaddy and Grandma like me?"

"Don't you remember, honey? I told you already that you were coming to live with me. Don't you worry; you'll see Arthur every weekend. I'll let you go over there when I come to see my mama, which I do every Sunday. Now go get some food. We got to hurry."

"How soon is Sunday?"

"Well, today is Wednesday, so that's Wednesday, Thursday, Friday, Saturday, and Sunday. It's the fifth day from now, if you count today."

I was exhausted. I was confused. I heard what she said, but I didn't believe it or know how to interpret it. Good or bad, I had known no reality that did not include the companionship of my brother.

From the moment I was born, I had an older brother. When my father died, when my mother deserted me, when we left behind all we knew of Greensboro and then of Crossville, Tennessee, we still had each other. To this day, I do not know if the aunts and uncles conferred with the grandparents about our nighttime noises and our daytime delinquencies. I suspect they did.

I imagine a series of secret phone calls, a secret plan devised for our own good, and a decision to lose no time in instituting a new order.

Back then, I didn't have enough understanding to even cry about it. Somehow, I still expected the summer to end and Mama to reappear to take us back to our old life in Greensboro. That she had been separated and divorced from Arthur Blair for two years was not something I knew or would have objected to, had I known. Debbie and Eddie and Mama and Arthur and me together would have suited me just fine. There was no love lost between me and Arthur Blair.

I left the room and went to the kitchen where Aunt Pauline greeted me.

"No time for Chinese checkers tonight, I suppose, not with you going on off to church with Dolores and then going on over to her place," she said. By the time she had finished speaking, I was in her arms. I was crying and trying not to and trying not to show it.

"Sh-h-h, sugh, it will be okay. You'll see." She hugged me hard. Then she pushed me gently away from her. She pulled out a chair for me, and she fussed with the food, organizing it on the plate for me like she had at lunch. But this time, none of it looked good to me although the glass of chocolate milk she placed next to my plate did tempt me a bit. Just as she put the last scoop of beans on my plate, I remembered the snake. I tucked my feet up under my thighs and sat Indian-style on the chair.

"Now you eat," she said. "You'll get plenty of food at Dolores's, but I'll tell you a secret, and I'll deny it if you say I said so—she ain't a very good cook!"

She giggled after she said it, and her eyes disappeared behind her crinkles. Then she pulled out a chair and sat down next to me. She didn't leave me to eat alone. I was glad for that. Already I had begun to look for the little things that would get me safely from moment to moment. I had much to discover about my new world, and until my mama came to get me, I'd have to figure out things on my own, without Arthur there to help or hinder me the way he always had.

I still didn't feel hungry, and Aunt Pauline complained in a friendly way, "You're going to be wanting that biscuit along about midnight, sugh. And that chicken and gravy ain't something you're going to see every day. Better fill yourself on up."

I laughed at her gentle probes. I was laughing when Aunt Dolores came into the kitchen with my polka-dotted dress thrown over one shoulder. It was the dress my mama bought me right before I went to Tennessee to live with Grandma Morgan. It looked brand new because I hardly wore it while I was there.

"Does this still fit you, girl?" Aunt Dolores asked.

"I dunno."

She put the dress across a dining chair, walked over to the kitchen stove, picked up the teakettle, and poured hot water into the dishpan. She cooled it down with some cold water from the spigot. "Finish that food fast, and come on over here," she said. She had a washcloth already lathered.

I put my fork down and went to her. Aunt Pauline followed me and helped me strip out of my shorts and top. I climbed up onto the sink which had only one spigot and that was for cold water. I stood in the sink and Aunt Dolores scrubbed me down with that washcloth. Then Aunt Pauline rinsed me off with the pan of warm water. Every bit of me came under their scrutiny, and those few strands of silk I had started growing on my Venus mound elicited raised eyebrows, but no words. When Aunt Dolores's eyes touched my body, they felt cold and critical. Their touch matched her words.

I was only ten, three months away from turning eleven, but she said of my flat chest, "Ain't nothing there to be shy about, honey. Not like I had when I was your age." I felt the sting, and when I looked to Aunt Pauline, she smiled just enough that I could tell it was a smile. Her eyes were still open. They twinkled like they knew a secret. Their touch was soothing to my body, soft like the inside of a daffodil.

Aunt Dolores scrubbed at me, and when I was clean and gently patted dry by Aunt Pauline, Aunt Dolores tugged my dress over my head. Then she handed me my panties, so I could put them on. Next I put on sandals with socks while Aunt Dolores gave a tug or two to my hair to get it back into its ponytail, and then she had me by the hand and out the front door before I knew it was good-bye.

Aunt Marlene followed us out. "Good-bye, sugh."

"Your Uncle Robert's at work, and we have to go by his mother's house to get the baby and Saralynn before we go to church, so come on fast."

I did as Aunt Dolores said. She churned the car up the sandy lane, and as we passed by Uncle Douglas and Aunt Evelyn's house, I saw Arthur and Larry and Betty all out in the front yard. They were playing softball. Aunt Dolores tooted the horn, and before I could tell if he'd seen me, we had passed the house.

"I was close to my brother, too," she said. "Bernice, your daddy. He was older than me by six years, but we were by far the two youngest, so we played together a lot until he got older. I loved your daddy, and that's why I wanted to be the one taking care of you."

I didn't say anything. I didn't know my daddy. I didn't know her.

"I even named you," she said. "I did."

"You did?"

"Yeah. Well, I picked out the name 'Sandra,' anyway. I told your mama that I was going to name my first girl child that. When you were born, she used it. So when my first baby was born, I named her Saralynn. So, you see, I really named you. And now that you're going to live me with me, it's like you were my firstborn after all."

My Nancy Drew ears opened. I could feel the importance of this information, but I didn't know yet how to interpret it, so I could survive this new life she had all planned out for me.

"Does that mean I get to be your favorite?" I asked.

Chapter 28

Salvation

"I don't have favorites. I love all my children the same, only differently. Like God does," Aunt Dolores said. It sounded like she'd been thinking about it, had even figured out what to say, if not to me, then to herself and to her own daughters when they would ask about the limits of love later in life. It sounded like Grandma Morgan could take a lesson or two from her, if she were telling me the truth of herself. Something in my heart hurt, though. I thought of Arthur. I could see the lie she was telling, even if she couldn't. She did have favorites, for she chose me and not him.

"We're here at Mrs. Shuler's. You come on in and help me get Saralynn and the baby."

The house she'd parked in front of was one-story and built with cinderblocks that had been painted white. It had a green roof on it, and a porch that ran the length of the small house. I smelled fresh paint before I saw the newly-painted, white rocking chairs sitting out on that porch, one on either side of the two front doors, a white door and a brown door.

Aunt Dolores knocked on the white door, which was to the left, and an old woman opened the door slightly, stuck her head between the open door and the locked screen, and peered out at us. That woman was all face and no hair, bald against that white door!

I jumped back, startled, thinking for a moment I'd seen Grandma Blair.

Then the door swung open wide, and Mrs. Shuler's hair appeared. It was bright white, as white as the door, and pulled back into a bun at the back of her neck. She wore a long black dress, and I could tell she dipped snuff like Grandma Morgan because I could see the plug of it in her lip and hear the slur of her words when she talked.

Without smiling, she said, "Come on in." Then, sure enough, she stepped out on the porch and spit a stream of brown juice into the hydrangea bushes. They were blooming, and then several of their sky-blue pom-pom blossoms had streaks of brown on them.

Aunt Dolores refused to go in, saying that the church service was about to begin. Saralynn had already darted out. She was brown-eyed and round-faced with brown curls. She didn't speak to me, but she watched me hard for a moment or two, then rolled her eyes and grinned, one quick one. "Is that the girl you said you were bringing home?"

"Yes, Saralynn. That's your cousin, but she's going to be your sister. Come on to the car." Aunt Dolores scooped up the baby Raina and took the bottle and handful of diapers Mrs. Shuler offered her. I just watched. No one said anything to me directly, and I didn't have much to say to anybody. We all headed back to the car, Aunt Dolores and her two daughters ahead, and me following.

I hadn't helped with small children since Mama had taken Debbie and Eddie with her to Florida and left me and Arthur behind with Grandma Morgan, but it didn't take me long to fall back into old habits. Aunt Dolores could hardly get over how the baby took to me. Saralynn, who was five, wasn't quite so friendly, and she made sure she got into the front seat and left the back for me and the baby.

I was watching how things were unfolding. I was looking to see how Aunt Dolores would love us all the same, only differently. I figured the front seat was part of the difference she was making for Saralynn. I wondered what difference she'd make for me later on.

I saw the church as she turned right off the highway into a dirt parking lot and drove around several lines of cars before she found a parking place beside the large, unpainted cinderblock building. Aunt Dolores drove a two-door, black Chevrolet that only had front doors. Saralynn hopped out of the car fast and ran around to her mother's side. Aunt Dolores practically had to push her away, so she could get out of the car. Then she pulled the seat back, so the baby and I could get out.

"Well, I do declare," she said, as she looked into the back seat and saw that I had already taken the rubber pants and diaper off Raina and was pinning a new diaper on her.

"You got any more rubber pants? She messed these up pretty badly," I said.

"Look at the little mama," she said.

We finished with that business fast, and I could see she was already beginning to see my worth. I had learned my lesson well from Granddaddy Pope. In this new world, I had to make haste to show my talents. I didn't want to be put out again. I wanted to settle in until my mama came and got me and Arthur and took us back to Greensboro or Florida to be with her and Debbie and Eddie.

I followed Aunt Dolores, who had the baby, and who held onto Saralynn's hand. I looked at the church as we approached it. It wasn't a small chapel like the one I entered alone on that long ago Easter adventure in Greensboro. It was a gray building that squatted on the ground and had circular slabs of concrete for steps, which led up to double doors. Knots of people, men mostly, hung around the sides of the church and were smoking cigarettes. I heard a deep voice or two and low rumbles that sounded like muffled laughter.

Inside the church, there were hardly any places left on the hard slat pews. What seemed to me to be hundreds of people were crowded into the church. Young women held babies on their laps, and old women kept grown children in tow while men in white shirts, with no ties on, sat here and there next to this woman or that one. A few older boys, who looked especially uncomfortable, lolled on the pews, and many children, as young as me or younger, were seated near overseeing adults.

The church was stiflingly hot, and fans, with full-color pictures advertising the crucifixion of Jesus on one side and Evans Funeral Parlor on the other side, were pushing the hot, humid air back and forth. Most heads turned, and most people stared, like they had a right to when we entered the church. Before I could stare them down, the pianist started playing, and everybody in the church snapped to attention. Someone in the pew we stood close to, slid over fast, and there was room for all of us. The sound of shuffling feet in the back of the church told me that the smoking men had entered, and then I saw them as they dispersed throughout the church and found their rightful seats, silently.

The only things left moving were two or three restless babies, who were in danger of being squeezed to death by their mothers, and the fans. The fans never stopped moving, not even during the prayer. I know because I kept my eyes wide open the whole time I was in that place. I'd never seen so many grown-ups in one place before. I'd never heard so many people singing. I'd never seen angry, young men in blue suits, slapping the pulpit and promising to save me from things I never even knew I was in danger of. *Later in life, when I read Jonathan Edwards, I would remember these angry young men and realize they were his descendants, and that the story, which they were telling about a hateful, revengeful God-the-Father, hadn't changed for three centuries in my little town.*

We stood and sang and sat and prayed and, one by one, the singing quartet of preachers took his turn behind the pulpit to tell me what an awful person I was and how I could save myself by admitting it. Aunt Dolores looked at me, knowingly, several times during the service. She had sad, dark brown eyes and eyebrows that didn't curve. They made a diagonal line from the inside corners of her eyes to the outside corners Those eyebrows, turned down like that, made her look even sadder. I took her at face value because I already understood longing.

"When God destroys the world with fire, yes, with fire," one of the dark-haired, blue-suited twin preachers shouted, "where will you be? Will you be caught in the fiery flames and then cast eternally into the fire of hell? Or will you be safe in the arms of Jesus in the heavenly mansion he has gone before you to prepare? The choice is yours. God says so. All he requires is for you to love him more than anyone, more than anything, and to serve him with all your heart, with all your mind, with all your soul."

The preacher surveyed the group of us. His eyes were like Grandma Morgan's had been when she'd search my face to find the truth or a lie in it. And she got it right most times.

I kept my eyes on him. I looked at him hard. I'd learned from Grandma Morgan that if I couldn't look a person straight in the eye, then that meant, for certain, that I was guilty. I didn't feel guilty. I didn't want to die, and I certainly didn't want to burn alive forever, not if it was any hotter than sitting in that church was. I felt his eyes stop on mine for a moment and then keep going. It wasn't me he was looking for, after all.

I relaxed deep into the pew, so deep that I could feel the flesh on my butt and the back of my legs press through the openings between the slats. I tightened up a little bit, so I wouldn't get pinched and endured the rest of the sermon quite well. Then the invitation came. That's what he called it, the preacher, just like he was inviting me to a birthday party or something.

He said, "Now as my brothers and I sing the final hymn 'Just As I Am,' I'm going to issue the invitation to you to come forward and be saved from eternal damnation." The piano started playing, and his twin brother joined his other two brothers and walked to where he stood. They started humming, and then they started singing for real, harmonizing and blending and bending notes like they had a bunch of fiddles and banjos and bass guitars for voices.

He said, "I want every head bowed and every eye closed. I want every heart opened to the spirit of Jesus. Harden not your hearts, but listen for the summons. Jesus is calling to you to come to him."

The singing began, and the four of them harmonized in voices that pleaded, "Just as I am, without one plea, but that thy blood was shed for me, oh, Lamb of God, I come. I come." I heard rustling sounds, and then the brothers were humming again, and one of them was talking and praying, and saying, "Praise the Lord," and "Thank you, Jesus."

I had my eyes open already, but I had to raise my head to see what the commotion was all about, and I saw three women and one young boy, who looked about my age, at the front of the church. Two of the women were crying, and all of the people, including two of the singing quartet were on their knees.

I looked across and saw Aunt Dolores had her eyes open, too, but she wasn't looking up front where the action was. She was looking at me. It was a look that had a demand in it, and I looked down fast. I didn't like the place. I didn't like the way the singing riled me up. I didn't like the threats. I didn't like Aunt Dolores, but something inside me knew I had to make her like me, at least for the time being.

I thought about what the preacher said. I listened to my heart. I knew where it was from studying in school. I didn't hear a knocking there. I felt it beating, but I knew that was normal. I thought about all the bad things I'd done, especially what I'd done with my brother Arthur. Then I thought about all the bad things people had done to me, and I felt mad. Nothing I could think up made me want to do anything but leave that place forever.

I kept my head down until the preacher asked us all to open our eyes and sing a song of thanksgiving for those who had come forward and been saved. I looked straight ahead as hard as I could. I did not want to catch Aunt Dolores's eye again. Those people up front looked kind of sheepish to me, like they'd been caught doing something wrong. I wondered if they were hiding things like I was and if they really did feel free and washed white as snow, like the preacher promised.

Chapter 29

Chocolate Fudge, the Theft, and the Plan of Action

Outside the church the air had cooled. Heavy still with humidity, it enveloped me as I walked into the night. I wanted to find a place somewhere under a yellow bell bush or in a meadow to curl up and sleep and to awake to my lost mountains, to my stone home, to the taunts and challenges of my brother Arthur, to the dew on the grass on the way to the pond, and even to the familiar, tight-lipped face of my Grandma Morgan chewing on her tongue.

Aunt Dolores gathered her children and followed me out the door and to the car. The ride to her home was short in miles, but it seemed interminable to me because it added more miles of separation from where I wanted to be in Tennessee. The memory of Greensboro and Mama was fading, and honestly, I clung to Tennessee in my imagination because it was the fresher memory. I was afraid that lonely little town of Wisteria, that strange new people, and those new fears of hellfire and damnation would replace my past, and I would forget there were other places and other people I once loved and who once loved me.

The car lights illuminated a small white cinderblock house, much like Mrs. Shuler's, and I would learn later that Uncle Robert and his brothers built both. The house was tiny, and the room I was given to sleep in with my cousin Saralynn, who wasn't sure she liked the idea, was tiny, too. I fell asleep fast.

When I awoke, it wasn't to the sound of songbirds or roosters or the voice of my brother or Grandma Morgan. It wasn't to the smell of pan-fried potatoes or to the scent of deep, summer-green grass or tiger lilies.

I awoke to the sound of voices in the room right next to mine, which turned out to be the kitchen. I awoke to the smell of fatback almost burning and to an empty bed that had already been abandoned by Saralynn. I awoke to the sight of myself, which appeared suddenly in the mirrored wardrobe right next to the bed when I turned over. I jumped at the sight of it, so unexpected it was to see someone there.

Then my heart shrank at the greenness of my eyes and longed for the brown of my brother's or blue of my Grandmother's.

"Sandra!" a voice totally foreign to me called out. "You get on up and come to breakfast."

I dressed in a flash and entered the room from which the voice had come. A dark-haired man with dark brown eyes already sat at the table with Saralynn, and Raina was in a high chair on one side of him. His skin was white, and he had black chest hair showing at the top of his shirt and curly black hairs all down his arms. Aunt Dolores was still at the stove, scooping up fatback slices and placing them on a brown paper bag to drain some of the fat.

"Go give your Uncle Robert a hug, honey," Aunt Dolores said.

I looked at the man and remembered him as a vague, quiet presence from my long-ago summer Sundays at Grandma Pope's. I went over to him, and he smiled and asked, "You ever had a bear hug?" His laugh was high and happy.

"No sir." I had no idea what was a bear hug was until that moment when he put his arms around me and squeezed me and squeezed me and squeezed me until I felt like I couldn't breathe and like I would never be free.

He let me go, and then laughed his high, sweet laugh again. "Now, that's a bear hug."

I looked at him and could see he meant me no harm. His eyes held no hidden meanings like Aunt Dolores's did. They danced. Hers cried. *As the years passed, sometimes I would want to wipe away her tears, and sometimes I would simply walk away from her, leaving her to cry alone, instead of pulling me into the drowning pond with her.*

"Sit on down and eat your breakfast," he said. I liked him. I sat next to him.

"Sandra was at church with us last night when five people were saved, weren't you, Sandra?" Aunt Dolores asked as she brought the steaming biscuits to the table and placed them alongside the molasses jar and the fatback.

"Yes, ma'am. I was."

"Who all went up?" Uncle Robert asked.

"Thelma—" she started.

"Again?" he asked. "Didn't she go up earlier in the week?"

"Yes, come to think of it, she did."

"And doesn't she go up just about every other Sunday?"

"Well, yes, but listen there were others, too. Betty Sutton and her boy went up. And a woman I didn't know from Wilton, and oh, yes, Eddie Phillips," Aunt Dolores said.

"Humph," Uncle Robert said. "I'm surprised to hear he even came to our church. Most of those Phillipses go to the Presbyterian Church in town. Must have had something on his mind he didn't want his daddy to hear about to go all the way out to our little church."

"He came with Darleen Holly."

"Oh, well, that explains it. He must have been putting on a show for her family, so's he could keep on seeing her. They don't let her go out with just anybody."

"Robert! Stop talking bad about folks." Then she turned to me and said, "Your uncle is a deacon in the church, and he really loves God."

"I love God. I love Jesus, too," said Saralynn and smiled hard into her mother's face. Then she looked over at me and asked, "Do *you* love God, too?"

I stared at her for a moment. I knew what to say to please Aunt Dolores, but I couldn't bring myself to say it just yet. "Could you please pass the biscuits, Uncle Robert?" I asked. And he did. *It was a strategy that would become second nature to me. No, it would become first nature, for I would not even remember that something unpleasant had happened that would cause me to change the subject. My mind would simply learn to take me elsewhere.*

"Little Saralynn was saved a year ago. She is the youngest child in the church to be saved, but she said she heard Jesus calling to her to come to him. She just got up one morning and said that and asked to be saved, so she could go to him. And we prayed and Preacher Hart came and he prayed and she was saved."

I could see it all in my imagination. Saralynn leaned onto Aunt Dolores's arm, and Aunt Dolores hugged her while I took a big bite of a biscuit. Aunt Pauline was right about Aunt Dolores's cooking! I needed the molasses if I was going to finish the whole biscuit. It was dry and tasted like baking soda. "Please pass me the molasses." Uncle Robert did. I never answered Saralynn's question.

I ate the biscuit and the salty, salty, salty, slightly burned fatback while Aunt Dolores ate and talked. She'd described what she called the "conversions" of just about everybody in the church by the time breakfast ended and we'd finished the dishes and cleaning the kitchen. She took the dishtowel I'd used for drying, and she spun it around itself and popped me on the rear as I was leaving the kitchen.

"Ouch!" I squealed.

"Oh, that was just a little love tap," she said. "Your daddy used to do that to me all the time and when I was just about your age, too." She laughed, but her face darkened. "You keep on listening to your heart, and when you're ready, you let me know, and we'll call Preacher Hart for you, too."

She'd gone back to talking about getting me saved.

"Yes, ma'am," I said. I started to leave the room again.

"No playing till you get your room cleaned, and then come on back here, and we'll make some chocolate fudge."

"Fudge? What's that?" I asked.

"Lordy, young'un, you mean you don't know what fudge is? Who-o-o, who-o-o! Well, it's is just about the best chocolate candy you'll ever eat."

I remembered Grandma Blair and the Hershey bars. I remembered the Ex-lax, too.

"Like Hershey bars?" I asked.

"Better!" she said.

She was right about the fudge. It was better than Hershey bars, even better than Hershey bars with almonds. She showed me how to make it, step by step, and Saralynn and I took turns licking the spoons and scraping the pot after she had poured the cooling liquid into a long flat pan to harden. Late in the day after Uncle Robert had gone to work the second shift in Wilton at J.P. Stevens Textiles, she cut the fudge into squares and gave us each two apiece. After supper, we had another one each. By then there were only two pieces left.

"Well, we have had more than our share, so don't nobody touch these two pieces. Robert didn't get any, and we need to save them for him," Aunt Dolores said.

I listened. I got ready for church again because it was another revival meeting night. In between the bath and waiting to get my hair combed out, I went to the refrigerator to get some cold water. The fudge was right behind the water jar. I broke off a tiny corner and ate it fast before I put the bottle back in. I must have made two or three more trips for water before we left for church, and each time, I broke off another piece. At first, I told myself it was just to even up the candy, so it wouldn't look like anybody had been into it.

"Let's go!" Aunt Dolores yelled, and I dashed out the door and sat in the back with the baby Raina again.

I had already memorized the progression of events in the service the night before, and things went the same way on my second night in church. The songs were different, and I had a moment or two when I felt panic because I was afraid I'd be discovered, not because I was a sinner but because I was a thief. When the invitation came, I thought hard about going on up just to get it over with and to make things a little easier if Aunt Dolores discovered I'd eaten so much of the fudge she'd meant for Uncle Robert.

Honestly, every time I thought about the fudge, though, part of me couldn't wait until I got back to her home, so I could trim a little more off. I remembered the irregular shapes of the candy created when I broke off a corner here and there. I told myself I'd use a knife next time and even up both pieces.

Of course, I'd eat the parts I removed to make the pieces even. Maybe she wouldn't be there when Uncle Robert ate the candy, and he'd never know how big the pieces had originally been. My mouth watered at the thought of getting more, and I sat and plotted how to slip back into the kitchen after everybody was asleep.

The show ended. The fans stopped. We were back at Aunt Dolores's, and I helped her get the baby ready for bed.

"Normally, we read the Bible and pray together every night before we sleep, but we don't need to do that this week because of the revival. But do remember to say your prayers before you fall asleep."

"Yes, ma'am," I said.

"Yes, Mama," Saralynn said.

I waited until she was sleeping. I knew to watch for even breathing, like I used to do when I wanted to be sure Debbie or Eddie were napping before I slipped out to play with Arthur. Saralynn went to sleep fast, but not before reminding me to pray.

I slipped into the kitchen. I opened the refrigerator. The light seemed to fill the room, and I pushed the door almost shut to dim it.

I reached in and found the bowl where the candy was. It was like my fingers could smell it.

I found a knife. It was a large butcher knife I'd seen Aunt Dolores use to cut the cooled fudge. After placing the edge of the knife just so, I pushed down on it to cut the fudge. The whole mangled square shattered! It lay in eight or ten pieces, like a glass that had broken. I scooped them all up and shoved them into my mouth. That fudge was better than anything I had ever tasted, that *particular, broken, stolen fudge.*

When I'd swallowed the last melted morsels, I looked at the other misshapen piece. I didn't dare try to even it up. Mournfully, I put it back into the refrigerator and went off to bed. I was still deliriously happy, and thoughts of discovery and retribution could not intrude into my happiness. I slept, and no one even woke me to call me to breakfast. I did hear low voices when I awoke. I rolled over and startled myself again with my own image in the mirror. The sight of me brought back my theft! My stomach tightened. I was breathing hard. I forced myself to slow my breath down, so I could listen to the voices.

"I think she probably did it," Aunt Dolores said. "I'll question her about it."

I lay in bed and put my plan together. I didn't particularly like it here. There was something I couldn't put my finger on, but there was something wrong with these people, especially with Aunt Dolores. I felt like I was sleepwalking, and she didn't want me to wake up. I wasn't about to be shipped off again to just anybody, maybe some place where my mama would never find me. I knew what to do to save myself, and I got up out of bed and put my plan into action.

Chapter 30

The Accusation and the Escape Route

The room went silent when I entered it. Uncle Robert left. I don't know where Saralynn and Raina were, but I was abruptly left alone with Aunt Dolores. She looked sadder even than she usually did. Maybe she said, "Good morning," but that was the extent of it.

I could feel her anger. I could sense her sadness. It flowed into me and felt like my own. I looked at her, and I was afraid. I looked again, and I was mad. Again, I looked, and I wanted to cry. But I did not know if I wanted to cry for her or for me. It would continue that way until the day after I graduated from high school and left her home forever.

That morning I did not know I could leave. I did not know I would ever have power over my own self. I never had.

How could I know that feeling or even know that such a feeling existed? I barely know it now as I sit recalling that encounter. Aunt Dolores wanted to be my savior, but she could not even save herself. She became my jailer, and I have spent my life looking for saviors, and leaving them the way I eventually would leave her when I realized they, like her, had become my jailers. I would continue that way until I realized I had become my own jailer.

That morning I knew nothing of this. I only knew I had to avoid her anger.

Breakfast was Kellogg's flakes and milk. And there were cold biscuits and molasses. She let me eat while she worked around the kitchen. I saw her looking my way a couple of times. When I was almost finished with my food, she said, "Sandra, I need to ask you about something."

I looked her straight in the eye and told the truth. "If you're going to ask me if I want to be saved, the answer is yes, I do." *I meant I wanted to be saved from her.* I knew she'd interpret it her way, and I let her. I needed to survive. I had no idea that eating that candy would get me into so much trouble, but I did not intend to admit to it, and I'd picked up enough about her ways to know that she didn't like liars.

"Well, no, I wasn't going to ask about that just yet, but hallelujah!" she shouted. "I'll call Reverend Hart right away." She was out of the kitchen fast and into the living room where the phone was. She must have roused Uncle Robert on the way, and then Saralynn and Raina showed up, too.

Uncle Robert said, "Honey, what your Aunt Dolores just told me makes me so happy. Come here and hug my neck." I knew what he meant, but it sounded funny to me, and the picture in my mind of me hugging his neck like a necktie made me smile. I went on over and hugged him, and I saw Saralynn hanging in the doorway, looking glum. Raina was squatting down next to her, looking serious.

When Uncle Robert let me go, Aunt Dolores was back in the kitchen. She was off the phone and said the preacher would be by in about a half an hour.

"That's just enough time to get this place straightened up. Saralynn, give me a hand." Saralynn whimpered.

"What was that?" Aunt Dolores admonished her. "Would Jesus like that behavior? Now, snap to! And, Sandra, you go get your face washed. Change out of those shorts, and put on that skirt and that blouse I laid out for you. You're too old to be wearing shorts. And Robert, will you take care of Raina?"

"Whew-oo, somebody sure needs to," he said. He laughed and scooped her up.

Preacher Hart arrived shortly, just as he said he would. The whole family was sitting or standing in the living room. Preacher Hart sat across from me. I stared above his head at the empty walls, which were painted a dull white. Aunt Dolores didn't have any pictures at all on them!

Grandma Morgan had portraits of Uncle Alfred who was shot down in the Korean War, and Aunt Delilah, who died when the barn door struck her in the head, next to a picture of Jesus walking on water on the Sea of Galilee, all hanging on her living room wall.

I conjured up that picture of Jesus.

The day was hot and sticky. "Humid," they called it. Grandma Morgan would have said it was a "close day." I sat on the couch, which was covered in beige plastic that was hot and slick except where roses were etched into it. I thought of the cool, linoleum roses that covered Uncle Will's kitchen in Greensboro. I shifted on the couch. The plastic stuck to the back of my legs.

Preacher Hart took out his Bible and read from it. It was a verse I'd already heard a couple of times at the revival, *and one I would memorize later on, along with others, for Bible drills.*

"For God so loved the world," he read, "that he gave his only begotten son that whosoever believeth in Him would not perish, but would have everlasting life. For God sent not his son into the world to condemn the world, but that the world through him might be saved." He stopped.

"Sandra," he said, "Do you believe that Christ can save you?"

"Yes sir."

"Do you have any sins you want to confess?"

I could still taste the chocolate fudge. Its richness flooded the memory of my mouth. I looked up at Aunt Dolores. She was large-breasted. I saw the playing cards from Uncle Will's pantry when I looked at her. She was naked right there in the living room in front of me! I blinked. She had put her shirt back on. I thought of my brother Arthur and how I'd let him rape me.

I looked Preacher Hart in the eye and said, "No sir."

"Then let's get down on our knees and pray so God will save you."

My legs had stuck to the plastic couch and stung like I was peeling giant band-aids off them when I stood up. I didn't let out a sound. I knelt on the wood floor. He knelt beside me.

"Please pray," he said.

I prayed, "Now I lay me down to sleep. I pray the Lord my soul to keep. If I should die before I wake, I pray the Lord, my soul to take. God bless Ma—Aunt Dolores and Uncle Robert and Saralynn and Raina and my brother Arthur. Amen."

I opened my eyes. I was done. That was easy, I thought.

"How do you feel?" Reverend Hart asked.

I felt numb, but I remembered this part from church. "I feel fine. I feel like Christ came down and washed away my sins," I said.

"Praise the Lord!" he said. "Now I'll pray." And he did, giving thanks for my salvation.

It was 1959. July 11. That's what Aunt Dolores wrote in the front of the white Bible she gave me: *Sandra Pope, Saved by the Grace of God on July 11, 1959.*

It was a lie. I wasn't saved. And I wasn't safe. I was almost eleven years old. I would sit in church for seven years, at least twice on Sunday and once on Wednesday for prayer meeting, and try to hear the knocking at the door. I would go up to re-dedicate my life several times a year and feel nothing stir inside my heart. Something was amiss for me and would remain so. I would begin to think that I had "hardened my heart" and Christ had gone away forever.

That fear would last for nearly half a century as I followed one thread and then another to try to unravel the secrets of my past, and in the process, I would discover the Divine where one always finds it. But I didn't know any of this then. I only knew that I had to please Aunt Dolores.

There were hugs and congratulations. Then the preacher was gone. Uncle Robert went off to work on one of his projects. He was a builder, by passion, and a textile mill worker, by necessity. Saralynn had disappeared again. Raina was put down for a nap. It was just Aunt Dolores and me again.

"Remember this morning I said I had something to ask you? Well, I still do."

Maybe the punishment would be less because now she thought I was a Christian.

"Yes, ma'am."

"Saralynn was using a word today that's a bad word. She never talks like that, and she said she learned it from you."

I must have looked blank. I felt blank. I had no idea what word Saralynn thought she'd learned from me that Aunt Dolores would object to. Then I remembered.

"Was it *bikini*?" I asked. I have no idea how I knew anything about bikinis. I had no newspapers and no television at Grandma Morgan's.

Aunt Dolores laughed. Then her face went serious. "What about bikinis?"

"We were talking about swimming suits, and she said you made her a two-piece one, and I asked if it was a bikini. She didn't know what a bikini was, so I told her it was like wearing a bra and little, bitty panties. Then I showed her what the bottom would look like."

"How'd you do that?"

"Easy. I just folded my panty top down."

"Sandra, good girls don't bear bikinis. And you shouldn't be showing your panties to anyone on purpose. That bathing suit I made for her is not a bikini, and she only wears it when we go to the creek, not anywhere else in public. We don't believe in putting our bodies on display. God doesn't like that." She looked at me straight in the face. *I wished I'd studied the faces of those women on the Uncle Will's cards more.*

Then she asked again, "And you didn't use any bad words, nothing that started with the letter 'f'?"

"No ma'am. I didn't." I hadn't used any of those words since I left Greensboro. I had almost forgotten them. Several days would have to pass before I could forget them again. Every time I looked at Saralynn, they would pop into my mind and march around in big bold letters for hours.

"Well, I believe you. I don't know why she'd say you did, but we'll have to ask her cousins from next door. It must have been one of the boys. You go out and play."

I turned to go.

"Sandra, I almost forgot. Did you eat up that fudge I left for your Uncle Robert? Saralynn said she didn't, and there weren't more than half a piece when I took the dish out of the refrigerator for him."

I stopped at the screen door. Saralynn was sitting on the other side. She had some pie pans, full of mud that she was playing with. She'd been listening to our talk.

"No, ma'am," I lied. I never touched it." I opened the door a little to go on out. Saralynn didn't budge.

"Can I play?" I didn't want to play, certainly not with her, but I needed an escape route. Nancy Drew would have understood.

She brightened. "Sure. Come on. I'm making chocolate fudge."

I sat down next to her. I helped her fill the pans up to the top with dirt. Then I found a stick, so she could cut pieces for each of us. I was playing, and I could see myself playing. But I wasn't having any fun. I felt numb.

"I'm too old to play," I said. She looked at me like I didn't make sense.

I opened the screen door and went into the house and never played again.

Chapter 31

The Inquisition and Testifying

I spent the afternoon moving from one room to another and looking for something to read. I missed Nancy Drew. Aunt Dolores had some books around, but she said they were not quite right for me. That's when she gave me the white Bible with the inscription in it and said, "Good Christians read the Bible, Sandra. You may as well get started on it."

I opened the book. The pages were thin, and the words were small. I tried reading some of it. Aha! At least I knew how to read in columns. I must have looked daunted, though, because she said, "You don't have to read it front to back right away. Just let it fall open some place and start reading there. That's how I do it lots of times. I get answers to my prayers that way."

I did as she suggested and found myself somewhere in the Old Testament reading. I had made my way through several pages before I asked her, "What does *beget* mean?"

"What are you reading, child?"

I showed her, and she laughed. "This means that one person was the father of the next person mentioned."

She paused. Then her face got serious and sad. "Do you know how babies are made?"

I looked at her, blankly.

She asked me again, "Do you know where babies come from?"

I listened carefully to her question. I knew where babies came from because I had seen enormous pregnant sows and cows and horses, and then I'd seen them skinny again with their babies all over them.

"No, ma'am. I mean I know where they come from, but I don't know how they got there in the first place," I said.

She laughed a quick, short laugh that she stopped in the middle of. "Put that down for a minute, and let's talk. Do you know what it means to have a period or a monthly or to menstruate?"

"Oh, my mama told me all about that before she went off to Florida, and she left me some napkins and a belt, but I gave them away to Aunt Toni Gayle once when Uncle David made her cry," I said.

"Oh. So, you don't need to use them yet?"

"No, ma'am, I don't."

She breathed out in a loud way. "But you know that you will someday start to bleed down there?"

"Yeah." I didn't know what she was getting at. I wanted to be sure I said the right thing, and she sure seemed like there was a right and a wrong answer to everything, the secret of which she'd only reveal once I had gotten it wrong. I'd learned that very first day of school with the dentist that people try to trick you into making a fool of yourself. Somehow that makes them feel smart. So I kept quiet.

"Once a month, Sandra, after you reach a certain age, an egg is put inside your womb. That egg can turn into a baby if it gets fertilized."

I was completely befuddled. I wondered how the egg got there. Was I supposed to put it in? I imagined it would be like a chicken egg, and I didn't know how something that big could get inside my stomach and stay whole.

All I knew about fertilization came from watching Grandma Morgan put a white powder, she called fertilizer, on the plants in the garden. She never let me help do it because she said it would burn my hands, and she always wore old gloves when she did it. But I wasn't about to ask any questions because even then I knew that the questions you ask tell a lot more than you mean for them to. Aunt Dolores seemed to like to talk, so I just waited for her to reveal herself.

"Your womb is a little pouch below your stomach," she said, and she poked my belly right below my belly button. "Right about there," she said.

"Every month your body gets your womb ready to have a baby. When there's no seed to grow, the body uses blood to wash all that preparation away. The blood comes out between your legs. That's why your mother gave you the napkins."

I understood about the napkins catching the blood, but I still didn't know how babies were made.

"The seed gets put in your womb when a man and a woman have sexual relations," she said.

She knew I didn't get it. She was talking about seeds, and I understood how they grew when they were put in the ground. But she was also taking about eggs, and I knew seeds didn't turn into eggs. I had planted enough to know that. Still I kept my silence.

"Did you ever see your brother Arthur naked?"

I knew I had to answer. "Well, when we used to take baths together."

"You know how he was different between his legs?"

I started to breathe faster. I was getting scared. I simply nodded my head.

"Well, a man uses that part of himself to put the seed in the woman, and as long as they love one another, and they are married, it is beautiful and God blesses them. When the woman gets the seed, it starts to grow into a baby."

"Oh."

She must know about me and Arthur. He'd put his seed in me more than once. I must be PG! I didn't want a baby. I didn't want her to know I was PG! I wasn't married. I was a bigger sinner than I thought I was when I stole the fudge. I didn't want to talk with her anymore or listen to her anymore. I wanted my mama!

"So, don't ever let any boy put his seed inside you. Not until you are grown up and married. Okay?" She looked sad again.

I felt awful. "Yes, ma'am."

"Good. And tell me when you get your first period, so I can help you."

"Yes, ma'am." I felt dizzy. I needed to leave the room. I wanted to go to sleep.

I got up to go.

"Oh, and, Sandra, remember you'll need to testify tonight at church about your conversion."

I'd heard enough testimonies to know what she meant. I dreaded it. I'd have to stand up, PG as I was, in front of everybody, and lie about being saved.

"Yes, ma'am. I need to go to the bathroom."

"Okay. You're excused."

I had my pants down in a flash. I looked at myself this way and that. I'd seen how big the sows and cows got before they had their babies. I didn't seem to be getting fat yet. I stood on the side of the tub and leaned way back. My stomach made two little pooches, one on each side of my belly button when I did that. *Oh, God, I thought, I'm going to have two babies! I'm going to have twins!* I stood up straight again. My stomach looked flat. I leaned way back and there the two pooches were again. I hated Arthur. I hated Aunt Dolores. I hated the world. I wished I'd never heard of chocolate fudge.

I went outside and walked around the house several times. Saralynn had tied a piece of string to a tobacco stick. Straddling it, she rode it like a pony, around and around the house. She passed me several times before I took off toward the woods at the back of the property. Aunt Dolores had warned me not to go there because the woods were full of snakes, but I needed to get away for a while.

As soon as I entered the woods, I felt better. The lime and chartreuse colors of springtime that let light through the leaves had changed already to the green that is almost blue, the color that leaves become in deep summer. Even the delicate leaves were thicker and opaque, no longer translucent. I loved words that described light. I loved the stories of halos and burning bushes and Paul being blinded by the light on the way to Damascus. I didn't understand then that I held light inside each of my cells. But I had an experience in the woods that day that equaled any enlightened peace I've felt since.

Each place I needed to put my foot down was cleared by the time I lifted it and was ready to place it on the ground again. Each leaf, each tree trunk, each bird was more colorful, more beautiful than I remembered any being before. I watched as a path opened up in front of me and closed behind me. It was as though there was a wind blowing the grasses aside, but I felt no breeze. I came to a small clearing. The air felt cooler there. I smelled sweetness and a cool moistness, unlike the warmth of humidity that hung in the air elsewhere. I expected to see water because the ground felt cool like it does near a stream, but I saw none.

A deep feeling of peace came over me. The earth here, the ground itself, held that peace. Sitting on the ground calmed me, like it did when I sat in the woods at Grandma Morgan's. The trees were different and so were many of the plants, but I felt at home among them. No, I felt alive among them. I can't say I forgot where I was, not for long anyway. I heard Aunt Dolores calling me, way too soon, and I felt the fears return. But then, it was like I had two parts of me. The Sandra I was when I was around Aunt Dolores and the one I had always been when I was alone. No, not alone. In nature, with the Mother. I would find that sweetness and that peace in Nature, and find it and forget it many times across the years.

With Aunt Dolores's voice came memory of that world she lived in. Came fear that I was PG. Came loneliness and feelings of being different from all around me. Came loss of life, of my Sandra-self, as I tried to figure out and fit into her world. I stepped out of the woods and hurried toward the house. I would not tell her where I had been. I felt sick and empty all at the same time. Like someone had flattened me out. I would have to be silent and strong for a few more days until Sunday came, and I could see Arthur and tell him I was PG and ask him what to do.

I entered the house like I'd just been outside on the swing set. The sickly, sweet smell of flesh frying hit my nostrils. I looked at Aunt Dolores who was standing over the stove on which she had a large black frying pan. I could hear the grease popping. I was certain she was frying breasts, large round breasts like the ones on the cards in Uncle Will's closet. When she smiled at me, I nearly fainted.

"I'm frying up some chicken for dinner," she said.

It didn't smell like any chicken my Grandma Morgan or my mama had ever fried, so I didn't believe her. *I was sure she was frying human breasts, so I just stared at her.*

"Don't you like fried chicken?" she asked.

"Yes ma'am, I do, but I feel sick," I said. I was afraid to look into the skillet as I rushed by toward the bathroom. I threw up as soon as I got to the toilet. She was at the door asking if she could come in, but I had locked the door, and I wouldn't unlock it. I flushed and said I was okay.

Then I sat down to pee. Before I tossed the toilet paper away, I sat with my eyes closed for a few moments, trying to figure out what Aunt Dolores had said about the blood. Then it came to me: *"The blood comes out between your legs. Your body uses blood to wash the seed away."* Blood! I opened my eyes and looked again at the toilet paper in my hand.

There was no bright red blaze of color. The paper was completely white. I dried again and again, but every time I looked, I still could see no blood. I knew, for sure, I was pregnant.

Surprisingly, testifying in church that night was easy. I was a liar. I was a thief. And I was PG because I had let Arthur rape me.

But somehow none of that mattered. I stood up in front of a couple hundred people, and the words I knew Aunt Dolores wanted me to say, just flowed. *They continued to flow for years. I became everything she wanted me to be, at least, on the outside. Inside, I hid myself away, waiting for something or some time I could not even know I was waiting for.*

Chapter 32

Betrayal, Perry Mason, and Letting My Fingers Do the Walking through the Holy Pages

My betrayal of my mama may have started with Aunt Dolores's quick quizzes. Each day seemed to have one or two questions that would come at me fast. The questions came when I was least expecting them while I was sitting in front of the television. I had had no television in all my eleven years of life, except for a few months in the summer before I went to live in Tennessee. Grandma Morgan only had a radio, and on Saturday nights, we could tune in one station that broadcast out of Cincinnati, Ohio, wherever that was.

Having a television that first summer in Wisteria was like experiencing a miracle daily. I could lose myself in grownups' problems on *The Edge of Night* or *The Guiding Light*. There was an older woman who thought she was pregnant, but Aunt Dolores said she was too old for that. I didn't understand, but I felt the woman's fear. When the woman found out she wasn't PG, though, she played with dolls. That I couldn't understand. I hadn't played with dolls since I was in the second grade, except for dressing and undressing the big-breasted, evening-gowned doll Aunt Shirley gave me and that I left in Tennessee.

Just when I would begin to tire of the sadness of the adult women who, in that way, reminded me of Aunt Dolores, just at that very moment, *Lassie* would come on. I could be a child again for a half hour or so. Then Disney washed over me and filled me with childhood energies as I watched cartoons and with adolescent urges as I watched Annette Funicello and wondered, like every other flat-chested girl in America, when I would get breasts. Somewhere in all that television, Aunt Dolores would suddenly have a question for me. She made me wish it were Saturday night, and we were watching Perry Mason. That was her favorite show, and she'd never take a chance on missing any to question me.

"Did you do well in school when you lived with your mama?"

"I don't know." I couldn't help looking at her breasts when she talked. They were large and pointy.

"What were your report cards like?"

"Okay, I guess. I passed." I did remember Mrs. Poole's comment on my final report card for third grade: "Loses her temper occasionally." I could still see the beautiful script in which she wrote those ugly words, just because I had said Clara's face looked like a sow's rear end. I didn't think it was fair for her to write that on my report card, especially since she'd punished me by making me stay in at recess for a month and not letting me go with her to the bookmobile.

That report card was the one I had to take with me when Mama took me to Tennessee to live with Grandma Morgan, and it besmirched my reputation there from the beginning, especially with Grandma Morgan. I held Mrs. Poole accountable for prejudicing my fourth-grade teacher, Mrs. Copeland, against me and causing me to get that paddling in front of the class on the very day I wore my poodle skirt to class.

I wondered for the first time as I sat there trying to avoid Aunt Dolores's questions, where I got that skirt. Surely, Grandma Morgan did not buy it for me. Could my mama have sent it?

I didn't tell Aunt Dolores any of this.

"Did you miss much school?"

"Sometimes we had to stay home to take care of Debbie and Eddie if they were sick."

"Dot kept you out of school to take care of the children?"

"Sometimes." I knew she had some information I hadn't meant to give her. It was all normal to me. Grownups made their older children take care of their younger children. Even Aunt Dolores did that. But I could tell by the way her voice changed, and by how she wouldn't let me just go back to watching TV, that she felt she'd struck gold. I tried to change the subject.

"Could I please go get us some moon pies and nabs and RC colas?" I asked, knowing Saralynn would chime in, and the begging would end up either with an angry "NO!" and the end of TV time, or with everybody getting goodies. Aunt Dolores was fond of sweet foods, too, so usually we got them if Uncle Robert wasn't around. There was a tiny country store across the street that also sold gas to people. RC's were a nickel each and so were nabs and moon pies. My diversion worked more than once that first few months when the Mama quizzes got too hot for me.

But Aunt Dolores was at me all of the time. If she wasn't asking me something about my Greensboro life, she was telling me something about my mama—something bad about my mama.

"Sandra, I am just concerned about you, honey. You see, I think it is just terrible that Dot took you to her mama's and threw you away for two years. You must have been real lonely."

"Not really." *Never would I tell her about the nights Arthur and I cried together, about how we held each other and how the holding led again and again to more than just hugging somebody's neck.*

"You didn't cry at all?"

"Sometimes."

"Did your mama write you? I would have never taken you and left you there, but if I had to, I would have written you every day."

"She wrote Grandma, I think."

"You *think*? Did she call?"

"I don't remember."

"Then she must not have. Or you *would* remember. Right?"

"I reckon."

"Honey, I respect you for trying to protect your mama, but you are forgetting that I know Dot. I knew her before you were born. I know what kind of woman she was. It hurts me to say so, but I have to protect you, Sandra. She was a bad woman. I know."

I looked at her. Nothing in my memory of my mama made me think she was bad. She wasn't the tormentor of the Red Wriggler girl. She never called anybody bad names. She never shot arrows into someone's windowpanes. She never let her brother rape her. She cooked spaghetti with green peppers I could still smell and made devil food cakes and bought me pretzels and pretty clothes, *maybe even that poodle skirt.* I got real quiet.

"Now, you listen, child. It's for your own good to hear what I have to say. Once, I went up to Greensboro to see your mama. When I got there, your daddy's car was gone, but I decided since I'd driven all that way that I'd get out of the car and check the door anyway. It was that Portland Street house where you lived when your daddy was alive. I knocked on the door, and nobody answered, so I walked around the house. All of the shades were pulled down tight on your side of the house. I was about to go when I heard a noise. I stopped. I turned and saw that one of the shades was bowing out on one side.

"I got real flat against the wall and was able to see into the room. What I saw, child, sent me running away fast from that window. Sent me back to the car, crying my heart out. And I am sorry to be the one to tell you this, but you have to know the truth, or she'll make you into a bad woman also."

I stared at her. I still didn't get it. She could see that I didn't know what to make of her story. So she started up again.

"Sondra, your mama was completely naked, and she was sitting on the lap of a man who was not your daddy. She was cheating on your daddy right there in their own bedroom! Right in front of my eyes, she was being unfaithful to my brother Bernice, to your daddy. And now that he is dead, honey, and God has delivered you to me, I just can't let you go back to her. Not ever. I know what I am saying is hurting you, but it's less hurt than living with her would bring you, child."

But I knew she was lying. Maybe not about what my mama was doing. Maybe it was her brother she was naked with, the way I had been naked with my own brother. I was caught. I could never be with my mother again unless I admitted I was already just like her or wanted to be. Or so I thought. I didn't know I had been bad when I let Arthur rape me until the Stevens boy got caught for doing it and sent to the penitentiary. I didn't want Arthur to go to the penitentiary. I didn't want to stay with Aunt Dolores, and I didn't want to lose my mama forever. So I just stood there and cried.

I cried, and Aunt Dolores reached out and hugged me to her. I felt no comfort there. I felt no safety there. I felt smothered by her large breasts, and I couldn't get my breath because I was crying so hard. She let me go when I got the snubs. I hated her. I hated her for lying, maybe not about my mama. But I knew she was lying about loving me. I could feel her hate, even in her hugs. I didn't understand it, but I could feel it.

Was it me she hated or just my mama?

Aunt Dolores never even asked me about Arthur Blair. Not then. I would have told her all she needed to know if she wanted to keep me for herself. But she didn't know that my mama had gone back to him. Neither did I until months later, when my mama actually showed up, when she came to see me and brought Debbie and Eddie -- and Arthur Blair. Mama said she came as soon as she could after she heard we never went back to Grandma Morgan's when school started. Aunt Dolores had already set me against her by then. Aunt Dolores had convinced me that to go with my mama meant I would never be saved and would burn in hell forever.

Had she known my mama was on her way? Was that why she worked on me so hard?

I sat in the living room with the four of them and with Uncle Robert, Aunt Dolores, Saralynn, and Raina. Across from me was my mama.

"Come here, Sondra," Mama said.

I didn't move.

"Go on. It's okay, Sandra," Aunt Dolores said.

I got up and walked a couple of feet and stood in front of her. Mama stood up. Then Mama hugged me. I melted into her arms. In that instant, I knew I would go with her anywhere! Then Debbie hugged me, and even Eddie, who was close to four, joined Debbie and hugged me.

It was Big Arthur Blair's turn, but I wouldn't hug him back when he circled his hairy arms around me. And Aunt Dolores must have noticed when I pulled away first.

"Sondra, baby, I love you so much. You go get your things and come on home with me now," my mama cooed. And I turned to do as she said.

Then he spoke. "Good girl," Big Arthur said. "You do like your mama says."

I stopped and stared at him coldly.

"You're making the right choice," he said. "You must be remembering all the good times we had together."

I saw the garden hose in my mind and the belt around his waist as he stood in front of me. I stood and stared at him.

"Baby, go on. Get your things," my mama said.

I backed away and went into the little bedroom I'd been sharing with Saralynn. I started to pack my things. Aunt Dolores came in. She was crying. She walked around and around the little room.

"How can you say you're saved by Jesus and go back and live in sin with her? Sandra, you are making a terrible mistake. Listen to me! Sit down on that bed," she ordered me.

I did.

"You haven't told me all the truth yet, have you, young lady?"

She towered over me. I was frail, tall and fine-boned. She was large, big-boned, and nearly 5' 8".

"Why do you hate Arthur Blair so much, and don't deny it! I could see it in your eyes. What'd he do to you, child?" she demanded.

I looked up at her. I was afraid of Arthur Blair.

But I was more afraid of Aunt Dolores. He hit me, and I had pretty much learned to read when the blows would come and how long they would last and even how to get out of the way of his anger and not get hit at all, some of the time. But Aunt Dolores didn't hit me, and yet she was about to hurt me more than he ever had. It would take me almost a lifetime to figure that out, and even then I'd look for the blessing in the pain.

I could have said, "He beat me with his belt most days." I didn't.

I could have said, "He dumped my food on the floor, and he beat me with the garden hose sometimes." I didn't.

I could have said, "He beat my mama bad." I didn't.

"Did he ever touch you down there?" She nodded toward my legs.

I understood her meaning, and her concern about me being touched "down there," reminded me that I was pregnant; I was sure of it, and though the months had passed, I hadn't had the courage to talk with anyone about it, not even little Arthur, mostly because I never got to be alone with him.

"Never." I didn't tell her how I used to walk around beneath the tall slat steps while he sat higher up, so I could look up the leg of his swimming trunks.

"Are you sure?"

"Yes, ma'am."

She shifted and walked across the small room. I stood up and started packing again. I still planned on going with my mama. My heart wouldn't let me do otherwise.

"What are you doing?" she nearly shouted it.

"Packing."

"How could you possibly think God wants you to go live with them? I know they say they have changed and say that they'll make a good home and keep you all together, but they're lying. I know they're lying. You know they're lying. *God* knows they're lying."

I stopped. I listened. I needed to. Between the fudge, being PG because I was a fornicator, and faking a conversion, I knew I was already in too deep with God to close my ears to her.

Then she scooped up the Bible and pushed it into my hands. "Let it fall open, wherever it chooses, like I taught you. Then close your eyes and point. That will be what God's saying about this."

I took the book from her hands. I let it fall open like she said, like I'd done before. I pointed with my eyes closed. Then I read the passage. I remember it went something like this: "They have lied. They run through the streets, committing every iniquity; they have refused to return."

"See?" She was triumphant. "God is telling you that they are lying. They haven't returned to one another."

I cowered beneath her. I read the words again silently. I felt suddenly caught in all the exaggerations of the past few months. I knew God was telling me *I had lied.* I knew God was telling me I had committed every iniquity. I was the one who was about to refuse to return.

I didn't understand the hold Aunt Dolores had on me then. *I wouldn't even begin to understand it until the eve of my fourth marriage when I was fifty years old.* But I did as she guided. Her opinion of me somehow mattered beyond all reason. It was like I had to convince her I was good, instead of convincing or asking God to make me good, so I walked out into the living room. I looked straight at Arthur Blair. Somehow that made it easier for me to do what I had to do.

"I ain't going with you," I stated flatly.

Mama cried and quivered in her voice when she said, "Sondra, what are you doing? Of course, you're coming."

"I ain't," I said.

Mama was crying hard suddenly and couldn't talk. Debbie and Eddie started sobbing, too. Arthur Blair got mad instantly. I saw his eyes flash at me.

He was on his feet and in Aunt Dolores's face, demanding, "What did you do to her? A minute ago she was ready to come, and now she is staying!"

That was when Uncle Robert moved over next to Aunt Dolores who was talking, too, but by then I wasn't listening much. I do remember Uncle Robert's calm voice and then the silence that followed.

"You are no longer welcome here," he said.

There must have been more or some magic I can't recall, but memory tells me that was all there was to it.

I watched as they walked to the car in the twilight. *I watched from some place far off. I had, indeed, refused to return. I felt my fate was sealed. But She did not disappear completely or forever. She could never do that. I would be under Aunt Dolores's physical control for seven long years, and by the time I left at seventeen, I would be so emotionally scarred that another three decades would pass before I could begin to write and pray and dream my way to recovery.*

Chapter 33

Becoming a Goose Girl and Sundays with Arthur

Aunt Dolores sewed for me. By the time school started, she had created a wardrobe that would allow me to enter the sixth grade with no shame, she said. Supposedly, I'd be the best-dressed kid there in my long-waist, cotton dresses that had gathered skirts and white collars with ribbons running through buttonholes, which Aunt Dolores had made with her new buttonhole attachment. She chose prints with red backgrounds and blue flowers and matched red checks with solid reds.

She found browns and greens that were pleasant to her, but too grown-up for me in an era when girls wore bobby socks and pastel Peter Pan-collared shirts with stitched-down, box-pleated skirts or circular flannel skirts, like my poodle skirt that I had left behind in Tennessee. Though I was as skinny as a string bean and flat-chested to boot, I let her cover me up—"You're much too old to go outside without a blouse on," she admonished early on. "And you can never wear shorts again because we don't believe in showing our bodies, remember?"

I hid beneath those colors. Inside those yards of fabric, I almost disappeared. Aunt Dolores was trying to turn me into a goose girl, like the one I'd read about in the folk tales book I got from the library. That girl was beautiful, and her grandmother covered her up and sent her off to take care of the geese until she was grown and smart enough to take care of herself in the world of men.

But my eyes betrayed me and undercut Aunt Dolores's efforts to turn me into a goose girl. They announced my beauty, my pain, and my knowledge beyond my years, and they trumpeted my depth to a world that could not interpret well what it saw. Large and lime-green to blue or gray, my eyes changed with the colors that surrounded them and held glimmers of who I truly was, of the world I had already swallowed before my exile. *(Green eyes, greedy gut, eat the whole world up.)* Some saw and turned away from my gaze. Others saw and tried to enter there and found the way closed.

By high school, the one who looked out through my eyes, and could sometimes be caught looking, was degraded and misunderstood. I had, it was said, bedroom eyes. Perhaps. By high school, I would lay aside the goose girl garments and don the tight skirts and sweaters of the day. Still, I had played the goose girl part so long, that I easily became the seductive, but untouchable Southern Virgin. Never mind that I was no virgin or that I thought my brother Arthur had made sure of that.

But all that came later. I was almost eleven when I visited little Arthur at Uncle Douglas's and Aunt Evelyn's the Sunday after I refused to go with my mama. It was the only time we had been alone together since that first night at Granddaddy's Pope's house.

When I arrived, Aunt Evelyn and Uncle Douglas were in the living room. They sat beside each other on the plaid couch that was placed in front of the double windows. He had his left arm stretched across the back of the couch and around her shoulders. They often sat like that, even in their car. Neither of them got up when I knocked on the screen door. Aunt Evelyn called to me from the couch to come on inside.

"He's in his room. You need to talk to him," she said. She must have heard from Aunt Dolores already about my refusal.

"Yes, ma'am."

He stood by the window at the far end of the bedroom he shared with Larry. It was a small window and had been pushed up to open it. He looked out through the screen, down at the yard. His back was to me. His sandy blond hair had been cut close to his head, so I could see the pink skin beneath. I was still two or more inches taller than he was and would remain so until high school. Then he would only grow to 5'8" and stop.

"Arthur?"

He didn't answer.

"Arthur?"

He didn't answer, but he did turn toward me. I walked the few feet from the doorway to where he stood. I sat down on the bed near the window, and I looked out, too. Next to me was a box. It was filled with his clothes.

"Did you see her yesterday?" I asked.

"Yes." It was a dreamy whisper.

"Well, I'm not going with her."

"I know. She told me."

"What about you?"

"I want to go," he said. Again, that whisper.

"Well, I don't. I remember how he beat me. He beat you, too, but he beat me almost every day of my life, and I ain't never going back to that."

"I know he did. But she didn't."

"No, but she can't stop him. She can't even stop him from hitting her. How can she help me?"

"She can't."

"You go on with them if you want, but I ain't never going to let him hit me again. Aunt Dolores is strange in lots of ways, but she doesn't hit me, and neither does Uncle Robert."

"I ain't going back either," he said.

"But you said—"

"That I wanted to go. But I won't go if you don't."

"But you knew I wouldn't go, and you are already packed—"

"I'm going to Granddaddy's to live."

"What? Why? I thought you were so lucky to get to be here with Larry and Betty."

"Me, too. But Aunt Evelyn is mad at me because I won't tell her I love her more than I love Mama. I won't. I can't. So, I have to go back and live with Granddaddy."

"He scares me."

He licked his upper lip. It was a quick swipe of his tongue upward. I hadn't seen him do that since we left Greensboro.

"Yeah, me, too."

"You have to go?"

"Yeah."

"Forever?"

"Maybe. At least until I can say I love Aunt Evelyn more than Mama."

"Could you?"

"Say it? Or mean it?" He looked hard at me. His dark, dark brown eyes showed his hurt and anger. I could hear Mama singing, *"Brown-eyed, steal a pie, run home and tell a lie."*

"Say it. Just say it."

"Maybe. But not yet. She wouldn't believe me now anyway."

"They taking you over there?"

"Unless you can convince me otherwise. Isn't that why they sent you?"

"I ain't even going to try. I don't even like Aunt Dolores. I certainly don't love her, and she don't love me either." I paused. "Tell you what. I'll help you carry your things. Let's just walk over there."

"Right now?"

"Yeah."

"Nah. I already made her mad enough. You just go on out, and when I'm over there, come on down. Okay?" His eyes were pleading.

"Okay, but there's something else I need to say before I go. Something that's eventually going to get me into a whole lot more trouble than you're in."

"What?" Arthur looked at me, and more than curiosity filled his eyes. I could see his fear and his concern.

"I'm PG."

"What?"

"PG. You know, *pregnant.*"

He was astounded. He stared at me like I was all there was in the world. I hated my situation, but I rather liked the attention.

"Aunt Dolores told me all about how babies are made, and what we did when you raped me is the way babies get made." I said it with authority because I truly believed it to be true.

"Me? The daddy?" He shook his head. "No way."

"You? Of course, you! Ain't nobody else, that I know of, that's touched me there but you!"

"But it's been months since that—that—since we got here."

"So?" I couldn't believe how dense he was. He just didn't understand like I did.

"So, if you were pregnant, your belly would be sticking out some," he said, and he held his hands about six inches out in front of me. "And as far as I can tell, it's still completely flat."

"Look at this," I said, and I unzipped my pedal pushers. I let them slide down to my ankles. I put his hand on my lower abdomen, and I leaned backward. "See," I said. "See how it splits into two bumps? I'm going to have twins, I bet."

"Well, if those are twins, they are tiny ones. I didn't even know you'd started your periods, but it don't surprise me I don't know, the way you got all private and stuff before we left Grandma Morgan's. When was your last period?"

"What are you talking about? I ain't never had a period. That's how I know I am pregnant, ignoramus!"

He stood with his mouth wide open with not a sound coming from it, and then he started laughing like a crazy person. He was howling at me. I yanked my pants up fast and started toward the door. I would tell everybody right then and there, and that would fix him. He grabbed me by my arm.

"He—hee, wait," he said. He was holding his sides. "Wait, Sandra. Listen, you can't be pregnant if you never started your periods. I know what I am talking about. Here let me tell you how it really works."

And he did. Painstakingly. I got it the first time, but he went through it again. First, the period; then, the rape; and then, the baby.

"Okay, what if the first egg doesn't get a chance to get out before it gets fertilized, smarty?"

"I suppose that could happen, but it's been months, and believe me you would be showing and your breasts would be, too."

Automatically, both of my hands went to cover my breasts. They were flat, but just the word "breast" made me feel naked.

"Okay, but what about those pouches?"

"Muscles maybe or poop in your belly!" Then, he howled again. I turned to go again.

"Wait. Remember, you promised to come see me at Granddaddy Pope's real soon. Don't stay too long over here. Just wait until you know I am there." He was pleading again.

"Okay." I left the room and turned into Betty's room instead of going back to the living room. I decided to believe Arthur, and the relief I felt turned to excitement when Betty pulled out her Superwoman comic books for me to read.

Arthur must have been gone for a couple of hours when I remembered my promise to go on over there. I jumped to my feet and ran out of the room. I raced down the sandy lane to Granddaddy's. Aunt Dolores was sitting on the steps. Granddaddy and Grandma sat on the front porch in two rocking chairs. Granddaddy's arms were folded across his middle, but Grandma was shelling butterbeans.

"Oh, there you are," Aunt Dolores said. "Good, I won't have to go looking for you. It's time to go, or we'll be late for Sunday night service at the church."

I saw Arthur come to the screen door. He opened it just enough for me to see his face. I knew he had been crying.

"But I didn't get to play with Arthur."

"There's just no time now. You'll get to see him next Sunday. You should have come sooner."

I looked toward the screen door. His eyes echoed her words.

"I know. I'm sorry."

"What held you up, child?" asked Grandma.

"I got to playing with Betty," I said in as low a voice as I dared use.

"Reading comic books again?" Aunt Dolores asked and frowned.

"Wouldn't be reading that trash over here," Granddaddy said.

I heard the screen door close.

"Arthur." It was Granddaddy. "Come on out here."

"Yes sir."

"Say goodbye to your sister."

"Goodbye."

I walked up the steps. I put my arms around him. I stood close to him. He felt far away. I hugged his neck.

"Bye, Arthur," I said and felt like I was saying farewell to someone I wouldn't see again for a long, long time.

Aunt Dolores would keep her word and take me over there most Sundays, but he'd be out playing touch football or baseball or basketball with Larry and older friends of his, older friends who would watch me grow up. One or two of them would have the courage to ignore the rumors and ask me out, and Arthur and I would double date a few times. But when the young boys discovered for themselves that my eyes might be open but my legs were shut, that would be the end of that. Such was the power Aunt Dolores had over me. Such was the guardian within who protected me—finally.

Part of my protection was my estrangement from my brother Arthur. I know that, but my heart hurts in recollection of those early days together before our wounding caused us to wound one another.

I am nearly sixty at this moment when I write these words. I often visit the creek on the farm that was Granddaddy's and is now Uncle Douglas's and Uncle Clifford's. I never visit Uncle Clifford or Aunt Pauline or Uncle

Douglas, even though when I park next to where the creek once babbled, I am only a few hundred yards from their homes.

I get out of the car and let myself be seen. I drive slowly by their houses, go up the road, and turn around, so I can drive slowly by their houses again. These ones, who called themselves my aunts and uncles and who laughed and cajoled me to hug them after they brought me back to the Fatherland in that long-ago past, these same aunts and uncles, who knew me and supposedly loved me enough to offer to raise me instead of returning me to my mother, do not reach out to me now. No one ever comes out to stop me, and I cannot bring myself to knock, uninvited, on their doors.

I know the opportunity to visit these old ones will slip away forever soon. Like the creek of my childhood, which once flowed clear and sweet, and now lives only in an underground stream of memory beneath the present-day, polluted swamp that marks its place, these aunts and uncles, who tried to save me once, will disappear; for they are old, and they will die to me soon, except in memory, as I must have died to them already.

Chapter 34

I "Develop" and I Disappear

The leaves had changed right after my mama had gone. I had been with Aunt Dolores for five months. I understood that soon I would be going to court, so Aunt Dolores could get custody of me and Granddaddy could get custody of Arthur. Things hadn't worked out for Arthur. He still refused to tell Aunt Evelyn he loved her more than he did Mama.

According to Aunt Dolores, my mama was the worst kind of evil, and I would be far better off without her in my life. What Aunt Dolores didn't know is that I was already as bad as the evil she was trying to save me from.

I worried about many things during those days before the court date—about seeing my mama again, about seeing Big Arthur, about being put on the witness stand and having all my secrets hounded out of me. But two days before the court date, something went wrong with my body that took my mind off all other worries. I had gone to bed one night with a flat chest and had awakened the next morning with *it*. I thought the mosquitoes had bitten me bad.

"Aunt Dolores, something is wrong with my chest," I had reported. "I think I got a bad bite."

"Come here, child, and let me see."

"No, let's go in the bathroom." Uncle Robert was sitting right there in the living room, after all.

"Okay."

She went in first. I closed the door behind her. I lifted up one side of my shirt, like Donna Ann had that day in the girl's bathroom back at Homestead High. I showed her my breast. A sudden caramel-colored nipple had raised itself overnight.

"Oh," she said. "Well, it looks like you've started developing."

"But—"

"What?"

I lifted the other side of my shirt. I was still as flat on that side as I had been all my life.

"Oh!" she said again and nearly giggled. It was twitter, at the very least, but she swallowed it and made it sound like a hiccup. "Well, I don't know. Let me think." She sat down on the toilet seat and looked over at me. "You can put your shirt down, honey. I think we'll just call Addie. She's had a daughter grow up. She'll know what's going on."

Aunt Addie said she'd be over within half an hour. That was enough time for Uncle Robert and Aunt Dolores to whisper behind their bedroom door about my single breast and for Saralynn to ask what was going on.

Later in life, I'd think back on it and feel proud that I started womanhood off as an Amazon. But back then I knew nothing of Warrior Women, even though I had been pretty handy with that bow and arrow back in Greensboro.

I stayed in the bathroom. I sat on the toilet seat and twirled the toilet paper roll until I had un-spooled most of the paper. Then I took it off the rack and stood up to roll it back on. I saw myself in the mirror. I flashed my single breast just as the door opened, and there was Aunt Addie. I jerked my shirt down fast, but not before Saralynn, who was hanging behind Aunt Addie, saw me. I scowled at Saralynn and turned away.

Aunt Addie smiled at me. "Hey, sugh." When she talked her lips had crinkles around them the way Grandma Blair's had. And she smelled like Grandma Blair, too.

She pulled the door shut. "Now let me just take a little look-see at your chest. I bet you are just becoming a young lady." I did as she asked.

"Uh, huh. That's what it is. Well, congratulations!"

"But—but there's just one."

She smiled again. The crinkles disappeared. "The other one will catch up in a couple of days. You'll see."

It hadn't. Two days later I sat silently in the back seat of Aunt Dolores's car, dressed up in birthday clothes and on my way to court because I had agreed that my mama didn't deserve me. I was eleven, I had one breast, and I had gotten clothes for my birthday. I wore a yellow, short-sleeve sweater and a red-and-green plaid skirt that had a line of yellow thread weaving its way through it. Aunt Dolores insisted they were the best clothes I had, and I should wear them for such a worthy event as that one—when right would finally win out the way God wanted it to. The only thing I liked about that outfit was the size of the sweater. If I slumped just right, it bulged and hid my single breast.

When I got on the elevator to go up to the courtroom, just before the doors slid together, Grandma Blair stepped into view. Her hair was cut really short and was brighter red than what I remembered. I noticed that the red on her nails was still the same shade as the red lipstick that edged the unfiltered cigarette she had poised between her first two fingers. I started to smile as I looked from her hand to her face. She screamed at me, "You hateful little girl! You're killing your mama and my son!"

Aunt Dolores pulled me back from the elevator doors, and they slid shut.

Then I sat in the courtroom. I tugged at my skirt of many colors. The real Sandra had gone far away, and this new one Aunt Dolores was creating was someone I didn't even like. It appeared that nobody else did either. So I sat silently and still and waited for the day to be over. I let my mind drift back through fields and along paths I walked in Greensboro and to other by-ways I wandered along in Tennessee. I forced myself to stay in those places, especially when Mama took the stand. From a long way off, I saw her through the fields.

She was little. I had grown so much in the six months since I had seen her that I was almost as tall as she was. She shook when she cried, and her voice got so high she had to stop talking for a while. She had on a dress I'd never seen. It had little bitty black-and-white squares, and it had a black collar and matching black cuffs. She was pretty. My mama was pretty. Pretty like a doll in a far-away window. *Sandra kept slipping farther and farther away, and Mama kept getting smaller each time I saw her. Sandra disappeared. I would try to recover her, and I would lose her again and again across the decades. She would come to me often, but always in disguise, so I did not recognize her.*

"Sandra. *Sandra!*" Aunt Dolores was whispering, but it was loud. I startled to attention. The courtroom was noisy. The judge was gone from his desk. My mama was at the back of the courtroom, standing with Arthur Blair, and Aunt Dolores was leaning over me, talking, "Your mama has your report cards, and it doesn't show that you were absent lots of times like you said you were to take care of the kids. Why is that?"

I looked up at her. Beside her, Granddaddy Pope towered. He stared down at me with his cold, steel blue eyes, and next to him was Attorney Fredericks. I looked around, searching for Arthur. He was standing between Uncle Douglas and Aunt Evelyn. I wondered what that meant, but I couldn't catch his eye.

"Sandra, did you lie to me?" Aunt Dolores demanded.

"No ma'am." By the time she had reinterpreted my life with my mama, making Mama the same Evil the minister said the Devil was, I would have said anything Aunt Dolores had wanted me to say. I no longer knew the difference between truth and lies. And every time I let the Bible fall open to look for guidance, Aunt Dolores read and interpreted the verse so that it seemed like God was agreeing with her.

She still didn't know my real reason for not going back had been my fear of Big Arthur. She didn't know my reason for agreeing with her about my mama had been to throw her off my track because I stole the fudge and had fornicated with Arthur. As long as we were talking about my mama's evil, my doings with my brother Arthur that first night at Grandma Pope's in the bedstead that lightning struck, might go unquestioned. That seemed to work. Aunt Dolores never asked me once about Little Arthur and me. I hoped this report card thing wouldn't put her back on my trail.

"Well, I don't think your mama could've changed the report cards," Aunt Dolores said. "And the lawyer says it's going make a difference. It's starting to look like you'll have to talk with the judge in his chambers."

She sounded like Della Street. I was on TV. I looked around for Perry Mason and could not find him, but I felt Nancy Drew look out through my eyes to size up the situation.

"Well, there's other things I can tell him that'll make him see things my way," I said.

I was eleven. Aunt Dolores and Attorney Fredericks looked at me oddly. She screwed up her face and said, "What did you say?"

"Never mind," Attorney Fredericks said. "Let's get your brother, and I'll take you in there. Now, Sandra, I can't stay. What you have to do is answer the judge's questions honestly and show respect."

I winked at him. "Certainly," I said, and I reached out and took the hand he offered me.

He escorted Arthur and me into the secretary's outer office and left us. She took us into Judge L. Richardson Preyor's chambers. The chairs were leather. The room was hot. Arthur was making strange faces at me. I leaned back and rested my head against the tall back of the chair and closed my eyes.

"Well, look at that!" Arthur said.

I opened my eyes, surveyed the room, and turned my face toward him. "At what?" I saw nothing remarkable in the room.

He reached over, and with two fingers, he tweaked my breast. "That!" he said and laughed.

"Get your hands off me!"

He tweaked me again, and I jumped up.

"Leave me alone."

"Look at that, look at that, look at that. Wait a minute! Where's the other one? Let me see. You only got one! Just wait till I tell Larry!" He howled in laughter.

I turned my back to him. I folded my arms hard over my chest, trying to squeeze myself into invisibility, the *same invisibility I felt inside*. I turned back toward him. I was enraged. I kicked him in the shins. I kicked him hard. I kicked him, and I screamed at him.

"You better shut up, Arthur, or I'll tell the judge you raped me, and after that night at Grandma Pope's, I got witnesses who heard you, I bet. You'll be sent to the penitentiary!"

Arthur was shocked into silence. His face was flushed, and instantly, he was crying. Just as I stood in triumph over him, the door opened and Judge Preyor came in. He looked first at me, then at Arthur, then back at me.

"You can sit right here, Sandra," he said.

I sat down, slumped forward, and looked him straight in the eye. Nothing he could say could make me go live with my mama, not as long as she was Evil, not as long as she lived with Big Arthur.

Chapter 35

He Beat Me, He Beat Me, He Beat Me

Judge L. Richardson Preyor had his long black robe on. From his chair behind his large dark desk, he loomed over us, but he smiled. Decades later in life, he would become friends with my first cousin Mervin and confide in him that this was the most difficult case he ever decided in his North Carolina Superior Court career. He would die before I could tell Mervin to let Judge Preyor know that he made the right decision.

"Tell me what it was like to live with your mother." He looked at Arthur. Arthur looked down. He looked at me. I stared him right in the eye, both my eyes on one of his, his right one, the way I saw Perry Mason do when he wanted to make someone confess.

I would tell my story. I would tell it all. *He beat me, he beat me, he beat me.* I would scream it. As long as she was with *him*, surely he wouldn't make me go because *she let him, she let him, she let him. She let Little Arthur, too.* I opened my mouth.

"She was evil," I said. *Who was that talking?*

"Evil, Sandra? What did she do that was evil?"

"She went out with men. She bought herself pretty dresses. The men came asking for her." *This was not my story. My story was of the beating. The letting, the letting, the letting.*

"Did you see these men? Did they hurt you?"

"I saw Bishop."

"The bishop?"

"Just Bishop. That's what he called himself. I didn't let him in. I locked the screen door."

"Where was your mother?"

"I dunno. Me and Arthur were watching Debbie and Eddie. She was gone. So was Big Arthur."

"Your daddy?"

"No. My daddy's dead."

"Your mother's husband, then?"

"Big Arthur." I turned toward my brother Arthur. "This is Little Arthur."

"So Big Arthur and your mother were gone when Bishop came?"

I listened from afar as I told this story. I was telling a different one in my mind, but it couldn't get out of my throat. *He beat me. My legs were bleeding. My dog was strangled. He raped me. No, not him. Him. Who? Him. Him. Him! With the mimosa tree. Again and again. He did, he did, he did.*

"I don't remember. I just know she was bad. She was evil. She committed adultery. She broke the Ten Commandments, and she runs around in the streets refusing to return." I stumbled over the words. They all came out in a jumble.

"You saw her being—evil?"

"I just saw the pictures on the cards, but Aunt Dolores saw her. Naked. Not with my daddy and not with Big Arthur either." I stared at him again. "God doesn't want me to live with Evil. I just know he doesn't."

"No, he doesn't," he said. "He certainly doesn't."

He left me alone for a while. He was talking with Arthur, and I was listening, but they must have been talking in another language. At first I thought it was pig Latin, but I could have followed that pretty well. It went on for a long time, and I was getting madder and madder that they were leaving me out. I was practically huffing and sitting straight up on the edge of my chair when, finally, he turned back to me.

"So, do you understand that, too, Sandra?"

"What?" How could I understand? I turned to look at Arthur. He was smirking at me and looking over at my chest. I froze and then slumped forward in the chair. As I did, I took great care to round my shoulders.

"No, sir," I said meekly. "I don't speak anything but English."

He had a puzzled look on his face, but he looked kind enough at the same time.

"Well, Sandra, I have decided that you will stay with your Aunt Dolores and Arthur—Little Arthur—will stay with your grandfather or your Uncle Douglas until school is over in May. Then you must go to wherever you mother is living and spend the summer with her. At the end of the summer, after you've had a chance to get reacquainted with her, we'll talk again, and you can decide whether you want to live with her or your aunt. That's my decision."

I won't go. "Yes sir," I said.

I expected him to go back into the courtroom and announce his verdict to everyone like Perry Mason did, but he didn't. He must have forgotten that part. Instead, he escorted us out of the room, and we waited in the hallway for a while. Attorney Fredericks had disappeared. My mama was nowhere in sight. Nor was Arthur Blair. I sat on one bench with Aunt Dolores and Uncle Robert, and Arthur sat across from me with Aunt Evelyn and Uncle Douglas. He was looking pretty smug. I knew he was happy we were going to be with Mama the following summer, but in the meantime he was making his way with Aunt Evelyn, too. I moved closer to Aunt Dolores, just to spite him. Closer, but not too close. She'd bathed and everything, and she was clean, but I didn't like being too near her. She couldn't help it, I know, but I didn't like for her to touch me.

Before I knew it, I had fallen asleep on her shoulder, and she was shaking me awake. Attorney Fredericks stood in front of us with Granddaddy Pope.

"It's pretty clear. You have temporary custody until after the summer. Sandra and Arthur are to be with their mother then. I wouldn't worry too much about it, though," he said, and leaned in close. "A woman that'll give her children away once don't want them anyway, and a woman that bad won't be able to take care of these children they way you do, and they're good kids—aren't you good kids?—and they'll know the difference. They'll want to come back and be with you. Won't you?"

I looked at Aunt Dolores. I nodded vigorously. Arthur stared at the attorney, and then he gave a single nod of his head. Aunt Evelyn smiled the biggest smile.

"They've been dragged from pillar to post since my brother Bernice died. Is there nothing we can do?" Aunt Dolores asked. She made "Bernice" rhyme with "furnace" and said it with fire in her voice.

Attorney Fredericks shook his head.

"Can't promise a thing. Really can't. That report card thing hurt us too much. But come the end of summer, we'll try again. We'll see what we can get. But for now, this is the deal. And it's not really so bad a deal. It gives the children a lot of time to get used to being with you."

"I won't go," I said.

I felt everyone look at me. I shrank back, but I said it again. "I won't go."

Attorney Fredericks looked me hard in the face. "Well, Claude, isn't that one strong-willed? Guess that's some proof that she is your granddaughter."

Granddaddy Pope took his turn staring me down. I didn't flinch from his gaze, and this time his eyes had lost their steely sharpness.

"I won't," I said.

"If the court says you have to go, you will," he said.

"No." I said it straight to him. "No, sir, I won't."

I was back at the creek, and he was telling me to get my clothes and stop playing my nasty games, and this time, I said, "No." And I liked saying it. That "no" found a secret place to hide inside me and love me. From time to time when I opened my mouth, it would surprise me and jump out just in time to save me.

Chapter 36

The Mustard Seed and the Cross

But summer didn't come fast, and Aunt Dolores made it clear to me that my sixth-grade year had better be a good one. She wasn't above bribing me to make sure.

"Grades matter," she said. "You'll have a nice surprise at the end of the year if you get all 'A's and 'E's."

I dreamed of a new bicycle to replace the used one I had left behind in Greensboro. I longed for another poodle skirt, a hair dryer, even a Mickey Mouse watch. I knew my achievement was all tied up with what the court might think, and I was willing to play it Aunt Dolores's way for more than just the reward.

I still feared Big Arthur. I didn't believe Mama had left him for good, but in all my fear of him, I didn't lie to myself about my other reason for not wanting to go to Mama's. I harbored some deep hurt and resentment toward her for leaving me with Grandma Morgan and taking Debbie and Eddie with her. I wanted to punish her, and evidently, so did Aunt Dolores who picked up on that theme early on. She played it more than once during that first year.

"How could a good mother leave her children? It don't matter what the trials and tribulations were, a good mother would trust in God, who gave her those children to care for, and she would keep them with her." Aunt Dolores would be talking while driving me to the store with her.

Or she would be driving me to church. "I know my brother, if he hadn't died so young—he weren't more than twenty-seven—he would have kept you with him, no matter what. And I can tell you this much, he would have left her, had he lived. I know he would have. He didn't have to say it in so many words. I could tell."

Or she would be handing me another dish to dry and put away. "Your Uncle Thomas and Aunt Iris tried to get your mama to let them have you after your daddy's funeral. And Douglas would have taken Arthur. I was barely married then myself, or I would have wanted you. Your daddy would have wanted us to have you. He never intended to have that woman raise you. But she refused us all," Aunt Dolores reported. Every activity I engaged in with Aunt Dolores came with lessons.

To top her lessons off, I got lessons from church. By the end of that year, I'd been in church over a hundred times, and testified more than five times (*lied about the state of my soul, though I tried more than once to remedy it by going to the altar*). You might say I was somebody else, someone new, somebody truly resurrected. I knew it wasn't so, but I got so carried away playing it that way, that somewhere along the way I forgot the other Sandra. There was little to remind me of her.

I had all of Uncle Robert's family to call "aunt" or "uncle" or "grandma" or "cousin," all of them strangers a few days before I began addressing them so intimately. I had the kind gazes and smiles of a church family. My mama never wrote me. She never called. Neither did Grandma Morgan. Or Aunt Toni Gayle or Uncle David. There were no pictures of those other times and places, none except those I carried in my memory or manufactured in my imagination.

Even Arthur had changed into somebody else and was back living with Aunt Evelyn and Uncle Douglas. No more Mama's boy, I reckoned. And when I went to see him on Sundays, he'd be out playing football or some other game with the boys. I only tried to play with them once or twice. I didn't like getting pushed around. I didn't like playing anything except Monopoly every now and then, or jack rocks, or marbles. I didn't even like music when Betty played records for me on her pink phonograph. I did like books, any kind of books. That made it easy for me to do well in school, and I liked doing well. And that opened the door to teachers along the way who would see more than they let on and who would try to save me. And some would, for a while.

That final day of school, I had gone up to Mrs. Pridge's desk to get my report card, and she had opened it to show me the sturdy "A"s and "E"s marching up and down the columns. I had walked to the bus and held the report card with both hands, respectfully, like I did the Bible. The bus stopped. I climbed down the steps, I looked both ways, even though the bus had its lights blinking and its stop sign out, and I crossed the country road to the Aunt Dolores's house.

That house would still be there, though she wouldn't be, forty-six years later when I moved back to this little town. Of course, the house would be smaller, and for me, the whole town would be haunted by the Sandra who got left behind. She's the real reason I have come home.

That sunny and windy May day long ago when I had finished sixth grade under Aunt Dolores's guardianship, I rushed into the house, glad to be bringing home the final report card and ready to get my reward. Saralynn wouldn't start school until the next year, so I was the only one who was even eligible for such a reward. I felt special.

"Here's my report card!" I said it with glee.

Aunt Dolores looked at me. Like I said, her features made her face look permanently sad, even when she smiled. But then she wasn't even smiling.

I walked across the room, passed through the French doors and went to where she stood with her back to me as she faced the kitchen sink. "Look! All 'A's and 'E's!" I felt jubilant. I felt smart. I felt better about those grades than anything else in my life at that moment. I felt the clean honesty of knowing my subjects.

She took the card I offered, opened it, and nodded approvingly at each mark. "You really did well. You earned your reward," she said. "I'll be right back." I watched, and then followed as she went through the small room I shared with Saralynn. The room was a mess. All of my stuff was pulled out of the wardrobe and out of the chest-of-drawers and stacked in piles on the bed.

"Oh!" I said, as I remembered that the end of the school year brought more than my reward. "When?" I asked. I raced after her, and the Sandra I had become, grew anxious and even sad. A year is a long time to stay in one place when you are only eleven. It was plenty of time to learn the names and titles of new relatives, to make friends with Judy Bryce and Debra Everett, and to get all "A's" and "E's" from Mrs. Pridge, even though she couldn't control the class, so she could be a really good teacher.

I caught up to Aunt Dolores. She turned from her bureau and used her hip to push a drawer shut. In her hand, she held two small white boxes. No bike in those, I thought. Still, I turned a shiny face up toward her and smiled. She sat down on her bed, which was covered with a handmade quilt, full of blue and red plaids.

"Go on. Sit down. Open them," she said and handed them both to me at once.

Something slid around inside the small boxes, something heavier than the boxes themselves. Jewelry, I thought, like the snowflake bracelet from Aunt Shirley, but I was determined to act surprised anyway. I opened the larger of the two boxes first. Inside was a silver cross that had a round crystal where the vertical column intersected the horizontal one. "So pretty!" I said. It was.

"Hold it up to your eye," she said.

"How?"

"Like this." She held it up in front of her right eye and peered into the round clear crystal. "There's something inside."

I loved secrets, mysteries, making discoveries. I loved the Nancy Drew of it. *Something in me wanted to be a part of the greater mystery, to make sense out of my world.* I took the cross back from her. Its silver chain hung down. I looked inside the crystal. There printed on a tiny piece of paper and magnified by the clear crystal was the Lord's Prayer. "Our Father, *my lost father,* who art in Heaven, *was he there, my daddy, in heaven? Why there and not with me, and would I ever go there, so I could be with him again?*"

"What do you think?" Aunt Dolores interrupted my reverie.

"It is beautiful," I said. Then I remembered my manners. "Thank you," I said, and I hugged her neck.

"Well, you earned it. You be sure to thank your Uncle Robert when he comes home." Aunt Dolores saw Saralynn leaning against the doorjamb, and little Raina just toddled in past her. "Come on, Saralynn. You're going to school in the fall. Come and celebrate with us." Saralynn smiled. Her dark, dark, nearly black eyes suddenly had light in them. She smiled! Maybe she liked me a little, after all.

I picked up the second box, shook it, made a smiling face back at the three of them, and opened the box. This was a bracelet. From it dangled a little glass orb. It puzzled me only for a moment. "A mustard seed!" I exclaimed.

Aunt Dolores smiled. "Yes. Do you remember the verse?" But before I could say it, Saralynn did. "O ye of little faith. Had ye but faith the size of a mustard seed, ye could move mountains."

"It's from the Holy Land," Aunt Dolores said. "The mustard seed is, and it is floating in water from the Red Sea."

I slept that night with a box full of clothes at the foot of my bed, the Lord's Prayer necklace around my neck and the mustard seed bracelet around my wrist. I had the power to move mountains and part the Red Sea wrapped around my wrist and a secret message from God hidden inside the cross.

The particular mysteries and powers of these amulets lay beyond my understanding. To me, it was all a sort of magic, like blowing all the seedling sentinels off that dried dandelion and sending them into the air had brought me a television, years before in Greensboro. I half-expected to wake up the next day and find my clothes put back into the wardrobe or find my mother and my real father sitting on my bed together like they must have once, at least, long ago after he convinced her that she should nurse me.

When I awoke and saw the box of clothes was gone, I was only half-disappointed when I looked into the wardrobe and saw that it was still empty on my side. I pulled on my Nancy Drew disguise, slipped into her mind, and began to figure a way to avoid staying with my mother for the summer.

I was thwarted in my first attempt. Granddaddy Pope, Uncle Douglas, Aunt Evelyn, and Arthur had arrived and were waiting outside for us. Uncle Robert and the whole family were coming, and we were going to drive separately. Everybody was in the car except me.

I stood inside the house and screamed, *"No. No. No. I will never go."*

I sat on the plastic couch, the same one I had prayed on when Preacher Hart came to save me. Granddaddy Pope opened the screen door and stepped in, only so far as to allow the door to close behind him. He had no badge, no billy club, no gun, no judge's robe, no Bible, and no pulpit, but when he spoke, he carried the authority of both church and state.

"I've been talking with Attorney Fredericks. There's no way out of this mess you got us all into. Either you get in the car on you own volition," he said, "or I will pick you up and put you there, and make your tail raw in the doing of it. I will not let you break the law and disgrace the Pope name any further."

I was a smart kid. I knew what "volition" meant. I knew it was a long ride to Jacksonville, Florida, especially for someone with a raw tail. I knew when I had to look defeated. Nancy Drew called it "feinting"—not the falling-down kind, but the trick-you-now-by-doing-what-you-want-but-I'll-win-in-the-end kind.

I balled up my own will as tightly as I could and made it as small as the Lord's Prayer had to be to get inside that tiny hole in my necklace. Only I didn't add a magnifying glass so others could peep inside at the truth of me. And I took my belief in myself, which was as close to faith as I could come, and made it as tiny as that mustard seed and covered it with so much logical clarity that no one could get at it. Then I let it fall down into the deep well of myself where it stayed protected, and I forgot about it until I was able, decades later, to untie my will from the demands of others, release my belief in myself, and let it grow and flourish.

In the meantime, I got into the back seat of Aunt Dolores's Chevrolet. I smelled fried chicken that Aunt Dolores had prepared for the trip. I was hungry already for it, but I knew not to ask just yet.

Chapter 37

Savannah Slums and the Sunshine State

The interstate by-pass took us past the slums of Savannah, and everywhere I looked outside my window, I saw clotheslines running from multi-storied, ramshackle wooden buildings that looked like they might topple and collide with the cars flying by them below. I saw dark black faces at windows and on fire escapes, and though I had seen black people in the tobacco fields and barns where I worked my first summer in Wisteria, I had never seen so many crammed together.

I heard the ugly angry word spoken again and again in disgust by my aunt as we passed by these other outcasts. My uncle only shook his head and said, "Uh, uh, uh," and kept his eyes on the road ahead. That made me look at the faces more intently as we blurred by. Those faces moved and talked and laughed and were attached to bodies that walked and to hands that gestured, to feet that jumped ropes and to mothers' arms that hugged children.

Spontaneously, as I looked at those houses alive with people, more people—black or white—than I'd ever seen living in one area before, I began to hum and then to sing, "Jesus loves the little children, all the children of the world. Red and yellow," and Saralynn and even Raina joined in with me to sing "black and white. They are precious in his sight." And by the time we finished the song with "Jesus loves the little children of the world," Uncle Robert and Aunt Dolores were singing with us, he, with his sweet tenor voice and she, with her alto, harmonizing as we drove out of Savannah, leaving the slums behind us, and drew closer to the Sunshine State.

We had chicken with Holsum white bread as we sped toward my new home. We drank iced tea from old mayonnaise jars. We only stopped once, so Uncle Robert could fill up the car, and we all could go to the bathroom. Somewhere, ahead of us or behind us, were Uncle Douglas and Aunt Evelyn with Granddaddy and Little

Arthur. We didn't caravan with them the way I supposed we would, but Uncle Robert seemed to know where to meet up with them.

I fingered my Lord's Prayer necklace, twisted it up over my nose, and looked inside through the tiny magnifying glass at the words. I had done this several times since we began the trip, and this time I noticed that the metal post had started to crack. It wasn't metal at all, or if it were, it was a soft one. I let the necklace down to my chest gently and placed it inside my blouse, hoping Aunt Dolores wouldn't notice I had almost broken it. I twisted the mustard seed glass, inside which the seed lay floating in a splash of Red Sea water.

Then I fell first into reverie and then into dreams in which the Red Sea did not part, and I went under the water. I could see the red, red water from the surface, see through it, and see myself held down by the weight of it while the cross floated up, broken and visible.

I missed the rest of Georgia and was pulled awake by Raina tugging on my ponytail as we crossed into Florida. The sun was spreading golden white light on the trees, the houses, and the faces of those who zipped by my window. Aunt Dolores was driving, and she and Uncle Robert had their windows down. The air flowed over me like a warm flannel gown. We were close to the ocean, and I had never seen it before. Aunt Dolores was talking with Uncle Robert about going to see it before they left.

I sat up on the edge of my seat and said, "Yes, yes! I ain't never seen it either. Let's do go." They quieted immediately. I looked from one to the other before I slunk back into my seat.

"We were just wishing out loud, honey. We really don't have time to go. We got to turn right around and drive back home, so your Uncle Robert can try to get in and get some sleep before working two shifts tomorrow to make up for missing work today. Maybe your mama will take you there this summer," Aunt Dolores said.

Then she rolled her eyes at Uncle Robert. I could see in the rear-view mirror, and I let my eyes meet hers once, in accusation, before I turned my head and cried. No one stopped the car or reached out in any real way to comfort me except for encouraging the two-year-old Raina, who tried to hug me, to go "hold the baby."

"Hold the baby," Aunt Dolores said, and Uncle Robert chimed in laughing. So did Saralynn.

"Kiss the baby," Uncle Robert said, and Raina kissed me.

The ridicule worked. It didn't comfort; nor did it heal, but it galvanized my will, and fully awake, I snorted once to clear my throat. I picked Raina up and held her in my lap, and I restored the proper order in which I was the helper Aunt Dolores wanted me to be, and Raina got to be the baby again.

When we drove up to the address where my mama lived, I saw Uncle Douglas's big Mercury parked outside a small house in the side yard of a bigger house. I looked at the big house, and I remembered the 1302 Portland Street house with its two stories, many columns, and its second story porch that was rotting and falling down so that we weren't allowed to sit on it.

I looked at the big yard and saw the green grass alight with the golden sun. I saw in through the side windows. Someone was moving inside the house. My mama and Portland Street with the ocean nearby! For just an instant, my heart swelled with hope. Then the news came in through Uncle Robert's open window.

Uncle Douglas's voice was deep and he boomed, "She's not here. We knocked on the door, and no one came. We looked in, and the place is empty. She's gone."

I started to object because even from where I sat, I could see the house was not empty. But I was slow to speak to him. He looked too much like Granddaddy Pope. I watched and listened, trying to detect something in what he was saying that made sense with what I was seeing. Then he pointed back toward the little house. That house! That's where my tiny mother had lived before I arrived that day, and from which she had disappeared.

Decisions were being made in a hurry. Those decisions would affect me, my mother, my brother, and even my half-brother Eddie and half-sister Debbie for the rest of our lives. They were being made by men and women, who were my daddy's kin, and they were being made for my own good, a "good" they assumed they knew well enough to act on for me.

"We came to where we were told to come. She's not here. We did our part. I say we leave," Uncle Douglas said. He was talking to Aunt Dolores, who was still in the car.

I saw some movement again inside the big house, which was about a hundred feet away from where I sat in the car parked at the curb. The sidewalk was right there. The Chevrolet had only two doors. *Had I had my own door, would I have pushed it open and stepped outside to stretch my legs or to run on that sidewalk toward that vision of a fancy Portland Street house and open the door and find my mother inside?* I couldn't get out of the car or my situation, so I drank in all the information I could.

"She must not care at all about them, or she would have been here when we arrived. Imagine not even leaving a note," Uncle Douglas said. "We could ask around, but I don't want to leave Arthur anyway, and I know you don't want to leave Sandra. Daddy says we have met our legal obligation, and you know he knows the law, what with all the laying up on that front porch and reading law books he's done. So, I say, we just let Daddy call Attorney Fredericks, and if he says okay, then we're gone."

My heart was conflicted, confused. Since I was there, I wanted the doors to that big house to open, and I wanted my mama to emerge. As we rolled away, I saw an old woman come out on the porch and wave vigorously at us, like she was trying to motion us to stop. Aunt Dolores was at the wheel, spelling Uncle Robert, and she kept driving.

"Sugh, it looks like you won't have to stay after all. I guess God has answered our prayers," Aunt Dolores said. "Praise him for saving you from all the sinful influences of such a woman who could desert her own children. Would you say a prayer of thanksgiving to him, sugh?"

I sighed. "Our Father," I began, "who art in heaven," *and where is my mother, I wondered, as the words droned on through my open lips and my heart closed hard against them, harder than the soft metal of the broken cross that lay against my chest. My heart closed against Aunt Dolores, against my mother, and against myself.* "Thy kingdom come," *was this his kingdom and I so bad as to be kept out?* "Thy will be done." *And was this his will? That I should be separated from my mother, from myself?*

Attorney Fredericks affirmed that we had done all that was legally required. All the grown-ups congratulated Granddaddy for his legal mind. I saw Little Arthur, dwarfed in the back seat of the Mercury where he sat next to Granddaddy. As Little Arthur leaned his head against the window of the car, I caught his eyes for just a moment before he turned away from me forever.

We drove back to Wisteria, without stopping to see the beach, and Uncle Robert got back in the car about five o'clock in the morning and went to work at his job in the textile mill thirty miles away in Wilton. The next day I was in the tobacco fields by seven, where I would be three days, and then four days, then five days a week every summer until I turned sixteen and started working at Cohen's Department Store.

Years later, my mother would tell me that she had moved to a bigger house that summer, so she would have room enough for our visit.

"It was ignorant of me not to tell my attorney where I was, but it never occurred to me to do that back then. I just told my old landlady when you'd be coming and to tell you where I was. My heart broke, but there weren't nothing I could do about it. The Popes had brainwashed you, and I just had to get on up everyday and go to work. I had a job I had to keep and Debbie and Eddie to take care of. That was the year before Arthur Blair took them away from me, too."

I still don't know how bad it would have been to live with my mama. Years later Debbie told me stories about being left alone at six or seven to care for Eddie, who was two years younger than she was. She recalled times when there was nothing to eat, even though my mama was working. More than once, Debbie said, Mama told her, "If you go next door and borrow a cup of flour and an egg, I'll make you some pancakes."

When I ask my mama about those years, her eyes fill up with tears, her voice sounds like a dirge and her shoulders slump.

"I have done some wrong things in my life, and I'll not go back over them. That man sitting right there," she will say as she points to Raeford, "knows everything about me and so does God. Raeford is my husband and he has a right to know, but not to judge, and God is my judge and he has forgiven me. But I will say this much to you, Sondra, the Popes didn't do right by me. They didn't even try to find me."

There are other stories about my mama being addicted to Valium and to dog racing. The only times I have seen Mama genuinely excited were when she was catching a fish or recalling a dog race or doing a "snake dance" to a country song. She whoops and hollers and becomes somebody through whom the life force zings. It's a bit embarrassing to watch, though. It feels intimate, like watching someone having an orgasm.

Chapter 38

The Virgin Years

I was a perfect child, the new Sandra, for the next three years. In my white chiffon dress, I graduated from junior high with honors, and I went on to George Johnston High School, the consolidated high school for my third of the county. We had moved out onto Highway 117 into a new house Uncle Robert had built, and I had to get up early to catch the bus on time.

Edmond Clancy drove my school bus. He was a skinny, wiry boy, a bit hysterical when he laughed, and something way down inside of him that wasn't sure of itself showed on his face. It made his sweet smiles painful to experience.

George Johnston High School was only six miles from our new house on Highway 117, but it took almost an hour of winding around dirt roads to farmhouses set back behind old oaks or pine trees to get to school. Where the pines had been sold to the paper companies, old farmhouses that had not been painted for years nor fully visible to passersby, stood baldly exposed in the middle of plowed fields all winter and most of the spring. By the time school was out, they would have greenery around them, tobacco or corn seedlings mostly that would grow tall and conceal them again for the duration of the growing season.

When Edmond Clancy looked at me, he seemed exposed like those houses in the winter when they sat upon the barren earth, and everything that could conceal them had died away. Spring felt far away when he smiled at me.

I was fourteen, a freshman, and he was a junior, old enough to have a driver's license and drive a school bus with sixty or more kids on it. I knew he was going to ask me out long before he did, so I practiced on my pillow, in case I needed to know how to kiss. Although I wanted to be asked out on a date, I wasn't sure I wanted him to be the one, but I carried myself primly like Aunt Dolores demanded, and the other, handsomer boys didn't come near me.

My hair had been long and flowing in the spring of 1961, right before the love affair with long hair began in the sixties, but in the summer before I began high school, I had it shorn. With my long neck, my fairly flat chest, my skinny body, and my big, green, and sometimes forbidding eyes, I was not on the top of the popular boys' list. And it wasn't just my looks. Other less attractive girls managed to snag some dates with seniors, but not me, and I didn't really mind.

I had become born-again, but not as a Christian. I was *a secret born-again virgin,* and *virgin* was apparent in my movements, in my voice, in my eyes, and in my choice of people to be with and places to go. *That was the case unless I had a momentary relapse into a Sandra, who had been around longer than this new version, not a freer Sandra like I thought during the late sixties, but a Sandra who had been groomed by all around her, even Aunt Dolores, to open to men and to be seductive even when I was being virginal.*

The first stair step onto the bus was high off the ground. I had to grab the bar with one hand, hold my books with the other, and lift one leg rather high to place it on that step. Aunt Dolores had upgraded my outfits since I was in high school, and I fit in better with the crowd. The skirts she made for me from the material I bought with my tobacco earnings were tight.

They were tight enough, so that when I stepped up into the bus, my skirt would slide up my leg. In that instant when the flesh above my knee and of my inner thigh flashed, the full-grown woman inside me, one who had already known orgasms, made herself known. At the same time, the *virgin* exiled any feelings of sexual excitement from my face and my demeanor. The step was simply too high. That was all.

Aunt Dolores had given me the code to live by when I started my periods. Those weeks when I lived thinking I was pregnant had put the fear of sex into me, and I knew I had nowhere else to live except Aunt Dolores's house and by her rules. The most important rule was simple: *Good girls don't put out.*

Strangely, I felt like a good girl. And it was a relief. All of that early activity with Little Arthur was a part of the fabric of that other life. Here, with Aunt Dolores, a different strand of who I was emerged, and I was sorry when it seemed it was time to start dating.

Aunt Dolores brought it up when I was just eleven. "Sandra, I know you are going to want to start wearing make-up and dating in a little while, so I'm telling you now. You can wear light lipstick when you are thirteen, double date when you are fourteen, and single-date when you are sixteen. Those are the rules. And you'll have curfews you must always keep. Understand?"

"Yes ma'am," I said.

She didn't understand that I wasn't studying dating or wearing make-up. All I wanted to do was read or paint or draw or daydream. I knew already what dating pointed to, and I wasn't interested.

It didn't take long, though, under her tutelage and around the other girls, to want go out with guys, just to fit in. Aunt Dolores even taught me to flirt. It started at Joe Sutton's store. Preston Halstead worked there behind the meat counter sometimes, and sometimes he pumped gas for us. He came into my life about the same time as Edmond Clancy, and I guess in Aunt Dolores's eyes, they were vying for my attention. Looking back, I wonder if something very different was going on.

I went into the store with her to help with the baby Tracey and with R.A., who was still a few days short of two years old. Both Tracey and R.A. were born in the same year. I pushed the cart through the store and minded Raina and Saralynn, too, while Aunt Dolores wandered here and there, looking for what she needed. It was a small country store, and the prices must have been higher than at the Foodtown in Wisteria, only a mile away, but Joe Sutton gave us credit, and sometimes we needed it.

I had dawdled in the aisle by the Nabisco vanilla wafers I was supposed to be getting for a banana pudding, which Aunt Dolores was going to make as part of Easter supper. When I reached the meat case, I saw Preston standing there, leaning against the meat case and holding his hands out over the counter with some pork chops displayed on white butcher paper for my aunt to inspect.

She stretched over and smelled them, looked up at him, smiled big enough to show her teeth, and said, "They are fresh! Wrap them up."

He beamed back and said, "Yes, ma'am." As he turned, he saw me watching and stopped. She saw him looking in my direction. I wasn't particularly impressed or interested, but I noticed he had dark black-brown eyes like Uncle Robert, black hair, and olive-colored skin. Aunt Dolores saw the look pass between us, and she blushed. I swear she did.

She turned red, but she caught herself and introduced me to him, him to me, like I'd been taught in Home Economics 101 was the right way. She must have had the same class when she was fourteen. She was thirty-two at the time. He was twenty-two. I was fourteen. She was married. He was single. I was single.

Back in the car, she asked me, "What took you so long to get back there?"

Puzzled, I looked at her. She went on. "Well, it doesn't matter. I've wanted to tell you about him for a while. The minute I saw him, I thought you might like to know him. He's only been working there a few weeks, but I found out he is single and well-mannered."

I wasn't looking for a boyfriend. I shivered. It was cold in the car. The heater didn't work well, but she mistook my shiver for something it was not. She laughed. It was a laugh that was ugly around the edges.

"Oh, yes, he is tall, dark, and handsome, isn't he?" she asked.

"I suppose." I was more interested in getting a new dress for Easter and eating banana pudding than I was in Mr. Tall, Dark, and Handsome, but I did encourage her a bit. "Dark and handsome. Maybe not tall."

She laughed, and it was that coarse laugh again. She caught my eye in the mirror, and teased, "Somebody's got a boyfriend."

Saralynn took up the teasing, and even Raina, almost four, taunted me, "Somebody's got a boyfriend."

I had my secrets. At least, I still thought they were my secrets, and I believed that having such secrets gave me the power, like magic, to see when other people were keeping secrets. I looked Aunt Dolores straight in the eyes when she caught mine again in the rear-view mirror.

"Yeah, somebody sure does." I only thought it. I dared not say it out loud.

It didn't end there. She coached me on what to say to get him to ask me out. And right before Easter came, there were cosmetics, and oddly, a beautiful silk slip, the most beautiful one I have ever owned.

"Try it on," Aunt Dolores said. "I'll come in the bedroom with you, and if it doesn't fit, I can send it back in time to get the right size. I obeyed.

Sliding that silkiness over my head and pulling it down next to my flesh made the woman in me sneak out for an instant. I got a glimpse of her before she disappeared. She looked a lot like that full-breasted doll I had left in Tennessee. Aunt Dolores must have seen her, too, because she said, "Goodness, how grown you look! That slip gives your little body a shape. Good thing nobody will be seeing that." She laughed. Then got serious. "Will they?"

I was befuddled. Of course, no one would be seeing it! It was a slip, not a dress, after all. My face showed my confusion as I screwed it up and looked at her blankly.

"Not even Mr. Dark, and Handsome, not matter how dark, and handsome he is." She laughed. It was that laugh again, but it also had a ring of sadness in it. Aunt Dolores was large, overweight by seventy pounds or more. She looked longingly at me, and smiled her sad smile.

Edmond Clancy kept driving our bus, and under Aunt Dolores's direction, I kept making my moves at the meat case. It was a race, really, to see whether Edmond or Preston would ask me out first. I didn't mention Edmond much to Aunt Dolores because I didn't trust her. I did everything she told me to do to get Preston to ask me out, and it all felt embarrassing and unnatural.

Preston had an easy way of talking with her, but whenever I was around, he would clam up. I saw him talking with Betsy Barden, who had red hair and blue eyes and was a year ahead of me in school. He seemed to have no trouble at all smiling and carrying on, and neither did she. He even looked like he knew how to flirt. I told Aunt Dolores.

She was furious. "How dare he carry on with another girl like that right in front of you," she stormed. "You can't let him get away with this. I'm going to drive you right back up there, and you are going to let him know he can't treat you like this!"

Honestly, I didn't care how he treated me. It wasn't that I liked Edmond Clancy more; it was just that I didn't care enough about either boy to work so hard at doing what it seemed to take to get a date. Even if I were to get one, I didn't know what I'd do with it. But Aunt Dolores was in charge, so I listened carefully as she explained about Mr. Rockefeller, and I rehearsed my lines well. She left Raina and Saralynn with Tracey and R.A. in the Chevrolet. She and I went inside, ostensibly to get some grocery items we had forgotten earlier.

She stayed near the front, looking at the shelves, and she shooed me back to the meat case.

Well, I strutted right up there just like she said, and I told him off.

"I don't know who you think you are, Mr. Rockefeller or some other millionaire, who can just play on a girl's feelings and do whatever he wants to do, but I won't have any more of it. You have been flirting with me and every other girl who comes through that front door, and I am not the kind of girl to put up with it. You can just go out with anybody you choose, but don't you ever talk to me again." I said it. No, I *shouted* it.

"You were supposed to whisper, or at least, lower you voice! I am so embarrassed, I don't know whether I can ever go back into that store." We were flying down the highway, back toward home. She slowed the car and pulled off the road. She turned the car around and headed back to Joe Sutton's store.

"You are going right back in there right now and apologize for making a spectacle of yourself in their place of business. You are to tell both Mr. and Mrs. Sutton how sorry you are."

I couldn't stop crying. I had done as I was coached, yet I had failed. I didn't understand what to do or how to do it, but I knew I had to apologize. Alone. That time Aunt Dolores stayed in the car. I cried all of the way through the apologies. Preston must have seen me from the meat counter at the back of the store. He must have been mortified. He called two days later to invite me out for Saturday night, but Edmond Clancy had beaten him to it. I had to tell Aunt Dolores about Edmond when I scheduled Preston for Sunday night of the same weekend. She snorted!

"You little hussy!" she said. "Stringing two guys along like that! And who are you double dating with? You aren't sixteen yet, young lady!"

Later she relented. My girlfriends at school were pretty impressed by my wiles. Not me. I didn't know what girls did on dates. I did know what virgins didn't do, and I knew from Little Arthur what guys wanted girls to do, and I knew what my body was capable of doing. All I really wanted to do was sit in the library and read, or lie in the grass and look up at the clouds. I wondered if boys liked doing that, too, and if so, if I'd ever meet such a one.

Chapter 39

First Dates

When Edmond Clancy arrived, I was still in the bathroom, fussing with my hair, so Aunt Dolores opened the front door. I emerged a few minutes later, clad in a shiny silk, two-piece outfit that consisted of a sleeveless pink-and-gray-striped sheath dress and a solid pink jacket with three-quarter length sleeves.

It was a cut-down, hand-me-down from my New York cousin, who was ten years older than me. I wore black pumps that had just the hint of a high heel, and of course, I was wearing a girdle and stockings and all the other appropriate underwear to bind the flesh down where it fluffed out in the wrong places, and to push it up in the right places.

At fourteen I was so skinny, I didn't need any underwear at all— nothing jiggled when I walked, but Home Economics 101 and Aunt Dolores's Virginity 101 teachings still held sway. My vulnerability was carefully strapped down and sealed away, so that before I could have removed all that wrapping, I would come to my senses. I wouldn't be swept away by a moment's passion like some girls were, according to Aunt Dolores.

"Yes," she had said. "You can single date with Edmond Clancy, but sit here, and let's talk before you call him back."

She indicated the foot of the bed in her and Uncle Robert's room as the place I should sit. She closed the door and sat down beside me, making sure she could see into my eyes. It felt too personal, too private, and that knot inside of me, where I hid all that was not allowed, trembled. I feared all my secrets would bubble up and expose me. She began.

"Most boys will take 'no' for an answer if the girl says it like she means it," she began. "They know that it's rape if the girl doesn't agree, and even if she does agree, and she's underage like you, it's statutory rape. That puts the fear of God into them. Or the fear of the state penitentiary, anyway." She looked straight at me. "You do know what rape is, don't you?"

"Yes ma'am." I looked away. Remembering. Trying not to remember.

"Look at me." I did. "Boys will only go so far as you let them, but they can't stop themselves once their passion gets them going, so you have to make sure it doesn't get going. Honey, they will try to touch you everywhere they don't have a right to, but if they are good boys, and I think Edmond Clancy is a good boy—he comes from a good family—then they will take 'no' for an answer. You understand?"

"Yes ma'am."

"They might beg and plead with you and even tell you how bad it hurts them and how much they love you, but good boys want you to stop them, and they won't respect you if you don't. And listen, I don't know what your girlfriends tell you, but you can get pregnant the first time. And even if you don't, it's a sin, and God sees everything."

I could smell their bodies, hers so near, and Uncle Robert's scent still in the covers. I used to make up her bed in the mornings before I left for school, but one day after I found a round gold metal package, she hadn't wanted my help. I knew what it was the minute I saw it, but I pretended I didn't. *The whole bed sparkled like there were thousands of those containers catching the light of the sunshine coming through her bedroom window. I wondered what was happening to me or if that was just the presence of God in the sheets, blessing her marriage bed.*

"Are you listening?"

"Yes ma'am, I am. I won't let him touch me wrong. I might not let him touch me at all. Debra Everett says she never let a boy even hold her hand until the third date."

She snorted. Then she acted like she needed to blow her nose, left to get toilet paper, stopped to pick Raina up for a moment, got busy with her, and left me sitting on the bed thinking about rape and the blessing and beauty of sex within marriage—like a gorgeous rose she had once said. I began to sense the presence of power in my body and the feeling of fear in the room. After a few minutes, she came back and stood in the doorway.

"Love between a man and woman is a beautiful thing when God blesses it in marriage. And it's the devil's work, and it is ugly and awful outside of marriage."

It was like she had felt my questioning and tried to answer it with her Bible talk. I looked up and nodded.

"Well get up and call him! And let me see you smile. You've got your first date! This is just the beginning."

I called Edmond Clancy to tell him I could go out with him, but I didn't smile. I knew I had to find the excitement, at least enough to feign it, or Aunt Dolores might see the woman in me who already knew what lay beyond handholding and first kisses.

"Great. I'll pick you up about six on Saturday evening, and we can go bowling."

"Okay." I hung up the phone and wondered what to wear. I had never been inside a bowling alley.

Aunt Dolores stood there in the hallway as I started fast toward my room. Her mood had turned gloomy again.

"Just think before you leap," she said. "Don't go rushing into the arms of your own doom like your mama did before you."

When he arrived before I was ready to go, Aunt Dolores invited Edmond Clancy into the den instead of the living room or parlor, as we called it. I couldn't believe it! She worked in dried tobacco all fall to get the furniture for that room, so we would have a proper parlor (since I would be courting soon, she had said), and when we had a use for it, she forgot about it. Luckily, I had straightened up the whole house before Edmond Clancy came because I had imagined he would somehow see into all the rooms, even the closets, in some kind of grand tour that would certainly not happen.

Nonetheless, I had to be sure everything was folded and put away neatly. Aunt Dolores's family was a bit messier than I was used to, having lived with my mama and her mama, where cleaning was always going on. With Aunt Dolores, cleaning was a last-minute panic activity before an invited guest came, and if someone came unannounced, they got held up at the door, while others scurried to pick up the soda bottles, the toys, maybe even a dirty diaper that was "about to be picked up and put away anyway." That night of my first date, I was relieved as I remembered I had cleaned everything thoroughly.

"Hi," I said as I walked into the room.

He sat on the couch on the plastic covering that Aunt Dolores had sewn herself. Winter or summer, spring or fall, I perspired on that couch myself. The couch in the parlor had a fine brown fabric covering. I would certainly take him into that parlor when he brought me home! He stood up as I walked into the room. Good manners! Did he learn that in woodshop or FHA? Or from his mother?

He said, "Hey" when I came into the room, and he made the mistake of trying to smile. His face contorted most painfully, and I am sure my own mirrored his disfigurement back at him.

"Well, let's go," I said.

"You certainly are dressed up nicely."

"Thank you," I said, as I noted his casual madras shirt and tapered dark slacks. The slacks stuck to the back of his upper thighs, puckering his pants at the knees in front. So, the couch made him perspire, too! The route to the door was only a few feet across the room, but the kerosene-burning stove was situated so that we had to dodge it to get out.

We moved toward the door, and there in the middle of our path was a naked Barbie doll, its breasts pointing to high heaven, its long legs stretching endlessly across the wood floor! "Oh!" I said in shock before I caught myself.

He stopped before her naked bounty, also. Then, I simply stepped over her, like she wasn't there, like she didn't have a woman's naked body, like I wasn't naked beneath my binding garments, like I didn't even bathe naked, didn't know nakedness, didn't recognize it, and had not just squealed out loud in its presence.

I reached for the doorknob and opened the door for him. He hesitated only a moment, dodged the heater, stepped over the doll without looking down again, and stepped outside as I held the door open for him. Before I closed the screen door and joined him on the porch, I noticed his pants weren't stuck to the back of his thighs any longer.

The bowling alley was darker than I thought it would be when he suggested we go bowling. Aunt Dolores had warned me about going to dark places with a boy, and when she had, again I felt the darkness inside me, that little knot where I stored away all those moments, those feelings, that body knowledge that I then knew was my sin, my darkness. It collected there before I could call it by its name—my original sin.

In the bowling alley, I looked around me, not knowing what to do or where to go. I felt the darkness in the corners of the room. I felt it gather itself and come to attention when I looked around, as if it recognized that dark spot within me, and like water trying to find its level when more is added to the mixture, redistributes itself and reaches a higher level.

Quickly, I sought Edmond Clancy's face. There was living confusion in his contorted smile. His cheeks jig-sawed, and when he opened his mouth to speak, his lips worked hard to form the missing pieces of the puzzle against the background of his teeth and tongue. Something hopped back and forth in his eyes—hope and certainty of disappointment, shifting from one moment to the next, walking across hot coals of his own fears. But there was no darkness in his eyes.

"I—I have never bowled," I sputtered. With that simple truth spoken, the light returned to my mind, to the room, and the original sin shrank again and scrambled to hide in the corners of my soul. *Here was not going to be a chance to re-enact itself. Aunt Dolores was wrong about me. I would not rush to my own destruction.*

"Oh," he said, and he took charge. I was outfitted with socks and shoes that looked awful with my just-one-degree-short-of-party dress, and I was handed a bowling ball. When I tried to lift it with one arm, my elbow bent backward like my arm had a green stick break.

But I bowled. We bowled. For several hours. Or days. He smiled his crooked smile, and I lifted the ball with two hands, using slow-motion exaggerated movements, which allowed that my part of my brain that controlled my muscles to catch up and connect with the newness of the activity. The roar of the ball rolling down the hard wood lane, the clack of it as it guttered or sometimes hit a pin or two, kept me separate from Edmond Clancy and curbed my fear of him, my fear of what my body might do if longing were reborn in it, like Aunt Dolores warned would happen, by his boy's body coming too close to my girl's body.

Chapter 40

Good Girl/Bad Girl

She was sitting in darkness in the den when I came home.

I didn't invite Edmond in. It was a few minutes before my ten o'clock curfew time, and I think both he and I had enough of one another for one evening. The porch light was on. Edmond walked me up to the door, I pushed the key into the lock and opened it, and I turned around to say goodnight.

Suddenly I felt her there. In that place where a mother's loving energy and care should have been, was a sudden stabbing pain, shrill, as it vibrated through me but audible only to me, I thought.

I looked at Edmond. He hadn't noticed anything.

"I had a good time," he said. "Thanks for going out with me." Then he waited.

"Me, too. It was fun. And thank you."

For the first time that evening, he reached out and took my hand. His felt cold, doughy; mine, bony inside his surprisingly fleshy hand. He squeezed mine once and let it go so fast; it fell to my side. He looked up at the porch light, laughed, turned and shot down the steps.

As I turned to go into the house, he called, "Sandra, let's go out again. I'll call." He did not wait for me to respond. Maybe he was afraid to. He was in his daddy's Pontiac, the headlights were on, and I shielded my eyes. He made a three-point turn and was gone.

My daughter Ana, who at two years old joined her twin Dani to set me on my search for my mother—and for Her—had my first grandchild recently. She told me she had read studies that show the bonding between mother and child occurs within the first thirty minutes after birth. If it doesn't happen then and isn't addressed adequately later, she said, the relationship would always be difficult, broken. Perhaps my mother's refusal to nurse me, to claim me as her own for the first three days of my life, perhaps her desertion of me when she left me with Grandmother Morgan, and perhaps my refusal to go with her when she tried to get custody, were all outcomes of those lost thirty minutes.

I couldn't have known then as I stood at the door after that first date all that I know now, and I wouldn't have had the words to say it. But I knew, in ways that words would take years to capture, that what waited inside that room for me was not kindness, not the gentle curiosity of a mother wanting to know about her daughter's first venture into the world of romance or wanting to innocently re-live her first date through her daughter. Had Aunt Dolores been sleeping, had she been indifferent, I would have been far better served.

What waited for me inside that room that night was the beginning— no—the continuation of the theft of my soul. It would still take years for me to understand why Aunt Dolores hated me and was so unconscious of her own inner self that she thought she loved me. By the time I figured it out, I would need, as I continue to do now, daily conscious connection to my own higher self, to the divine within me—to Her, who was always with me, even when my world would not let me know her or have a category for her that would enable me to know that I did not know her, so I could long for her.

It was her absence I felt. Dolores gave me that. It began long before my return from that first date, but that is the moment I became aware of the hole in me, the hole in my world, and I continued to fill it with Dolores's beliefs about me.

"It's about time you got inside here, young lady!" she said when I stepped in and closed the door. "You better be glad I didn't come out there on that porch and drag you in here right in front of that boy, who, by the way, you won't be going out with again!" She was talking in low, grunting sentences, and she hadn't risen from her reclining chair. Uncle Robert had gone to work already, and I knew the children were sleeping. "How dare you tempt me this way, breaking your curfew the very first time I let you go out?"

"But—"

"No, don't you dare talk back to me," she raged.

I had to walk past her to get to my room. I moved toward her.

"I'm not done with you. Where do you think you are going?"

"I need to go to the bathroom."

"I bet you do! You slut!"

"I—I just need to pee. I didn't do anything wrong." I was crying and shouting at the same time.

"Then how come you come traipsing in here two hours late? Tell me that!"

"I'm not late."

"I looked at the clock just before you came up on that porch and woke me back up. I ain't crazy. It said ten minutes to twelve."

"No, ma'am, you aren't—"

"Don't be correcting my grammar, Miss Smarty-Pants. I know how to speak right."

"I—I wasn't." I pushed past her and rushed into her room. I picked up the alarm clock. It was one of those wind-up clocks. The time was 10:05 p.m., exactly. I rushed back out to the living room and showed it to her. "Look!"

"You change the clocks now to cover up your bad behavior? You'll never go out of this house again. I should've known I couldn't trust you to be anything but your mother all over again."

"Stop!" I screamed it.

I hadn't seen my mother since the court appearance when Judge Pryor had talked with me in his chambers and told me I had to go to Florida and live with her for the summer. I had come back from that disastrous Florida trip, the court had awarded Aunt Dolores custody of me, and I had penned a poison letter to my mother that Aunt Dolores had not only approved of, but had dictated half of.

I studied hard. I worked in green tobacco all summer from the time I was eleven to make money for clothes, I took care of the children, I helped clean the house, I cooked, and I helped feed ten thousand chickens daily, sometimes twice a day. What did this woman want of me? I had even faked a conversion for her.

Still something inside me knew I was what she called me, not because of what Edmond Clancy and I had done, for we had done nothing except endure a very awkward four hours together, trying to believe we were having a great time. I knew I was what she called me because of what me and Little Arthur had done. I had never spoken of it, would never confess to it, and she could not have known it unless our sounds had been discovered that first night we spent at Grandma and Granddaddy Pope's home in the bedstead that lightening struck.

By then, I didn't really believe we had been discovered. The Popes being the Popes, I figured they would have talked to one another about it, and Aunt Dolores being Aunt Dolores, I reckoned she would have brought it up during one of her infamous "bikini" talks. She hadn't, so I felt like she had no proof. Still, somehow, she knew. She could sense it, like I could sense her dark intentions toward me, even though she swore she loved me. I was a slut, no matter how well I played, and liked playing, the born-again virgin.

I resisted her anyway.

"Look at your watch," I said.

"What!"

I flipped the light switch on.

"Look at it, please." I could see she was going to. Curiosity was about to win out over her need to be right about me being a bad girl. I stepped back, further away from her. She looked at her watch. She looked at the clock. She looked up at me. Then she looked away.

"You better get to bed. You got church tomorrow."

Slowly, I backed down the hall until I was almost to my room. Then I turned and dashed inside. I locked the door. I left the light off. I pulled my clothes from my body and put them on the chair beside my bed.

In the dim light of the room, I looked at my young girl flesh, naked in the night. I felt desire, old desire, rise in me, felt it begin as a warm flush that spread to every cell, then it localized in my chest, *in my heart*, for a brief instant before it coursed downward and burst into flame between my legs as I wrapped them around the iron bed railing and rocked my born-again virgin self in safety, back and forth atop it, until I flew away amidst the flamingo-pink mimosa blossoms. As I flew upward, something happened that was more than identifying with her negative image of me, more than releasing tension, but I could not put words to it until now.

I was Rumi, in great grief, holding onto a pillar and swinging himself around it, mourning the loss of his beloved and speaking spiritual truths poetically and spontaneously that others wrote down as he twirled. I was in the center of my own self, somehow returned there, opened to a spiritual experience that denied the dirtiness of everything "slut" signified.

I was spiraling inward to the ancient center of my being, like a pilgrim walking the great labyrinth at Chartres, like a Tibetan monk sand-painting a mandala, like a Druid finding her way to the center of the Celtic cross where everything was magnified and glorified, a living prayer to "Our Mother-Father who art in Heaven." And there I remained in my own divine center, entering there through my own divine body, the same body that she taught was dirty, that the church taught was defiled, and I believed that with my mind, while my center split open to a place of light and love, as I followed the only route I knew to get there, and wondered, even then, at fourteen, what was wrong with me that I could only find glory that way.

Chapter 41

The Devil's Grippe

Uncle Robert woke me that Sunday morning but not in his customary way.

There was no sweet tenor starting off softly and building to wide-awake deafening loudness as he sang, "You can't get 'em to bed and you can't get 'em to bed and you can't get 'em to bed at ni-i-ight. Then you can't get 'em up and you can't get 'em up in the mor-r-rning!" He simply knocked loudly on my door and called from the hall, "Time to get up. Now, Sandra." Drowsy still, I dragged myself from the bed. I was wearing the silk slip. I must have put it back on after my naked flight the night before.

Except for that one time when I asked Aunt Pauline instead of Uncle Robert to take me home from the dried-tobacco tying fundraiser for the First Original Free Will Baptist Church, Uncle Robert had never been mad with me. I was having cramps so badly that time I couldn't stand up at the tying horse any longer, and I wasn't ready to talk with him about such a problem.

"He felt hurt," Aunt Dolores said when Aunt Pauline told him instead of me. And for about a week after that, he hadn't been the one to wake me up. I'd hear him calling the other children, but if that didn't wake me, Aunt Dolores would do it herself. After a while, I was back on his morning wake-up call list, and he always sang that same song before he knocked on the door. Only once did he have to come into my room and sprinkle me with cold water to get me out of bed.

But today was different. He hadn't knocked on the door. He hadn't sung to me. I sat on the side of my bed for a moment. I never had a housecoat until right before I went to UNC-G for that first year of college. I just pulled on some everyday clothes from the day before, clothes that could double as work clothes soon when I'd have to put on some boots and slog through the poop of ten thousand chickens to give them breakfast. But not before I got my own.

When I passed by Aunt Dolores's bedroom, the door was shut. She wasn't in the den or in the kitchen. And Uncle Robert had disappeared. I knew my Sunday morning duties, so I began to do them. First, I made a pan of biscuits: flour, lard, baking soda, salt, and water. As soon I stuck them in the oven, I lugged the iron skillet onto the electric burner.

I cut the fatback into thick slices and placed them in the skillet. Then I turned on the burner and started with the meat in a cold skillet. Keeping the temperature on medium meant the skin would be crisp, and the fat wouldn't burn. That's when I turned around and really began to wonder where everybody was. Only Raina had wandered into the kitchen. Then R.A. came toddling in with just a diaper on. Tracey would still be in her crib.

I walked back down the hall. Shoes still had to be located and polished, clothes organized and maybe ironed, baths taken, and hair combed, and nobody was making any progress but me. I swung R.A. up onto one hip and stopped in front of Aunt Dolores's door. It was open. Saralynn sat on the far side of the bed at the foot with Raina right next to her. Tracey was standing up in her crib. Aunt Dolores had her back to the door, and Uncle Robert sat in a slat-back rocking chair on the opposite of the bed. He was looking at Aunt Dolores.

"What's wrong?" I asked. Aunt Dolores often got sick, especially since she had those last two babies—R.A. in January and Tracey in December.

"Like you don't know," Uncle Robert said.

I started around the foot of the bed, so I could see Aunt Dolores's face.

"Just hand me R.A. and go on about your business," Uncle Robert said.

I felt like I had suddenly wandered into the wrong family, like I didn't know the people around me the way I thought I did. He stood up and took R.A. from me. I looked at Aunt Dolores. Her dark eyes looked up at me from her red, swollen face. I had seen that puffy face before—once when her daddy died just after she left him alive at the hospital and came home to rest herself for the long night ahead. When the phone call came, she broke down.

She grieved almost more about not being there when he died than she did about him dying. She must have needed some last moment of reconciliation with him. When her mama died, Aunt Dolores was still in the hospital, but she had just left the room. That hurt her more than when her daddy died, and she cried harder and longer for her mama than for her daddy.

"Did somebody die?" I asked.

"No, nobody died, but you 'bout broke your aunt's heart with your shenanigans, and made her so sick, she can't get out of the bed. And here you come acting like you don't know what's going on," Uncle Robert said. He was a quiet man, and this speech seemed to heave itself from inside him and left him looking queasy.

"Aunt Dolores, are you okay? What is he talking about? You know I didn't do nothing wrong."

"Don't try to defend yourself!" Uncle Robert said. "Just leave her alone."

Aunt Dolores was crying again. Hard crying. Raina began next. Then Saralynn. Then R.A. started crying, and I put him down. By the time I left the room, everybody but Uncle Robert and me was crying.

I smelled the fatback when I entered the hall. The smoking grease was smutty black. I grabbed the skillet right before it caught fire, and I fished the fatback out of the grease and put in on top of the paper sack I had laid out to drain it on. We could still eat most of it, especially with some molasses.

The biscuits fared better. They were a little too brown, but edible. I pulled the pan out and put it on top of the stove. I could hear all that crying through the kitchen wall. Aunt Dolores's room was right behind it. I pulled at one biscuit. It came cleanly away from the bunch, and I tossed it from one hand to the other until it cooled. Then I stepped out the kitchen door onto the screened-in porch.

The box in the corner that held our boots from the chicken house didn't stink yet. The day hadn't got hot enough and probably wouldn't because it was March and cool though the weather was changeable. There was a crate of Pepsi's right next to the boot box. The sodas were cool from the night, cool enough. I took one, without permission, and I capped it on the bottle opener Aunt Dolores had nailed to the side of the house.

I sat down on the only chair out there. It was a kitchen chair from our old set, the one chair that had escaped the dump. The yellow, plastic vinyl seat was split open, and the stuffing was coming out. I usually sat there to pull on my boots before feeding the ten thousand chickens, but on that morning, I sat on that chair in the sunlight, held my Pepsi between my legs, and raised that hot biscuit to my mouth. I let some Hansel and Gretel crumbs fall to the floor. I'd finish the biscuit, I thought, eat it all a crumb at a time, and then I'd be able to follow the path of clues and figure out what was going on inside the house.

I sat there long after I had finished my biscuit, swilled down my Pepsi, burped quietly, and placed the empty back into the crate. I sat there until I heard them in the kitchen. I huddled just out of sight of them, all of them there but Aunt Dolores, who must have been in the bedroom still. I overheard the answer to Saralynn's question, "Why ain't we going to Sunday school?"

"Because your mama is sick, and I ain't leaving her."

"What's she got?"

"I don't know, but it looks to me like all that crying weakened her. She can't move without her back hurting her, and I can't get her to the doctor by myself, especially since I don't have nobody to leave you with."

"Sandra can—"

It must have been a look that stopped her because I didn't hear Uncle Robert say anything. That was when I slowly, quietly, slipped the boots on, and I made my way through a chicken house and a half before I saw Uncle Robert enter. I had been careful not to spill any feed, and I had dragged my hand through every watering trough to clean out the chicken poop and the wood shavings that got in them when the chickens roosted atop them.

He picked up the other wheelbarrow and the coal bucket. He went to the feed bin, opened the chute, pounded on the tin side and held the wheelbarrow in just the right spot until it was mounded with feed. He coughed once and tossed his head as the feed dusted up from the barrow. He let the chute slide shut with a clang, dug the shovel end of the coal bucket into the barrow, and pushed it to the opposite end of the house from where I stood working.

I finished the row I was working on, parked my wheelbarrow, and left by the side door before he could stop me. When I stepped out into the yard, I could feel the chicken poop caked to the bottom of my boots. As I was knocking some of it off on a railroad tie that Uncle Robert had put by the chicken house for that purpose, I saw the big sleek car drive up. Even though I didn't know its name, I knew that the only person who drove a car like that was Dr. Moore. I slunk back toward the house, dumped the shoes in the box on the screened-in porch, and managed to get down the hall to the bathroom before Dr. Moore was at the door. Saralynn answered it, and by that time, Uncle Robert was back in the house.

I took a long bath, and with all that commotion at the other end of the house, everyone was so engaged that I got the bathroom all to myself. I was still in some kind of numbness. I could hear what was going on around me, but I didn't feel like I was in the same house with all of it. It wasn't even as close as a television screen to me. I was in a faraway place, and I was to stay there for quite a while.

It was the other Sandra, the bad girl, who they hated, not me. I knew that, but what I didn't know was how they knew she existed. I had tried so hard to keep her to myself, and I was certain that I had done nothing to reveal my other self. Somehow Aunt Dolores just sensed her.

When I finished my bath, I dressed in my room and sat on my bed. I was starting to get really hungry again, and I knew I had to make Sunday dinner and help with supper. Dr. Moore was gone. I walked down the long hall toward the kitchen. Her door was open. I looked in. She was looking out at me.

"Come on over here, Sandra," she said.

I didn't want to. I didn't want to go near her ever again. But Uncle Robert was sitting in the slat-back rocker, urging it forward and backward with the slightest motion, and he was staring at me, too. Together, they drew me inside the room.

"Sit down, child," she said.

I did. I sat on the bed.

"I want to pray for you. Uncle Robert and I want to pray for you."

Uncle Robert slid out of his chair and onto his knees. I followed his lead and got down on my knees, closed my eyes, propped my elbows up on the bed, and pressed my palms together like I'd learned to do right after I arrived in Wisteria.

"Dear Heavenly Father," she began. Then she reached over and put one hand on my head. "This lost one is one of yours, too. She is one of ours, Lord, but she has fallen again by the wayside. Help her find her way back, dear Lord. Help her see her willfulness is not your will, but her own.

"Help her to see that when she disobeys, she causes sickness and disease to come into the world. Help her, Lord. Convict her heart, O God, so she will see that she has sinned, if not in deed, then in thought, and in deed, too, when she shows disrespect to her elders, like she did to me last night, and me having taken her in when her own mama didn't want her, didn't even show up to get her when we drove her all that distance to Florida.

"Help her to see that she must always in mind and heart and body and deed, be free from insolence, and never talk back or act up like she did last night when she accused me of lying, when all I had in my heart was love for her, and concern for her, and the desire to protect her from all manner of evil-doing, Lord.

"Convict her heart, O God, so she can see what it is she has done, and how it has brought this tribulation upon my head because I have stood up for her, O God. I have taken her as my own and promised to train her in your ways. Help her to see that I must pay for her mistakes, for her bad ways, and that this sickness that has been visited upon me, is my punishment from you, O God, for failing at my task. Forgive her, Lord, and give her another chance. Amen."

"Amen," Uncle Robert said.

"Amen," I said just as a loud knocking came from the outside den door.

"Who could that be?" Uncle Robert said.

"You stay here," Aunt Dolores said to me. "Robert, get the door before the kids open it to heaven knows who."

I was crying. The old Sandra. The new Sandra. All of who I was, crying. Pretty soon I'd have the snubs.

"It's okay," she said. "I forgive you. Now, sh-h-h! Listen."

From the bedroom we heard Uncle Robert's voice. "Well this is a surprise. Come on in and sit a while. Dolores's not well, but I'll let her know you are here."

"I am sorry for just dropping by like this, but I wanted to see Sandra. What's wrong with Dolores?"

It was Preston Halstead's voice! He wasn't due for my second first date for hours!

"She got the grippe," Uncle Robert said. "That's what Dr. Moore said. She's been kind of upset for a while, and I reckon things can come on you fast when you're not feeling like yourself."

"The *grippe*?" Preston asked.

"Yeah, the grippe. Real bad though. Dr. Moore called it something else, but when I asked what he meant, he told me it was like the grippe. Said she had a real bad case of it, too. Bad enough that he said the old-timers called it the Devil's Grippe."

And while I was recalling what Aunt Dolores said, I heard the words she didn't say that *I had caused her to have the Devil's Grippe. My Nancy Drew mind wondered if that made me the Devil in whose grip she was. I pretty much felt like it was the other way around.*

Chapter 42

Visiting Hours

Preston's voice filled me with embarrassment and dread.

"I'm sorry to hear she ain't well. Could I pay my respects to her?" Preston asked.

"I don't see why not. That medicine she got worked right fast," Uncle Robert said.

Aunt Dolores heard them from the bedroom, too. I was still on my knees, but I shot straight up when Aunt Dolores took her hands off my head fast.

"Close the door!" she ordered. "Get me my hospital jacket."

I slammed the door shut.

"Dolores? Hon?" Uncle Robert called from the den. "Are you decent? Preston wants to say hello."

I was up and at the closet, pushing aside her few Sunday dresses and Uncle Robert's Sunday suit. I knew right where she kept the bed jacket, way at the back of the closet. I felt cool air rush up toward me as I reached way back into the closet. The pipes for the plumbing were back there, and the hole Uncle Robert had cut for them was too big, so air from beneath the house rose up through the hole.

The hospital jacket was silky and quilted, and it was emerald green. It wasn't the normal kind of stuff Aunt Dolores wore to bed, but she'd got it and a couple nightgowns right before R.A. was born, and she used them again when Tracey came that same year. Lace that was two inches wide rode up around the neck and down the front of the jacket, and the bed jacket was fastened with green, pearl buttons that snuggled into the lace. She had pushed herself up in the bed, but not without making a face full of pain, and I had stretched around behind her to help get her arms through the sleeves. Then she fumbled the pearl buttons closed.

"Dolores?"

"Yes, bring him on in, but don't nobody expect me to be up to much."

Maybe it was the medicine that made her eyes glow or maybe that green color was just right with her reddish brown hair and set off her brown eyes. I don't know, but when the door opened and the light from the picture windows in the den flooded across the bed, she beamed.

"Why, you don't look like you been sick a day in your life," Preston cajoled.

"I reckon the medicine is working because I sure was feeling like I was dying just a few minutes ago."

"Well, I'm surely glad you didn't. I am," he sputtered the words out fast; then he went silent like a radio somebody had turned off suddenly.

"The doctor said I got the grippe, but I told him that it had me. It felt like it had a real hard hold of me right there on my lower back."

Preston laughed and looked as she pointed to her lower left back. She had to twist a bit to point, and I noticed how she moved like Grandma Morgan did after she'd stayed late with Granddaddy Morgan when he came home from his apartment in town. It was a smooth, floating movement that had rhythm that originated from some place deep within. And the stretch caused the bed jacket to gap slightly, but enough to show some white breast skin.

Preston's dark eyes shone as he watched. Uncle Robert was sitting on the bed next to her, shaking his head "yes, yes" to all she said. He reached over and patted her hand. It was like the sickness itself was another presence in the room, a presence that somehow brought people together. I could sense it like it was an outgoing person, but not one I trusted as I watched from the shadows in the corner on the opposite side of the room. Tracey jumped up and down suddenly, bouncing and saying, "Baby out! Baby out!" Everybody laughed, including me, and Preston saw me for the first time. I had stayed in the shadows to hide my face, which always got red when I cried.

He sputtered again, and as he spoke, I watched his eyes. They lost their sheen, a luster like the shine of chocolate pudding when it's cooking. When he looked upon me, his eyes looked waxy, dull like pudding after it sets.

"Hey, Sandra. I came by early."

"Well, that's fine," I said, glad I had taken a bath and dressed up a bit already. And then I asked Preston, like I would have anybody who came to visit me, "Would you like to sit down in the den or in the parlor? And I could get you some iced tea." I started toward him, toward the door. "And would anybody else like some?"

Preston didn't move from where he had taken up his post. "Well, I—er, I was hoping to see you and sit around and get to know your family a little better, too. I've seen them all in the store, but we never have much time to talk."

"That's mighty refreshing," Uncle Robert said. "Not many boys— young men—these days would do that. They show up a minute before they're supposed to, with some place they have to be a minute after they arrive. It's mighty nice of you to think that way."

"But now with Dolores sick—it's okay I call her that, isn't it? I just got so used to hearing it in the store. With her sick and all, is it okay I am here?"

"Yes, yes. Yes, it's better than fine you're here, and it's okay to call her Dolores. And call me Robert. We're all mighty close up in age."

Tracey cried out again, "Baby out! Baby OUT!"

"Well, almost all of us," Uncle Robert said. He laughed and said to me, "Hand her over here."

I walked across the room and did as I was told.

"Go get Preston a chair. We'll just have to sit right here even though it's not a proper sitting room because even though I can tell you're feeling better, Dolores, I'm not about to move you."

"Oh, Lord, no. The difference I feel is like night and day from what it was right before you came, Preston, and I can sit up for a while, but don't anybody go moving me!"

I stood listening and looking from first one of them to another. They sounded different from me. They looked different. They certainly acted different than I did. I felt like I was in another country. I'd had some French lessons in the seventh grade, and I felt like it must be France. This hadn't happened since Judge Pryor and Little Arthur had talked in another language, but that was a secret one. This one started to sound familiar, like I had heard some of the words before, but not many of them. Still something was even more familiar, maybe the rhythms of it, like a drum beat every so often.

"Sandra. SANDRA!" Uncle Robert had raised his voice again!

"Oh!" I said.

"Get Preston a chair."

"Yes sir." I went into the kitchen and got a chair. It was one of the red dinette chairs that had replaced the yellow ones. The plastic squeaked when I squeezed the padded back to pick up the chair. The metal was cold against my arms as I hugged the chair to my chest to carry it.

That coldness surprised me and alerted me that spring had slipped away for the day, and in its place, winter had rushed in. Still, I just wanted to go outside and take the chair and sit in it. I wanted to go outside without a sweater and feel whatever cold there was and let it chill my skin, give me goose bumps, shrink my skin, and squeeze me back into a child's body, a little girl's body, all the way back to a little baby girl's body. But I wanted to take my face, my grown-up face that people said had turned so pretty, and my hair that, before I had it hacked off, had grown into a long veil of honey brown and let it swaddle me in my mother's arms.

I wanted to go all the way back into the birth canal they talked about in health class, to come again into the world that could see my beauty and want to love me in the right ways, not the ways that Little Arthur wanted me, or Preston wanted Aunt Dolores.

And I wanted blue eyes, not big green ones, next time, small blue eyes that everybody would look at and love and not see through them into me. And suddenly, as I entered the bedroom, all I wanted to do was sit in the bathtub again. I wanted to feel the warm water around me, and I wanted to pee in it without holding back.

"Here's your chair," I said. Just as I was about to set it down, I saw something shift on the foot of the wooden bedstead. I blinked. It moved again. I stood with both hands still on the chair. My eyes adjusted to the light, and I could distinguish the red maple color of the wood grain from the swamp-brown color of the snake, which had stretched itself out and reached from one side of the bedstead to the other!

"Sandra, put the chair down. Sandra!" Aunt Dolores was yelling at me. The snake shifted. Was I the only one who could see it? I raised my eyes, moving only my eyelids, freezing my body in place, and I stared into Aunt Dolores's eyes.

I lifted my chin slowly and stretched my mouth wide like I was about to smile or grin. I felt my tongue touch the back of my upper teeth and dip slightly, and I hissed the initial sound of "Ss-" through my teeth, and then grunted the rest of it, "NAKE!"

"Snake, snake, snake," I muttered and slammed the chair down and stood up straight.

Preston saw it the minute I was out of his line of sight and said, "Oh, my God—goodness—it is a snake. Right there on the foot of the bedstead!"

But as soon as he said it, the snake was gone, and nobody saw where it went, but me. It slipped right into the closet, and I would have bet, if anybody had asked me, but nobody did, that it went right out that hole in the floor Uncle Robert had cut too big when he had run the plumbing pipes into the house.

I knew it was gone, so it didn't scare me, and anyway, I knew it wouldn't come back right away. And even if it did, it wouldn't be coming for me; it'd be after her. Even if later on I did get scared, I figured all it would take would be some old rags stuffed around those pipes to block that hole. Nancy Drew knew just what to do.

Aunt Dolores was clutching her green lace bed jacket tight around her throat, no more breasts playing peek-a-boo. With that quilting, hm-m-m, just about the right size to ball up and fill that hole, I thought, in my first moment of conscious jealousy since I heard my sister Debbie and my brother Eddie talking in the background when Grandma Morgan had phoned my mama before letting us go to Grandma Pope's. And that wouldn't be the last time I felt jealousy, nor the last time I wished I could call back that letter that had resurrected my dead father's family.

Uncle Robert was up on his feet. He pushed Tracey toward me, but I stepped aside, and she ended up in Preston's arms. R.A. and Saralynn and Raina were rushing into the room when it would have made more sense to rush out. In the end, there was such a scramble that nobody noticed I left the room.

I picked up the butcher knife off the kitchen counter where I had left it after I had hacked the fatback into thick slabs for Sunday breakfast. The knife was still greasy. The pan of biscuits still had a couple of cold ones in it, and I picked them up, too. I walked out the back door, letting the screen door slam. The cool air felt good, but not cold enough. I caught the unmistakable rotting odor of dead chickens in it. Uncle Robert had picked up the dead birds and stacked them close to the house in a wheelbarrow. Later he'd bury them. I walked fast to the edge of the woods. Sheltered beneath the pines was the pump house. Out of the sun and in deep shadow, it was just where I wanted to be.

Chapter 43

Discovery and Abandonment

That knife was never sharp enough to cut fatback rind without me hacking through it. I took the knife by the handle and played its cold greasy blade against the inside flesh of my wrist.

How did I know to seek out that tender spot, that place where the skin thins and the veins lie so close to the surface that they blue it? Perhaps an instinct to die, as strong as the instinct to live or as strong as a baby's instinct to tug on its mother's nipple, exists.

Perhaps that dark side of being human, that knowing one could be otherwise, that one could be, has been, elsewhere, perhaps that holy urge to blend with the divine, got warped when the world turned me inside out by denying me mother love when I was so young, a love which would have allowed me to blend with all that is.

Perhaps the hatred of the body, the refusal to recognize it as divine, pulls the body toward death, so that when one seeks death, it is the body seeking a way out of a living death, and spilling blood is as close as we can come to feeling the flow of the universe for which we long.

I only managed to break the skin about paper-cut deep because the knife was dull, and of course, I knew it would be, but I also knew how to sharpen it later. Just that little cut and knowing I *could* go deeper was comfort enough for the moment. Then I held the knife up high and thrust it point first into the flat roof of the pump house. I pulled it out and placed it on my lap like I might have a kitten. The motor whirred on at just that moment. Either someone had flushed a toilet or was running water in one way or another.

I turned around and with my back to the house, I sat cross-legged, making sure my pleated skirt covered my knees. I stared into the trees, through them toward the sky, and I felt the vibrations beneath me stop and the cold of the day swoop down as the sun disappeared behind giant clouds.

Somewhere inside the house, life of a different order was going on. For the moment, I was glad to be outside of it, for solitude was so much easier than being amongst the others, feeling alone and trying to play the part of being included. A lie. The "me" they wanted to include did not exist, and the one I was did not dare to show herself, for she knew she was not wanted.

I drifted. Then I munched on first one biscuit and then, the other. The sky grew thicker; a strong wind pushed the clouds around me and blew into my body through my thin garments. I loved the invasion. I welcomed the cold, so cold, colder and colder moment by moment, and I laughed out loud when I saw it there—a tiny, fragile flake of snow floating down before my open eyes. Then another, and more, until this early spring day was about to end in flurries, and that snake wherever she'd ended up would have literally been stopped in her tracks, her blood cooling while mine still boiled.

The whole lot of them must have noticed I was gone after some time had passed. I could imagine that someone needed something I normally was called upon to do, or Raina glanced out the window and asked, "What's *the girl* doing on the pump house?"

I heard him call from the window. Uncle Robert. Then I heard her, too. Aunt Dolores. I sat as still as a monk in meditation, a state I knew nothing about from the outer world at the time but one which I would learn of and seek out later in life. I heard them. At first, they were still speaking French. Then the English words started to slide in, a few English words for many French ones. Then more and more English until I understood they wanted to me to "Get down off that pump house and get inside here *now*!"

I didn't move. Maybe the cold had caught up with me like I knew it would the snake. Maybe I was frozen. I wondered what that would be like or how that would be different from what I felt each day when the real Sandra slipped farther and farther away from all of them and knotted itself deep inside me until it disappeared into a pinpoint. *Still there. Still there.*

So far away then. So elsewhere, that I did not feel him approach. It would be like that for the rest of my life. *It is like that now. I do not know someone has come upon me until they touch me and then...*I screamed. I jumped. I grabbed the knife and held it by its wooden handle with both hands. "Don't touch me," I screamed. "Not ever! Not ever again!"

I saw him turn and run. It was Preston, and he didn't even go back inside the house. He was in his car and gone, gone, gone! Good! I knew where to find him, too, if I ever wanted to, and so did she. She.

Then. It was *Her* right in front of me. She materialized with her coat on, and her bed jacket lace was sticking out from the collar. Her coat was black, and she'd pulled on Uncle Robert's chicken-poop boots—his red galoshes. Her hair whipped her face, and covered it, and she called my name again and again, softly, almost cooing it.

"Sandra. Sandra. Sandra."

At first, I could not understand why this angel was wearing Aunt Dolores's clothes and those smelly boots, but then the wind swept her hair off her face, and I knew it was no angel coming for me. It was Aunt Dolores!

And she was sick, wasn't she? And I had caused it, right?

Then Uncle Robert was right behind her and he was saying, "You are going to kill your aunt with your shenanigans, making her come out into the cold to get you. You better put that knife down and get back into the house or I will let her wring your neck just like I did those sick chickens!"

Love. That was it. His love for her. For her. Not me. Not the knife. He didn't love me or the knife.

I screamed, "Go away. Go away. Go away! I didn't want her to come out here, and I don't want her or you or anybody near me! Just leave me alone."

"Sandra." It was Aunt Dolores's voice. "Just put the knife down."

"Down?" I looked at the knife. I still held it with both hands.

"Down? Like this?" I jabbed it into the roof of the pump house. "Or like this?" I jammed it in again and again and again, without stopping.

Then with one powerful jab, I stuck it in the pump house roof and left it there and screamed, "Can't you just go away?" I jumped off the rooftop and fled fast beyond them into the house. I was in my room with the door locked before they could reach me.

Aunt Dolores didn't even have to call Reverend Roberdeau. He was out visiting between Sunday morning and Sunday evening services, and since none of us had been in church, we'd already created quite a stir in that small congregation. Uncle Robert was a deacon, and Aunt

Dolores taught Sunday school. Saralynn and Raina and I sang in the youth choir, and little R.A. sometimes joined us. So, we'd all been missed—even Tracey because she was just about the prettiest baby Aunt Dolores had ever had, and everybody said it out loud, even in front of the other children.

Nobody bothered with me once I was inside my room until after Reverend Roberdeau came. Aunt Dolores was in bed again, and the whole family, except me, continued to cluster around her. I could hear them through the wall. My bedroom was on the other side of hers and Uncle Robert's. I just lay in my bed. I didn't feel much of anything. My room was cold, and that was to my liking. We only heated the front part of the house. If I got too cold, I could just pile on some quilts and huddle beneath them.

But Reverend Roberdeau came, and that meant I had to be called out of my room. I came at the first call because I was alert again, sensing danger nearby, and I knew better than to embarrass them any more than they'd been already by the way I acted around Preston.

I didn't care about Preston. I never had really. Aunt Dolores had pushed him on me, and I had just done as she had wanted me to do. I joined the circle of prayer around Aunt Dolores's bed, and she said she felt so much better than she imagined she would when she had taken sick the night before.

"Even being outside in the weather chasing this young'un didn't seem to set me back none," she confided to the minister in front of all of us as she pointed to me.

"Chasing Sandra in the snow?" he asked, like it was the most outlandish notion he'd come across all day.

"Yes sir, Sandra got herself pretty upset earlier today when she thought she saw a snake in the room. Even made that boyfriend of hers—Preston—think he saw one, too, for an instant or two until we got everybody settled down. Then he could see that it was just the way the light shone on the foot of the bed. She had everybody in such an uproar that it took us just about forever to calm them down. And Sandra was so scared she was sitting on the pump house outside with the butcher knife to protect herself! But she's okay now, ain't you, sugh?" Aunt Dolores asked.

"Oh, yes ma'am, I am," I said. I grasped my left wrist with my right hand, my fingers curling around the top side of it, and with my right thumb, I covered the place I'd cut on the inside of my left wrist. It smarted a bit from the dirt or salt on my thumb. "Oh, yes, ma'am."

"Well, let us pray for you, too, and ask forgiveness for you causing your aunt to go out in the cold and risk getting even sicker," Reverend Roberdeau said.

"Yes sir, let's do that," I said, and we did.

Chapter 44

Clear Pools of Blue Light

Keeping my eyes focused on my penny loafers, I entered the bus on Monday morning and avoided Edmond Clancy's gaze, but I could feel it. I couldn't believe I'd been out with him just two days before. I sat far back in the bus, so that he could not catch my eyes in the rearview mirror when he checked it at each stop. I felt like everybody on the bus could see into me, could see beneath my clothes and knew my shame.

When we reached George Johnston High School, I rushed off the bus, and even though he turned to see if I would look at him, I could not. Only when I was inside the building, did I feel safe. School was like that for me. I could blend in. I loved George Johnston High School, and it loved me back in mysterious ways.

The namesake of the school, who had been the local patriarch and would be my benefactor through his heirs later, was both a Revolutionary War hero and a slave owner. At the time I attended the school in the early to mid-sixties, the Johnston home place was dilapidated, a regular ghost mansion, where Halloweeners staked themselves out to scare whomever dared to step upon the property for a requisite holiday thrill. The grand oaks in the front yard had Spanish moss hanging from their limbs, and moonlight added to their mystique.

The sad truths the place hid would not be known until years later when the mansion was restored and a small museum added to house the Johnston family artifacts. Even then, the re-enactments at Christmas and the master's ledgers, immortalizing behind glass cases the sale of this human being or that one, would not be condemned as records of inhumane acts, but hallowed as History. That same Johnson family later became my benefactor.

The school itself was a square, brick, one-story structure built around a center square of land that we could look out on from some of the hallways. Each leg of the square had rooms on both sides and a hall running down the middle. Even so, it was a small place. My graduating class only had ninety-seven students, and it was the largest in the history of the school to that point.

Entirely Caucasian still in 1962-63 during my freshman year, George Johnston was a consolidated school that housed the hopes of the local whites, who wanted their children to get a good education and go to college. Those of us who were the children held that goal somewhere within ourselves also. Most of us did anyway or had it mysteriously placed there during some moment of covert action by a teacher who knew more and could see farther than we could.

What interested most of the students at that high school time of life was the flow of others as they came and went through the halls during class changes and at lunchtime. Upperclassmen boys would position themselves along the walls; and many of the newcomer freshmen girls would travel around and around the halls, promenading like the young virgins dressed in black I would see a few years later, linking arms with their mothers, walking down the *calles* of Madrid after siesta.

We girls walked in two's or three's, wearing our stitched-down, box-pleated skirts with matching sweaters and Peter Pan collar blouses in lighter matching hues. Some of the more daring wore tight skirts, nylons, and loafers. The clothes Aunt Dolores made for me put me in the daring group most of the time, but that Monday I wore my most unattractive skirt—a camel-colored, thin-wale corduroy A-line skirt that was too long and too big. I wore a white shirt, and I buttoned up a dark black cardigan over it. I carried a big blue wool coat with me because I knew Aunt Dolores would make me if I didn't take it on my own. I'd stuff it into my locker as soon as I got to school.

I avoided all of my friends, except for a quick hello. I let my teachers call on me, and I even raised my hand to answer questions. It kept my mind busy and kept suspicions about my reclusiveness to a minimum.

But when lunchtime came, with its rush toward the small cafeteria, its long line waiting for Monday's hamburgers with chili, and its regular sitting places, I had no choice but to join my friends.

"You're not talking much today," Carolyn giggled. "Didn't you have a date on the weekend?"

"She had two of them from what I heard," Sally called out.

"She doesn't look happy about it," Bonnie said. "You okay?"

"Yeah. Just tired. Aunt Dolores was sick," I said.

"Oh, no. Did you have to stay home and watch the kids?" Carolyn asked.

"No. I went bowling with Edmond on Saturday night. She got sick on Sunday."

"So, no date with what's-his-name, that guy at Sutton's?" Sally asked.

"Preston. He came over on Sunday. But we never went out. He stayed around all afternoon, though."

Judy Bryce stood up. She was a pretty girl with curly hair and a real figure. Her mother sewed for her, too, but her clothes were less beckoning than mine were. I liked her and hoped she would ask me to walk with her.

Debra Everett came up about that time and said, "You look done. Let's walk."

I wanted to disappear, not to walk the gauntlet, but I didn't want to keep talking with the other girls either. I got up. Debra Everett said nervy things when we walked around. Once she'd asked a guy if he liked fried chicken. When he answered that he did, she stuck out one of her arms and said, "Well, grab a wing!" She embarrassed me, but she later married the boy and stayed married to him all her life.

"Not today," I said. Debra Everett walked off. Judy Bryce was still standing there.

"I have to go to the bathroom first, but then we can talk if you want to," she offered. She was that kind of sensitive girl.

I looked. The shortest route was right by the table where Edmond Clancy usually sat. He was looking straight at me. I looked away. "You go on," I said. "I'll meet you at my locker."

I walked across the back of the cafeteria and took the door nearest the ice cream and snack bar. Some days I just used my lunch money for an ice cream sandwich and saved the fifteen cents I had left over. But that Mrs. Smith, Mike Smith's mother, made hamburgers and chili better than Ghaynelle's, a local cafe and after-school hangout.

I reached my locker, opened it and fussed around with my books. I had re-stacked them a couple of times when someone's gaze surged over me as I turned around to look for Judy. I felt the force of sudden attraction like a wave nearly knocking me over before I looked right full in his face, staring into his eyes the way I would learn later in life never to stare at a dog when one challenged me on my long solitary walks.

I didn't know those things then, and just when I had decided that I never wanted to date again and before Judy could get to my locker and save me, the shock disappeared. Calm settled over me. I became liquid and poured into his being through his eyes, eyes that had become clear, deep pools of blue light and invited me to rest within them forever.

"Sandra. Sandra!" Judy touched my arm as she spoke my name. "Still want to talk?"

"No. Let's walk," I said. She looked shocked. She was one of the few girls who didn't do that.

"Okay."

I put all but my notebook, my literature book, and my shoulder bag back into the locker and managed to keep the big blue coat from falling out. He was still looking. I was still floating, and I walked away while I also stayed behind.

The first time we circled the center quad and came up the hall where he had been standing, his look slammed into me again. The same calm blending with him, like he was me, followed that. I soared and fainted into his eyes again. *If she noticed, Judy did not say so. She kept talking to me about other things, and I kept answering as if I were interested or listening.*

The second time around. The third time. Each time, the sudden jolt, the electrifying dissolving, the blending, and the calm followed one another in a continuous pattern.

I would have to date him. He called me forth. He claimed me. He knew me. And then the fear came. He knew me already in the Biblical sense of that word. He saw the Sandra beneath the born-again virgin, and I wanted him to see her, wanted to offer her up to him, had already done so, just by my way of looking at him, and he, too, had already taken me, first by force, a sudden thrust that took my breath and stripped away my disguise. I wanted to merge with him, already knew merging; he could tell I did, I was not a virgin, and he had entered there already.

Together Judy and I would circle the center quad one more time before the bell rang us to class, and our tall, lanky, and aging principal, Mr. Wood, would stand outside his office to urge us on to class with a bemused half-smile and nod of his head. I worked in his office the last period of the day, and I wondered if he, too, would see I was different. *I wondered, but I didn't care.*

Fifth period was right after lunch—English with Mrs. Tyndall. She was a wooly-headed woman in her sixties, whose hair was gray streaked with fading, red dye. She loved all of us and laughed at our jokes with her mouth open, her bad teeth displayed, and her bosoms shaking. She reached for one of her bra straps, digging deep within the neckline of her blouse or dress as often as she reached up and adjusted her cat's eyes glasses, punctuating most sentences with one gesture or the other. She guided us toward the future with her *Reader's Digest* vocabulary tests, her insistence that we write and write and write, and with her love of the *Our Town* and Shakespeare.

I loved her, and I was one of her favorites because of the autobiography I had written early in the fall. Writing came easily to me, just as reading had, and unlike most of the students in my class, I had a story to tell even then. My autobiography told the story of the death of my beloved daddy, the desertion by my mother, the rescue by my aunt, and my fortune at being saved by God and going to school at George Johnston where I was so well cared for. *It was not the story of my life as I would come to know or tell it later, but it was the story I needed to believe then, maybe as much as I need to believe this version now.*

I scintillated that day after my lunchtime visitation. Even Jimmy Sanderson, who usually looked right through me and kept his attention on Linda Ann Potter, one of the class beauties, noticed me. I saw him look casually in my direction when I was answering a question, and then I saw him turn again in surprise, like he was seeing me for the first time. I glowed. I smoldered. My green eyes glistened. I floated to the board. I felt free. Known. Acknowledged. My blood no longer beat at my wrists, longing for release.

By the time I reached sixth period and Mr. Wood's office, the transformation into Cinderella was complete. He smiled a full smile at me, and when I typed up the bulletin for the next day, I did it without making a single error. Mr. Wood noticed and smiled again, this time to himself, a confident, self-congratulatory smile, the kind I would understand years later when, as a teacher, I too, tried to rescue students and felt my own pride swell at their achievements. I was simply a pleasure to be around. Then the bell for home rang.

Each step toward the bus, toward Edmond Clancy, toward Aunt Dolores and that other life sucked the joy out of my body. I could not help that I did not want to be with Edmond. There was nothing wrong with the boy, nothing he did or didn't do that he could change to make me feel otherwise, and nothing I could do that would make me feel otherwise.

He didn't look straight at me when I got onto the bus, though he watched out of the corners of his eyes. I kept my eyes looking down, and when I realized how dumpy I looked in my over-sized skirt and black and brown color combination, I was struck even more by Clear Pools of Blue Light's look at me. He could see right through my disguise! I smiled at the thought just as I got up to get off the bus.

Edmond Clancy surely thought I was smiling at him, at last, and his relief broke into a big full-face grin that twisted his features but lit up his sad eyes.

"Bye," he said.

I didn't want to, but I answered back. It was simpler that way.

"Bye to you."

The yard was greening, despite the snow flurry on Sunday. The pine trees in the front yard were already full of pollen, and the hillside, on the left of the ranch-style, gray shadow-shingled house that Uncle Robert built, had been newly plowed. I could smell the fresh scent of broken earth above the low notes of chicken poop and dead chickens. As much as nature sang to me, and though my own heart wanted to join in the song, I felt myself deaden as I climbed the steps to the house. What madness awaited me there, I did not know, but I feared it. I longed for the security of school, for the new feeling of being found by someone who could really see me.

Chapter 45

If He's the One

She called me from her bedroom. As soon as I opened the front door, she called my name.

"Yes?"

"Come right on in here after you get your coat off."

"Yes ma'am."

I hung my coat, the sapphire-blue wool coat that had come from my cousin June who lived in Schenectady, New York, and had already tried to leave her husband twice and kill herself. Her mother, my Aunt Addie, the one who had reassured me when only one of my breasts popped up overnight, had put a stop to that.

(Aunt Addie had gone straight to the hospital when she got to Schenectady. "I didn't even take my hat or gloves or coat off. I sat right down beside her and told her the truth. 'You ought to be ashamed of yourself,' I said. And she broke right down and cried, and that was the end of all that nonsense.")

Though Aunt Dolores had cut the coat down for me and was proud of her work, the coat still fit awkwardly. It was a Sunday coat, really, with big floppy sleeves and a taffeta lining that was always cold and rattled when I walked. I hadn't worn the coat all day, and I was glad I had remembered to get it out of my locker. I hung it in the den closet.

"Yes ma'am?" I stood in the doorway.

"Come sit here," she said and motioned to the spot on the bed next to her. She was wearing a regular cotton granny gown with a high neck and no lace. I secretly called it her granny wolf gown. The green genie bed jacket was stored away. Uncle Robert was already at Stevens Mill in Wilton, and the other children were strung all over the house, including Saralynn who always followed close on my heels off the bus.

I sat down.

"Your Uncle Robert and I talked, and now I want to talk with you about Preston. You know we both really like him, and you need to call him and apologize for your bad behavior yesterday. I think you scared that poor boy to death. He is just the nicest and smartest boy, not really a boy at all, honey, a *man*; and your Uncle Robert and I think the two of you would be perfect together. We felt just like he was family already when he was here yesterday."

I looked at her. I fingered the sleeves of my sweater. My wrists were pulsing again, the blood screaming against the skin. I rubbed them hard, but I kept them covered and rubbed them with my thumbs, first on one side and then on the other.

"Don't be nervous, honey." She placed one of her hands over both of mine to still them. She patted them. "It's got to be a bit scary for you. You're so young, but you'll know if he's the one. And if he is, don't pass him up. True love is rare, and when it comes, even if it's inconvenient, you have to let it have you."

I was shocked. My body drew back from her. I tried to get her in focus, to get her notions in focus. Her face wavered; so did her voice. I concentrated hard to hear and got most of her words.

"If you...marry...I know you're young...Aunt Pauline...fourteen...Now... babies...well, no babies for a while...Uncle Robert and I will sign for you."

"What?"

"Well, if you want to marry him. We'll sign. You can't do it legally until you're eighteen. But as your guardian, I can sign so you can."

"But I don't love him."

"Well, maybe not yet, honey, but later on you might, and we just thought we wanted you to know you didn't have to, you know, if you felt things, you didn't have to—to wait until you're eighteen. You might not be able to wait. I mean he's a man, a young man, but he is a man, and well, he might not be able to wait, but if he knew he could have you, that we would sign, and then he would be willing to respect that. I mean you couldn't expect him to wait until you were eighteen. That's four years. And I don't want any more babies coming into this house, not from me and certainly not from you. So you go call him and apologize!"

She was suddenly angry with me. She was giving me away, and she was angry with me. She was afraid of me. Afraid I would embarrass her and get pregnant? Afraid I had chased Preston off for good? Was that it? Did she know what she was asking me to do? For her?

Did she know? Did she know that she wanted him, not me? What about Uncle Robert? Did he know? Didn't he see how Preston looked at her when he came into her bedroom? They were good people, church people, a deacon and a Sunday school teacher, and they were giving me away at fourteen!

"Well, okay. I'll call right away. Do you think he's home?"

"Yeah. It's Monday. He doesn't work on Monday."

"I didn't know that," I said and looked at her. I stood to go. I reached her door. "Okay if I close your door? I'm a bit nervous."

"Sure, sugh! You go on. It will be just fine. Just come back and tell me what he says."

"Okay."

I found his number fast. I chased the kids out of the den and into Aunt Dolores's bedroom. I made sure Saralynn closed the door. I dialed him. I heard the click as someone picked up the phone.

"Hello?"

It wasn't Preston. It was his mama! I slammed the phone down. I couldn't talk with her. I didn't know what he had told her about me. I didn't want to know. I sat there for as long as I dared. I closed my eyes.

I was back at school. I was taking a geometry test, and I knew all the proofs. I was taking notes in biology class, and I could take them even before Mrs. Bidden could write them on the board. I knew what she would say. I was reading a poem I had written in English class, and Mrs. Tyndall was nodding at me and smiling. Everywhere I looked, in every class, at every turn in the hall, Clear Pools looked back at me, urging me on to my next success. I felt blessed that he had come into my life at just the moment when I needed to have a reason to get away from Preston.

"Sandra? Are you still on the phone?" The question came from behind the closed door.

"Oh, no, ma'am. I'm not."

I went to her door and opened it. Tracey and R.A. were jumping on her bed. Saralynn was trying to round them up, and Raina sat in the rocking chair, watching me. Her dark black eyes never ceased their hard looking.

I knew what to do. I would speak to her of love. Maybe she was right that it would come to me early, but not for Preston.

"So what happened?" she asked.

"He didn't answer."

"Well, call back later."

"I don't love him," I said.

"How can you know you don't? And even if you don't now, you might later on!"

"I don't love him now. I won't ever love him."

"Oh, sugh, I must have scared you with all my talk. I didn't mean you had to marry him right away. And I just know he would never hurt you. You just need to give it some time. He is so very smart. Such a good person. Just the right kind of man for you."

"I don't love him now, and I never will because I love somebody else!" I blurted it out.

"What? Who? That silly little Edmond Clancy? I only let you go out with him, so you could see how he doesn't hold a candle to Preston. Now you are too smart not to know what I am talking about, and besides he doesn't respect you or he wouldn't have brought you home so late, and he did, I know he did, no matter how you tried to trick me and say otherwise. Oh, mercy. God have mercy on me. There goes my back again!" And she shrank back and slid down into bed.

"I don't love Edmond Clancy. I don't even like him."

She looked up at me. She had the quilt up under her chin. Her face showed her pain. I knew she was hurting. I moved closer to the bed. I picked up Tracey, who had begun to cry.

I shushed her and turned to Saralynn and said, "Take R.A. into the other room. And you go with them, Raina. Have you guys had your Pepsi and your Nabs yet? Get mine out, too. Just go." And they all did because I was the one who most often took charge of them.

Still holding Tracey on one hip, I reached over and touched Aunt Dolores's head. "I don't mean to make you sick again. I just don't love Preston. Or Edmond. But I do love this boy I saw today at school."

So there it was. I didn't want to feel what I felt, except when I felt it, and I didn't want to have to act on it, to get married. But if that was what Aunt Dolores had in mind for me, if that was the way things had to go, it surely wasn't going to Edmond Clancy or Preston Halstead.

"What's his name?" Aunt Dolores asked incredulously.

"I—I don't know."

"What?!"

"I just saw him today for the first time. I turned and there he was, and I felt this love for him, and I could tell he felt that way about me, too."

"You silly little girl. Just like your mother you'll end up. Not got the good sense God gave you. No judgment whatsoever. You go out there, and you call Preston and apologize and don't say a thing about any of this other madness. If he asks you out again, you better say yes. And leave the door open this time, so I can hear you." And then she groaned.

I called. He answered. I apologized. He didn't ask me out, but he said he would call me again some time. "Don't do that," I whispered. "Please don't."

Chapter 46

By the Light of the Moon

I don't know what went on in classes that week, except that my hand was up in the air often, and my voice sounded confident. Each time I spoke, I sparkled and drew looks of interest from all the good-looking boys and glances of *who-does-she-think-she-is* from the girls attached to those good-looking boys.

Andrew was his name. The one who mattered. Andrew Smith. The one who lit me up. And he looked at me with those clear pools of blue light each time I came within reach of his gaze, but he did not try to talk with me or send a message by one of his friends. He left me to swoon on my own, to worry myself about how to get him to ask me out.

Nighttime. That was when he would come to me. When everyone was asleep, and I was sleeping, too, he would slip into bed beside me. My body would curve into his and begin to awaken, as memory of Little Arthur and deeper memory of something I could not locate still governed me in that half-asleep state.

Perhaps it was the archetype of divine lovers, I would think over the years when I pondered those nightly visitations. Perhaps I had connected to the universal pool of love. I would drift in it, sometimes awaking and arising to examine my naked body and to sit in nothing but my slip with my legs sprawled open and my mind afire.

Or I would open the window on the early spring nights and let the cool damp air bathe me, sometimes slipping the straps down from my shoulders and pushing the slip beneath my breasts which I bared to the night, gave to the dark pool of night that his blue eyes became during those nocturnal visits. Nighttime. My body was left aching, but I would not dishonor our love and seek the release of the bedstead.

I would linger in the ache of memory and longing, sometimes falling asleep in bed; other times, I stayed on the stuffed chair by my window until I was called by Uncle Robert to "Get up, get up, get up, you lazy head. Get up, get up, get up, get out of bed." He had returned to awakening me with song, but he always did so from the other side of my closed bedroom door since I was a big girl, old enough to be married off.

Wednesday came. No approach. No call. Just looks. *And nighttimes.* As Thursday came, I was certain he would make his move and ask for the weekend date. I moved closer to him during my rounds of the halls at school. He held my gaze from the moment I turned down the hall, where he lounged against the lockers with a couple of his buddies, until I passed by him. And if my body was right in what it felt each time I passed, he turned and watched my backside as I moved beyond him. I did not dare look back the way some girls might. But I felt him there, his look gliding over my skin.

Judy was aware of what I was doing. She's the one who got his name for me. She warned, "He's fast. He's not going steady, but he keeps going through girls. I wouldn't go out with him myself, and I hope he doesn't ask you."

I left her standing there and walked the next round by myself. From the moment I could see him on that last round for the day, he was looking elsewhere. A girl—who was it?—was standing in front of him, and she was tall enough to reach his eyebrows and cover his eyes. He didn't shift or turn to see me as I walked by. I didn't feel his eyes on my body after I passed him. Judy had waited for me by Mr. Wood's office, but she was mad. She had one hand on one hip and cradled her books with her opposite arm, so I could see she was waiting just to tell me off.

But she saw my face, and she didn't.

"What's wrong?"

"He was talking with some other girl. Some junior girl. You know the one that has short brown curly hair and wears those light blue-rimmed glasses?"

"Humph! Well, he doesn't deserve you, and anyway he's way too old for you. Somebody told me he should have graduated last year and didn't."

"I don't care about all of that! I can't help how I feel about him! I have never felt this way, and I know even though I can't say why, but I do know it is love." I didn't want to cry right there in front of everybody.

Judy understood and she pulled me by the hand to a little bench outside where we could sit. The day was warm again—no more sudden spring snow flurries—just warm winds and a few daffodils, just enough to say the earth was alive again, were waving beside the flag pole, *a quick hello from the future when they would reappear as Wordsworth called them forth from memory, and I would be grateful I had survived such tough times.*

Even as Judy reached out to me, I tried to stay far off in my mind. At first, I argued because I knew she would expect it. I didn't really care what she thought. She wasn't the one Aunt Dolores was trying to marry off.

"My mama said she'd drive us to the talent show over in Rockville on Friday night. You want to go with me?" she asked.

"You don't think he's going to ever ask me out, do you?"

"I told you already that I hope he doesn't. You deserve better."

"What do you know about what I deserve, and why do you hate him so much?"

"I told you already, but you don't listen."

"I don't care that he's older than me. I need somebody older. I'm older than me. I mean I am mature, more mature than other girls my age. Serious. Like you, but different. You are book serious. I am serious in my mind."

"Oh, you reminded me! I have a book you got to read. I'll bring it tomorrow. It's called *Catcher in the Rye*."

"Why are you talking about books and talent shows when I am about to married off to somebody that I don't know and don't love, and the person I do love is going out with somebody else?"

"This book is about a boy who goes looking for love, but he doesn't know that's what he's looking for. His little sister is the only one he can be himself with."

I just looked past her and waited for the bell.

"And anyway," she continued, "she can't make you marry anybody. She may have to sign for you, but you have to sign, too. So don't."

Silence.

"If it ever gets that far, I mean," she said. "And it won't. I just know it won't."

The bell rang. I didn't have her certainty. I felt the hate behind the love that Aunt Dolores professed for me.

"So, go with me to the talent show! We'll have fun. I'll ask Carolyn to go, too. I mean, you go with us if he doesn't ask you out."

I didn't answer.

We went to class where I forced my dazzle. When no one noticed it wasn't real, I learned how to get on in the world when the world doesn't want who you really are. So, the boys still looked in my direction, and the girls still gave me their *Well-I-do-declare* glances. The school part was breezy. Going home would take more out of me, and getting there with Edmond Clancy driving the bus wouldn't make it any easier.

I spoke to him when I got on the bus.

"Hi, Edmond." I sat right behind his seat. Right where he could not help but see me in all his mirrors. I don't know why I thought to do it. It just came natural. I even made sure I crossed by legs a number of times, even though I was quite comfortable and had no need to do so.

I didn't want him to ask me out. I hoped he wouldn't. But I wanted to know that he still wanted to. By the way his sad eyes watched me, he proved he did. I smiled. I encouraged him to look at me, and then I regretted it almost as soon as I had done it. I felt mean. I felt lonely. I felt angry. So I looked away for the rest of the ride home, avoiding his eyes most times when he searched for mine. I seemed to know just how often to look up to keep the peace between him and me. I needed that peace before I encountered Aunt Dolores.

Aunt Dolores let me be for most of that late afternoon and evening. Busy sewing with her new Kenmore and figuring out the smocking attachments, she seemed glad to keep to herself and leave me to mine. I didn't have to come face to face with her even during dinner because since she was up and about again, she was trying to diet.

I served white rice and stewed tomatoes to everybody but the baby Tracey, who got strained peaches with her rice and then a bottle of half-water, half-Carnation condensed milk. I put her to bed before Bible time. Aunt Dolores kept the schedule religiously. Every night at eight o'clock, except Friday night because *Rawhide* came on then, she read to us from the Bible and from some Bible storybooks. That Thursday night I held R.A. on my lap, like I generally did, and the girls found their own places on the couch. As she sat in her platform rocker, Aunt Dolores assumed her ministerial face, though she was only a Sunday school teacher.

She read to us about Ruth and Boaz that night. I knew the story and liked it pretty much because I felt like Ruth, even though Dolores was my aunt and not my mother-in-law. Still, somewhere deep within, I knew I had made a choice much like Ruth when I refused to go with my real mama and stayed instead with Aunt Dolores. That Ruth did the right thing was clear to me and to Aunt Dolores. I knew that part of the story well. What had struck me, in all the times I had heard the story before that night, was Ruth's reward for her care of her mother-in-law, who I guessed needed her more than her own mother did.

That particular night, though, Boaz interested me, and my imagination filled with images of Ruth bending and bowing to pick up the leftovers from his fields. I could see him standing far off behind some trees, which I imagined must have been palm trees. He was standing there out of sight and watching her as she worked, gleaning what others had left untaken. His eyes were the eyes of Andrew. Her body was my body receiving Andrew's approving looks. And her reward should be my reward—a Cinderella marriage to someone who would care for me like Boaz cared for Ruth.

After the prayer that always followed the Bible readings, I headed off toward my room to study a couple more hours before I went to bed. Aunt Dolores shooed Saralynn and Raina off to the room they shared, and she put R.A. in his bed next to Tracey's crib. I immersed myself in biology and then in *David Copperfield*, losing track of time and aware of Andrew only occasionally when I would look up from my desk into the mirror across from it and imagine him seeing me the way I could see myself. I was still Ruth in my mind's eye as I soaked in all I could from the books I read, from the education I was receiving, secretly preparing already, so that if marriage did not save me, education would.

I always said good night to her before I went to bed. There was a standard hug and a kiss on the cheek that I had routinized and minimized as much as I possibly could and still call it a kiss and a hug. I walked toward the den where she was still sewing.

"I came to say good-night."

She turned toward me. It was a slow, lumbering turn, designed to save energy, cause as little distress to her back as possible, and still get her head pointed in my direction. Her painful movements wrenched at my heart, but my face did not show it.

"Well, come on over here."

I did.

"Look at this work," she said. She held up the bodice of a navy blue dress she was making for Raina. She had used red thread for the smocking and had sewn red rose appliqués on the collar. It was pretty, not quite professional, but good.

"See what you could be doing if you hadn't given up on sewing," she said.

"Yes ma'am."

"I never understood why you stopped. You even tied Priscilla Miller for the 4-H contest last year with that reversible outfit you sewed, didn't you?"

"Yes ma'am, I did." Aunt Dolores had sewn that outfit for me, most of it anyway. I just couldn't stand to sit at the machine. My mind died when I sewed or it turned to thoughts of sadness that I wanted to avoid. I much preferred to read. It took stabbing myself, mostly intentionally, a couple of times with the electric sewing machine needle, letting it plunge right through my index finger, for Aunt Dolores to take over. I still had to model the outfit she made and pretend it was my own, though, and even back then I was too shy to be in front of all those people, lying and showing off that way.

"Well, I did what I could," she sighed.

"Yes ma'am, you did." Just let me go to bed, please, just let me go to bed. *Maybe he will still come to visit me there; maybe he will choose me instead of her.*

I leaned toward her and gave her a quick kiss on her cheek. It felt warm, soft.

"Good night," I said and stepped back.

She checked my action by raising her hand.

"Just a minute," she said. "Preston called today and talked to Uncle Robert and me. He wanted to see how I was doing, and he asked about you, too."

"Oh."

"Yes, he said he knew you were upset and that he hoped you were okay."

"I'm okay."

"He didn't say whether or not he'd be calling you, but I told him he should feel free to call you anytime. I don't think he will, though. You really scared him off. Too bad. He was such a nice man."

"Yes ma'am."

"So, has your new love paid you any mind this week? Or your little boy Edmond, has he asked you out again?"

I steeled my will against her. The lies came easily then.

"Oh, yes, Edmond did ask me, but I told him no, I was already taken. I was about to tell you, but we got so busy. Andrew—that's his name—Andrew Smith. He's from Rockville, asked me out for Friday night, and I said yes but that I would have to check it with you. So can I go?"

"Are you double-dating?"

"Well, yes ma'am, we are. His sister and her boyfriend will be going along. I'll have them all come into the house and meet you if you like when they come."

"No, that won't be necessary." She paused. Her hands were so much more delicate in their look and touch than her face. Her hands feathered across the sewn fabric, loving each stitch a bit as they passed over it. "But I would like to meet the boy before you go out with him."

"Yes ma'am. I'll have him come in and spend some time before we take off, but we're going to the talent show over in Rockville in the elementary school auditorium, the one Larry and Little Arthur are in, so we have to be there by seven-thirty. Okay?"

"Okay," she said. "I just wish it was on a night when your uncle was here, too. And by the way, what grade is this boy in?"

"He's a twelfth grader, but he had to repeat the grade because he got sick or something and missed a year, and somebody else said he didn't start school until he was almost seven. I reckon that makes him old enough that you would call him a man," I said. In long proud strides, I crossed the room and was out of sight by the time she could have lumbered around and called out to me in a loud whisper, which I could hear but which would not wake the children.

"A *man*?" she said.

"Good-night," I called back as though I thought that is what she had called to me.

Chapter 47

The Morning After

I rose early on Friday, laid out my undergarments, including a new, padded bra that Aunt Dolores had ordered for me from the Sears and Roebuck catalog, my silk slip with the delicate straps and lacy top that I only wore on special occasions, new stockings and panties from Christmas, and a lightweight girdle. I picked the tightest and shortest black skirt I had and paired it with a bright orange sweater that I buttoned up and wore without a blouse.

I put my makeup on twice to darken it, and I wore black Capezios, thin leather shoes that were dance shoes for ballet classes that neither I nor the other George Johnston girls, who wore them, ever had. We just wore the shoes, shoes too thin and too expensive for everyday use. I used more of my tobacco earnings for them than Aunt Dolores thought fit, but they made me feel elegant and move gracefully.

On the bus, I let Edmond Clancy look at me and believe I had dressed up for him. His face had Friday urgency in it, too. I scooted past him with a devilish grin and rushed into school, heading straight for Andrew's locker where he lingered during lunchtimes. He wasn't there. I stayed until the first bell rang, rushed to my locker, and then to class. Between every class I passed by his locker, and when, even at lunchtime, I did not see him, I despaired. He had not come to school! My last minute determination to get him to talk to me and say the magic words (*You want to go out on Friday night?*) was in vain.

Judy caught up to me at the snack bar where I had decided to go for the ice cream sandwich lunch. I bought two of them. She joined me. A quick smile from her, the new book pushed toward me so that I had to put my ice cream sandwiches in one hand, and a nod of her head toward the double doors, and we were outside.

"You're going to love that book, but hide it from your aunt. If she won't let you wear shorts, go to dances, go to the movies, or to Ronnie Rhodes's swimming pool, you better believe she won't like that book. But all the freshman up at UNC-G read it. It was required summer reading, and then they talked about it during the first week. Ann's there now, you know." Ann was her brother's girlfriend.

"Yeah. She like it? The school, not the book." I'd talk about anything but what was on my heart.

As she bit into her single ice cream sandwich, she nodded "Yeap." She had peeled the paper back and torn it off at the halfway mark. Holding the bar delicately, she licked around the edges of it where the ice cream had squeezed out after her first big bite. Then she said, "She likes both. The book and the school. I think I might go there myself. How about you?"

"I don't know. If I don't get married off before then, maybe, but nobody's going to help me pay for it. I know that. I'll probably just get married."

"Oh." Silence. "You going with us to the talent show tonight?"

"Yeah. I'll go."

Judy looked at my second ice cream sandwich, which I had just opened. "How do you get away with eating like a horse and staying so skinny?"

"Worry," I reckon. "I just worry the weight off." I broke the second sandwich into two parts and handed her one. She laughed and took it.

It wasn't until I was walking out the door that Friday night that I had to tell Aunt Dolores about my change in plans.

"Whoa!" she said. "Not so fast. Remember I'm supposed to meet this—this *man*."

"Oh, he got sick and sent a message by his sister. I thought I told you. That's Judy Bryce and her mother instead, waiting to take me to the talent show. Okay?" I stood at the door, knowing that she was quite capable of saying no and keeping me from going for no reason other than I hadn't asked earlier or in the right way. Judy knew that, too, so if I had to go outside and say it, it wouldn't be as embarrassing as it might have been. It had happened before.

Aunt Dolores just smiled at me, almost like she understood the whole story and felt kindness toward me, almost like she was the person she longed to be and felt love toward me like she told everybody. If so, it was a confused love, a conflicted love, that hurt me more often than it built me up.

"Go," she said. "Go on. You got the money for it?"
"Yes ma'am."
"Well, go before I change my mind."
I did.

The old auditorium building still stands at the former site of the Rockville Elementary School, which had been Rockville High until the county consolidated the high schools. The white frame auditorium is big for the area and can seat about three hundred people. It is used occasionally, most often for the February celebration of Martin Luther King Day, still a primarily black event in that small town of six hundred and in this small, rural county. But I have gone there a couple of times since I returned. During the celebration, above the glorious oratory about Dr. Martin Luther King and louder than the voices of combined gospel choirs, I heard the noise from that night long ago and felt the ghosts of that talent show night arise and leave, to wait nearby for a quiet time to return.

The gymnasium, too, still stands and is used for peewee basketball. It sits on the right corner of the lot, far off Highway 117, which used to be the main highway running north and south until Interstate 40 came through. At the back of the lot beside the gymnasium is the site of the old playground. The concrete slab where the merry-go-round was anchored may be visible from the auditorium steps, especially when the grass is mowed or dies back in winter. I've never had the courage to go up close and look for it since I returned.

What I remember from that time long ago is muddled inside me. Those here with whom I have talked about these events, say it was a quiet night when the horror took place and that the talent show came a year later when I was already going out with Neil Norris. Perhaps.

Perhaps the terror was so real for me when I discovered what had happened that my mind believes I was there, sitting in distress and longing. Perhaps my mind melded the past and the future and left me unable to distinguish the real from the imagined presence of danger in the men I met before and after that. I do not know, but this is how emotion has recorded those events in memory, so this is how I record them in words.

Mrs. Bryce never sat with us girls when she took us places, and this time, in particular, she had other things on her mind because Judy was quite a pianist and would be one of the contestants. Carolyn and I peeled off from our little group and wished Judy good luck as

Mrs. Bryce rushed her toward the backstage area. We pushed down the aisle, looking for front or near-front row seats. Ronnie Rhodes would be the MC, and Janice would sing. In addition, Little Arthur, Larry, my other cousin Rudy Pope, and some boy I didn't know whose name was Neil Norris and who was a friend of Larry's, would be pantomiming a new British group called "The Beatles."

Settling into a seat in the middle section, a few rows back from the stage, I looked around to see who else was there. Carolyn had already spied out Ralph Greer with a group of boys sitting farther back. She had had a crush on him from the first day she arrived at junior high, three years earlier. Carolyn was a giggler and smiled easily. When she did, her smile took up half her face and announced itself to the world as "happiness." I hardly smiled, but I liked sitting in the glow of her giggles and smiles.

I was starting to content myself with knowing that Judy and I were the only two at school who knew about my crush, as Judy called it, on Andrew. Maybe she was right, but I sure felt a lot toward him, a lot more than I ever did toward Edmond Clancy or Preston. I actually felt close to him like I did to my brother, Little Arthur. Anyway, I was telling myself, suddenly feeling positive around Carolyn's infectious happiness, only one week had passed, not even that, only one *school* week had passed since he first noticed me. Who knew what might happen next week or the next one?

Maybe he already had a date with the girl with curly brown hair and those cat's eye, blue-rimmed glasses. Maybe he was just gentleman enough to want to break it off easily with her. I sank back into my seat and laughed and clapped and loved the first half of the talent show, but when the lights came up for intermission, I looked to my left and saw Andrew. He had his arm around that girl's waist, and she was smiling hard into his face.

He touched her back lightly after he released her from his half hug, and I felt his touch the way I had felt his eyes on by backside when I strolled past him in the halls of George Johnston. When intermission began, Andrew and the girl slipped out the side door into the night, and I kept a keen lookout to see if they returned at the end of intermission, but I saw them nowhere. Nothing could bring me relief or pleasure for the rest of the evening.

Even when the "Beatles" tuned up, and every other girl was on her feet screaming, the way they said girls did at real concerts, I stayed put. It wasn't real. It was just my brother and cousins and some other guy. They weren't really singing. Even their hair was fake! They mimicked life while real life was killing me. That's how my heart spoke to me. But when the news broke on the Monday after the talent show, I took a lesson from those counterfeit Beatles and went back to mimicking life myself.

I don't know how long the girl with curly hair and the cat's eye, blue-rimmed glasses had lain under the merry-go-round before someone saw her legs sticking out and went to tell someone else, so that eventually the sheriff came. I do know that Andrew's sister was sent to school that Monday, and that she must have heard the story in the halls of George Johnston where the rest of us had heard it by lunchtime. *Why was she there? How could her mother have left her to what she must have known would come?* She caught me looking at her once right after the bell rang for fifth period. She had his eyes, too, and my heart closed up on me as the rumored details took up permanent residence in my mind.

("*It must have happened when we were all inside watching the talent show.*"

"*He shoved her so far under the merry-go-round that only her feet were showing. Her bare feet, my mama said, so she must have lost her shoes when he dragged her there.*"

"*I used to play basketball in that gym when I was at that school. It's spooky to think about somebody murdering somebody right under our noses and right on my old playground.*"

"*She probably screamed out for help, but with all that racket inside, nobody was going to hear her. If he had to do what he did, he didn't have to kill her.*"

"*Somebody said he just shoved her slip into her mouth, and she strangled to death on it.*"

"*Yeah, that's what I mean. He could have let her yell. Won't nobody to hear her anyway.*"

"*My daddy said it was the fault of all that rock and roll music they were playing that got the boy too riled up.*"

"*Aw, that's not so. That music wasn't even played until after they was gone cause I saw them there in the auditorium before intermission.*"

"Yeah, but as loud as it was, he could have still heard it from outside. My daddy said it sounded like quite a ruckus when he drove by. He said he didn't even have to roll down his windows to hear it."

"Ain't nobody got to act that way, no matter what they been listening to."

"Maybe she got him started, and he couldn't stop himself. My mama says girls have to be careful because boys can't control themselves."

"I don't believe he meant to kill her."

"No, but he sure meant to do what else he did, and that's enough to send him away for life.")

Aunt Dolores knew, too, by the time I came home.

"Did you hear?" she asked.

I nodded.

"You must have a guardian angel watching over you. You know that could have been you, don't you?"

The single thread of a scab on my wrist where I had made the slightest cut with the dull knife had just about healed, but my wrist started throbbing. *I felt like she was me.* I went to my room. I didn't speak to Aunt Dolores for several days except when I couldn't avoid it. She didn't pick at me.

Once I did overhear her say to Uncle Robert, "I don't reckon I need to say much to her. By the way she is moping around, I'm pretty certain she got the picture about how serious this dating thing can be. At least she's older than I was."

I had wanted to be the girl with the curly hair and cat's eye, blue-rimmed glasses, whose name I will not let myself invoke. Let her rest where she went so many years ago. I had wanted to be the one on whom he looked.

Something inside me was broken in ways that left me that unprotected. My time with Little Arthur had taught my body lessons, the record of which boys could see in my eyes, and something else, something before memory, something before I knew I was separate from the world, something I could not recall then, and can only know now from dream life and from speculating about black holes and from sifting through the ashes of the past to discover, something else, too, had left me vulnerable. Aunt Dolores knew, but she was not able or ready to tell her story for another thirty-six years. So, I coped. I mimicked life.

I was fourteen that April, and though I didn't go out with another boy until late fall, life still brought little inner peace.

Chapter 48

Attempted Kidnapping

A few weeks after Andrew disappeared, as did his sister a day or two later, I was called out of class with a summons that said, "Your mother is here to take you home. Be sure to get your books."

I did wonder why Aunt Dolores had come for me, but I figured she needed some help with the children while she did something or maybe I had a doctor's appointment I had forgot. She had been at me lately about my cough.

I didn't see her waiting outside the office like she generally did. It occurred to me that she could have already gone back to the car because managing two little ones was a lot for her, especially since she seemed sick most of the time. Lately, she bled a lot, even lost a job at the sewing room she needed. Maybe she'd have to get another D and C. That would be hard on all of us, and from what Aunt Dolores and Uncle Robert said right in front of us, money was tight. They were still paying off the hospital bills from the last two babies. Summer was coming, and I was glad I'd be earning some tobacco money soon.

I looked out at the spring day, and I saw a car parked right at the school's double doors. I saw my mama sitting there in front of my wide-awake eyes, right there in the passenger's seat!

I almost ran the other way. She seemed so cold behind the glass window, which wrapped around the front of the new car in a way I wasn't used to. The man driving was not Arthur Blair. That may be why I did what I did. I walked toward the door, I pushed it open, and I stood there on the sidewalk. Peering beyond the man who was on my side of the car, I leaned over to see her face. She peered at me. Her tiny head was afire with bleached blonde flames.

"Get in the car, Sondra," she said. Her eyes were green and swollen, rheumy with nights of crying. They matched my own.

I straightened.

"I've come all this way for you, Sondra. Just get in the car, and I'll take you home." She was starting to cry. Then she was crying out loud and yelling, "For goodness sake, Sondra, I am your mama. I won't hurt you. Just get in the car!"

I was backing off slowly, a half Capezio at a time, moving backwards to the door toward which I did not turn, but which I knew would swing inward if I could just sink my back against it.

"Stop right where you are," he ordered.

The authority in his voice stopped me.

"Now come back here and get into the car."

("Edward? Right, Mom?" I asked her after I moved back to Wisteria. "Edward Burroughs. Right?"

"Yeah, that's right, but you knew that because I told you about him one of those times I went out there to L. A. 'Burroughs,' that's what I called him—just Burroughs because his daddy's name was Edward, too, and we lived with his parents after we were married. That's where I learned to raise honeybees."

"That's when you came to Wisteria to get me, just after you were married?"

"Yes. Burroughs made me do it. He couldn't stand listening to me cry anymore. Big Arthur already had Debbie and Eddie. Well, shit, and pardon my French, he'd had them for years, and I knew there was no way I'd ever get them back. I was wrong about that, too, because now that they're grown, I got all of my children back, except Little Arthur, and he knows he's welcome anytime. But back then, I thought if I could convince you to come home, then Little Arthur would come, too. You two were always so close.

"You were so skinny when I saw you with that long made-over dress on, I just broke down and cried. You looked like you were scared to death of me. I don't know what you were afraid of. I was just your mama, and I missed you, but you acted like I was trying to kidnap you.")

When Edward Burroughs ordered me to stop, I did so, but only long enough to know I could never live near that man. I might not have known when I was in danger of being raped and killed, but I knew right off that something was wrong with that man. He didn't look mean, really. He looked like he was seeing more than just me and the school behind me, and I guess, he looked scared, plain scared of something I could not see. *Was he scared of me?* So, I turned and ran back into the school, straight through the outer office, and into Mr. Wood's office.

("Tell me, Mom, was he that one that killed himself?" I asked.

"You know he was. All the husbands I ever had, five up until this one, died, but Lord'a mercy, his death was the most horrible of all."

"He shot himself, right?"

"He took that gun and put it right in his mouth while he was sitting up on our bed in his mother's house, and he blew his brains out. We knew he was in trouble. We'd been trying to figure it out and get him help. But he was so tormented, he couldn't stand it, I reckon.

"I picked up bits of bones and teeth out of our carpet for weeks afterward."

"I'm so sorry," I said. "Wasn't there something about him being used in drug tests?"

"I don't remember telling you that, but, yes, there's no doubt about it. The military tested him with something while he was in Greenland, and nobody told him about it. He thought he was going crazy, and he kept having flashbacks. Then that guy up at the CIA jumped out of a window, and that was the first time we started to get the real story.

"The whole thing came out. That's the only reason I got a pension from him right now, Sondra. The army knew they had to make it right somehow, not like that little piddling check makes it right, and I'd much rather have Edward back. That was before I met Raeford, but you know what I mean. If they hadn't known they'd done wrong by Edward, they'd never have paid me a pension. The insurance sure didn't pay a thing. Said they wouldn't pay out because it was a suicide.

"Weren't no suicide. The army killed Burroughs, just as surely as if they had picked up that gun and put it in his mouth and pulled the trigger themselves. Yeap. They sure did. And then they had the nerve to tell me if I got married again, I'd lose that little pension, and you know it's not much, but I can't afford to lose it. But the government changed all that about a year ago. And you better bet that Raeford is sure glad of that.

"He said now that we are finally married after twenty years of living together, he never wanted to see or hear that old Burroughs name again. But I don't feel that way, and I told him he oughtn't either. Edward was a good man, a kind man. Nobody but maybe your daddy treated me any better than Edward did. But, Sondra, all the men I married treated me like I was a queen, every one of them but Big Arthur, and he did in the beginning. But he was always rough. He liked to hold me hard by my hair. If I hadn't been so ignorant, I would've had sense enough to know there was something wrong with that.")

Mr. Wood sat behind his big desk, pen in hand, and looked up at me with a question mark between his eyes. When I didn't speak right off, his shoulders slumped, and his head sank forward in a gesture, that wasn't exasperation, but close.

"Sandra, why did you come bursting into my office like that?"

"It's not my mama. I mean it's not Aunt Dolores. It *is* my mama, and she's trying to make me get into the car."

He got my meaning pretty fast, but by the time he'd reached the double doors, they'd vanished. I wouldn't see or hear from her again for several years. Each time I did, it would be a shock.

By the end of that week, Aunt Dolores put me in the car and took me to see Dr. Lanier. My cough had gotten worse, and I was running a fever. I think she expected him to look at me and hand her a prescription for penicillin, but he told her I had to be hospitalized. That didn't set well with her.

"You see what comes of acting the fool and sitting out in a snow storm," she said to me right before she went to the bathroom to change another pad. She was still bleeding badly. I wished it was her going to the hospital instead of me, and I think she did, too.

Chapter 49

Pneumonia, Pleurisy, Anemia, and Anorexia

With a tray of food that had just arrived sitting in front of me, I sat up in the bed at Johnstonsville Memorial Hospital. Aunt Dolores was walking around the halls, looking for Dr. Lanier who, the nurse said, was making his rounds. I had uncovered my dinner plate. Steaming hot and waiting for me to dig into it was chicken and pastry, string beans, collard greens, milk, and blueberry pie, but I placed the round metal cover back over the plate because Dr. Lanier had just walked in. I put my fork down to wait for him. He saw me do it.

"So, I caught you with your fork in hand. I guess you've taken to eating again. Good," he said. "You got to eat to keep getting better." Then Aunt Dolores popped back into the room.

"I been looking for you, Doctor," she said.

"Mrs. Shuler," he said. "Looks like this young lady is getting better." Even though I was the only one in the semi-private room, the nurse had pulled the curtain that surrounded my bed, and the four of us were shrouded inside its folds.

Dr. Lanier simply pushed the tray on its rolling table out of the way. "This won't take but a minute. Don't want to let your dinner get cold, do we?"

I managed a weak smile.

He listened to my heart, my lungs, and when he told me to breathe deeply, it still hurt. Wherever his hand touched, felt warm, but the stethoscope was icy cold.

"Hm-m-m," he said. "That pain any less?"

"Yes sir, I believe so."

"Still hurts though, doesn't it?"

"Yes sir."

"Well, you are a brave little one. How about your back side? Those shots for anemia can be pretty painful."

"She knows she has to do what she's told, Doctor, so she can get well and come on home, and as a matter of fact, that's what I wanted to talk with you about," Aunt Dolores said.

"She's been a mighty sick young lady," Dr. Lanier said. I could feel the smile drain out of his face, out of his body. The warmth, too, disappeared and snow flake flurries rested on my arm where he touched me.

"I know, Doctor," Aunt Dolores said, "but she *is* getting better."

He touched my hand, looked at my fingernails, and turned my hand over so that my palm was up. Then he lifted his eyes from my open palm and my wrist, and his look was full—fatherly, like I imagined Mr. Drew looked at Nancy—and his eyes were brimming with what he knew about the secret me. I looked down at the tray, but I stole a glance at my wrist. There, still, was a faint, faint trace where the tiny scab had been, a silky trace so faint that it was visible only when it was held in the light, exactly the way he was holding my hand. I relaxed my arm. It moved out of the light slightly, and the little line of sheen was gone.

"Yes. She is better."

He patted my arm, sighed, and stood up. The nurse pushed back the curtains. I touched the metal cover on my food. It was still warm. He made some notes on the clipboard he held and handed it back to the nurse. He turned to go.

"Dr. Lanier, I said I need to talk to you because I want to know when I can take her on home." She followed him out the door.

The nurse slid by them and was gone. My food was right there within reach, but I did not uncover it. Aunt Dolores and Dr. Lanier stood outside my open door.

"I can't afford to keep her here any longer. You said she was better, and I need to get her on home."

"She is better, but I can't release her yet. She is not strong enough."

"I can get her well at home. All you are doing is giving her pills. I can do that at home."

"She is getting shots twice a day, as well as other medications, and the nurses and I are monitoring her several times a day to be sure that she is getting well."

"But you said she was better."

"She is, but she still needs to be here a while longer."

"Well, I can't afford it any longer, and I know I can take care of her at home."

"You aren't a trained nurse, and she is still in danger."

"Can't you just give her pills instead of shots? Or are you just trying to run your bill up?"

"Mrs. Shuler, she came in here with pneumonia, pleurisy, anemia, and she's terribly skinny. That's how sick she got under your care! For goodness sake, let us help her get well before we send her back to you!"

That's how sick she got under your care!

"I want her out of here now!" Aunt Dolores demanded.

Though I strained to hear what was said next, I could not. Dr. Lanier had lowered his voice, and all I heard, at first, was the low rumble of it. Then I heard Aunt Dolores as she began to cry. That was a familiar sound to me. Unmistakable. I saw her turn and walk off. She didn't say good-bye.

Dr. Lanier came back into the room. *He knew.* He saw me sitting there with my food still covered. I looked up at him, fear in my eyes, my lips pulled downward into a frown.

"I am sorry you had to hear that," he said. "I bet you completely lost your appetite now."

I bet you completely lost your appetite now.

He knew. No amount of chicken and dumplings or blueberry pie was worth losing his favor. *That tiny line on the inside of my wrist had become a lifeline for me.*

I pushed the tray away. I sank back into my pillow.

"I'll have the nurse take that and put your bed back down," he said.

As if by magic, the nurse had reappeared. "I got it, Dr. Lanier. I heard," she said. "And you want to have her on glucose again?"

"Not if she eats supper." He turned to me. "You will try to eat supper, won't you? You don't need to worry about anything. Just eat your supper for me."

I nodded. By then my bed had been rolled down, and the blueberry pie had been rolled away. I turned on my side because my rear end was so sore from the anemia shots I couldn't lie on my back for long.

I didn't get my supper at Johnstonsville Memorial Hospital that night, so I couldn't do as Dr. Lanier had asked. By nightfall, Aunt Dolores had gotten him to sign a release form to another doctor from the neighboring county, and I was transferred by ambulance to the Sampson County Hospital.

To this day, she claims she saved my life by transferring me, and I still haven't learned what Dr. Lanier said to her when he lowered his voice and sent her crying down the hallway. Whatever it was, whatever he knew, he decided to keep it quiet. When I recovered enough in the Sampson County Hospital, I was sent back home to live with Aunt Dolores until I graduated from high school three years later and left.

Many times since I first held the knife to my wrist and made that almost imperceptible cut, I have felt the blood push against my wrists, seeking escape from the physical body that got me into one imprisoning situation after another over the years. I never sought the sharp edge of a blade or the deep sleep of narcotics, though.

My love of learning, of reading, of mystery, led me other places, away from that original wounding and closer and closer, then farther and farther away from it, until I landed eventually in the labyrinthine center of myself where I came to know that those visions of myself, hanging from this or that light fixture, from this or that second or third story balcony, or that those times when I sat, fully clothed, in bathtubs and recalled the blood-filled water in "The Death of Marat," or reeled on the edge of one mountainous precipice in the Sierras or another, feeling the urge to fall into the abyss, all those images of death were cries to Her to bring me new life. And she did. She does. Daily. But, always, I must do my part. I must ask.

So, when I say that I returned home to Aunt Dolores, and that I did not know the presence of the Divine Feminine then, I do not mean to lie. I did not know I knew it then. Even in its degraded form, even as Aunt Dolores lay in the bed again and again during my high school years, claiming some phantom unkindness of mine put her there, I sensed with something other than my mind that more was at work there than I could understand, and wanting to know what it was, my love of mystery, kept me alive and seeking until the Divine revealed itself.

Chapter 50

The Numb Years

The first morning in Sampson County Hospital, I awoke with a start, still feeling like I was in my dream world, and there was a shadow leaning over me!

"Who—who are you?" I screamed.

"Sh-h, sh-h, Sandra! Sandra! It's Aunt Addie."

"What are you doing here?" I was shocked that she had been there watching me when I was sleeping and that I had not known nor felt her presence. From that moment on, I've been shocked and frightened when someone wakes me. My husband stands across the room and calls my name. He knows not to touch me or I will scream.

"Dolores's sick and in bed again, so I came by to see you instead," Aunt Addie said.

"What time is it?"

"Early. But I had to come by before work."

"Oh."

"Sandra, you can't keep doing this to Dolores. She can't take much more. She's so worried about you dying that it's killing her."

"Yes ma'am."

"You have to get well. You have my personal doctor here to help you, and I just know if you try, you can get yourself well."

More than anything I wanted to be away from all of them, but I didn't want to die to do it. I never meant to get sick. All I really wanted was to be at school or at work and away from everything else.

"Dr. Lanier said I was getting well."

"Well, it looked like he just might let you die, Dolores said, and that's why we moved you here to my doctor because I know we can trust him."

"But I was feeling better until—"

"Until they quarreled in front of you like a good doctor would never have done? I know about doctors and hospitals, and I know about young women who want to give up on living."

She picked up my hand and turned it over to make her point. I snatched it back and put it under the cover.

I never meant to kill myself. I knew that knife was dull. I just wanted a little bit of the blood to come out so I wouldn't explode. I didn't even feel any pain when I cut myself like that, not nearly as much as I did during my monthly, and anyway I had a diagnosis of pneumonia, pleurisy, and anemia, not suicide.

I didn't want to die. There were awards to be won still, clubs to become president of, continents to explore, men to marry and then to scorn, and babies to bear and love and guide. The future must have been encoded inside me. That encoding and Aunt Addie together would not let me die.

"I'll get well. All I have to do is eat and take the shots. That's what Dr. Lanier said. That's what the nurse here said, too." I came as close as I dared to sounding defiant. Something in that last statement silenced Aunt Addie. She was smart enough to see that she had gotten what she wanted and wise enough to let me think I had won the argument.

I had lots of visitors while I was in the hospital. The one that surprised me the most was Pamela Sue Smith. I knew her from algebra class, where I often got caught talking to her because she would ask me questions about the in-class work. Mr. Horton, brilliant and wall-eyed, would always catch me and not her.

Pamela wore her skirts tighter and shorter than I did, and she hooded her entire eyelids with eyeliner and eye shadow that was nearly black. When she came to visit me, I didn't know what to talk about with her after we finished giggling over Mr. Horton always catching *me (Did he think I was talking to myself?)* and not her. I pulled out a magazine I had gotten off the hospital reading cart.

"Look at this hairdo," I said. "When I'm well, I'm going get my bangs cut this way." Though my hair had grown fast since I cut it off the summer before, and it almost brushed my shoulders, it wasn't nearly as long as the model's. I thought the look would work for me and look better and better as my hair grew out.

She agreed. "You would look great that way."

Eventually my body healed though it carried the seed for chronic fatigue syndrome, which would plague me later in life until my spirit also healed.

I went home. Though I felt numb about most things, I was excited that my illness had brought me the support of my friends who had made me vice-president and president-elect of a new club while I was in the hospital. It was in the Future Business Leaders of America, in that friendship circle, and in school that I would hide until I graduated and left. My life looked normal, always an ironic word for me, except for a long hiatus from having a boyfriend while my girlfriends were all coupled up.

Then, seven months later in the fall of my sophomore year, my cousin Larry introduced me to Neil Norris. Neil was already in his twenties, and I knew that would please Aunt Dolores, and the truth was, he pleased me. He was good-looking, and he smiled a lot.

On our first date, I noticed he had some initials on the dashboard of his black and white, silver-finned 1957 Chevrolet Malibu. There in the middle of the black dashboard were two gold letters: S P. (*Sandra Pope? How could that be? That was our first date.*)

I didn't ask until our third date.

"I knew you'd ask sooner or later. It stands for Sally Parker. She was a girl I dated a while back, but she was crippled and nearly died in an accident when she went out with someone else. She can't use her arms or legs, and she doesn't know anybody from before."

I couldn't ask more. I said weakly, "I'm sorry."

"It's been a while, but I just never could take the letters off. Maybe now I won't need to," he said. He fingered the letters slowly. Then he slipped his arm around me and brought me close to him. I let him kiss me. I kissed him back. I didn't know enough about men back then to wonder if he thought of her when he kissed *me, whoever "me" was.* I just kissed him and we kept dating and the gold letters stayed. Even if he had removed them, their outline would have remained etched in the black leather of the dashboard.

Neil and I had been dating regularly, every Friday, Saturday, and even Sunday night for about two months when we went on a double date with my cousin Larry who was dating Pamela Sue Smith. We were at the Sundown Drive-in Theatre in Wilton, me and Neil in the front seat, and Larry and Pamela somewhere in the back seat. I didn't dare look back to see, and I was glad the movie's sound was loud enough that I didn't have to hear much. They sat up after a while.

"I'm hungry," I said to Neil.

Neil and Larry headed off to the concession stand to get some hotdogs and French fries and fountain drinks, and Pamela thought she would set me straight on a few things.

"I think Neil is kind of cute," she said.

I didn't really like Pamela. I might have once, but as I turned to look at her in her new hair style—the one from *Teen* magazine I had shown her and that she had expropriated before I returned to school from the hospital—I knew I truly disliked her about as much as everybody else had *loved* her hair. I didn't trust her.

"He is cute," I said.

"Well, what do you think will happen between you two?"

"Oh, we'll be going steady before the month is out," I bragged the way I had heard other girls brag.

"Oh, sure!" She said. Then she laughed really loudly.

"I'm not kidding."

"I know. But that's what makes it so funny."

"Wait and see."

"You are so ignorant! Boys don't ask girls like you to go steady. You haven't even kissed the boy all evening. Why would he want to be with just you? A boy has to have something that keeps him coming back for more."

I wanted to ask her how boys could keep coming back for more from her when she already had given them everything she had. I wanted her to know I wasn't anywhere near ignorant, but I didn't want to let her know how I knew what I knew, so I couldn't dig too deeply into her. Besides, it wasn't in my nature to be mean, and I didn't really know what she and Larry were doing in the back seat besides some heavy making out.

I just shrugged my shoulders and said, "You'll see."

When the hotdogs and fries and sodas were downed, I slid up close to Neil. He had gotten in on the passenger side of the car, so he didn't have to sit behind the steering wheel, and he put his left arm around me. I rolled my head toward him, and I opened my eyes, those big green eyes that once made my mother fear me, and those big green eyes that made grown men look twice at me, even in the presence of their wives, even in church. And I smiled at him as he fell into them. "I love you," I whispered into his ear, right before he kissed my open mouth.

That much penetration was all he would get for the two years we dated. I never went further than French kissing. That, too, wasn't meanness. It was how I was. I still didn't trust myself not to open to him, like I had to my brother before him. I often felt desire for him, but I always took it home with me, and he only pressed me one time for more than hugging and kissing.

That double date with Larry and Pamela Sue Smith was in mid-November, and before December came, Neil and I started going steady. I wore his big Wilton Hill class ring, filled with paraffin, on my finger to signify that I was taken. And on the first Monday I wore it, I turned around toward Pamela Sue Smith during Algebra class and waved my hand in her face. I did it right under Mr. Horton's gaze, but he used his walleye to my advantage and pretended he did not see me.

Neil was safe, safe as any boy-man would be for me. Every since Andrew had raped and killed the girl with short curly brown hair and blue-rimmed, cat's eye glasses, I saw him in every male before I met Neil. As long as Neil stayed safe, I stayed with him.

I must have been safe for him, too. I must have filled SP's place and given him something pleasurable to do on weekend nights and some idea of a future to hold onto while he worked at the meat market in Wilton in the daytime. I was dead to myself, so it made perfect sense for me to step into the role vacated by someone else, who though living, was for all the world's purposes dead, too.

Chapter 51

A Surprise Vacation

There was a rhythm to life during those years I went steady with Neil. Although Aunt Dolores lay in the bed again and again during my high school years, claiming I put her there, I lived as though life were normal, happy even. I did grow cold to her, and when she took to her bed, I no longer asked what I had done or what I could do. I just slipped into the routine of taking care of the kids and the house, and I learned to walk right past her door, even when it was wide open and she was lying there, sobbing.

Every time I did otherwise she would tug at me and tell me how much she loved me and how much it hurt her that I was fighting with her, *which I did not do,* and how concerned she was for my soul. She would drag me into such emotional turmoil that I would cry for hours. These bouts ended with me apologizing and promising to do better and never really understanding what had brought on the disagreement and her sickness or why it hurt so badly when she accused me of wrongdoing.

She did consider it wrong-headedness when I had a different point of view and expressed it even mildly. So, most of the time I held my tongue and kept my thoughts to myself. But I had lived in several homes by the time I got to her house, and I saw how people did things differently and how people thought differently, and somehow that made me feel like there was more figuring out to do than I saw or heard going on about me.

But in Aunt Dolores's house, her way was the right way, and she was always ready to back it up with a verse from the Bible or with insights she'd gained from dreams she had. So, most of the time, I stopped expressing myself to her and the rest of the family.

Not until early in my senior year did I even confide in anyone about how she broke down every now and then and blamed the episodes on me, saying I had upset her. In two years of going steady, I never once complained about her to Neil. He did not care to linger when he came to pick me up although he was friendly, and his bright smile earned him much latitude with Aunt Dolores. So, thankfully, I was able to keep my life with Neil separate—until the summer before my senior year when Aunt Dolores decided to include him in a special treat for the whole family. It was odd how it all came about and how it ended so badly. I only half understand it even now.

There was never enough money in our household; each school fee, each new pair of shoes for this child or that one, was a talked-about and worried-over expense. We always had food to eat, clothes to wear, and money to buy heating oil, but vacations were luxuries we didn't know. Stories of beach trips and even some cross-country driving tours by other classmates were stories as far from my experience as my own tales of riding motorcycles down canyons in California to the ocean, or hitchhiking from L.A. to New York to fly to Paris, or driving my Volkswagen bus from Fez to Marrakesh are distant from the experience of my students at the community college where I have taught in this small town since I returned. Wild, unimaginable almost, are my stories, and certainly, only somebody else does such things.

But the Appalachian Mountains were only two hundred miles to the northwest of Wisteria, and the beach was no more than fifty miles to the southeast of us, and one time Aunt Dolores managed to get us out of town for a few days. Unfortunately, the trip had its shadow side.

School was out for the summer. Aunt Dolores was excited. The whole family piled into the car and went into town. Uncle Robert went off to Ricky Blakemore's hardware store, and Aunt Dolores left me and Saralynn in charge in the car while she went into Woolworth's. Minutes later she emerged with hot cashew nuts, hot Spanish peanuts, and chocolate fudge for us to share while she went to the bank. We weren't used to so many treats at once.

R.A. was three by then, and he stood up in the front seat of the car. Saralynn sat up next to him while Aunt Dolores and Uncle Robert were gone. I was in the back seat, serving up the treats, with Raina on one side of me and two-year-old Tracey on the other side. Something mysterious was going on, and try as I did, I could not quite figure it out.

But Aunt Dolores was happy that day. She was out of bed, her face was not blotched from crying, and whatever had put her in bed for the previous three days was forgotten by her and never clearly known by me.

I had just about divided up the treats, making sure to save some for Aunt Dolores and Uncle Robert, especially some fudge, when she came rushing back to the car. She wasn't just smiling—she was grinning from ear to ear. She had to tell us the news, even before Uncle Robert got back to the car.

"We're going to the beach! We're going to rent a cottage right at the beach and all of us are going." She reached over the back of the seat and dug deep into the bag of cashews, but before she allowed herself to sample them, she had more to tell.

"You all know I haven't been myself lately, and I asked your daddy"—and with a nod in my direction—"and your uncle if we could please go down to the beach for a few days and just relax and enjoy ourselves. He said he didn't think we had the money, but if there was a hundred and fifty dollars in the account when I checked the balance today, we'd go." The nuts went into her mouth, and she smiled even as she chewed them.

"The beach?"

"Will we swim?"

"Where'll we sleep?"

"Who'll take care of the chickens?"

"Can I bring a friend along?"

"Yes, the beach! Yes, we'll swim—well, we'll play in the waves, anyway. And we'll sleep there. There won't be any chickens because they get picked up Tuesday, and we can catch and clean the runaways before we leave next Friday!"

"So, there was enough money in the bank?" I asked. Money was such a big issue always. I was skeptical.

"Yes. More than enough." She was still smiling when she looked up and saw Uncle Robert coming toward the car. Right in front of him was a black man who passed our car without looking our way. All the windows of our car were down, and R.A., who was still standing on the front seat, said, "There's a ----!" He used that word I cannot bring myself to put in print. And he pointed.

"R.A., don't talk like that. And don't point," I demanded.

Aunt Dolores looked almost cross, not quite, when she turned to me, "Don't you scold him. He is not your child, and he only spoke the truth."

That was how I always got into trouble with her. I would forget myself and contradict something she believed or something the children did or said. I was embarrassed and ashamed of R.A.'s behavior, but I said no more.

Fifteen years later when I came back for a secret visit, as soon as I drove into town and saw a black person, my inner voice spoke the awful word. Again and again, when I saw black people, the old word that I abhorred would return. The energy of the place still held the hatred stereotype. I had taught lessons in high school against stereotyping and hatred, and I never uttered the hateful word from the time I arrived in Wisteria at eleven years of age.

Finally, I had to call my therapist, Joan, in California and ask what to do with the screaming in my head. "Just tell the voice that we don't use that language any more. Tell it we honor all human beings." I did, and eventually the screaming stopped.

That day long ago in Wisteria when we were about to take our first vacation, and I was already in trouble with Aunt Dolores about that hateful word, Uncle Robert opened the driver's door and swung himself into the car behind the steering wheel.

He caught the tail end of Aunt Dolores's stern look at me, but before he could ask about that, he saw her face light up and the same grin, which I'd noted earlier, return.

"So...?"

And everybody, including me, starting laughing, or hurrahing, or talking at the same time. Aunt Dolores's voice raised above all the others.

"You all quiet down now."

"Why is everyone so happy?" he asked. He was a mild man most of the time, hardworking, and careful with his words and his money. He laughed more easily than Aunt Dolores, but he was a man and he hadn't had all those babies so fast, so it made sense that he'd have a greater sense of ease. And he got out of the house a lot. Oh, he was always working, always building something, another chicken house, a new floor for the church, a house for his mother. But he had a real sense of accomplishment about him, and I liked him for the most part. And he was gone at night because he worked at the textile plant on the second shift. Sometimes he'd pull an extra shift, so he didn't cross my path too often.

"Is nobody going to tell me what's going on?" he asked.

"Oh, Robert, I know I wasn't supposed to say anything until we talked, but I was just so happy when I saw that we had the money that I just couldn't help myself, and I told the kids. That's why everybody is so excited!"

"You shouldn't have done that."

"Well, I know, but it doesn't really matter because we would have told them right away anyway, but I'm sorry I didn't let you tell them, too." She turned to us and said, "Children, we wouldn't be able to do this if your daddy didn't work so hard, so everybody needs to be sure and hug his neck." That time she didn't add "and your uncle" for my benefit. I was still in trouble.

R.A., the closest to Uncle Robert, hardly understood what was going on, but he was actually a loving child, despite his ugly remark, and when he was told to hug somebody's neck, he set right to it. He had Uncle Robert in a bear hug that normally would've lasted for several moments and ended with Uncle Robert tickling him and laughing his high, sweet tenor laugh.

Not this time.

"Now you set yourself down, R.A." Uncle Robert had already begun to turn on the car, and he was reaching for the gears on the column. "Nobody's going to the beach."

"Oh, he's just kidding us," Aunt Dolores began.

"The money's not there," he said, deadpan. No smile.

"It is, Robert. I just checked like you said to. I got the slip right here where Mrs. Baker wrote down the balance." She scrambled for her purse and she showed him the slip.

"Well, it won't be there by the time we need it for a beach trip. I wrote a check for ninety-five dollars three days ago, and it must not have cleared."

Uncle Robert had not yet pulled out into the road. The windows to the car were still down. Aunt Dolores stared at him.

"So, you knew there wouldn't be enough money when you sent me there? Why didn't you just say so? Why make me go through all of this?" Then she began to cry.

"I didn't know. Well, I wasn't sure. But I know there can't be that much if that check went through. I thought there might be barely enough, but if I subtract the ninety-five dollars I paid for the new tin to patch the roof on the chicken house, then there's not enough."

Her body started to shake. We all slunk back in our seats. She began to sob. Loud moaning sobs. Grief from a thousand disappointments and betrayals wracked her body. Uncle Robert said, "Sugh, sugh, now don't cry." She put her head down on the dashboard and would not be comforted.

Halfway down the block, a man and a woman came out of Rexall's corner drug store and looked in our direction; they turned and went the other way. Uncle Robert eased the car out onto the roadway, and none of us so much as crunched a cashew on the way home.

Chapter 52

Topsail Island and the Payback

I don't know what promises were made or what deals struck or where the money came from, but by Sunday, we were on the way to Topsail Island. All of us went except Uncle Robert, who stayed behind because he said he needed to clean out the chicken houses to get ready for the next batch.

"And, just think, I'll have the whole house to myself for several days, and nobody will bother me when I put my country music shows on." He said that for my benefit.

I couldn't bear Porter Wagoner or Minnie Pearl or some of the other stuff he loved to watch. I knew he was just teasing, though, because those programs didn't come on until the weekend, and we'd be back by Saturday afternoon. Still, I liked it when he laughed, so I didn't contradict him. I figured out later that he stayed home to pull double shifts at the textile plant to pay for our vacation treat.

We did have an extra guest that Aunt Dolores had put in a special request for—Neil! I guess that was part of the deal. He was coming along to protect us and be the man of the cottage. He drove his new car—a red and white 1958 Mercury convertible, and I rode along with him, sitting as close to him as I could without making it too hard for him to change gears. We caravanned. Aunt Dolores and the children went ahead of us, leading the way to Topsail Island.

Topsail Island is off the North Carolina coast, with the inland waterway on one side of it, and the ocean on the other. Except for a small bridge over the inland waterway, it would have been possible to miss the fact that we were on an island.

Long and flat, it had only a few scrubby trees, and most of the cottages were low-budget ones—nothing like the three-story houses that line the coast there today, despite the constant threat of hurricanes. The water on the ocean side was blue, not like the Pacific with its cobalt blues, but respectably blue and even green in places where the sandbars extended for hundreds of feet into the ocean.

The cottage was small and set back a street or two from the beach. It was old and the wood on the porch had warped the way the front porch at Granddaddy Pope's house had. Too green when it was nailed in place, the wood had dried and popped its nails up, making splinters in the process. Aunt Dolores, R.A., and Tracey slept in one bedroom; Saralynn, Raina, and I shared another bedroom; and Neil had the couch. Not once did I even consider slipping into the living room to be with Neil.

For two days I had been carefree and nearly gleeful as Neil and I took long walks and explored the island. I chased sand crabs, waded far out into surf, and walked on sandbars that kept me never more than waist deep in warm, warm, wonderful water. I led the way or Neil did, and the fun was more about freedom and sea breezes and sea gulls and whitecaps never before experienced than it was about touches or looks or kisses.

I was in love, but not with Neil. I was in love with the sea, with the vast ocean, and the line of horizon beyond Neil, where I knew the water stretched beyond my vision toward Europe and Africa while beneath its blue-green surface, sea creatures of unimaginable beauty and variety swam and danced and lived on mountain ranges higher than the Himalayas.

My scant knowledge of the ocean, gleaned from *National Geographic*, fed my imagination, and I turned away from all other worries. I became unselfconscious, even in my bathing suit, and I cared little that my hair was wet and salt-filled, long and stringy. I laughed. He laughed. We found our way back to the others when it was lunchtime, or dinnertime, or when the sun was setting behind us and throwing long golden shafts across the surf.

I managed to escape sunburn without any intervention from Aunt Dolores, but by the night of the second day, both Tracey and R.A. were cherry-soda red, and Saralynn was Pepto-Bismol pink. Neil, Aunt Dolores, Raina, and I escaped the sun's pain. We were instantly chocolate brown. Aunt Dolores bathed those with sunburn in cool water to which she added freshly brewed, unsweetened tea, and I helped her.

"Why don't you just talk the fire out?" I asked.

"I don't want to be misusing God's gift. I mean we are here having fun, and we could just get out of the sun, and that'd keep us from burning. It ain't like we have to be out in the fields working or like we burned ourselves accidentally."

But when the tea bath did not completely alleviate the pain, Aunt Dolores took each burned child, one at a time into the bedroom, and she did her fire doctoring. Before she began, she pulled me aside. "Don't be chattering about this with Neil. If he asks anything, I'll tell him what I need to later on."

Neil had no questions. He was in the kitchen where, like he promised, he was cooking some steaks he brought. He taught me to make a tossed salad, something that was new to my family and me, and he hardly noticed that Aunt Dolores wasn't there. He made garlic bread and baked some potatoes, all very high-class fare for my family's country palate. It was a first time, too, that we had sour cream and chives and Thousand Island dressing.

He even grilled hot dogs for Tracey, Raina, and R.A. The food was a hit, and so was the beach trip in my opinion. By bedtime, the children slept peacefully, their burns having already healed. By morning, their skin would lose its red color in favor of tan, and no one would complain of pain.

Wednesday morning Neil cooked eggs over-easy and served them with some leftover steak, and I made hot biscuits to go with it. We cleaned the kitchen, and Neil and I headed to the beach before the others.

We climbed out on a jetty where the island curved toward the inland waterway that was way down from the cottage. An hour later, we were still exploring. I looked up. Saralynn was coming toward us. Neil said something funny, and I turned toward him and laughed. When I looked back toward Saralynn to wave her on over to where we were, she was racing the other way.

"Saralynn," I called out. "Come on back. We've found some starfish." But she did not turn around. The wind of the sea must have filled her ears and carried my thin, high voice away.

"Sandra, come here," Neil said. I crossed the jetty and joined him. There in the tide pool were seahorses, tiny little creatures with miniature horse heads! I *beamed into his face, and he said, "You are my nature girl!"*

Always, even in my most sophisticated moments later in life, I was that— a nature girl, loving the dirt and the trees and the breeze and the water. Years later I would discover my mother and I were alike in that way, too.

Neil was right but also wrong. I was a nature girl—but not his nature girl. Something in me shifted, and I knew I would have to let him go.

I had no definite plan, but playing house, cooking and sleeping in the same house, full days spent together and yet so far away from him, all hinted that a different plan would soon emerge, and it would not include him. In retrospect, I see it so clearly and see the role that Aunt Dolores unwittingly played to break us up, even though she so completely misunderstood what was happening between us.

Carrying Tracey astride one hip, Aunt Dolores came around the jetty with R.A. and Saralynn and Raina marching behind her, almost militarily. Neil's back was to her, but she was right in my line of vision. I jumped up, almost like I had done something wrong, but really I was wondering what was awry. I had already scanned and had seen that all of the children were with her, so no one was lost or drowned! When I stirred and stood so suddenly, so violently, Neil turned, too, to see what had so quickly drawn me away.

It was anger. Now that Aunt Dolores was closer, I could tell. She was mad, not sad, not hurt, not sick—not yet. She saw us, and she stopped short.

"We're leaving as soon as we can get packed and get the cottage cleaned," she said. "That means you need to start back—now." She turned and walked off, and as she did, the line of children turned too, still nearly marching, and followed her off down the beach.

I looked at Neil, my face holding bewilderment. He returned my look and stood straight up, the tide pool at his feet no longer engaging either of us, and his face held puzzlement. I shrugged my shoulders, shook my head, and walked toward him. "I never talk about it much, Neil, but sometimes she gets that way. Suddenly, she will just snap and change everything. It usually means she is about to get really sick." I reached for his hand.

"And somehow, and I don't understand it and probably never will, she always says I caused it."

"What? How could you cause her to be sick?" he asked. "And why have you never told me any of this before? She's certainly been sick before."

"I haven't told anybody much of anything about her. I don't know what to say about it. By the time she gets sick and tells me how it's my fault, I guess I believe it really is, and then I feel ashamed. And evil. So, why would I tell anybody about that?"

"Well, let's go, Sandra, but if she gets sick this time, it certainly wasn't from anything you did. I can tell you that much." He shook his head, but as we turned to go down the beach, he held onto my hand.

I knew that he wanted to hold onto me forever, but something in that moment troubled him, too. He saw how much I was hiding from him about my real life, my real self. The puzzlement in his eyes would quickly grow and cloud his eyes when he looked at me.

Our get-away wasn't as easy as Aunt Dolores prophesied. We didn't escape her scolding while we were cleaning. "I can't believe how you, Sandra, and you, too, Neil, have just slipped off every day and left me to do everything with the children.

"I know you need time to yourselves, but all day long you have left me to look after the children. Do you think that I planned this trip just so the two of you could have a premature honeymoon, and I could go back home more exhausted than I was before I came? I brought you two along as a gift, but also because I thought you were mature enough to see that I needed a break and that I needed your help.

"I am ashamed of you mostly, Sandra. You could have helped Neil see his responsibility, but you just ran off, and I was even willing to put up with it, but you couldn't behave yourselves and act decently, or should I say 'morally'?"

With that Neil's broom stopped brushing sand through the cracks in the wood floor, and my hands froze in the hot dishwater. I turned abruptly toward her.

"What are you talking about, Aunt Dolores? We didn't do anything wrong or immoral!"

"Saralynn, take the children outside and close the door behind you. You two, meet me in the living room. Now!" she shouted.

I sat on one end of the couch, and Neil sat in the middle, not close enough to touch me, and he didn't speak to me or look at me before Aunt Dolores entered the room.

"Do I have to tell you what I know or are you going to admit it?" she asked.

"There's nothing to admit," I said.

"Neil?" she asked.

He shrugged and did not look at her.

"Well, I worried that you might be slipping into the living room, so I checked several times a night, and as near as I could tell, you weren't. At least, I couldn't catch you, but now I think I must have been wrong about that after what Saralynn saw."

"What are you talking about? What did Saralynn say she saw? We were just looking in the tide pools!" I was astonished.

"You want me to spell it out, do you? Think I won't? Well, I will certainly say it to make you admit it if you have no shame and want me to."

"I have nothing to be ashamed of, Aunt Dolores!"

"Saralynn saw the two of you. She saw you, Neil, pull your pants down, right out there in broad daylight, and she saw you, Sandra, look at him and laugh! What am I to think about that kind of familiarity and in public? Even if nobody else was around, or you thought nobody else was, God was."

"What are you talking about? Nothing like that happened! Why would I do something like that? Neil, tell her nothing like that happened!"

He sat mute. He didn't look at her. He didn't look at me. He looked at the floor.

"Neil, tell her."

Still, he did not answer.

"Call Saralynn in here," I demanded.

"I will not humiliate her that way," Aunt Dolores said. "Saralynn saw what she saw. She knows what she saw, and evidently, at least one of you is not willing to raise your voice in a lie about it. Get ready, and let's go."

It wasn't that simple. It wasn't that easy. I didn't stop protesting. She turned a deaf ear. She swore that if I said anything to Saralynn, she'd ground me forever. For over forty years, I have wondered why Neil did not speak up. I have wondered what Saralynn did see, for I know she did not see what she reported. I have wondered if someone did travel from one bed to another during the nighttime and if Saralynn did witness something there that her mind closed itself to.

I have wondered if the nighttime vision descended upon her in the full light of day when she saw Neil and me laughing in the sunshine. Did she see him as he had been, however briefly, the night before, laughing at someone else as he disrobed? Did she see me in the light of day instead of Aunt Dolores in the darkness of night?

Or was she simply curious and sensitive to the same broken, repressed sexual energies that being around Aunt Dolores stirred up in me? Saralynn was old enough that she had been given the "Virgin Talk." Perhaps her mind out-pictured its opposite and made Neil and me the players. I don't know, but I never asked her, and I never forgave Neil. I paid him back on the way home.

Both cars were finally packed, and this time Neil and I led the way. He kept the convertible top up, and I sensed that he wanted more separation from the others than he had needed on the drive down. I scooted over on the seat until I was sitting right next to him, but contrary to his normal custom, he did not put his arm around me. I remained next to him, and after we had traveled for ten or fifteen minutes, I checked to see how close Aunt Dolores was behind us. She was within view, but the road ahead of us seemed to stretch on, uninterrupted by stop signs, so I felt safe.

I slipped my left hand onto his right leg and began to massage it, something I had never done before. I turned my head slightly to see if he was responding in any new way. His face was the same in profile as always, except the smile he always wore was missing.

"Neil, are you okay?" I asked.

"Uh-huh."

"I'm sorry you had to go through all that."

"Doesn't matter, really."

"Why didn't you speak up and tell her the truth?"

"Huh?"

I had begun to work my hand further up toward his thigh as I spoke to him. Neither television nor movies nor anything I consciously recalled from living had taught me those moves. I was in new territory, but I felt like a pro. I had my hand in between his legs by then.

Perhaps my girlfriends had spoken of these things to me. Perhaps I had witnessed these actions some time along the way when I showed up some place unexpectedly or even when I was sleepwalking. Perhaps Arthur and I...I do not know.

Using both hands, I unzipped his pants. His eyes cut to the rearview mirror. I saw the pain on his face, the look of conflict. I didn't stop. I was holding onto his nakedness, its warm soft velvetiness, still slightly soft inside my hand. He never looked at me. I never checked the rearview mirror. I hadn't planned this behavior.

Something inside me simply slipped into an older way of being. I was holding onto him because I was afraid of losing him. Because I knew I would soon send him away. Because he left me alone to stand up for my other, my better self. Because Aunt Dolores had called forth this other me, and no matter how I tried to be otherwise, she would always see this other me. So I became her. I showed her to Neil just that once. And then I left him because I knew he could not protect me from myself.

I saw the intersection coming, but I did not remove my hand. I knew she was right behind us, and I saw his gaze lock onto the rearview mirror. I saw her pull along beside us, saw Saralynn on the passenger's side with her window rolled down, heard Aunt Dolores call out, "We're going on by Rockville to see Mama before we go home. You two can go to the house and get your car unloaded. I guess you don't need chaperoning anymore."

I let him speak. I did not look toward her. I did not move my hand, though I felt his nakedness melt away.

"Yes ma'am," he said. She drove off.

We rode in silence. I removed my hand. I did not zip his pants for him.

Chapter 53

How Did a Good Girl Like Me
End Up in a Place Like This?

Neil unpacked the car, all the while making comments about how nice the trip had been. He asked me what I wanted to do on the weekend.

"Maybe we could go down to the Cliffs," he said.

"Hm-m-m," I answered.

"Did you get everything out of the car?" he asked.

"Yeah," I said after I looked up at what we had placed on the porch.

"Any of that too heavy for you? Cause if it is, I will help you take it inside."

"Nope."

"Bye, then." He climbed behind the wheel of his car, the new one without the initials "SP" on the dashboard, without the reminder of either Sally Parker or me.

No kiss. No hug. Hardly a wave.

I did my chores early before Aunt Dolores came home late with the children, who were all excited because they went to Ghaynelle's for hotdogs for supper. It was one of those rare times when Aunt Dolores said it was too late for Bible study, so I was free to go to bed. I did.

The next morning I was met with cold stares from most everyone in the family, including Uncle Robert. He must have heard Aunt Dolores's version of the story.

I slipped away and found a spot on the ground in the backyard where I was close enough to the house, so that if someone looked out the window, they wouldn't see me unless they looked straight down. The windows were high up in the house, and I knew I could hide there and still be out in the open, lie back in the grass, and look up at the clouds. That's what Mrs. Price, a George Johnston English and history teacher, said all of us should remember to take time to do all our lives.

And I have. I have followed clouds in verse and books and all across the continent to the Pacific coast of California and further, to the island shores of Maui, Kauai, and Oahu, turned around and found them across the continent again moving over the Atlantic to Europe and Africa.

Today, I sit here in that same little Southern town, looking up at the same Carolina blue sky where bright, fall sunshine illumines fantastic shapes of cumulus clouds that roll across this same patch of sky where I looked for answers, for inspiration, for understanding four decades ago.

I look back at this white, illuminated computer screen that has lines of letters that push out across it, each one making its part of the story, and each one shifting shapes and bringing other stories forth, the woman in me slipping through the openings in the "a's" and the "o's," looking still for the oracular moments of revelation, of rapture.

The bugs were always bad in summer, and I didn't last long on the ground. But I lay there long enough to make a decision.

Neil didn't call Thursday or Friday, but he did show up at the regular time for our Friday night date. Aunt Dolores made sure she came out of the kitchen and spoke to him. She wasn't trying to be friendly. She just didn't want him thinking she was too embarrassed to confront him. No smile masked her hostility. No veil covered the judgment in her eyes.

"Hello, Neil," she said.

"Good evening, ma'am," he said.

She walked back into the kitchen and, uncharacteristically, she closed the door. I smiled at him faintly, and we left. It was *Cleopatra* at the drive-in in Wilton with hamburgers, French fries, and cokes during intermission.

We watched the movie from opposite sides of the front seat, both of us absorbed in the plot and glad for the diversion from one another. Ordinarily, romantic movies brought us closer together. Neil didn't ask if I wanted to see this movie, and if he had, I would not have objected though Aunt Dolores would have.

The movie had been out a couple of years, and with my bangs, I was already imitating Cleopatra without realizing that was the origin of my *Teen Magazine* model's hairdo. As soon as the movie was over,

Neil turned the car on and put it in gear. I had to work at Cohen's Department Store the next day, so Neil knew I wanted to be home early.

"I'll take you right home," he said.

"Fine." *No detours to the cemetery for making out.*

The drive home was thirty minutes long, thirty long minutes of the Top Ten hits on the radio, so I was surprised when Neil, not only walked me to the door, but also waited while I unlocked it and then asked to come inside.

"Of course. But be quiet." I had opened the den door, and there was no door at the end of the hallway between the den and the bedrooms. Had I known he planned to come inside, I would have opened the other front door, the one that led into the living room or parlor.

Before I could turn around from locking the door, he placed his arms around me and drew me back toward him. This was new. I had never been hugged from behind like that. At first, his hands were around my waist, and I let myself rest against his chest while he burrowed his face into my hair and kissed, then nibbled, my neck, my ear, my cheek, turning my face toward his till he could kiss my lips. I twirled around in his arms, and he held me tight and pushed himself against me more vigorously than other times.

I felt the fire in him, in me, and then there in the den, *with her open door not more than fifteen feet away*, he slid down onto the hardwood floor, and wrapping himself around me, he guided me down and pulled me atop him, then together rolling over, all held together by kisses, till he pulled away, lay on his back, unzipped his pants, turned back to me, exposed. The break in the rhythm, the light in the room, the clouds in the daytime sky and the decision I had reached, re-constellated.

The fire in me became anger; the anger masked the sadness of betrayal; and the sadness filled all the places where love would not flow.

"Stop!" I hissed it in a low hoarse voice. "Stop now!" I pulled away, sat up. Aunt Dolores had taught me well. He reached up, tried to pull me to him, grabbed my hand and pulled it downward.

I gagged as though it were I, and not her, who had swallowed my slip in the moonlight. The fire between my legs was no longer passion but terror, remembered terror. I sobbed.

He let me go. "Sandra, Sandra, I'm sorry. I thought after that, you know, what you did in the car—"

"How could you?" I hissed in hoarse whispers. "How could you think I wanted this?" I stood up, stepped over him, and left him lying there. I went into my room, and though I did not sleep, I did not come back out until the following morning.

I dressed for work, and Aunt Dolores drove me there. Little passed between us, and I was glad to have work to occupy me for the day. Neil would have to work also, and that meant he wouldn't try to see me at the store.

I was on time, but no one was out in the store when I got there. Then Pamela Sue Smith came from the back of the store where Aaron Cohen had his office. She'd only recently started working next door in the Bargain Store. Then she walked over to the cash register and started setting up sales receipt books with carbon paper. She was still wearing my hair-do.

When Aaron appeared, I said, "Good morning."

"Oh, by the way, you're working the Bargain Store today."

I looked at Pamela Sue Smith, and she tossed me a triumphant, Cleopatra look that came right off the barge and marched through the streets of Rome.

"Yes sir," I said. I was the top register girl usually. The Bargain Store was right next door, and it was not air-conditioned. I'd worked it a few times, and I liked Miss Mary who was the regular there, but it looked like it was going to be a hot day.

A voice inside cautioned, "It's best to stay out of harm's way." And "harm's way" meant Aaron Cohen, who liked young girls and had nearly cornered me once already. I had told no one.

Who was there to tell? His mother? Like she didn't already know, and like it wouldn't get me fired? Aunt Dolores? She'd be sure I brought it on myself, and something in me feared she was right because my body liked the heat; my body liked it when Aaron tried to corner me, even though my mind and my behavior denied it.

The Bargain Store, then. Good. I would hide out there during the day, waiting until the time was right to call Neil.

"Miss Mary is out, and that puts you in charge over here," Aaron said he as walked ahead of me to unlock the door. He opened the cash register and put the cash for change into it while I watched him count it out.

"I'll be working here, too, part of the day just as soon as Mother gets to the store," he said and smiled. It was unpleasant to see him smile, but every time he came over to check on things during the day or so I could stock some of the tables or shelves, *I gave him a look I knew was seductive, and he gave me that smile. My world felt shaky, like too many people had sensed some secret part of me, and their awareness of it was calling it forth.*

The day was almost over when Aaron came to help close up.

"Go stock those shelves while I close out the register," he said.

"Yes sir."

I didn't see him walk up to where I was, so when I turned around and he was practically touching me, I screamed. Not a loud scream, but a scream. One hand was at my mouth to quiet me in an instant, and the force and manner with which he did this, pinned me against the wall of shelves. His other hand was up my dress and inside my panties almost at the same time he covered my mouth. He held me down there in his hand and squeezed me. I gasped. He laughed, removed both his hands, and was gone out the door in a jaunt.

"Lock it up," he yelled back to me, "and bring the keys on over."

That was all there was to it. But he knew it could have been more. That satisfied him and humiliated me.

Uncle Robert was waiting in the car when I came out of the Bargain Store to deliver the keys next door. Aaron was out of sight, and his mother took the keys from me. I walked to the car and rode in silence to the house.

Once inside, I went straight to the telephone table. It was one of those fifties' designs that have disappeared because with mobile phones, most people don't sit in one place and have a conversation. Ours was a combination chair and table that was placed along the wall in the den. The phone was on the table portion and below it was an enclosed area that could house and conceal the phone book. It didn't give me much privacy, but no one was right in the room when I picked up the party-line phone and listened. No one was talking. I dialed Neil's number.

"Hey," he said.

"Listen, Neil, don't come over tonight. I'm breaking up with you. I'll give your ring back to Arthur who can give it to Larry to get to you."

"What? What are you talking about? What are you saying? Look I'm sorry about what happened. It was a mistake. I won't do that again." He was sincere. I knew that.

"I never want to see or talk with you again," I said, and as I hung the phone up I saw the Portland Street house, the homestead, and the Tennessee hills flash by.

I never did see or talk with him again. Oh, he called back. He talked to Aunt Dolores. He called again. He talked to Uncle Robert. But I wouldn't talk with him or see him.

In the five years I have been back in this town I have not sought him out, though recently the desire to see him has surfaced. Perhaps the forgiveness of those I hurt along the way and their healing and my healing are as important as the secrets that I am seeking to discover to help me understand my original wounding.

I just phoned my brother, Little Arthur. His only daughter Alana, who is twenty-eight, phoned me back, though he did not. She tells me that she was very close to my brother Arthur, that he drove her to dance lessons and other places when she was growing up in a house with four brothers. She wonders who I am and what I am like because Arthur told her often that she reminded him of me.

And in that comment I know he missed me and now I miss him, too. I miss the brother he started out to be before the pain began. Now, she says, he has asked her not to call me or see me without telling him first, "Out of respect for him," he says. And she is a good daughter and will not go against his wishes. She tells me also that he is not sure how or if he will respond to my calls. I have not called either one of them since.

Now another voice joins the chorus: Does he fear me? Does he remember how inappropriately we were intertwined, he and I? Does he feel the shadow of the past fall across the life he has built so painstakingly since he closed the door on our dark deeds decades ago when he stopped returning calls and stopped visiting our mama?

Chapter 54

Senior Year: Sex and Scholarship

I was no longer the young girl who cried when her mother left her in Tennessee, no longer the young girl who disguised her emotions and covered her face with dirt to hide the redness left by crying hard and long. I had learned to leave and not to grieve, at least not to grieve consciously.

So, when Neil, like all the other men I left after him, did no more than call a time or two and never came to see me, I took that behavior as permission to move on with my life. Junior year was over. I looked forward to a summer of work on the high school annual and in Cohen's Department Store. I was alone, not coupled for a few months, and that suited me fine.

It didn't last long. Larry had another friend he wanted me to date, a young man four years older than I, who was in the same class as he was. Bill Rollins. He was blue-eyed, blonde, tall, kind, and sweet. And he was a writer who was on his way to UNC to become a journalist. I still had no idea what I was to do with my life, but I was a talented writer, so my teachers said.

Mimic that I was, a year later, I would tell my anthropology professor adviser that I wanted to be a journalist. She nearly threw me out of her office. I didn't really even know what a journalist was. I grew up without reading newspapers and magazines. I thought I wanted to write, and I thought that because I was told I wrote well, because I liked writing, and because I liked doing things well.

To get to that awful interview with my college adviser, however, from my junior summer, I had to make some changes fast. I went to see my high school adviser, Mrs. Lou White and told her that I wanted to go to college. I cried. I felt it. I meant it. I wanted to escape the life that Dolores had created for herself and was trying to bequeath to me.

"I do not want to get married and have four kids and sit in a rocking chair on the front porch of a little brick bungalow, which is the highest aspiration my Aunt Dolores has for me, as far as I can tell,

Mrs. White. I know I should have started preparing for this sooner, but I thought I was supposed to get married as fast as I could, and that college was for others, not for me, because we couldn't afford it anyway."

I confided about Dolores's breakdowns. I told Mrs. White about Dolores's willingness for me to get married at fourteen. I had read enough, talked enough with other girls my own age, and taken in the lessons of my teachers, so I knew that kind of thinking went against what the school encouraged—college for all its capable students. Mrs. White listened. She checked my records. I had taken most of the courses I needed. I was third in my class. She could help. She would help.

I worked that summer. I saved my money. I forgot Neil. I felt justified. After all, he only called a few times. Then he stopped. Perhaps I had been convincing when I said he should never come. Perhaps he was relieved that I was gone from his life. Perhaps his heart was broken. I do not know. In the meantime, Mrs. White began to gather forces on my behalf. It wasn't difficult. I had made a good impression on my teachers, I had assumed a leadership role in several clubs, and my friends were all situated in the most popular clique. I started to come to the attention of the town fathers.

Larry and Pamela Sue Smith started to date again in the middle of the summer, and Bill and I sometimes double-dated with them. The back seat antics were more and more embarrassing, and I was mad with Larry anyway because he was supposed to be going steady with Jennifer Graham.

Aunt Dolores became very interested again in what I was doing on my dates. I ignored her questions, as much as I could and just did the things I knew were required of me, and for the most part, she stayed out of my way, too. She still held some sway over my beliefs, and I did feel scared that I might slip up and get pregnant before I could get away from her.

In that regard, Pamela made me nervous. I didn't like being around her and Larry when they were doing whatever they were doing in the back seat. I didn't want to have to compete with her or keep up with her. I liked Bill, and he didn't put pressure on me, but something in me knew I could be down in the front seat doing all— and maybe more—than what Pamela was doing in the back seat and doing it better. I had to put a stop to that downward slide toward old behaviors.

"Oh, that Pamela is really fast," I said to distract Aunt Dolores on one occasion when she questioned me about my dating behaviors. "She embarrasses me."

"What do you mean?"

"Oh, you know what I mean! She is down in that back seat almost from the minute Larry picks her up. It's almost like Bill and I are single dating expect for the sound effects!" I was bold, but I wasn't overstating.

"I thought he was going out, even going steady, with that nice girl, Jennifer Graham."

"He is or was."

"And he's taking Pamela Sue Smith out, too? And acting like that? Well, he better be careful or he just might find himself facing a paternity suit with a fast girl like that," Aunt Dolores proclaimed.

I knew I had gone too far. I didn't like Pamela, but I wasn't really sure she was doing more than heavy petting. Aunt Dolores's version of dating was that any petting would lead to sex because guys, and sometimes girls, would just lose control. I wondered how she could be so sure, but I also knew that Pamela's best friend Glenda had recently gotten pregnant.

I had gone to visit Glenda. It was sad to see her sitting in her bedroom at her mother's house, her belly big before her. She showed me a gallon jar that was half full of silver dollars, round like her belly, and told me she was saving them for the baby. It hurt to see how little she was prepared for the life she was about to bring into the world.

I felt pain for her, and pain for the child, and pain for myself, too, for the child I had once been inside my mother's belly, a mother, who was also unprepared to mother. And a part of me worried that I still might slip up, and a part of me knew I wanted to show Pamela up in one way or another—either by outdoing her in the front or maybe, maybe, in some other way that would be safer for me.

"Well, maybe Pamela could get pregnant. I did hear a rumor that she was caught by Erick Rouse's mother having sex with him," I said.

"That's it. You can't go out with Bill anymore if you double-date with Larry and that girl, and I am calling my brother and telling him that Larry may be dealing with a paternity suit soon if he doesn't watch it." She made the call.

So I saved Larry and myself. Pamela and Erick ended up married some time after I left the South. That's one way to tell the story. Bill Rollins didn't quite see it that way. I called him to tell him that I couldn't go out with him anymore if we doubled with Larry and Pamela. He was shocked. He and Larry were best friends. *Maybe nothing was happening in the back seat. Maybe it didn't bother him if something were. He was a nice guy, but maybe some part of him was wishing something more were happening in the front seat.*

I liked Bill Rollins. I liked his tenderness. I liked the fact that he was going to college, and I would be going there soon myself. I wanted to keep seeing him, but I did not want to end up pregnant and I did not trust myself. I held my ground and hung up the phone.

The next day I was working at Cohen's Department Store. Bill worked at the Jakes Pickle packing plant in Sutton, a few miles down the road from Wisteria. He worked all night, and before he went to bed, he came by Cohen's Department Store. I was working the bargain store more and more with Miss Mary. From the back of the store, where I was re-stocking the shelves, I saw Bill enter by the cash register. Miss Mary, who was in her fifties, was kind and smiled a lot. She laughed softly at something he said or did and pointed to the back.

"Can we talk?"

"I can take a break in about five minutes. We can go down to the Rexall's and get a coke. Meet me there," I said.

"You look so pretty in that color." It was blue. Carolina blue.

"Thanks." I smiled.

I finished what I was doing and stopped by the cash register to tell Miss Mary I was going. She smiled hard at me.

"That's a really nice boy," she said.

"Yeah. He is."

Bill waited at Rexall's. He had ordered my coke. We sat apart from the others in the store. The conversation was short, and I read the essence of it in his eyes more than in his words. He loved his friend. He didn't want to hurt him. He liked me. He didn't want to hurt me. I remember the end of the conversation.

"But what if he loves her? What if he loves Pamela?"

"I don't believe Pamela loves him. Otherwise, how could she be doing what she's doing with Erick?"

"I don't know about her. I just don't want to tell Larry he can't double date with us if he takes her out. He really might love her."

I knew he was saying what he felt. I knew he wanted to love like he imagined Larry might love Pamela. I wanted to love that way, too, and be loved that way. The longing in his eyes let me know that he did not yet feel that way about me, and that absence of feeling made me want that particular kind of love more.

"I can't go out with you if we double with him." I paused. He looked down. I stood up.

"I'll pick you up tonight after work," he said.

"Can you just pick me up straight from work? I don't want to go back home first."

It was the best I could do to sympathize with him, to suggest that I was under pressure that I could not resist and that I was sorry I had gotten us into this mess.

"Yeah. I will." He stood and walked me back to the store.

As a couple, we lasted until that November ice storm that came upon the town suddenly when Bill was home that Thanksgiving. He had kissed me at the door, and I had thought he had gone. I was already in my nightgown, a rather flimsy white affair, another gift from Dolores, more for a trousseau than for a young girl's winter nightwear. The house was cold because we didn't run the heaters at night. I had no housecoat, so I wrapped myself back up in my coat and went to the door when I heard a knock.

"The rain has frozen on my windshield," he said as he stepped inside the living room. "Could I please have some water to pour over it?"

"Sure." I left him, trying to stay warm in the cold room, and went to get him a large pitcher of water. I returned quickly with the pitcher.

"Thanks," he said, and he reached down to kiss me. I kissed back. Like I meant it. He put the pitcher down on the floor next to him, slipped his arms beneath my coat and drew me to him. It was the sweetest kiss. He was both embarrassed and attracted by my lack of clothing. He held me as long as he dared or as long as I dared to let him.

"I'll leave the pitcher on the porch," he said, "so as not to disturb you again."

"Okay," I said, wanting more, not wanting more.

I stood behind the closed door. I heard his footsteps. He stopped at the top of the stairs. He paused longer than it would have taken to put the pitcher down. I waited. I did not open the door. He didn't knock. Then he was gone.

The older girls and college life took him elsewhere. I wrote to him all that year, even as I, too, began to find other companions and to stay very involved in my school life. I was president of the Future Business Leaders of America, the new club on campus that was full of fun and life and drawing everybody who was anybody at the school into it. One of those it drew was Ronnie Rhodes, a bright young man whose parents were divorced and who had a flair for the theatrical.

He and I became companions, and many thought we were boyfriend and girlfriend. On some surface level, we imagined as much ourselves and went to dinners and plays and movies and out looking for old historical houses together. He was the activity coordinator of the Future Business Leaders of America, and he created White Elephant Sales and Early Bird Breakfasts. I was fast emerging as both a scholar and a leader. In each other we sought refuge, and for that one year, our senior year, we found it together. I think we both were scared of sex, and each of us felt somehow protected in the company of the other. Without Ronnie, I would not have survived that final year at Dolores's.

The following summer my friend Alyce, with whom I was living, took me to Bill's home, so I could give him my new phone number just in case he wanted to call me. Alyce talked me into going. Oh, I wanted him to call me, but I was too shy to try to make it happen. There he was in the driveway washing his father's car in the sunshine. He smiled. He took my number. He never called.

Chapter 55

Graduation and the Abyss

My mother was there when I graduated. I invited her. She was there in Johnston Auditorium and heard them call my name to receive the George Johnston Scholarship, a full scholarship that would pay my way through the University of North Carolina at Greensboro, where I had been accepted. And again, she heard them call my name, this time to award me a full scholarship from the Veterans Administration, which I received on the basis of need and scholarship and because my daddy died in a veterans hospital. Dolores was there, too, and afterward she said she felt so sorry for Dorothy Best when my name, *Dorothy Sandra Pope*, was called because she just knew that poor Dorothy Best must have thought it was her name they were about to call.

I don't know who the man was that accompanied my mother. I sat in the front yard at Dolores's for a few minutes with them, and then they were gone. Tears. No gift. No plans to visit more.

The day after I graduated, I asked Dolores to drive me to the bank, from which I withdrew my savings. I went home, packed my belongings, and my friend Alyce and her mother came and picked me up. I was driven ten miles, ten country miles away, and lived with Alyce for the summer before we both took off to UNC-G for college as roommates.

Alyce treated me like a sister, and her parents took me in like the lost child I was. Later that year when they discovered that Alyce smoked cigarettes and that under her influence I did also, they expressed great disappointment in me. Her mother told me something about myself that helped me along the way thereafter.

"I thought you would influence Alyce, not the other way around. You are very lucky, you know. I know you have had a hard life, but every time things got rough for you, there was someone there to help you out, even your Aunt Dolores, who I know made all sorts of mistakes with you, though I don't know why. You have a lot to be thankful for."

She was right. *Someone* always did reach out for me. Something was protecting me, though I surely suffered along the way.

I left Alyce's home. We roomed together that first year at college, but the summer after our first year, I had no place to go. Looking for something to do for the summer, I followed a job lead for a tutor into a local neighborhood and ended up at the Lumbee Indian Neighborhood Center. That tutoring job led me into Youth Educational Services, where I became a VISTA, and worked with, lived with, and fell in love with Martin, who became my first husband.

Up until the time that marriage began to fall apart, I felt I had control of my life, even though I had dropped out of school to save the world. I was living life, according to my rules. I was set on changing the world and being a positive force. In a way, I was trying to do for others what Alyce's mother had pointed out someone had always done for me. But once I let myself leave that first marriage that I thought would last forever and let myself leave the work I was doing with the civil rights, welfare rights, anti-war, and feminist movements, which had justified my departure from college, I fell into an abyss.

In the cold of January in a park in Fayetteville, as I talked with my companion who would accompany me across the country in my 1958 VW bug, I felt Dolores's presence. I looked at my friend's face, and the pores on his skin enlarged and his eyes were swimming in them. I knew at that moment that I had become the bad person (*as bad as my mother*) that Dolores and Grandma Morgan had predicted I would become. But, then again, maybe I wasn't bad at all, I thought, as I turned away and saw the landscape swirling around me. Maybe I had gone crazy like Grandma Blair.

I crossed the country in the cold darkness of winter, surviving a nighttime snowstorm in the Rockies that caused my windshield to ice up on the inside and my VW to stall. Yet the coldness and the stark, vast beauty of the world comforted me.

I had never been further west than Kentucky, and when I reached the Southwest, my heart, hurt as it was, expanded and linked my Tennessee years of nature-nurture with the first wide-open western sunset somewhere in Texas. The long trek into the future had begun. Nature became my mother, and then, for a few years in California, the university became my father.

I had left North Carolina, the land of the fathers, and though I had tried to leave the past behind me, something of it lived inside me. Each time I tried to overcome it, I failed. I created a world in which I was a victim; and sometimes, I victimized others as I struggled to free myself.

Book 3

Revelations

Chapter 56

Is That All There Was?

Nearly twenty years after I left North Carolina for California, I found my mother and began my interrogations of her. I was searching for the missing parts of my story that might explain my brokenness. When the story I could piece together was finished, I was not satisfied with what the linear narrative through time, recalled by Memory, revealed.

But that was the only story my mind could reconstruct to explain my exit from Wisteria right after I graduated from high school with enough scholarship money to get a Ph.D., my exit from college when I married at nineteen, and my exit from the South when that first marriage and the political revolution of my generation failed me. It was the only story Memory could produce to explain many of the years, ragged years that followed, which I will not recount in detail.

Suffice it to say that through every man I met, I sought spirit, I sought salvation, and I sought God. I began every relationship by falling in love, believing that this man could hold me, could transform my story, and could erase my past. I embraced his ways, his hobbies, his family, his friends. I told my story again and again—victim, lost child, motherless child, fatherless child that I was. And some of the men held me for a season, but sex, which always felt so initially bonding, eventually became bondage—the kind of experience where the body is present, but the spirit has fled. I always left— broken. I wanted to know why.

But wasn't my story enough to explain my brokenness? My mother denied me and refused to touch me or to nurse me during my first three days of life. My father, who was my defender, died before I was three. My stepfather beat me. My mother deserted me when I was eight years old. My aunt said she loved me, but she hated me for reasons Memory did not explain. My brother had sex with me from the time I was seven until I was almost eleven, and no adults intervened, even though one adult uncle and a grandmother slept in the same room with us! I wanted to die by the time I was fourteen, and when I couldn't bring myself to cut my wrists deeply enough to do the job, I made myself sick enough to die by refusing to eat. I created a perfect false self and hid my true self away. I failed my community when I dropped out of college. I failed myself when I left my husband, and I became as bad as my mother when I ran away with another man.

No, that was not enough. There was *more.* My body, not as object but as spirit blended with matter, knew there was. *I, the Holy I,* the body and spirit, through which Soul could move, knew there was. The missing part of my story felt present and real to me like an amputee feels the presence of an absent limb. I began to search beyond Memory.

When I was thirty-seven, divorced again, and my daughters were five, I found Joan Norton, a Jungian therapist, who lived around the corner from me in Silverlake. She was about my age, had children, and what I called "life experience." I liked her, and in the early years with her as my guide, I reared my children, developed as a teacher, and continued to write.

I have spent over twenty-five years searching my dreams, following my intuitions, and then my visions. At first, I mined the inner world for clues about what happened in the outer world and for information on how to live in the outer world. Eventually, I would enter the present, a time when I *rely* on Revelation. I do not just turn to it to find a thread, a clue, or a fact that might be verified in the other, rational, real world. I really don't care about outer world validation anymore, not on the big issues.

Here are some turning points in my story about going inward, developing, and relying upon other ways of *knowing.* It is the story of my return to the *Goddess* and her return through me and others like me.

I was forty-two, and I was thriving in worldly ways. Joan had guided me through parenting crises, job challenges, and relationship troubles. Always, she asked what my dreams were. Always, she supported me in anything I did that helped me to develop, to believe in myself: my reading, my writing, and my searching. When the outer world seemed under my control, I dreamed of her, of Joan. She came to me as an inner guide.

The dream: I am starting out on a journey. Suddenly, I am wounded and have to be hospitalized. I am sitting up in a large bed that is higher than most beds. *Is this a crib?* It feels regal somehow. I am very scared and very close to death.

Joan comes to me. She takes my hand and tells me that she is with me and that the journey will be safe. While the dream-Joan holds my hand, I wake myself up saying a word, a name that I had not seen, nor read, nor heard until that dream revealed it to me: *"Eurydice,"* I said.

I went to my desk and found my dictionary. I was able to sound out the word because I was an excellent phonetic speller, and as it turned out, this word was phonetic. *Eurydice*, I learned, was the wife of Orpheus, and she was bitten by a snake as she ran away, trying to escape a rapist who was a friend of Orpheus. Orpheus was off playing his lyre and did not protect her. She died and had to go to the underworld.

Orpheus mourned for her and gained entrance to the underworld by making beautiful music. Yes, Eurydice would be allowed to return to the upper world with him as payment for his beautiful music, but if Orpheus looked back at her while she followed behind him, then she would have to return to the underworld forever. About halfway up the winding road out, Orpheus looked back, and *She* began her long stay in the underworld.

I *knew* I was Eurydice. I knew I had been abandoned and left in the underworld long before. I also trusted the promise I was given by Joan, by the dream-guide Joan, that I would be safe. I understood this to mean that I could travel consciously in the underworld, where I originally had been pushed by those who used me and by those who would not keep me safe. This time, though, I would be safe — I could go there, but I could also come back.

Over time I learned to see the underworld as a realm of light and transformation, for I grew new eyes with which to know it, eyes unlike the eyes of the sun-god Apollo's son Orpheus, who was so mesmerized by the material world that he truly thought that seeing with the human eye and the human brain was the only path to truth, and so turned back to verify that Eurydice, was following him.

I was being asked, even then, to believe — *to experience* — the truth that lay in a dimension above and below and beyond and before and after and intertwined with the human dimension, and certainly, beyond the polarity of rational human consciousness. I continued to go to the underworld, the Otherworld, where all time is concurrent, and to search there for clues about my initial wounding. I remembered the time when *rape* first became known to me. The word itself came into my vocabulary when Beverly Hornsby, much like Eurydice, was grabbed while playing in a meadow. And the seductive nature of the rapist entered my heart and mind again when I was so enamored of Andrew that I could have been the one he raped and killed. On some level, I was.

I began to wonder who, if I were Eurydice, who was the rapist? Was it my brother, after all?

Again, the years passed. That question was answered in many ways on many levels, but never did I feel the answer was acceptable to my Nancy Drew mind. I was forty-seven. That was thirteen years ago. I was barely staying afloat during my daughters' high school years after I left another husband. And, yes, I left him for all the same conscious reasons I left all the other men I once loved. Yes, in some way, some Sandra sub-personality loved him and was trying to save him at the same time. While the details of each of my loves are interesting in themselves, I have learned all I can from them, and I have no desire to wander through those dead emotional landscapes yet again.

What draws me back in this search for healing to this time of life is that after he was gone, I became seriously ill. I was renting a house in La Canada, an upscale neighborhood twenty minutes north of L.A. As a veteran high school teacher, I knew how important high school was, and I sought the best public school I could find for my daughters and moved into the district.

La Canada was an affluent neighborhood with streets lined with mature live oak trees. Parents there had enough money to raise over a million dollars a year to supplement what the school got from the state and county. Located in the foothills above Los Angeles, the neighborhood was a safe and gorgeous sanctuary, just the place to rear my twin daughters, who were entering the seventh grade when we moved there. They were juniors when my marriage, my finances, and then my health began to collapse.

The disease I had was compelling; it was debilitating and left me sleep deprived. Called interstitial cystitis, it was diagnosed as irreversible, and I was told I needed to have my bladder replaced by a portion of my intestines. That solution might last for three to five years, I was told; then, I would probably need another such replacement. Fortunately, my doctor, an Asian man, suggested acupuncture for pain relief, and there began a path of learning about the body, a path filled with challenges and help from the unseen world that ultimately led to more than my physical body healing.

I was also fortunate because Joan's sister, Sally Norton, was a Traditional Chinese Medicine acupuncturist and Chinese herbalist, and I was able to have both Sally and Joan work with me on my healing. As I yielded to the frequent acupuncture and the herbal concoctions—one of which included earthworms—I began to improve.

The burning in my bladder, caused on the physical level by the degradation of the cells that line the inside of the bladder, started to cool. In addition to giving me acupuncture, Sally taught me a clearing meditation for my chakras. I changed everything about my life that I could change and still be a mother to be daughters. And one day I walked into a bookstore in Pasadena called "Alexandria II" and walked immediately to a book that was on the very top shelf, not at eye level, and pulled it off the shelf.

It was entitled, *You Don't Have to Live With Interstitial Cystitis*. Here, delivered to me, was an out-of-print book that delineated the nature of my condition and explained it, in what was then cutting-edge terms, as an immune deficiency disease and linked it to nerve damage caused during hysterectomy. The description fit my situation precisely. The prognosis was for recovery without surgery. The path to health included everything I was already doing and some additional supportive measures.

I meditated. I learned to pray. I prayed. I learned and practiced Chi Gong. I learned more about the chakras, those energy openings in our bodies that the Yoga and Indi traditions teach connect the physical body with the spiritual, emotional, mental, and soul bodies. I learned how each of these chakras governs different human emotions, body systems, glands, and human relationships. I read book after book about the body as energy, the body as spirit. As I made changes in my outer world that brought me peace, as I moved onto the path of learning about the body as a blend of matter and spirit, my body healed itself.

What is still compelling about this disease is that it will put in a short, much less awful, reappearance, when I let the outer world define me or if I engage in sex when I do not feel safe. I must continue all of my spiritual practices regularly, so that I will not fall into unconsciousness and mistake my body and the outer world for the only reality.

I learned all I could about the second chakra, which is the chakra that controls the bladder and relationships with others. The second chakra is the sexual chakra where "misdirected love leads to control, addiction, and the kind of lust that objectifies the other" (Matthew Fox), and to that, I add, it is also the kind of lust that causes one to objectify oneself and offer oneself to another as desirable object, a perfectly groomed, compliant object.

This chakra is designed to reconcile "matter and spirit, sexuality and mysticism, self and other," (Fox) so I wondered what my Soul through my bladder disease, through the hot pain I felt of introverted anger—of being *pissed off*—was trying to out-picture to me.

Through Louise Hays' book, *You Can Heal Your Life,* I had learned and accepted that imbalances that occur in the emotional, spiritual, or mental bodies and are not healed in those bodies, will manifest in the physical body as illness.

I asked my body to talk to me. I learned to listen to it, and as I did, my physical body healed, and my other bodies began to open. I listened with all my ears.

Chapter 57

Dreams Take Me Back to the Homestead

Answers came slowly to my inner world questions, but in retrospect, I see that my *knowing* developed according to a plan that was just right for me. My daughters were finishing their second year at the University of California in San Diego. I dreamed. I studied. I stabilized my finances. I was at the top of the class in my teaching.

I fell in love again.

I was in Joan's office.

"Joan, I had a dream about being back at Grandmother Morgan's homestead. It's a dream I've had several times over the years."

"Do you want to talk about it?" She held her pen in her right hand. My file folder lay on her lap. She placed the file atop a large book and was ready to write. We had done this many times before. She would listen and look at me mostly, but she'd also be jotting down what I had to say. Her voice was gentle; her expression, kind. She knew my secrets, fifteen years of secrets at that point, and she had held them for me, unconditionally, while I mined them for bits of myself, my Goddess self, for *Her*, though even as late as that dream, I did not know it was *She* who called me into service.

I had learned to record my dreams in bed before I moved too much and to use the present tense before the dreams fled. I read what I had written down.

"I am standing on the porch at the Cumberland Mountains home of my mother's family where I lived for over two years after Mom dropped me and Arthur off and disappeared. I can see the sandstone slabs beneath my feet and feel their coolness. From this spot, I can see across the rolling hills and into some of the faraway valleys because the house sits on a hilltop in the dream, though not in waking reality. I see two rivers through the trees.

"I know I am at Homestead House in Tennessee. I am down near the pond, the one that is cradled in the bottom of the hollow and whose hillsides are green and grassy. That spring when I was ten and learned what rape was, these hillsides were covered with wild violets.

"*This is more of a western than a middle Tennessee landscape, for the hills are brown and not covered by trees. They have either been stripped or they have chaparral on them. A woman (perhaps an aunt or my Grandmother Morgan), a child, and a baby are down in one of the hollows. I believe the woman is chopping wood.*

"*I sense movement and light. I look at the hills and see one of the rivers first. I realize now that it has been frozen. It glints and shimmers, suddenly exploding into liquid fire as the sunlight stokes it. I turn and see the other river. I realize they are racing toward one another. They have thawed suddenly and are crashing downhill with huge chunks of ice breaking off as they go, making the water rise rapidly.*

"*They will reach the spot where the child, the baby, and the woman are, almost instantly, and there they will collide, their two separate volumes of unleashed water, inundating the hollow. I scream to the woman, to the child. I use a megaphone. I tell them to run to higher ground immediately.*

"*I imagine that the baby has been left on higher ground in its crib, and that brings a moment of relief. I worry, though, that some wild creature has already eaten the baby, leaving behind only its partially gnawed head, the way the coyotes do with stray cats they find in the California foothills. I wonder how the woman and the child could have left the baby alone. They know these hills. I awake.*"

"Things are changing fast in your life and so much is coming to consciousness. How do you feel about the dream?" Joan asks. She looks at me, drawing me out. I feel safe in her *presence*.

"Some part of me feels threatened. All that frozen water suddenly thawing like that and rushing toward me. I feel like I am about to be overwhelmed by something from my past. The part of me that is watching is concerned about the baby, but that part also sees the beauty of the sudden brilliance as the sun's rays strike the icy rivers. I don't really understand the baby in the playpen part, but I feel like the mother should have protected her, that she should have known like I did in the dream that it was dangerous to leave her out in the open like that. The playpen feels like a prison, too, in a way."

"Do you remember telling me that your real mother left you in a playpen?"

"Yes, I do! Mom said that I was such a good baby, that I would sit and play quietly by myself for hours. She said she kept me in the back of the service station for months after I was born, and that when she did finally bring me up to the front of the store, everybody was surprised that she had another child."

"How old were you?"

"I don't know."

"Were you in danger when you were left alone in the living quarters behind the station?"

"Danger? I don't know. I don't know who was there besides my little brother who was two when I was born, and my mother, and my father."

"Your father?"

"Yeah, about whom I know so little. But I did find out that he was stationed near Oak Ridge, not at Oak Ridge, so I don't know about that theory I had that he was contaminated by something having to do with the atomic bomb and that's how he got cancer and why he died so young. He wasn't guarding Oak Ridge.

"He was a guard at a prison camp where German and Italian prisoners were being held, mostly Germans. It seems there were about 500,000 prisoners of war in this country during World War II. There was an agreement with the Allies that each of them would house a certain percent of the prisoners of war, so when a supply ship would go to England or maybe even Africa or Italy, they would bring POWs back in the empty ship. There were prisoners in Texas and some in Tennessee, and several other states.

"I got that much information from reading some books I found at the UCLA library, but my father's file, which I got through the Freedom of Information Act, was very brief. There was a fire in the 1970's and whatever else existed about him was burned."

"How do you feel about that?"

"Suspicious. Like it certainly would have been nice to get rid of his files if there were any medical records that showed he had some kind of exposure that might explain why he got melanoma at twenty-six and died within—what? I think it was six months of his diagnosis. And the way my mother described his skin, it sounded different from the melanoma I've read about. It was mostly under the skin, not the kind of lesions you see in the medical texts. So, I am suspicious still about what happened to him. I don't really know much more than I did last summer when I visited his grave and left flowers for him."

"Nothing more in the records?"

"Oh, I learned that he was a nail-biter. There was one medical record that said he went to the army doctor because his nails were infected from biting them. He must have been scared, don't you think? He was only five feet tall; he had a walleye and flat feet. I bet those prisoners taunted him horribly. Maybe worse?

"Worse? Like what?"

"Oh, I don't know. You know for me 'worse' often means some kind of abuse."

"You think he was abused?"

"I never thought about it. It just came to me."

"Is there anyone in the family you could talk with and find out more about him?"

"Maybe. I could call Dolores. I do have her phone number though we haven't communicated for a long time."

"When you were growing up with her, did you ever ask her about your father?"

"Not really. A little. She said some things about how much she loved him, but she didn't talk about him much. She did call me when I was nineteen years old and married for the first time. I never told you that story, did I?"

"Tell me, if you want," Joan said.

"I was living in Fayetteville, organizing neighborhood councils in the black community, and she and Uncle Robert and the family were living there, too, because the textile plant where Uncle Robert worked had moved there. She called me and asked me to come over to see her. She said she had something she had to tell me about my father, and she said she wanted to apologize to me. So I went. I was married, but I went alone.

"She offered me coffee from a stove-top percolator. I didn't remember her drinking coffee when I was growing up, but I said yes. I only had coffee occasionally, but that day I must have drunk four cups. She even commented on it. She didn't send her daughters out of the room, and I remember we talked about some fabric I had and some dresses that I had started to make for them for the Christmas that had just passed. I guess I thought I would make pretty dresses for them all, and we could spend Christmas together, and everything would finally be perfect. I never got the dresses finished, and Martin, my husband, and I spent that Christmas in Landenberg, Pennsylvania, with his family.

"I can't seem to come to the point."

"It's okay."

"Well, with the children there, listening, she told me that she had gone to Duke University for quite a while to see a psychiatrist because of some things that had happened to her when she was a child."

("They told me that I had the strongest faith of anybody they ever talked with," Aunt Dolores said. "That was what pulled me through that hard time."

"What was wrong with you?"

"Well, some things happened when I was a girl—your daddy did some things to me that were wrong, some things that hurt me, and I had to get over them. But the reason I wanted you to come here today was to tell you that I know I mistreated you some times, and it was because I was angry at him and didn't know it. So I took it out on you, and I want to ask for your forgiveness."

"What did he do?"

"You know we never had an outdoor toilet. We just went in the woods. He used to follow me and watch me."

"Oh!" It didn't seem like much to me.

"But what I want is to say I have forgiven him, and now I need you to forgive me."

"I do." I didn't feel it, but I did mean it. "I forgive you."

"You want more coffee?"

"No, I think I am done.")

"That ended the visit, Joan, but I promised to drop over the unfinished dresses later, so she could finish them for the girls. I did, but I haven't seen her since then, and that was thirty years ago!"

"Well, how do you feel about what she told you, Sandra?"

"I think there must be more than just being spied on."

"Could she tell you more?"

"She was only interested in getting my forgiveness back then. She might be willing now to talk about it. I hadn't thought about that conversation for years and years. And I guess since my brother and I had done much more, much worse, her confession didn't seem like much. It didn't seem like a reason to be so secretly hateful to me. There must have been more."

"And the dream seems to be saying that, doesn't it?"

"Someone who was too young to protect herself was endangered."

"And now that you are older and know about dangers and how to protect yourself, you are no longer frozen by fear. You saw a way to protect the baby in the dream, remember?"

"I saw an ax that could protect her from the coyotes, but not the waters, not if she stays in that playpen."

"What about that playpen? Does it have any more meaning for you?"

"Well, I said it was like a prison, and I said my father worked at a prison in the area. I thought how the hillside was covered with violets in the springtime when I learned what rape was and that someone had to go to the pen for raping a young girl in the area.

"This is almost too much to say. I have always thought of my father as my savior. He was the one who talked my mother into nursing me, Joan, after she refused to believe I was her baby and wouldn't nurse me for three days! I can't believe he would have hurt my aunt in *that* way."

I started to cry. She always comforted me with a touch on the shoulder, the forearm, maybe the top of the head, and the offer of a box of tissues. And her voice. The words didn't matter, just the sounds of her voice, the comforting sounds of a mother letting me know that it would be okay.

I calmed down.

"Let me get you some tea or coffee, and are you hungry?" Joan asked.

"I am. Yes. I would love one of your peanut butter sandwiches. With jelly. I never let myself eat them any place but here." I was still trying to stay too skinny.

She smiled. Laughed. Stood up. Touched my shoulder reassuringly. "I'll be right back."

We didn't return to the dream again. Small talk. As I was leaving, I said, "I have to know what happened. It's not the timing I'd like really, to have to hear this right before my wedding, but I must know. Maybe he did abuse her. Maybe that's why she hated me so much. Maybe the dream was telling me that he should have been in prison. Maybe he knew he was no better than the ones he guarded. Maybe that's why he bit his nails into the quick!"

Chapter 58

Nancy Drew Follows
the Dream Back to Aunt Dolores

I did call Dolores. At least fifteen years had passed since last I spoke with her, but she hadn't moved or changed her phone number.

"Aunt Dolores, this is Sandra."

"Well, hello. I haven't heard from you in years."

She hadn't called me either, but I didn't say that. My phone number had changed several times. Maybe that was why. "I know. How are you?"

"Can't complain. I have been in a wheelchair for years because of my knees, but I got them replaced and I am beginning to walk again."

"I'm glad you're better. And the rest of the family? Uncle Robert?"

"Oh, he hardly ages. And Saralynn and her daughter Catherine, who is all grown up and about to be married, are both fine, too. You know they live with us still. And you?"

"I'm well. I'm fine. I need to talk with you, though. I want to ask you something."

"Well, go on."

"Do you remember that you told me that my father did something wrong to you when you were a young girl?"

"Yes."

"Could you tell me more about that? Did he do more than watch you while you were in the woods going to the bathroom?"

Silence. I waited.

"Yes, Sandra, I've never told anybody but Robert, Addie, and Saralynn about this, and I never would have told you if you hadn't asked. But he did."

"What did he do to you? Did he abuse you sexually?"

"Yes. He followed me into the woods and he did."

"I'm so sorry. Did he rape you?"

"It was oral."

"Oh."

"I was only eleven at the time, and I never told anyone until I was married."

"You didn't tell anyone? Not even Grandma Pope?"

"He was her favorite, Sandra. I never told her. He was the runt of the bunch, and she always protected him."

My daddy was small and short like my mother. All of my other uncles were over six feet tall, and my aunts were tall and big-boned.

"I don't think Mama would have believed me," Dolores said.

"I'm sorry."

"She should have known what was going on, what with those boys killing off her chickens like they were doing, but she couldn't admit it."

"Chickens?!"

"Yeah. It's ugly, I know. And I really mean that I would never have told you if you hadn't asked. I took you in, Sandra, and I loved you. I really did. I still do. I always pray for you. I never meant you any harm, but when I asked you to forgive me once you were an adult and married yourself, it was because of what I learned at Duke. I went up there for years to talk to that psychiatrist because I kept having such breakdowns. First, I had to admit what your daddy did to hurt me. Then I knew I had hurt you because he hurt me."

"Thank you for telling me. You must have seen him in me all those years. No wonder we had such a hard time getting along!"

"I'm sorry, Sandra. I pray for you all of the time."

There was a long silence. I was shocked and couldn't even think of others questions to ask. *Only later would I wonder if it were fellatio or cunnilingus.*

"Oh, and I did find one of your yearbooks the other day. I'd like to send it to you," Aunt Dolores said.

"Thanks. I would love to have any pictures you have of me when I was young. I have nothing to show my daughters, except four or five pictures that Aunt Pauline had."

"Sandra, I don't mean to hurt you more, but Tracey got so mad one Mother's Day about ten years ago when I was crying all day long over you, that she went through all of the photo albums and tore up all of your pictures. She said she couldn't stand it any longer, how I ignored the good children I had and cried over you when you weren't even my own."

I was silent. So was she.

(*I wondered about that Mother's Day when Dolores was crying over what she said was the loss of me, but what I could sense then was really her recognition of her own failure. I wondered if, as Tracey found every picture of me in every album and found my annuals, my yearbooks, and tore each one up, trying to rid me from memory, did she rid Dolores's own demons from her? How did that work? I wondered. One demon exorcised for each picture destroyed?*)

"I'm sorry," I said to Dolores. "Thank you for talking with me."

Again, the silence.

"Well, I have to go. I do want to get that yearbook to you," she said.

"Let me give you my address." I did.

"Good-bye," she said.

"Bye."

I hung up the phone. I sat in my small kitchen in La Canada in a small apartment where I moved when my finances had fallen apart a couple of years earlier. The man I was about to marry moved into the apartments a few months after I did. John. He saw me before I saw him and planned to marry me before I ever met him. He was six months out of a marriage when he moved into the apartments to be near his La Canada family. Since then he had moved into an upscale condo on the La Canada golf course.

I sat near the sliding glass door on the small balcony, and I looked out over the oleander bushes planted between the San Gabriel Mountains and me. It was June. I was to be married at the end of July. The sun was warm already. The days were long. It would be a warm evening, just right for walking outside and being among people who didn't know me. I called John.

"Let's go some place pretty, some place over in Pasadena for dinner, and let's go early, okay?" I felt numb. I felt dirty. I felt ugly. I couldn't tell him anything about what just happened to me. I wanted to sit in the bright sunshine at a table with a white tablecloth and cloth napkins and crystal wine glasses and be served amidst the chatter and laughter of people I didn't know and who didn't know me, but whose lightheartedness would surround me. And I wanted a glass of wine. Maybe two. Good California wine.

"Great," he said. He was always upbeat and positive, or so I thought at the time.

"Okay. I'm going to shower and dress. Pick me up in an hour and a half."

My mind raced. And the unanswered questions came. Eleven! I thought. She was abused by my father when she was the same age I was when she took me in *and began to abuse me!* It wasn't sexual abuse in the sense that she touched me inappropriately, *but it was emotional sexual abuse!* Her great suspicions about my behavior on dates, her flirtations with my boyfriends, her dislike of me, those times when I could not grasp what was going on between us when she would say I was responsible for her sickness, that, *that was her payback for his abuse of her.*

And because of what I had learned about the energy bodies, about the blend of spirit and matter that we are, I could visualize how her body's lines of energy were wounded still by my father's abuse of her. I could feel how her wounded, unhealed system had closed around me and entrained my energy field to her, *making me a victim of his abuse of her.* This truly was a Big Payback.

No wonder she cried on Mother's Day, I thought, as I showered. She should have cried for what she did to me, for what he did to her, for what she did to herself.

I heard the sounds on the roof again. The workmen were back. I had heard them for days. They always seemed to stop right above my bathroom fan, and I imagined that they were somehow aware I was there naked in the bathtub. I felt my body respond again. Each time I imagined they could hear me, I moved differently, seductively. Then, I caught myself beginning this dance. I always caught myself before it went too far, so that if someone were watching, they wouldn't know I was aware of them or performing for them.

I remembered other such dances from across the years, moments when I took risks and exposed myself by walking half naked into rooms when the blinds were not fully drawn, or years before when I was still in the South during my first marriage to Martin, I remembered standing at the open window before a screen in the nighttime and baring my breasts to the indigo night outside my window. There were recollections of lovemaking in outdoor places where discovery was likely. I remembered almost becoming a go-go girl in a bar in Fayetteville.

This time I cried. I cried for the young girl that I was, whose behavior was sexualized so early and who lived in the presence of someone who said they loved her but who really hated her for sexual wrongdoings other than her own and who truly warped the young girl, warped me. And yet, somewhere deep inside, I remembered hoochie-choochie dancing like that long before I lived with my aunt. My dance with my brother? Even before that...It dawned somewhere far off, somewhere just beneath my conscious knowing, that some truth was trying to out-picture itself, to take over my behavior and make me expose myself, so I would recognize something.

I stopped crying. Then I dressed myself meticulously, wrote down what I could bear to write down, and waited for John to pick me up. Later, we would make love at his home, soon to be mine also, and I would be aware that the sliding glass doors, for which blinds had not arrived, allowed anyone passing by to see us, even in the dark. I would cry while we made love. He wouldn't notice, and I wouldn't tell him. Not yet. I wanted to talk with Joan. I needed to.

Chapter 59

Memory Fails Me, but Dreams Return

The next day was Sunday. I wouldn't see Joan until Tuesday.

I called my sister Debbie sometimes when I needed to talk. She and I had a telephone relationship that started when I first reconnected with my mother, and we'd met face-to-face several times when I visited Mom. We'd traveled together once looking for my brother Arthur. We found him, only to lose him again later. As I write this, I am still trying to get him to answer my phone calls. Perhaps he is smart not to do so, for I am angry with him again.

"Hey, Debbie, have you got your flights booked yet?"

"I was going to call you about that, Sandra. We're not coming. There are just too many strands that we can't weave together right now with the business. It is *the* time of year when we do a lot of business, and we can't afford to lose the income."

Debbie is a natural blond. Blue eyes. *Not the green-eyed-greedy-gut green eyes like mine.* And pretty. She's Southern Belle pretty. *Blue-eyes-beauty-spot-prettiest-baby-Mama's-got* pretty.

"Oh-h-h! I am so sorry you're not coming!" I was. I felt abandoned. My heart hurt. I walked over to the serving table where I had put a tiny picture of me when I was about seven. Next to me on the couch was Debbie, at three, and on the other side of me was Arthur, at nine. I picked up the photo, one of a very, very few I owned of any of us as children. I fingered it as we talked.

"Me, too, but I can't help it," Debbie said.

"Oh, I do wish you could."

"You sound so upset. I am so sorry. But is everything else all right?" Debbie asked.

"How could you tell?"

"Well, you usually call when you need to talk or when things are bad. Not me! I only call when things are good, which may explain why I don't call often!" She laughed.

"Do you have time to talk?" I asked.

"Yeah," she said.

"You know I have been trying to find out more about my father. I have been searching the army records and reading about the prisoner of war camp where he worked."

"Yeah, and didn't you visit Wisteria after you left Mom's last time you visited us?"

"Uh-huh and Rockville where he grew up and is buried."

"What else did you find out?"

"I called Dolores because I remembered she had told me something about his misconduct with her when she was a girl. I had a dream, never mind what, but I felt like I wanted to talk with her and learn more."

"What did she say?"

I related my conversation with Dolores. She listened. Asked questions. I said, "So my father was an abuser, and I ended up living with the one he abused when she was eleven—the same age I was when I went to live with her. I know Dolores didn't physically abuse me or sexually abuse me, but it feels as though she did. She certainly emotionally abused me. Just being in her presence, being captured by her punishing spirit, makes me feel like I, too, was abused by my father. Somehow she passed it along to me. It even makes sense in terms of all I am learning about our energy bodies." I didn't say more about that. Debbie was interested, but she didn't really want to find out about stuff like that from me.

Then Debbie said, "I know I was abused, too."

"Really? I am so sorry! What happened?"

"I always wondered if it was you and Arthur who did it. Or you. Or Arthur."

She meant Little Arthur. Our brother. And me!

Silence. Disbelief. Shock. Tears.

"Debbie? What? What are you saying to me, Debbie? That I abused you? Sexually? Are you crazy? I didn't even live with you after you were five years old."

"Sandra, I tried to talk with you about it the last time you were out here. Remember when we stayed up late one night talking?"

I remembered. I had been so sleepy that I could hardly stay awake, but she kept sitting on the couch, which was to be my bed, and talking. She was stretched out comfortably, and I was sitting on a little stool and leaning up against a wall. We had talked about Mom and wondered if she had had an affair with Debbie's daddy while mine was still alive. We did figure out that it wasn't long after my daddy died, that Debbie was conceived.

Mom did not have much of a mourning period, really. We had imagined that Grandmother Blair and Aunt Ida might have been ladies of the night, and maybe Mom was, too, and that was how they all met. But we pretty much discounted all of that. We both knew there was way too much sex in the air while we were growing up, and we were trying to tell a story, to find a story, that could make sense of it.

I was sleepy and ready for bed, but then she began to tell me the story of a snake, an anaconda, that she had when she worked for the North Carolina School for the Deaf. The children liked the snake, and she took it home to keep it overnight. She'd done it lots of times, but that particular time, she couldn't find the snake the following morning. She was animated as she told this story.

"See that beautiful pottery vase over there on the hearth?" she said and pointed.

It was glazed a cobalt blue, and she had placed a maidenhair fern in it. I got up to examine the vase more closely. There was a design in the glaze that was nearly serpentine.

While I was kneeling there next to the hearth, she said, "One day I was cleaning, and it was before I had potted that plant. I put my hand inside to dust that vase, and I screamed." She laughed as I jumped back.

"Yeap. That anaconda had coiled up inside that vase and gone to sleep. That snake had been missing for three or more months. It was winter, and I guess it might have been hibernating, but I always wondered if it had traveled around my house unnoticed and slept where it wanted when it wanted to sleep. I put a cover on that vase and a brick or two on top of that and took it out of the house and over to the school right away."

I was sitting on the stool again, struck by the story but sleepy still.

I held the phone receiver in my hand on that Sunday afternoon while I stood in my La Canada apartment. Just when I thought I had discovered more about the origin of my own brokenness (other than my early involvement with Little Arthur), Debbie was offering me up as the perpetrator, not the victim. I was the snake hidden in her midst.

"I remember that night, Debbie, but you never said anything like this to me, and I don't know why you are doing this!"

"It just came up again as you were talking. I needed to tell you like you needed to know what Dolores could tell you."

"Well, tell me then." I stood in my small kitchen. In a few hours I was going to dinner with John and meet his brother and sister-in-law for the first time. I opened the refrigerator door, pulled out an unopened bottle of wine, cradled the phone with my cheekbone and shoulder, and uncorked the bottle. I reached for a wine glass, poured it full, replaced the cork, and put the wine bottle away. I had started drinking more than occasionally again. It was all tied up with dating.

I moved over to the balcony and sat down. All the time she was talking, I was in shock. But I listened.

"Remember when Eddie and I came to Grandmother Morgan's with Mom, and I had a bladder infection?"

"Yeah." *I surely did. She screamed when she urinated. Mama put her on the back porch and let her pee onto the stones. It was cold out. I didn't understand why she had to be outside. And she had to take medicine. I remember it looked like chocolate, but when I tasted it, the chocolate flavoring did not mask its nasty taste enough to tempt me to take more. It certainly was not as good as Ex-lax.*

"I was about five years old, but I remember that one day you and Arthur and I were outdoors playing, and you made me promise not to tell something. I can't remember what it was."

"I don't remember any of this." *And at that time I didn't. Bits of it came back later in the conversation.*

"You told me that if I did tell anybody—ever—that the devil would come get me and take me to hell."

A vision appeared. I saw myself as the Red Wriggler girl's antagonizer, one hand on my hip, and my other hand pointing and wagging a finger at Debbie.

"I can see us together, Debbie, like you are saying, but I don't remember what I said or what it was about."

"I think somebody had done something sexual to me. I think that's why I had the infection. I think you did it. Or Arthur did."

"God, Debbie, this is awful. I have no memory of what could have happened." *And I didn't. And I don't. Just the vision.*

"I know Mom put me in danger's way a number of times. And I have wondered if that's why I felt like I was abused, but I have this other memory, too, and it makes me feel like something happened earlier, something happened then."

"Honest to God, Debbie, I have no recollection of anything other than a picture, which may not even be a recollection, of me wagging my finger at you. I remember the medicine, but I thought you had it when you got there, and I thought you had to go get more. And as far as what I might have been warning you about, all I can say is that maybe Arthur and I let you see us when we were sexual. I remember we always tried to protect you before."

I remember when you were born; you took her away from me. I remember when she left the homestead, she took you and Eddie with her, and she left me and Arthur and that turned out to be forever. But I did not and I do not remember hurting you in the way you recall.

I drank another large swallow of wine. White wine. Red wine hurt my bladder. I had learned to watch what I drank. I hadn't learned not to drink yet. That would come later. Silence between us.

"Debbie, I have to go to dinner with John's family in a little while. I have to get ready. I am sorry about all of this. And I am sorry you can't come to my wedding."

"Good-bye, honey, and I hope you are okay with all of this."

Okay? Okay! How could I be okay? She had attacked me and accused of horrid wrongdoing and Memory would not serve me well enough to exonerate myself or accuse another.

"I'm fine, Debbie. I'll call you next week."

"Bye."

I sat in Joan's office two days later, letting the chair, the room, the friend hold me. I wasn't crazy. There had to be something I was missing still. I told her about the conversation with Debbie.

"Tell me more about your relationship with Debbie. Wasn't her daddy the one that whipped you, abused you really, when you were growing up?" she asked.

"Oh, yeah, and when he died, she tried to tell me how much he loved me, and the only thing I could think, was 'He beat me, he beat me, he beat me.' But I never told her that. And our relationship seemed fine over the years. It's mostly been a phone relationship, but I always found it easy to talk with her that way, and I felt close to her when I did."

"What'd you talk about?"

"Mom, mostly. Making up stories about her life from the pieces we knew. Debbie knew more than me about some things, and I knew more about others. Still, all the pieces never added up to a whole story that could explain my mother's life or why ours were so broken. Mostly, we talked about how sex seemed to be so much a part of all of Mom's choices, even before the sexual revolution!"

"Why do you think Debbie told you this story now?"

"She's competitive. About everything. Maybe she couldn't stand it that I had begun to figure out some of my past. Maybe she is jealous that my life, my story, seems to be making more sense than hers. I mean she won't even admit that her father beat us all. Eddie, my half brother, says he got beaten every day. So does Johnny, Arthur Blair's son by his second marriage. That's not normal.

"I don't know, Joan, and then that night after our phone conversation, I had this dream about another baby being abandoned. I know we sometimes talk about babies as the new life starting up in us, but this one was in the refrigerator. John's mom knew it was there, but she wouldn't let me do anything about it."

"Was there more to the dream?"

"No, I didn't get to write it down, and I don't remember more."

"What personal associations can you make with the refrigerator?"

"Personal? Hm-m-m. Well, I have always been cautioned about old refrigerators and about how they should have the doors taken off them. Otherwise, a child could climb inside and suffocate to death. And then my puppy, my first dog, died when he was tied to a refrigerator. He strangled himself to death because he kept trying to get away from it.

"You remember that story? It was the time when it was storming, lightning was flashing and thunder was clapping, and Debbie's daddy, Big Arthur, told me that somebody's dog was howling. It was dark already, and I put off going out to see about him. Nobody offered to go with me. I was about seven. I fell asleep, and the next day I found my dog dead."

"There's a lot of sleeping and death, which could also be seen as unconsciousness, in these stories. And refrigerators generally hold something nourishing for us, keeping it fresh until we are ready to eat it to nurture ourselves," she said.

"So there may be something here that I am unconscious about that feels like death to know, but that will really nurture me?"

"Something like that. Can you make any connections with what's in the refrigerator? With what the baby might be?"

"Some small growing consciousness that I have put on ice but which may nurture me if I pay attention to it. But it feels like death to know whatever it is. That's what it felt like when Dolores told me what she did about my father. There I was in Rockville, buying roses to put on his grave, sitting by it, crying and talking to him and thanking him for saving me when he told my mother I was his child and she should nurse me—"

"Yes?"

"Joan, I have heard that story at least five times from my mother, and she always says, 'He brought me those yellow roses, and he got down on his knees and told me you were his child and begged me to nurse you.' Joan, my mother said that he told her I was *his* child, not *her* child! Do you think she had an affair, and when she saw me, and I didn't look anything like little Arthur when he was born, do you think she might have thought my father would notice the difference, too? Do you think she feared she would be discovered? Is that why she rejected me?"

"That's quite a shock, isn't it?"

I was trembling, then crying. I nodded, yes, yes.

"Do you want to stop for a while?"

"No. I want to finish this. I want to wonder out loud about it for a while longer."

"Can you think of anything else that might help you understand what happened when you were born?"

"She nursed me after that. Then she kept me *in the back room* of the service station forever! Could she have been trying to hide me from the eyes of those who came in who might see the resemblance between me and whoever my real daddy might be?"

"Is there anyone you can think of that it could have been?"

"Oh, goodness. I guess everyone is suspect where my mother is concerned. She is so over-sexualized that she doesn't know how to be with a man without flirting. She just naturally does it, no matter what the age difference is."

"So, who was around back then?"

"My Uncle Douglas and his wife Aunt Evelyn lived in the same back rooms for a while, and my daddy ran the station with Uncle Douglas, but I think that was some time before. I think my mom and dad ran this second service station by themselves.

"But I don't know what the timing was. Mom lived with Grandma and Granddaddy Pope for a while. I think the timing there is wrong, too. So, it couldn't have been anybody in that household. I know Dolores said my daddy was about to leave my mother right before he died because she ran around on him. Remember how Dolores claimed that she saw my mother in the arms of another man when she peeped through the opening in the shades at the Portland Street house when nobody would come to the door?"

"Yes."

"There was one other person I remember. A man named Bishop. I told you about him once, and I asked Mom who he was. 'Your daddy's friend,' she told me. She said, 'He used to come around and drink moonshine with your daddy. He was older than your daddy, and he wore these overalls, and he had these big old green eyes he always looked at me with. I couldn't stand him.' But maybe she had a reason for not liking him. Oh, Joan, I think I can't go on any more today."

"You've worked really hard."

"Yeah, but it doesn't feel bad. I don't feel like I am dying. I feel like I may be finally finding out what happened to me way back then that has frozen my will and held me back from all I know I am capable of doing and being."

Joan still sat in her chair. I had gone way over the time for my session again.

"Joan!"

She sat across from me. Her eyes held mine. Her soul held mine.

"I think I know who hurt me, Joan! I know who touched me wrong, who abused me! I can't prove it, and I want to, but I know it. It was my daddy, wasn't it?"

She looked at me, her gaze intense. "Well, that feels really big, doesn't it?"

"Yes, but it feels like the truth, Joan. It's clearer than the bright sunlight coming through that window! I wasn't his and he knew it and he couldn't hurt her because he loved her so much in that codependent sort of way that she is with men, so he hurt me. Like he did Dolores!"

I wasn't crying any longer. I had no desire to cry. I wasn't numb. That my father had abused me must have been something I had *known inside* forever, so it didn't even shock me to say it out loud.

"Are you okay?"

"Yes. I don't know why I am, but I am. I feel such certainty. I feel great. I *know* I am right, even though I can't recall it."

"Then stay with your inner knowing."

"I'll have to because I can't prove it. Not yet. Maybe never." I paused. Then I said, "But I sure want to prove it!"

The old Nancy Drew mind wanted to follow the intuitions *and* wanted to find the physical evidence. She always worked intuitively, but she also always got the proof. I wondered if I ever would.

Suddenly, I wanted to puke. Instead, I breathed.

We sat silently for a few moments. I spoke first.

"The dreams show it, Joan," I said. "Over and over they have shown it; I can see that now. But I want to remember it with my waking mind the way some people do."

"That may come." She paused. "That may not come. What's important is that you do *know*. You do have important validation from your dreams, from your father's history, and from your own patterns. And you have made this leap into awareness."

"No one but you will believe me. If I can't recall it with my mind, I don't know if I can believe it myself even though I know it."

I looked at her. She smiled lovingly. It would be a while yet before my mind found the peace my soul was offering, the peace that shone forth in her smile. I could live with the paradox, though, until I could begin the search through memory to find the proof. I was done for the day.

The queasiness had passed. I was hungry. "I'm ready for a sandwich," I said. "Lots of peanut butter and lots of jelly, too, okay?"

"Yeap," she said and laughed. I followed her into her kitchen this time, a rare privilege.

I think both of us would have liked a friendship outside the walls of the healing room, but both of us respected the cauldron, the container of that room, that hour or two of time together, that soul work, and held it above the human longing for day-to-day girlfriend companionship.

I took in the beauty of the intricate quilts on the chairs and the couch as I walked through the living room into her sunny kitchen, all her quilts, all that beauty, all the work of a master quilt maker. Some of the patterns were subtle, hidden by the brilliant colors. But once I found the pattern, I could see how all the tiny pieces of fabric had been cut and stitched precisely to fit.

Chapter 60

Nancy Drew Turns into Joan of Arc

So, I *knew* that my father abused me. I couldn't prove it, but my intuition kept developing.

I married John. My mother came. My sister didn't. My two daughters and John's daughter were bridesmaids. It was a lovely wedding in an idyllic outdoor setting.

But the marriage wasn't idyllic. My old patterns began to emerge after a year or so when I began to feel burdened by his demands. Sex became bondage. Add to that *his* patterns, which included being drawn to women who had been abused. And he took my creative ideas and used them as if they were his own.

John made nearly twenty times in one year what I did as a teacher, so I no longer worked outside the home. Ours was a very affluent lifestyle, but I pursued the quiet, meditative life as much as possible when family responsibilities and travel allowed. I returned to painting for the first time since Mrs. I. Smith's first grade class. I experimented with watercolor and oil painting and charcoal, took a chi gong class, recorded my dreams, read, and meditated and prayed. I had journaled for forty years, been in therapy and dream analysis for fifteen years, had read my way through three centuries of British and American poetry and much fiction for the same period, had written short stories and poems myself. I was a seeker.

I continued to want definite proof to confirm my inner certainty that my father had abused me. Then I began to have visions again. One of the early ones was auditory, not visual. I heard a voice speak to me. Just like Joan of Arc.

I was making a pencil sketch of Sai Baba, a Hindu avatar, who is an incarnation of the *Christos* energy. A friend of mine had introduced me to his teachings years before, and I had just begun to read his books. I was trying to find God/Goddess, but my early failure in the Christian Free Will Baptist Church in Wisteria made me turn to the Eastern traditions, to find first the *Christos* in Sai Baba and later in Kuan Qin before I could return to a Western church to seek the *Christos* a second time and then later be empowered to experience the *Christos* in Jesus and Mary Magdalene.

Sai Baba wears his hair in an Afro style, and his eyes hold this world and those beyond it and before it. I loved looking at his face. As I sketched, I felt love for his presence. And he spoke to me. It was 2001.

He said, "In five years you will be a healer."

Then I dreamed of him. He came to me and turned his back to me. It was covered with the folds of his white robe, though he is most often pictured in a bright orange robe. Despite the robe, I could see a hole in his back at about the location of his heart. He told me to put my hand in the opening. I had been studying chakras at the time, but I did not associate what I saw with chakras at first. I did as he instructed, and when I drew my hand out, it sparkled with light. I asked him if the hole in his back hurt, and he said he was well. Later, I realized that under his guidance, I had placed my hand in his heart chakra.

I was already deeply interested in healing because my body had healed itself through acupuncture and life changes that promoted spiritual harmony. I let the vision guide me as I considered various kinds of healing modalities to study. I had read Barbara Brennan's *Hands of Light* and was curious about her work. I looked at her website, saw she had a seminar in San Diego where my daughters were still in college, and I signed up for it.

In looking for the Brennan website, I saw other websites about healing and was drawn to one that Joan had mentioned to me called "Healing Touch." I went to that website and read about their classes and practices and about a practitioner and teacher, Steve Anderson, who taught classes in the San Diego area. Healing Touch was described as a heart-centered method of healing in which the practitioner used light touch to bring a person's mind/body/spirit/ and emotions back into balance so the body could heal itself.

The first night I entered the large auditorium at Scripps Hospital, I felt both curious and skeptical. I had grown up with Dolores, who was a fire healer and believed in the laying on of hands. She was sicker than most of the people in my community, and she hurt me more than she healed me. Still, I was interested. The Sai Baba vision sustained me.

I spoke with the Brennan student who was stationed at the information table. I let my intuition be open. What she said about the program intrigued me, but something about her eyes made me remain skeptical. I shrugged it off. I went into the meeting room and chose an aisle seat about halfway back from the stage and near the door. Next to the seat I wanted for myself was another empty seat and beyond that sat a middle-aged man. The room already held about four hundred people, and there were only a few seats left.

"Is this seat taken?" I asked, indicating the one closest to the aisle.

"This one next to me is," he said. "But not that one."

"Thanks." I sat down.

A few minutes passed. I was fifteen minutes early, unusual for me. A woman in the row ahead of me turned around and looked past me to the man.

"You may not remember me, but I am a nurse here at Scripps, and I was in your Level I Healing Touch class about a year ago," she said. "I'm Julie Merritt."

"Sure, I remember you," the man said.

Another woman three seats down in front of the man turned around. "Oh," she said. "You're Steve Anderson, aren't you? We haven't met, but I remember you from one of the Healing Touch International conferences."

At the name "Steve Anderson," I turned around and looked at the man. Here in this auditorium filled with around four hundred people, I had sat down next to Steve Anderson, the Healing Touch Practitioner and teacher I had just read about on-line! I waited until the three of them finished talking.

"You don't know me either," I said, "but I just visited your website and read about your work. I didn't recognize you until you started talking. I mean I just didn't even really look carefully at you until then."

He laughed. "That's an old picture of me, isn't it?" Before I could protest, he asked, "Are you a student of Barbara's?"

"No. I'm here to see what she offers. I have read her book *Hands of Light*, and I'm looking for a program that will teach me how to work with healing energies."

Just then a vibrant, red-haired woman appeared, and Steve looked up at her. She announced to him, "Barbara's coming back here to meet you!"

"Oh, no." He laughed. "She'll probably scan me."

I didn't fully understand what he meant, then, though I did know that Barbara Brennan could see the aura that is made of up interactions of the light and energy produced by the chakras. I supposed he was joking about what she would see when she saw his aura.

Barbara Brennan did come by. I don't know if she scanned his aura or not. I tried to stay out of the way. I looked down at the floor while they were being introduced. She wore beige, strappy, sandal shoes with heels over two inches high, closer to three. Her pedicure was immaculate, so her toenails looked like little red jewels. My own feet were covered in sensible supportive, though stylish and expensive, black leather Mary Janes.

Brennan had glamour about her—she was a pretty blond and was much thinner than her picture on her book. She was a former NASA physicist, who had taken what she knew about energy from physics and began to see the body as molecules in motion that could be reorganized for wholeness and health through intention and touch.

She had started her own successful school for certification in healing with a rigorous two-year curriculum. And there I sat, unable to focus on anything but the painful absurdity of those shoes, which she would wear for the next three hours while she talked and taught and walked the length of the stage during her presentation.

Brennan's greeting and conversation with Steve was brief. When he sat down, he introduced me to the redhead, Margie Phillips, his friend and also a Healing Touch Practitioner and instructor, who, in turn, handed me material on Healing Touch.

What a miracle to have been in a position to "scan" Barbara and Steve in my own primitive fashion at that seminar. There I was in the presence of the two teachers I was considering. The serendipity of that chance meeting with Steve Anderson and my continued intuition that the competitiveness I would feel around the star quality of Barbara Brennan would inhibit my learning, led me to become certified as a Healing Touch Practitioner. Steve Anderson taught most of my seminars.

Later in one of my Healing Touch classes, I met the woman who had been the volunteer at the information table at the Brennan seminar that weekend in San Diego. She had left Brennan's school because she was told she had her *heart* too much involved in her healing work, so she was becoming certified in Healing Touch.

I knew, then, that Sai Baba, who had told me in the vision that I would be a healer in five years and who told me in the dream to place my hand in his heart chakra, had guided me in making my choice to learn Healing Touch, which is a heart-centered approach to healing.

Chapter 61

I Visit the Fire Doctor

I continued to seek ways to know, in the world's way of knowing, what my father had done to me and how my mother could not have known. My sister Debbie and I had many conversations, postulating first this and then that. The one who held the truth was dead.

My mother, who lived, would listen to my questions, hear me review my findings, and later dismiss my knowing by saying to my sister that "I know Sondra thinks all those things really happened, but she has made it all up. Pope was never like that. I don't believe he hurt Dolores, and I'll never believe he hurt Sondra, no matter who tells me so."

I turned away from my family for a while, and my own development as a healer continued. I could *feel* the energy with my hands. This "energy" is called *prana* in India, *ki* in Japan, *chi* in China, *baraka* in one part of Africa, and *grace* in Christianity. This healing energy can be felt as sensation and used to help balance others, so their bodies will heal themselves. I remembered how Dolores and Robert and others in his family had healed burns — my kitchen burns and others' more serious burns. And I remembered I was promised that this healing art would be passed on to me.

"When you are older if you want to learn how to be a fire doctor, we'll teach you," Dolores once told me. "But you can't ask just out of idle curiosity. You have to ask because you want to use the knowledge to help others. You can never take money for fire doctoring, and you always have to go whenever you are called."

"Someday I might want to know," I told her. I must have been about twelve at the time.

At fifty-four, I was ready. I traveled back to North Carolina with John. We were on our way to France for the second time in a year. He had a business meeting in Paris, and then we were going to tour Paris, visit Mont St. Michel, the beaches of Normandy, and Chartres. I was especially interested in returning to Chartres where I had an unusual experience when I was twenty-one and bumming around Europe, trying to escape myself and my country.

Dolores lived outside Goldsboro, North Carolina, in a doublewide trailer that was really two singlewides that Robert had joined together years before. Though he was an amateur, Robert's carpentry work was that of a master, and the trailer appeared seamless. My heart hurt, though, when I entered the door. The poverty of my youth returned. The pain of the past still lived in my cells, and her presence called it forth. She was seventy-two and moved slowly because she had two knee replacements and numerous other operations. After she greeted us and after the formalities of introductions, she gingerly sat back in her chair, which she only partially reclined.

"I have been really sick for a long time with my back and my knees. I am a lot better, though, thank the Lord," she said. Then she looked at me like she was seeing me this time. "Well, you certainly have aged well," she said.

My mother's genes gave me a youthful appearance. All of the women in her family looked twenty years younger than they were. John's affluence bought me fine clothes and natural-looking blond hair. Those two assets allowed me to create a look that was youthful, graceful, at ease.

"Thank you," I said. "You look great."

She laughed, but she still had sad eyes. "I thank God every day I am alive after all the pain and operations I've been through."

"I'm sorry," I said calmly. Inside I was choking.

"Would you like a soda?" she asked. "Saralynn," she called to her first-born, who still lived with her and cared for her and Robert. "Bring some sodas out here for me and for them."

"Yes ma'am," she said. She hardly had to leave the room to get the drinks. The kitchen and dining areas were practically a part of the same room as the living room. Saralynn turned around and had two cans of store-brand soda. She'd already popped the tops on them. I reached out and took both. I handed one to John. I took one. It was hospitality appropriate for that time of day. Robert sat quietly in the room. When Saralynn asked if he wanted a soda, the familiar "No, sugh" was his answer.

They were waiting for me to talk. "Thanks for letting us come."

"Well, it's been a long time, but you have always been welcome. We never closed our door to you, Sandra."

"I know," I said. Saralynn and I sat next to each other on the couch. We had exchanged several e-mails before the visit, and I felt closeness to her. Saralynn had a daughter who was the same age as my twin daughters, and we both felt connected through that happenstance. I imagined that over the years, as she had lived with Dolores, she had come to know more about what happened between me and Dolores and blamed me less than others might. Anyway, Saralynn was excited about my visit. Dolores was afraid.

"Well, I already told you all I could about your daddy. Humph!"

"I believe that my father abused me, too," I said.

She didn't ask how I knew or how it happened or how I could have remembered it since I was so young, all questions my mother had asked me. I didn't say anything to further describe my knowing.

"Hah! You, too! That figures," she went on. "The whole bunch of them was rotten."

This was not the story I had heard during those years I lived with her. The story I heard again and again was about how my mother was rotten, and how wonderful Dolores's brother, my father, was. I wished Dolores had told me the truth, the whole truth, that day she called me over when I was in my early twenties. I wondered why she didn't tell me then, but I didn't ask even though I wished I hadn't had to wait another thirty years to find out.

I remembered that Mother's Day when Dolores cried so hard over me that Tracey found all of my pictures and tore them up, and I knew Dolores, too, had suffered because of her failure to tell me. But not the way I had. It felt like one more act of cruelty, of payback for what my father, not I, had done.

I wanted to get up and leave at that moment, but I remembered what I had come for.

We talked about her other children. About my daughters. She saw their pictures and said, "They sure are pretty girls."

I talked briefly about my Healing Touch training. Then, as she had told me long ago was the tradition, I asked for the secret.

"Aunt Dolores, you once told me that if I wanted to know how to heal burns, you would teach me. I'm ready now to know."

"Ha!" she said. "So, that's why you've come!"

"Yes," I said, but John jumped into the conversation.

"That's not the only reason. She really wanted to see you, too. She's talked about it for years," he said.

John meant well. He didn't understand the great wound I had received while I was in Dolores's care. He didn't realize how cruel it was for her to fail to reveal that my father abused her. I knew what John was doing, and I knew he was sincere, but he had a third-degree black belt in Aikido.

He was projecting his *ki:* he was sending out his personal power into the room to attract others to him. I wasn't attracted, but Robert liked John. I could tell, and Robert would be angry with me later when I left John and returned to Wisteria. But at that moment, Robert liked John, and somehow that extended to me.

"I'll teach you," Robert said quietly. "You know how the healing is passed on—from a man to a woman and from a woman to a man."

"Yes. Let him teach you." Dolores said.

"When you were talking about what you are learning in your healing work, I got a feeling of the spirit rushing in," Saralynn said. "Let's pray first."

Robert prayed. His words were the long-ago, ordinary words of prayer I had heard so many times as a child. Unlike Saralynn, I did not feel the spirit rush in. I understood why. The spirit was always present in me, or I should say that I was always lost in the spirit world, a place I went in an attempt to escape the pain, the remembered pain, the phantom pain of the abuse.

I let the inflections, the rhythms of Robert's prayer steady me. Then he and I went into the bedroom where he passed on the healing secrets to me. John waited in the living room and never asked me to violate the tradition of secrecy; nor did he ever ask to be taught to heal in that manner himself.

We left, accompanied down the driveway by Dolores, Robert, and Saralynn, and hugged by each of them before we got into our car. We drove up I-40, a concrete corridor through a tunnel of pines, toward the Raleigh–Durham airport where we would fly to D.C. and on to Paris the next day.

I would not get to revisit Chartres because his business commitments prevented him from accompanying me. My unwillingness to travel without him, just a year before I left him forever, kept me sitting in a café, drinking wine, instead of taking a tour bus to Chartres. That's how I was with every man I stayed with—completely enmeshed and unable to be without him until I left him suddenly forever. I wonder if the abuse which bound me to my father and his sudden departure when he died imprinted some awful pattern, one that I have re-enacted many times.

At any rate, Chartres would have to wait. By the time I was ready to see Chartres on my own, I would not need to revisit it; for I would know from experience that I already carried the same blueprint within my chakras that the architects used at Chartres, so it could open the human energy field to the divine feminine within.

Chapter 62

I Follow the Paths of Dreams and Visions

I continued to study and practice Healing Touch and started a healing ministry at the Hollywood United Methodist Church. Daily life in my marriage had challenges as I continued to feel that my ideas, my essence, was being drawn out of me as though I were John's connection to the collective unconscious. Unknowingly, he would repeat insights I had shared as if they were his own ideas, and he did this in his writing as well as in his conversation with others and me.

I remembered a lesson that I had learned from Joan years before. I had complained about someone not giving me what I wanted, someone who did not connect with me the way I wanted or did not connect me with what I longed to be unified with. She recognized that I was looking for God, for the Goddess in myself, though she did not use those words when she gently suggested that I might be going to the wrong source. She urged me to turn inward to the wisdom of my own body and mind.

With John, I started to monitor what I talked about. I did not let him seek the Goddess through me instead of seeking his own way of opening to guidance. I began to turn inward more and more, began to listen more to my body, and continued to follow the paths of occasional visions and abundant dreams. I also began to spend more and more money, not wastefully, but selfishly and secretly.

Daily there were dreams to follow. There were tree dreams. And tree visions.

I was sitting in my living room, and I looked out at the pine tree that soared past my second story patio. I saw Mary Magdalene's face in the tree. I asked her what she was doing there.

She said, "When Yeshua was killed, and after those of us who loved him fled, we lived for a while in a place of safety. But there came a time when I sent my essence into the pine trees, so that it would be present in the world and safe from those who would destroy it."

I have always loved nature and have always felt uplifted by Her. To imagine pine trees were imbued with the life force of Mary Magdalene, to discover that Her life force was still alive and I was connected with it, with Her through Nature, was a wondrous moment of revelation. Life went on, and I simply tucked this dream away, and when my path shifted, and time opened up, I would read more and more about Mary Magdalene, first in a book written by Joan Norton and then in Margaret Starbird's books.

There were often baby dreams.

A baby was given to me and taken away by Dolores. A wealthy woman, who sat on a park bench, gave a baby to me. A baby showed up at a picnic and turned out to be mine. And there were talking babies—babies who would show up speaking in complete sentences. Only once did I record what a talking baby told me: "Your diaper is soiled," she said. "You need to change it."

I recognized the new life in the image of these babies, and I took the command to change my soiled diaper to be an invitation to cleanse the lower realms, the lower chakras, my connection to Earth instead of racing away into the higher chakras, trying to get off the planet and abandon Mother Earth. I came to understand that the language of lower and higher was a barrier, that all chakras are equal and work together, and when they are in harmony, we can experience ourselves as both body and spirit, as whole, as part of the Whole, as part of God-Goddess.

There were vulva dreams.

Enormous, swollen vulvas, so full of divine feminine energy, carrying so much unrecognized, unaccepted divinity, that it became almost burdensome, embarrassing. Torn vulva dreams. Ripped clitoris dreams. Babies with ripped vaginas.

At each stage of my developing consciousness, I took my dreams and visions to Joan. I trusted her because of the way we had worked together in the outer world—she was my counselor, my mother, my sister, and my friend during my time of isolation in California and later in North Carolina. *I trusted her also because my inner world gave me assurance of her goodness*, and my Eurydice dream, years before, had identified her as my spiritual guide. Often she encouraged me to dialogue with my dream characters. Often I did, but I wouldn't dialogue with the talking babies until much later.

The summer before I left California, I had a *yoni* dream, though I did not know what a *yoni* was when I first encountered it in the dream.

Here is the dream:

I am in the car with Rev. Ed Hansen, the Hollywood United Methodist Church minister, and he is driving. He hands me a book. It is entitled, The Book of Life. *He tells me it is mine and that I am loved always. I take the book. The dream shifts. Rev. Ed is sitting on a picnic blanket with another minister. The two have spread the blanket out and are getting ready to eat their food in the quad at UCLA where all the older buildings are. High above them is a dove that is holding something silver in its beak. I come across the quad and call to them to look up. They do. "It's a beautiful sky, isn't it?" Rev. Ed calls back to me.*

I'm puzzled for a moment. I watch both men look up, and there is no look of surprise or recognition on their faces. I look up and see the dove is still there. I look down at my left palm and see an almond-shaped drawing appear. I have no idea what it is.

But Joan did. "It's a *yoni*, a universal symbol for the divine feminine," she said. "And so is the dove. It is the symbol for the Holy Spirit, which is considered the feminine divine energy. *You* get to see it," she said. "The men, even those as connected to divinity as Rev. Ed, don't see it. They can't bring the divine feminine into being for you, but that's no problem because it looks like you already have the knowledge, the wisdom as represented by your *Book of Life* to find your own way. You've also been given a promise that you are loved always. All that's pretty good recognition that you have made and can maintain your own direct connection to what is holy, I'd say!"

The cobra dreams began two years into my marriage to John and they continue.

A baby cobra bit me on the lips. I came to see that bite as a deeper initiation into the mysteries of the divine feminine. There were white cobras, huge cobras, small cobras, and blue ones. There were other snakes, too, black snakes, snake skins, baby snakes, and brown snakes with yellow rings as the new energies began to rise in me, demanding that I leave the shell of my old self behind and begin a new life, dedicated to the rise of the divine feminine energy, the *Wouivre* which was flowing through me the way it flows through Chartres.

Then more Dolores dreams came.
I follow her down the highway to the old house outside of Wisteria, North Carolina, on Highway 117. I lose her along the way.
Another time *I am in the old house and know there is a secret way out. I find it, but a blue spider with secret markings blocks it. I know the spider is poisonous and that I cannot get out that way, at least not yet.*
Joan suggested there was a story in whose web I was caught still, and the weaver of all stories was not going to give me access to the purely spiritual, unintegrated with the mundane. I came to see my entrapment of myself in an affluent lifestyle as detrimental as my early life entrapment by Dolores had been. I was being used, willingly, but I had reached a time of consciousness when I could no longer participate in the misuse of my energies.
I was fifty-four. I began to leave John.

One Sunday I received an e-mail from Bill Rollins, the man I had dated in the summer and fall of 1965, thirty-eight years earlier. He was a sports journalist and quite a writer. He had returned to Wisteria a few years earlier. We told our stories in e-mails until we fell in love, and I traveled again to Wisteria, to the Fatherland, leaving everything I knew and had loved for thirty-five years behind me, much like I had earlier when I left North Carolina and went to California. There was mystery at work in this re-connection with Bill. I needed to return to Wisteria, and I would never have done so on my own. A way was given me, an outer world reason that my human heart could understand: I was in love. Again.

I was excited to be back in Wisteria, this spot that had troubled my memory and imagination for nearly forty years. Many of my early short stories and a draft of a first novel were peopled by residents and locales in this town, and that writing was an attempt to solve the mysteries I needed answers to. But it was a shock, also, to return, and I spent the first nine months in deep grief because I missed my twenty-three year old daughters. I meditated. I prayed.

I had read Joan's manuscript on *The Mary Magdalene Within* several years earlier, and I reread it in its published form, one chapter at a time, as a daily meditation. I began to read Margaret Starbird's books on *The* Mary Magdalene. I started a Healing Touch practice. I began to teach at a local community college. I studied aromatherapy. By springtime, I started to revisit the old places and to try to find some of the old people.

The house on Highway 117 had been bricked; no longer was it the gray-shadow shingle house of my youth. The tall long-leaf pines that had filled the front yard were all gone, save one that stood to the right of the driveway. That one was ten feet around its trunk. It was a regal giant of a pine tree that reminded me of the Mary Magdalene pine tree vision and gave me assurance of her protection.

Despite that, the whole place felt cold. The side yard was strewn with beer cans, ale bottles, and X-rated DVD covers. There was a spiritual vacancy about the land that made me feel the way I do when I walk through the liquor department of a supermarket. Something cold and isolating was sucking my energy from me. Drugs, I thought. A drug house. And in a way, it wasn't even ironic to me that this house that had held so much pain, covered up by false understanding of the "Spirit," should have attracted these other negative energies.

I shielded myself with light and love through prayer, touched the Mary Magdalene tree, and I walked toward the house. It was clearly empty, and of course, everything about the place—the house, the yard—seemed much smaller than I had recalled.

The side yard had thirty-feet tall coastal maples and scrub pines right up to the driveway. The open yard that had led to the chicken houses was dense forest with tall shiny poplars, more coastal maples and pines, and a tangle of various weeds I could no longer name. The backyard had closed in around the house with new and old forest growth and underbrush that made me think "snakes" and turn away at first. But then I saw the old pump house. It, too, had been bricked. I walked straight through the underbrush toward it.

I stopped next to the pump house. It reached my chest, right at heart level, and I felt immediate compassion for that fourteen-year-old girl I was when I had enacted that terrible ritual. Forty years had passed since, both Abraham and Isaac, I had sought to take and give my life on that flat-topped altar above a well. I felt again the agony of that powerful early out-picturing of my desire, not to die, but like Isaac to be rescued by an angel of God; or like Christ, to be reborn; or like Mary Magdalene to be recognized for who I truly was beneath the powerful personal projection and cultural projection of hatred for the feminine that came through my aunt and from the Old South.

I felt cold, then weak, when, in memory, the vision of Dolores came toward me, not the angel I had hoped who could save me from death that had kept reaching out for me. But I knew back then that Dolores held truths that, like the angel that freed Isaac, could set me free. I had searched until I had finally found proof, but those proofs had still held me in thrall. It would take truth of a different order to set me free me from the demands of my Nancy Drew mind.

I touched the top of the pump house. It was warm from the springtime sun. I blessed the well beneath the ground, and I scooped up the energy of my Self that this place had held and returned it to my heart. Three times I did this. It came naturally to me. It was a *feng shui* ritual I had practiced in many hotels during my travels with John. When I arrived in a new place, three times I'd place my heart energy in the bed to make it my safe home. Three times I'd scoop it up again before we moved on to another hotel.

As I stood in front of the pump house and enacted this ritual on that sunny spring day, I was attended by whatever lay hidden in the tall grasses that grew up around the pump house, by a few errant blue jays and by the mixed growth of coastal maples and new pine trees beneath a cloudless, pale blue sky.

I turned, thus fortified, and walked around the house once. Then twice. Then again. I had no plan. I just followed my desire from one moment to the next and found myself up on the front porch, peering into the windows. The life, or rather *death-in-life,* that the house had once held, was gone. I felt no presence lingering there that drew me further.

I turned, walked to my car, and drove down Highway 117 to an intersection where I recalled that a road crossed the railroad tracks and led to Grandmother Pope's old farm. I even remembered the name of Grandmother Pope's road. It was Beasley Mill Road.

Chapter 63

The Land Reclaims Me

I had revisited Grandma and Granddaddy Pope's old farm two years earlier before visiting Dolores and Robert and receiving the secret of fire healing. That time I had asked John to let me revisit the old place alone. Gently, I had asked him to stay in the car. I had walked down the lane, aware of his presence, but trying to focus my attention in the moment, trying to connect with my purpose. I touched the land with my palms. I closed my eyes. I began to move back in time, to ask the land to speak to me.

Suddenly, a car door slammed. I was jolted back to the present. I turned and saw John walking down the road toward the creek. He had his camera with him. I raced toward him. "Let's go," I had said. "Now!"

"I was just—"

"I asked you to stay in the car, to let me have this time by myself. Now, let's just go." I had taken one look toward the creek and knew I did not want to stand there with John. It would have become his experience, his story, not mine, not even ours, like my life had begun to feel. He yielded in angry silence to my demand. We left.

This time I was alone. I could take my time and have my own experience, unchallenged and unthreatened by the needs or demands of any other or by my inability to close myself off and not become a channel for others to use knowingly or unknowingly. The ramshackle, unpainted, old family house made from green pine that had warped and weathered gray over the years was gone. It had burned, and Aunt Pauline's daughter had built a small house in its place. The spring day was still warm, though the sunset would come soon.

At the point where the two entry lanes met, they formed a triangular island of brambles. I stood at the point of this triangle, and white sand stretched out before me. Ages earlier, the land must have been covered by water, an inland sea or lake that deposited the beach-quality white sand in which no grass ever grew. The mica in the sand shone. I took off my shoes and stood on the land barefoot, digging my toes into the sea of warm sand.

Suddenly, I was caught in a vision as the old home rose up to supplant the current one.

The warped screen door hung open on that old house, and where its screening was ripped, someone had sewn it back together with bits of tobacco twine. The long porch, with its accumulation of old straight-back rockers and rattan couches that were no longer used inside, was empty of those who had rested there at the end of each warm day and all day long day on warm Sundays. At the left side of the porch was an old Packard that only worked when Arthur or I pretended to let it take us wherever we wanted to go.

I wanted to people the place with those from long ago and walk right in as an adult and say hello, ask all of my questions, and express all of my suspicions out loud. I wanted to move toward the house, to see if it were real, if I could somehow make the vision come alive. I leaned forward toward the house with my head, my arms, and my body, but I could not move my feet. I felt magnetized, held by the earth in that one spot.

A great in-rush of feeling, of sensation, of energy, flooded through the soles of my feet, up my legs, and spread throughout my entire body. The sensation lasted for only a few moments, but while it did, I felt like I was caught in a stream of brilliant light that flowed through me. I felt like I *was* brilliant light. I looked at the earth. It sparkled magnificently bright, far brighter than the sun had made it the moment before. And it all felt familiar.

The next instant, the earth returned to being a brightly lit patch of sandy ground. I could move. With my shoes still in my hands, I started forward. I looked up. The vision had passed. The present had returned. My body felt enlivened, light but full, as though each dry cell had suddenly been watered. I slipped my shoes on and walked across the yard and up the steps. Three quick knocks. Then I paused. I knocked again. No answer.

I left my car where it was and walked down the sandy lane back to the road. I turned left and continued down to the old creek. I still felt light. I felt guided. I had no fear. I stood on the road. The bridge had been replaced long ago by a metal culvert that carried the creek from one side of the road to the other. The creek itself was dark; its sandy bottom was gone, covered by leaves and other natural debris, and the water was dyed tea brown.

Across the road, the creek had invaded the forest. It was no longer a discrete stream of water; it pooled out. Years of flooding and pollution from the factories in Raleigh, the fouled run-off from the surrounding farmland, and beavers' dams had caused the creek bed to fill up with sand and debris; and instead of a creek, there lay a swamp with a brown, soapy film on its surface that dulled the reflection of the early orange rays of the approaching sunset. I stood on the roadside, looking for beauty, for the carefree fun of childhood when I was a visitor for a couple of weeks in the summertime before I returned to the fatherland and became a ward of Dolores.

A hawk suddenly dived from the top of a pine tree and came within inches of my head. I turned to her, saw the nest she was protecting, but still I loudly proclaimed, "I'm back. I have a right to be here. I mean you no harm. Move away and let me be."

Twice more she came at me. Twice more I yelled my command and stood my ground. When she had settled in the tree, I waited several minutes more before I turned to go. Now, I thought, I have announced my right to be here, have stood my ground, and I can go. As I looked back out over the swamp, the voice of the swamp rose inside my mind. "Find Arthur," it said. The greasy scum on the water held the dull orange reflection of the sun. The water was sour, so stagnant I could smell it in the dusk as the heat left the air, and water condensed into pockets of mist and rose.

My encounter with the hawk had emboldened me. I would not be caught by the demands of the past. I still felt the current of life that flowed through me and had made itself available to empower me. Out loud again, I answered the swamp, "When I am ready, I will," and I walked back up the hill to my car. I felt the presence of two powerful, opposing streams of energy each step of the way to my car.

The land enlightened me, uplifted me. The flat brown swamp water dulled me with its stagnant stillness. The shadowy surface absorbed even the light of the sun. The hidden depth could not be known by looking. And the danger of what lay beneath its brown surface could only be known by intuiting. Two ways of knowing were meeting in my body and asking to be harmonized. I was caught between knowing and proving, between my heart and my mind. I would have to learn to be as fierce as the hawk to protect myself.

Several days a week that first spring and summer, I went to sit and meditate at the creek. I still go there once a week. I always acknowledge the swamp. I even dug up some wild violets that grew along its edges and planted them in my yard at home, but I always sat looking toward the creek, my back toward the swamp, when I meditated.

Each time I went to the creek, I passed by Aunt Pauline's and Uncle Clifford's home as well as by Uncle Douglas's home. Eventually, I understood that I would not visit or interrogate them. They would not have the truth I was seeking. This I knew.

I did call Arthur again. I left messages several times. I waited for his call. I read. I prayed. I meditated. I walked the cemetery where my father lay. I dreamed. I found another returnee to Duplin County, who had a sanctuary garden in which she had built a labyrinth. I walked that. I bought a small brick home on an acre of pine trees.

I married Bill.

I wrote.

I longed to be back in California with my daughters.

I continued to talk with Joan every other week by phone. She was my lifeline.

Then a year after I had returned to Wisteria, I had another vision of Mary Magdalene.

I had asked for her guidance while I was meditating, and I heard her speak and saw her in a triple circle of luminous blue light. She said that Aramat, her "lesser angel," would attend me.

"Aramat." That was the name Mary Magdalene had used. She said she had two angels. One was named Ruth, and the other Aramat.

I searched as well as I could in books about angels and could find no Aramat. I, of course, welcomed this "lesser angel." She became my inspiring angel for writing this memoir. Always before beginning a chapter, I prayed to her for this work to be her work, Her work, and she has guided all I have written.

Six months after Mary Magdalene had given me this guide, I had a vision in which Aramat appeared—a column of light with wings—and held a mirror up to her name. It became Tamara! Again, I searched for the meaning of this name, and eventually understood it to be another name for the Goddess, and for daughter of the Goddess—Tamara.

I wondered about my visions, of course, and about their verity. Dreams came. And books came to reveal more of Her. Now I am certain of who Tamara is. Though some call her Sarah, others call her Tamar, and she is the daughter of Mary Magdalene and Jesus, and the twin flame, or mirror image of Mary Magdalene, as am I. As is every woman.

At every point along the way when the writing got rough, when it became graphic, when I feared the consequences of seeking and writing these truths, Tamara led me on, assuring me that this work was guided and blessed and necessary in order to clear me and make me a vessel for other truths.

"You, too," she assured me, "are the Divine Feminine, and even when you didn't recognize her, she was present in you, and, yes, you were a degraded version of her. What else could you be while she was in exile, in exile from your own heart and mind and in exile from every molecule of your body, which is her body, too? But as you have worked to come to consciousness about your own wounding, you have released her, too, for she was wounded every time you or any other woman was degraded and wounded. You are restoring and healing her as you restore and heal yourself."

That was a lot to take in, but many paradigms came to me along the way to help my mind grasp enough, so that it let go and let me learn how to listen and begin to see the world differently. But my human mind still had human questions, and my human heart still wanted human answers.

Again, my brother Arthur chose not to call me back, but his twenty-eight-year-old daughter called. Every now and then I e-mail her and send her pictures of my family. She sent me birthday photos that I shared with my mother on New Year's Eve. Arthur looks like he did in high school—just older. Whatever secrets he knows will probably remain with him because I don't see the family coming together again. Perhaps when my mother dies, we will all gather one last time, the way my mother's family did when Grandmother Morgan died.

Chapter 64

The Man in the Bathtub

I had a session with Joan right after I tried to contact Arthur.

"Joan, I have had visions again, wide awake visions about the chakras and about mandalas and about the labyrinth. Mandalas are like chakras, the visions say, and so are labyrinths, in that they are all multi-dimensional.

"You know how when you see a mandala it looks flat, two-dimensional? Well, they aren't. Like the Tibetan sand drawings of temples that look two-dimensional because we see them from a bird's eye view, all mandalas, like chakras, and like rose windows, too, are multi-dimensional. The labyrinth is also. It has lines of energy that rise up from it, and I can't quite visualize it yet, but I believe it, too, will form a globe, a ball of energy like the chakras do."

"You haven't talked quite this way about the chakras for several years, and certainly not mandalas or labyrinths before. Go on."

"Well, you know I have been reading about labyrinths because I walked that one, as have you, down in Laguna Beach; and in the sanctuary garden that my friend Kitty Bass has in Rockville, of all places, she built a labyrinth that I also walk.

"The whole area of sacred geometry is starting to fascinate me. I have begun to read more about Chartres cathedral, for example. You know I visited that cathedral when I was twenty-one or twenty-two, and I had quite an experience there, though I did not understand it. I am starting to understand that the sacred knowledge and the sacred geometry which guided the construction of the cathedral was specifically designed to connect to the human energy field to assist it in opening to other dimensional realities. So far, I only have a glimmering of what this means, but while I was meditating, the image of the rose windows and mandalas as far more than three-dimensional came to me. Then I read about labyrinths. One writer actually has a diagram of the Cretan labyrinth and shows which of the chakras each leg of the labyrinth balances!"

"This is really interesting."

"Yes, and it all connects back to my own body/spirit, my own chakra system, my own energy and other dimensional bodies."

"In what way?"

"I know you know this stuff, Joan, but here is how it presents itself to me. We are more than flesh and blood. The ancients knew this. Christians say we are flesh and spirit, but they present the two as being in constant combat. I don't think the body and the spirit are at odds with one another, except when the mind interferes with the higher role of the flesh and sets itself up above it.

"Now to make it personal, very personal. I believe I have held the energy of abuse—of rape—in my second chakra where my bladder pain is. The second chakra is linked to the emotional body. It governs our relationships with others, including our sexual relationships. I believe that lust and anger ripped me open when I was a baby. I believe that the lust and anger—being 'pissed off'—lodged in my second chakra. I turned the anger against myself. The lust activates lust in others, and I mistake that lust for love. Something like that."

"Are you remembering something, Sandra?"

"*Not with my mind.* I still have no conventional memory of my father's abuse of me, but I believe the energy blueprint exists in my body and that the work I do in meditation, Healing Touch, aromatherapy, and all the other ways I connect with spirit, keeps putting me back into balance. In the process the old imprints are released, and when they are, my *knowings* occur. The *knowings* are in the form of images. Sometimes the images are new to me. Other times, the images are old ones that I understand in new ways."

"Yes."

"Joan, do you recall that memory I have, one of the two memories I have of my father? The one where he is in the bathtub, sitting in yellow water, and I come in, sit on the toilet, and am startled by his presence?"

"Yes, I do. How old were you?"

"Not even two. He died in August before I turned two in October in 1950."

"I remember this story, but remind me again of the details. What did you see?" Joan asked.

"Well, I froze when I turned and saw him there. I *remember* seeing him there. I remember that time and one other time with him, the time I saw him in his coffin. Now to see a dead man, especially if that man is your father, is shocking. But why was I so shocked at seeing him in the bathtub? It wasn't like I saw his genitals—at least, I don't have an image of that.

"In the memory I see myself reach up for the glass doorknob, which came off in my hand as I opened the door. Then I see myself from across the room. *From the perspective he would have had,* I see myself on the toilet. I see my little checked dress. It sticks to me like it's wet. I don't see my panties anywhere. I see the shock, the pain, the tears on my face. And I see him in the tub from where I sit on the toilet. He looks at me full face. I can't see his body, except for his shoulders and his head. I see the water, though, and it is yellow, bright yellow, like he urinated in it. He was a grown man. Why would he sit in his own urine?"

"What happened next?"

"I don't remember. But I *know*."

"Tell me what you know."

"Well, it's all squashed together. I mean it is all out of sequence. At least, the urine in the water is. This is hard to talk about. It's hard to know and not be able to prove."

"I know. Just tell me what you want to when you're ready."

"Let me start over. I rushed into the house from being outside and playing. I remember the clear glass doorknob on the bathroom door. I must have been in a hurry, either because I had to go so badly or because I wanted to get back outside fast and play. I opened the door, and there he was. He must have grabbed me. That would account for the shock of remembering.

"He must have grabbed me fast *like he did Grandma Pope's chickens* and pulled me into the tub before I had time to urinate. And I must have peed all over myself and right into the bathtub. That must have been my urine and not his!

"And I must have tried to scream, but either nobody else was around to hear, or he held his hand over my mouth to quiet me, or maybe my mother did come. Maybe she did know. Maybe she was going to leave him—not the other way around like Dolores said. I don't know."

By then, I was sick to my stomach, and my bladder was burning just from remembering, like it burns every time I am in danger of being misused or of misusing myself.

"I understand. I understand."

Had I been in California, seated across from her, there would have been a different kind of time for recovery. Tea. Small talk. A peanut butter and jelly sandwich. A hug. Far away in Wisteria, there were words of comfort, of concern, and Joan would have let me go, but I wanted to continue.

"Ugly stuff, isn't it?"

"It doesn't bother me to hear. Your pain is so real, and you have every right to express it."

"But what if I'm wrong?"

"You'll know if you are."

"But I still can't prove he, or anybody else, abused me. He died within a few months of that—that time. He was diagnosed with melanoma, and he died within six weeks. My mother said it was horrible to see."

"Have you ever dreamed about him?"

"No, but I did have a vision once. I was looking at his army picture. He was in uniform. There was a backdrop of a hill and some trees beyond it. He had on wire-rimmed glasses, and his right eye turned toward the wall. Then I was on a pine-covered hilltop with my two daughters. He joined us there. He told me he was proud of me and all I had done with my life. I asked him why he had to go away, and he told me, 'It had nothing to do with you.'

"I suppose that could mean that what I *know* happened, didn't occur. Or it could mean he had to go away because of who he was, *not because of who I am,* because he was so out of control and didn't know how to redeem himself.

"I do know people can bring disease to themselves, unconsciously, when they are suffering spiritually. I have learned that imbalances manifest first in the spiritual body, then in the emotional/mental bodies, and then in the physical bodies, to separate the 'bodies' in ways they really aren't separate. Each body is intertwined with all of the others, like a garment that's knit with many threads, and each thread affects all of the others.

"I *know* that's why my bladder hurts sometimes. It's remembering the physical wound, and the spiritual wound is still healing."

"What more do you feel has to happen before it can heal?" Joan asked.

"I don't know. Maybe this. Maybe knowing. Maybe admitting I know. Maybe accepting what I *know* is true without having proof that others will believe, like Nancy Drew always finds after she intuits the truth. I feel well most of the time, but I feel the panic in that part of my body as I reconstruct that time. To me, that means there's something important and something unresolved. I am holding something in that needs to be let out."

"Your experience and behavior in the world does fit the pattern of abuse, Sandra."

"I know. And, Joan, I know someone abused me. I know whoever he was, he must have reached for me many times before that bathroom moment, for it feels as though it came naturally to him, and my shock at seeing him feels like I knew I was in for it when I raced in and shut the door behind me. I felt trapped, even though I had the doorknob in my hand, and obviously, the door wasn't locked.

"But maybe I thought I couldn't open the door because I did have the doorknob in my hand. I was only two! I was starting to make memories, though. Still, all I really recall with my memory is him in the yellow water, me with the glass doorknob, and me sitting on the toilet in that wet dress. The rest is gone." I paused.

"Joan!"

"Yes?"

"I just had an in-rush of knowing, like a current went through me. It wasn't the first time he hurt me, but it was the first time he hurt me in that way. It was the first time he penetrated me! That is why my body remembers it down there. It was new. I was older. Before that time, it must have been oral, like it was with Dolores. Sucking would have come naturally to me."

We parted after a few more exchanges. Twenty-five hundred miles away from Joan and her kitchen, I made my own peanut butter and jelly sandwich, and I was very generous with both the peanut butter and the jelly, just like Joan would have been. I sat in the sunshine on my back door steps, looked up at the sky and the pine trees, and ate my sandwich. The brick steps were warm beneath my bare feet, and the pines lifted my spirits.

That night I had a confirming dream. More and more, I looked to my dream life for confirmation and stopped trying to follow the clues into the outer world. The dream brought me horror and then peace as I let its deeper meaning sink into me.

Chapter 65

The Green Cobra Is Passed on to Me, and I Turn Lead into Gold

I slept uneasily that night because I dreamed of snakes. Snakes have shown up at key moments in my outer and inner worlds all of my life. I know that somewhere along the way, the snake got a bad reputation, probably because it was associated with the Mother Goddess traditions that Christianity came into conflict with.

Many scholars have documented this, and I read several of them to understand the role of snakes, specifically of cobras, as they continued to appear in my dreams. What I learned about their symbolism of rebirth and the power of the Mother Goddess reassured me, and I recognized something important and powerful was moving in my psyche when I woke from dreams of cobras.

The dreams themselves were often terrifying, and I often woke myself up when I had them. Such is the strength of several thousand years of maligning the Mother Goddess and her symbols. Of course, cobras are poisonous, and therefore, dangerous in waking life. But never in my dreams have they harmed me. Frightened me, yes. And I know it is wise in the presence of such power to be in awe, if not in terror. Terror certainly clears the mind of the mundane and focuses it on that which is important. Awe opens the spirit to the divine. So when the following dream came, it terrified me and woke me. I went into my healing room, a place where I felt safe, and the terror changed to awe. I returned to my bed to write down the dream and let it teach me its meaning.

Here is the dream:

I am with my colleague Michael and other people from work. We are addressing students. They are gathered on the ground around the old steps to Dolores's former church, the First Original Free Will Baptist Church in Wisteria. Michael tells the students something in a low-key way, punctuating his presentation with his direct gaze and his pleasant laugh. I add something.

Then a woman with long, dry brown hair, styled so that it does not move, addresses the students. She talks about the need to teach responsibility. She seems very old-fashioned in her dress and maybe conservative in her ideas. She is running for office. She is some kind of public figure. She uses the analogy of the rocker arms in engines to make her point about creating smooth-running students. She talks about three sets of rocker arms for an engine. One set runs at 100 rpm. Another set runs at 200 rpm. A third set has one rocker arm that runs at 100 rpm and one that runs at 1425 rpm.

As I listen to her, I wonder what all of this means. She says she usually has these items with her to demonstrate, but instead she describes them. In the dream, I envision them as metal semicircular disks that have the center cut out. I see them as if they are set on a conical stand. I look around. Only a few students still remain. They have taken advantage of the outdoor setting and have slipped away. It looks a little like Janss steps at UCLA to me.

I look back to the speaker. She stands on the top slab of the circular steps that used to lead into the church. In waking reality, these steps have been replaced by rectangular ones and a wheel chair ramp. I am standing on one of the original circular slabs, several steps below the speaker. I see a light green snake, with a slightly darker green horizontal stripe on it, crawl from under her hair at her forehead. It stretches its head out and then starts to move into the open.

A young female student, who has remained to listen, calls to her, "Ma'am, there is a snake in your hair!"

Just as the woman turns, the snake falls out of her hair. I am right below her. I am lying down. A green cobra drops toward me like it is going for my hair. I jump and I wake up.

This was the third snake dream in a week. The first one was a brown snake that I saw but could not catch as it slid into my closet in my bedroom. The second snake dream had two snakes, electric green snakes, entwined around a staff, like the staff that Aesclepius carries, like the twin streams of kundalini that rise from the base of the spine and encircle each of the seven chakras. Then came this third dream right after I had just talked to Joan about the knowing I had about when my father had raped me.

I went to my healing room. I wrote:

What have I evoked? Medusa? Certainly my revelations will petrify some people, but I really believe that for those like me, who were wounded before memory could name and record the event, for those my quest to know will be healing. I believe my growing willingness to rely on dream and on what the spirit body has recorded will also be healing.

Then I remembered Hathor. Hathor's headdress often includes a cobra, a symbol of regeneration, of rebirth. I wondered if I had gone too far in writing this book. I asked Mary Magdalene for guidance. She came to me in inner vision and in light. No, she said, not too far. "You are doing what needs to be done."

I asked for her protection. I was still frightened.

I returned to my bedroom. With the light on, I wrote the following:

"That was a terrible image I put forth about my father. Would I have been better off, would others have been better served, if I had never put the image on paper?" I asked Mary Magdalene.

"No, Sandra. Your body, your chakras held the energy of abuse. Your mind sought an image, a recollection that could *contain it. Your abuse was known and meant to be brought forth when you are able to dispel it, meant to be brought into consciousness. It is powerful knowledge you have gained, as is represented by the snake, and it is not going to go away. It does not have to be hidden in the way that the traditional staid woman in the dream hid it. Brought to consciousness, the information no longer is poisonous, and you do not have to carry it in your spiritual crown chakra either.*

"That is the old way—to hide the truth you know from others, if not from yourself, like the woman who talks about other topics, misdirecting her desire to tell the truth away from herself and admonishing the students to seek what she, herself, cannot see. The power of the snake is with the woman, but she cannot let it be seen. She hides the snake in her stiff, unmoving hair which covers her spiritual or crown chakra. She is rigid like her hair for, in her era, it would have been dangerous for her to reveal her power."

I continued to write though the voice faded. I understood. The young girl, the young, reborn part of me, saw the snake. She called it what it was, as I have. No longer are witches burned at the stake, and no longer do women, such as I, have to fear ex-communications like the one I had witnessed in Dolores's old church for a woman who had committed adultery. The old steps to the sanctuary, the steps to the holy place, have been removed. There are new steps now, new ways to encounter God/Goddess.

In the dream, Michael had stopped talking. He had stopped trying to make nice. All of the male students had gone away—not the female student. The feeling is that the women have to do this part of coming into consciousness by themselves. The men can go off and play hooky.

Then the voice became clear again, "Sandra, you don't have that avenue available to you any longer. You can't ignore the snake. You see the snake, and that means the old blind ways are not available. On the old circular slab steps, that are already gone and cannot lead you to the Divine, she is passing the serpent, the cobra, the goddess energy to you. She is the Mother Goddess, imaged in the style of your childhood years."

I still didn't understand the rocker arms, so I went to *Wikipedia* for some quick help. I saw that the rocker arms, as I had drawn them from the dream, (not like they really look in engines) looked like the crescent of the sun, the emblem of Horus, that Hathor wears on her head. And they also had the shape of the *menit*, the front part of an ornamental necklace that is shaped like a crescent and is symbolic of the uterus. This *menit* is often depicted touching the king, Horus, because it is through the Queen Hathor that he gets his power.

And the *knowing* came: only through bringing these wounds to consciousness, *including body consciousness*, will a vehicle capable of carrying the Goddess energy return *for that vehicle will be my healed consciousness, my wholeness, as it joins with yours and yours and yours.*

I slept again. And dreamed again. This time the dream was almost a direct confirmation of the story I had surmised was true about my father's abuse of me and my mother's neglect. I accepted that dream, with its almost one-to-one correspondence as a gift, given from the record, held in my body by the imprint made in the energy field. I imagine that this record, where every *hair on my head is known*, may be the mind or heart of Goddess/God, or what some call the akashic records.

Here is that dream, which came after the snake dream, which I wrote down around four o'clock in the morning:

I am watching the children. I am with a young Dolores. It is either Dolores or Eula (Grandmother Blair), a younger Eula than I ever knew, though, if it is her. Or it is my own mother, large like she always was when she was pregnant. There is a man around also. *This is the Portland Street house in Greensboro.*

One of the little girls comes into the room where I am. She has pulled the plaster off the door and walls of the bathroom and has been eating it. I immediately take control and stick my fingers down her throat and make her vomit.

Up come the plaster and paint and also the glass doorknob. I tell the others that she needs to go to the doctor, that the paint is old, and may be lead based, and therefore, toxic. They don't seem to have my concern. I say that, at least, they ought to call the health department and see what can be done.

No one wants to do anything for the little girl. She is bare-chested and running around in just her panties and her hair is cropped short and looks spiky and uncontrollable with a cowlick like little Sandra. I say that the lead will stay in her body and poison her if someone doesn't help her. They won't do anything. I say her stomach needs to be pumped out. Someone says that considering the mess on the floor, which they point out I need to clean up, there's nothing left in her stomach.

The dream felt like an exorcism, and it felt like Hathor's work, especially since my cowlick was so prominent in the dream, and Hathor is often portrayed as cow with the sun disk between her horns, or a queenly woman who wears the sun disk and horns on her head, or as a woman with a cow's head. Hathor is the goddess, called forth as Sekhmet to punish the humans who had lost their connection with Ra. Ra called her forth when he could not draw the people back to him by himself.

She was bloodthirsty, and once she was set on her mission, she was unstoppable. She killed thousands. When Ra was ready to forgive humanity, when he had enough of the bloodletting, he was unable to recall Sekhmet. Instead, he had to fool her into stopping the killing on her own. To do this, he had a field flooded with beer that had been tinted red by blood red ochre. Sekhmet saw it and rejoiced, thinking it was blood. She drank it all, and she became transformed into the Goddess of Beauty and Love, and her name was changed to Hathor.

The dream was teaching that by following my rage against the excesses of men, I, too, would eventually be transformed into the Goddess of Beauty and Love. I sent the dream and my understanding of it to Joan, and she called me back. Her message to me—it was, indeed, a dream of transformation.

She told me, "This is just what really makes your book, *your* book. It is more than a novel or memoir. It is some kind of new format, but this is really, really wonderful. The dream is extraordinary. I was just so struck by the barfing up of the lead because lead is related to Saturn, the Lord of Karma; so the alchemical association of this is that you have turned the lead into gold in your writing and in your life and moved beyond the limits of karma. Congratulations!"

I called her back.

"What else about the dream speaks to you?" Joan asked.

"The doorknob. The knob really was glass like it was in the dream. I remember that. Now I feel like it's a diamond really. Something hard and beautiful that refracts the light and has been hidden inside me since I was a small child eating the leaden part of life that poisoned me in that bathroom. And before. And, Joan, you know that for years I have not locked a bathroom door, not even in a public place."

"I remember that. You've talked about it before."

"Yeah. I'm afraid the lock will break, the handle will come off, and I won't be able to get out again. I thought I had locked myself in my apartment bathroom about ten years ago, when I lived in the Montrose apartment. I panicked and screamed for help. I was about to take the back of the toilet off and pound my way through the door when I calmed myself by breathing. I tried the door again, and it opened. The lock was fine. It was as though I had remembered something or re-enacted it."

"It may have been a memory surfacing or a moment that was suddenly symbolic of an internal state," Joan said. "What is so striking in the dream is how you, as the grown-up, are able to move beyond the limitation of the past, beyond karma, and when you do, the little girl with spiky hair appears. Didn't you tell me once that your mother kept your hair extremely short so that your cowlick didn't sprig up?"

"Yes! Once she even put Vaseline on my whole head and plastered my hair down. She made elaborate spit curls. I was about three years old."

"Well, this little girl is surely sprigging!"

After the call, I looked again at the *menit*. Often it was worn as a necklace with the *menit* worn over the goddess's front, and over her back a counterpoise was worn to hold the heavy necklace in place. That counterpoise is shaped like a *matrass*, the long-necked round-bellied vessel used by *alchemists*. I had missed that important detail until Joan guided me toward the alchemical imagery in the dream. The matrass on the back was located right where Sai Baba had asked me to place my hands into the white light several years before!

Hard as it is to tell these stories, I had received verification that I was doing the Great Work to heal my life. This confirmation gave me enough heart to dialogue with the talking baby and transform more lead into gold.

Chapter 66

I Talk to the Talking Baby

This is how I began my dialogue with the talking baby, and how it became *Her* revelation:

To the talking baby: You seem to want to tell me something. In my dreams for years I have always been so surprised, and even amused by the fact that you talk, that I don't ask you anything. I only remember one comment you made about my soiled diaper. All you have to say that will help me is welcome.

Baby: There is much to say.

The inner scene shifts. Mary Magdalene appears. The talking baby disappears.
I didn't understand why Mary Magdalene had come to me when I was trying to talk with the baby, but of course, I was thrilled.

Me: Thank you, Mary Magdalene, for sending your daughter Tamara to me.

Mary Magdalene: You are welcome, Sandra. She wanted to come. She asked to come. She, too, felt wounded. She is the guardian of all baby girls.

Me: Wounded? Abused?

Mary Magdalene: No, she wasn't abused the way you were precisely, but being female meant her value as the heir, was not acknowledged. The moment she arrived and was examined, her vulva, too, condemned her to the *less than* in that time. That is why I called her my "lesser angel."

Me: Why?

Mary Magdalene: It was an ironic, endearing, playful term. Rather like when you would answer one of your twin daughters' questions about why you did or said something for or about the other twin daughter. You would say, "Because I love her more," but you didn't really mean it. You were trying to bring that daughter's worst fear to the surface, so they both could understand that you knew they feared this. You wanted them to see that you could joke about it because it was so far from the truth.

Me: Like that.

Mary Magdalene: Tamara felt *less than*. So I called her my lesser angel to show her how absurd it was for anyone to think of her as *less than*. She understood my irony.

Me: You call her the angel protector of baby girls, but I was unprotected.

Mary Magdalene: Remember also that she is the Angel of Reversals. Remember the mirror revelation of her name to you?

Me: Yes...

Mary Magdalene: Remember the thirteenth fairy godmother and your intuitions about her role as the one to pull the young girl under, down into the unconscious, and teach her all she needed to survive in the world until I could re-emerge?

Me: Yes.

Mary Magdalene: That was a reversal, and Tamara's wisdom was what was imparted.

Me: So She was there? When...

Mary Magdalene: She held you in the seventh dimension while your third eye was ripped open before its usual human time for opening.

Me: Can you show me?

Mary Magdalene: You have already seen. Every time you closed your eyes in early childhood, she led you back through rings of blue light to the deep place of knowing you were safe and known and connected with me.

Me: Can you show me the baby being wounded?

Mary Magdalene: Only in the seventh and some sixth vibrational energy patterns, not in the images human memory records because your ability to record these was not yet formed. You had not the conceptual understanding that would allow you to make pictures and store them.

Me: The crib? The playpen I see in recollection?

Mary Magdalene: Let me take you back. You are protected and ready and loved and all that happened then is known now by your conscious mind, so it will not shock you into unconsciousness again. You can hold the energy of knowing.

That is why your clients, who were abused before and after memory, seek you out for their own healing. Higher vibrational levels through you are attracting them, and for their own good and healing, the same way lower vibrational levels through you in the past have attracted men who sensed your brokenness and used you. What they really sought was the healing of their own brokenness, which they sensed you held.

They could not receive it because they were still held by an older vibrational matrix in which their energy was only for taking from others, not seeking within themselves. This, too, will change.

Me: So we can travel back to the vibrational levels, both the lower and the higher ones?

Mary Magdalene: You believe still that you can know with your mind's memory what your body knows vibrationally, what your sickness, which was healed, taught you and what your behaviors, which out-pictured your wounding again and again, showed you.

You cannot apprehend this with your human mind in the sense of replaying a movie. Not now.

Me: Ever?

Mary Magdalene: You can know vibrationally where you went when the body was being accosted. If you want to know more about your earthly parentage and whether or not the man you think was your father, actually was, and whether or not that man or some other individual man accosted you, you have earthly ways to find out more.

Yes, the genetic testing is available, and your mother can tell you much more than she already has. Her memory carries some of the images you seek, but it will be a great shock to her to encounter them.

Suddenly I felt afraid. I wondered if I were making all of this up.

Me: Mary Magdalene, is this really you?

Mary Magdalene: Me. And you. And Tamara. And all that is. Another daughter you are to me. And, as with you and your daughters, she is the best I have to offer. Are you ready to see vibrationally? She can take you there.

Me: Will you stay, too?

Mary Magdalene: I always have. I always will. I can be no other place.

Chapter 67

The Rape of the Goddess

Tamara came to me as a whirlwind of colors with wings, filled with the rushing exuberant movement of a young woman. Joyous laughter in motion she was, and she swept me up into her being. This is what I saw:

I am entering a center channel, and it is expanding. It is a channel with funnel openings coming into it on either side. The central channel is light brown, and it has scroll-type writing or symbols on it. There is pressure on one side of the channel. I feel like someone is pushing down on me. I start to get images.

Mary Magdalene speaks to me again. "Sandra, those are images you formed later, not memory. Just let yourself go."

I do and I feel something—some energy intercede. I feel a fullness come and slip into inner spaces, and I see/sense myself going up. Then I emerge into a beautiful blue light. I know something is happening to my body. Pressure. A feeling of not being able to breathe.

A memory of a television special on abused children comes into vivid recollection. One fifteen-month-old child's experience has stayed in my mind, and that part of the program starts to replay. I see the baby, a picture of it after it was rescued. It is gaunt, skeletal, nearly dead. The narrator says the child existed only on semen for several months.

I feel as though I will vomit.

My mind will not shut off.

Did my belief that my father sexually abused me orally come from that moment of revulsion at the possibility? Dolores had said it, too. "It was oral." She was eleven. He was eighteen. Surely, if it were oral, it was fellatio. Was this real or was I still wading through ideas from others that had been put into my field, introjects? I wanted to run away.

Mary Magdalene again intervened. "Sandra, you are protected. Trust your intuition that comes from the outer world images, but let the images go. Do not search memory. The answers are not there. Stay with *this* experience."

Pressure. Color. Changing patterns of color. Blues. Then pure white in the middle of pure blue. I see a baby being pushed up through the water until it emerges. The scale of this is huge. I remember this place. *I have traveled here before.* Mary Magdalene does not call me back from this imagery. I do not know why. I am almost overwhelmed.

Then the colors again and changing shapes. Then the knowledge that She, Tamara, is taking my place, and that this is what it means to be loved and connected to the Goddess. Tamara has reached down and pulled me up into my expanded self, and she has taken my place. The horror of what this means hits me:

My father is raping the Goddess who appears in the form of Tamara, the daughter of Yeshua and Mary Magdalene. How could it ever be otherwise when one of us, who are emanations of Her, is abused?

Then I understand that it is She who my father, in his warped way, seeks through me. *And he is killing himself as he harms me, for he is connected to me; he is me, too, and what he does to harm me is mirrored back, through the intervention of the Goddess of Reversals, to him.* She did no harm to my father. She could not receive his willful negative energy because of her divinity, and his physical being could not transform the negative energy that was mirrored back to him and experienced by him in the instant he began to misuse another.

He would not survive this encounter with the divine. Perhaps that is what is meant when we are told that we cannot look upon the face of God/ Goddess and live. Perhaps it is our own unworthiness that turns back toward us and destroys us.

My father would die before I was two, and I would spend most of my life recovering from losing that part of myself that was his responsibility to activate to allow me to move, with protection and confidence, in the outer world. I was left with a wounded will that made it difficult for me to function at the level of my talent and ability. I was left with a wounded heart that could only attract men like him, men who were users or abusers, even though they wanted to be saviors or healers.

But the Christos energy in the form of Tamara had "interceded" and prevented the wound from touching my Soul! *For we are so loved, that we are so protected.*

Tamara could not see with my human eyes, but she saw through my third eye, which was torn open the moment the abuse began. She flowed into my human form, so she could see and hold the energy of divine protection for me. Her intervention for me left my intuition heightened for my whole life. This I *know*.

Mary Magdalene was still there guiding the "vibrational" journey. These things I "saw," I did not see with my human eyes. I saw with my inner vibrational eyes.

Me: Is this what happens for everyone who is abused? Does the goddess energy intervene?

Mary Magdalene: It is always present, but it depends on the Soul's purpose and even the age of the child. Babies always have this protection. Always Tamara is there. And, yes, she is there and there and there all at once and forever until my return and this return and even beyond that.

While you were away, you were protected and taught. When Tamara returned you to your body, she left her essence. She always does.

Me: And that essence? Is that the healing energy I feel?

Mary Magdalene: No. The essence is more like a genetic shift or a blueprint that can allow healing energy to enter that way. Healing energy can enter many ways.

Me: I feel like I am forgetting a part of the vision already, like I do my dreams if I don't write them down quickly. Can you help me remember?

Mary Magdalene: This is it, Sandra. The pathway created by Tamara's presence is what allows *you* to open to healing energies. It works differently for each individual, though the mind may make some generalizations. But the human idea that the *wounding* itself opens to healing energies is not quite all there is to it. And the wounding is not necessary for the opening to occur and for the healing powers to emerge or for you to wish to use them to heal others, although this is a pattern that some choose, as you know, from the story of Chiron.

The entry of the Tamara energy is one way to open the human to the healing energies and, in particular, sexual wounding always calls Her forth and it is her presence, *not the wound*, which creates an opening for the Divine Feminine to become activated. It can become activated in other ways. The wounding is not a part of the divine plan.

Me: I think I am remembering and understanding the lesson.

Mary Magdalene: Sandra, the choices to reject Tamara, and Yeshua himself, and me as The Magdalene, were human choices, not soul choices, as was your father's choice to fall into unconsciousness and misuse the trust you had placed in him. When these kinds of human choices, which arise when free will is distorted, are made, we reach out in ways we can to restore the Divine in humanity. We can leave traces of the Divine Feminine for you to discover and manifest. And we do. And you have.

Me: And my father?

Mary Magdalene: He was given other opportunities to release himself from the destructive pattern he had chosen and that his time and place allowed him to choose.

Me: The cancer? He chose that?

Mary Magdalene: Other choices he made created the cancer. That and other choices he refused to make. He held great anger, fear, and resentment inside his body.

Me: So he chose death?

Mary Magdalene: Unconsciously, as you would say, yes. I would say he did not choose life. He had brought with him into your dimension the remembered ways of blending with all else, and he failed to learn how to manifest these powers properly in your dimension.

He mistook the soul energies he held for physical and sexual energies; and he degraded himself and others, for he did not become conscious of the soul's intention behind his "seeking" impulses. The time and place into which he was born made it easy for him to fall into that destructive pattern, but that was not his mission or the soul's intention.

His spirit withered, and the disease came in.

Me: What was his soul's intention?

Mary Magdalene: To help break the pattern of abuse and misuse he saw from afar.

Me: For so long, I perceived him as my protector, and I mourned the loss of him! Even though he was dead and out of my life, I still clung to the belief that I was worthy and loved by him because of the story regarding my birth and his intervention when my mother would not nurse me. I believed that, had he lived, I would have been protected.

Mary Magdalene: Human consciousness is complex, and when it consciously joins with the divine, as it always may, it creates more of what is needed by all. What you believed could have protected you was an illusion, but you were protected always because you longed for it.

Your knowledge of protection and your desire for it, even the belief you held that your father was still somehow your protector from the other dimension, allowed you some freedom of soul movement and soul growth. Even the illusion of protection created protection, for the mind is in the service of the imagination.

Now you can release that illusion of the source of your protection. Under that illusion, you became strong, though, because you created protection for yourself through conscious connection with the divine. Again, then, in a reversal, you have learned the pattern of trust and that has freed you.

Me: Like through my love of Nancy Drew stories, I unconsciously developed my intuition, through my belief in my father's invisible protection, I unconsciously opened to invisible divine protection?

Mary Magdalene: That is how it has been for you. Again, your pattern is your pattern. It is not the only way.

Me: I want to say thank you. Thank you, thank you for reversing my belief that the wounding was necessary for the healing energies to emerge and that it was part of the divine plan. I could never reconcile that with the experience of divine love. And thank you for being present always, for these teachings. I must rest. Love and Light. Love and Light. Love and Light.

I took a short nap and arose feeling refreshed. I had housework to do. While I was cleaning the laundry room, I picked up a stack of books I had placed on top of the dryer several weeks before. I had put the books there, a temporary home for them, because I had clients coming and didn't want these rather esoteric books stacked next to my chair in my healing room.

I moved the books from the dryer and set them on a utility shelf, admonishing myself for leaving them on the dryer for so long. As I did, one of the books caught my eye—*Jung and the Lost Gospels.* The book came to me from an acquaintance who gave me boxes of books on healing that had belonged to her deceased mother-in-law. I had hardly handled the book before, but I took it into my room and sat down with it.

Planning to preview it to see if I wanted to read it after the book I was currently reading, I flipped it open. My eyes fell first on page 143, on which was recorded the creation of the woman Zoë, later called Eve and created by Sophia as a helper for Adam. Eve was raped by the chief of the rulers of the tyrant angels, but *"the shining spirit of wisdom that inhabited Eve, fled while this ravishment took place, so that only the human Eve was shamed, but not Zoë, the living spirit."*

Again, I had received immediate confirmation in the "real" world of my inner world story, for in remarkable ways, the story of Zoë and the tyrant angels mirrored the one Mary Magdalene had just told me about myself. It was a serendipitous affirmation that the spirit world operates for me in the manner the channeled voice of Mary Magdalene had described, and therefore, it was affirmation that my vision was "real."

Here is that story of Zoë and the Tyrant Angels, which was opened to me that day:

Sophia was the celestial mother of all things, and while alone in the darkness of an abyss, she brought forth a son by herself. Stephan Hoeller in *Jung and the Lost Gospels* says, when the child appeared before her, "She saw that he was a shape changer: he appeared in the shape of a serpent with the face of a lion and out of his eyes there came forth lightning flashes" (141). Sophia was sorry she had created him, and she repented. She called him Yaldobaoth, and he rebelled against her and created another world based on power.

Sophia, or Wisdom, decided to secretly aid those Yaldobaoth had created in his own flawed image. She came close to the earth and conveyed her wisdom and love to it, and placed her "splendid archetypal patterns" in the fabric of the world that Yaldobaoth and the tyrant angels had made and from them came forth archetypal man (142).

These archetypal patterns were revealed to the tyrant angels and to Yaldobaoth who claimed to be the one and only God. He and the angels turned from the archetypal Man in horror because it far exceeded anything they could create. When Yaldobaoth did create a man, it was a creature that could only crawl on the earth like a worm, and Sophia again intervened and breathed the life of spirit into him (142).

When this man, Adam, was attacked because he was so much greater than the tyrant angels and Yaldobaoth, Sophia created a helper, a woman, whose name was Zoë, later to be known as Eve, and placed this feminine spirit inside Adam so that the tyrant angels would not know that the divine feminine was present (143). The tyrants imprisoned Adam in a garden where he would be distracted from finding and developing the spark of divinity within him, so with the guidance of Sophia and other heavenly powers, the woman came forth out of Adam to help him find it, and the woman was known as Eve (142).

What Hoeller tells us next is what my eyes fell upon that day after receiving the vision of how Tamara protected me from the horror of experiencing the sexual abuse I *know* I underwent, but cannot prove:

"...The chief of the rulers recognized her as having the light of Sophia in her, and he was enraged. He pursued her all over the garden, and having subdued her, raped her, and she conceived two sons by him...

"But the shining spirit of wisdom that inhabited Eve, fled while this ravishment took place, so that only the human Eve was shamed, but not Zoë, the living spirit" (emphasis added)(143).

The answer to my question, "Is this real, Mary Magdalene?" came in this form, in a book I had ignored, a book written thirty years earlier that had, almost by happenstance, come to me. Here was a story that mirrored my own story and explained again how my living spirit had fled the rape and was still whole. Because of other such moments, like when I was so sick and was guided to the book on how to heal my unusual condition, I felt the presence of spirit saying, "Yes, this experience is real."

So have I come to accept that I was abused by the personal father *and* by the archetypal patriarchal energy that devalues the divine feminine and permeates the consciousness of male and female alike when the goddess is exiled.

I have come to understand that in other dimensions, beings move through others and blend in ways that only sex approximates for most people in this dimension. I know, too, that in some early worship of the divine feminine, when the Goddess was revered, physical intimacy was a part of spiritual initiation and opening of the chakras.

Even though this may have been what my father was seeking, none of this changes the damage done to me or to him by his degradation of the goddess. He had the power to seek the divine feminine in the world and to help restore her as others, both male and female, are doing today.

Instead, when my father raped me and my aunt, he raped the Goddess, the divine feminine in the human form.

That was the secret I had been living with. That was the black hole that distorted my life and had threatened to suck all of the light out of me.

Chapter 68

More Help from the Seen
and the Unseen Worlds

My life continues to weave together visions, dreams, and outer world experience. One world mirrors and heals the other, transforming me daily. Often the outer world experiences evoke some intuitive understanding, or conversely, some intuitive understanding clarifies some outer world experience. I visited my mother on New Year's Eve and the weaving continued.

My mother lives on a tiny tongue of land that juts out into a large clear water pond that is surrounded by pine trees. Years ago the seven-foot deep pond, which covers about three acres, was dredged out in order to get sand to use in building the Pee Dee River Bridge. Her house is a small affair and is almost completely surrounded by water as it sits on that little peninsula.

The den looks out through a small screened-in porch onto the water. She says that twenty-five years ago while she was still in Florida, she daydreamed about and then drew a small picture of a place just like the one she now owns. It was to be her retirement home, and it is. I believe her story. She has always had a different relationship to the world, an ability to telephone me or Debbie just at the moment we are about to call her, and often we find ourselves getting the same insight at the same time.

Beyond her back porch and down the three steps is a clothesline on the left. When there are clothes on the line, they partially block the view of the pond. Two days before my visit, my mother sat there in her little den while her husband Raeford showered in the late afternoon. The blue herons had returned and stalked along the banks of the pond for several minutes before something stirred and caused the herons to launch themselves into the blue South Carolina sky. Mama had been watching them, and seeing the old cleaning rags she'd washed earlier in the day and hung on the line. Raeford was to bring them in after he showered, but she wasn't willing to look at them a minute longer.

Up she sprang, out she went, down the rags came, and on the way back into the house, she slipped and fell. She cracked two ribs, fractured her humerus in her left arm, and fractured her left shoulder.

I arrived a day later to spend some time helping with her recovery. It was New Year's Eve. Early in the evening, the TV was off, and the talk went hither and yon. Debbie and I sat on the couch in the little den, and Mom and Raeford sat across from us. Somehow the topic of Grandmother and Granddaddy Morgan came up. Mom brought it up, I believe.

"I still can't believe my mama let Daddy treat us like he did. I know he was wrong, and I have forgiven him. I finally was able to forgive him for doing what no father should ever do, but it wasn't until Daddy got sick and was in the bed up at Jolee's, that I could do it," she said. Jolee is her youngest sister.

"But I did it. And I still can't understand why my mama let it happen."

My mama is eighty years old. She weighs sixty-nine pounds, is wizened, mostly skin and bones, but full still of energy and emotion. I didn't understand why she kept talking about Grandma Morgan that way. It seemed clear to me that Grandma was scared of Granddaddy, and I didn't like it that Mama was blaming her for what Granddaddy did.

"Grandma was scared of him, too, Mama. Granddaddy was mean to all of you," I said.

"Yeah, he was, but he treated me the worst. The way he treated me really was not the way a father should treat his daughter. It was almost unforgivable," she said. She folded her legs up into the chair and sat yoga style. She wore an over-sized sling on her left arm, which she had to keep re-adjusting. She didn't complain about the pain, though I know she hurt.

"I have forgiven him, but it took him getting so sick I knew he was dying, and seeing him helpless to make me forgive me. But it still comes back at times. I still wonder how he could have treated me that way. And how my mother could have let him."

I got up and went into the kitchen. It was time to prepare dinner for my mother and the others. I could have waited a little longer, but

I didn't want to hear any more about how it was Grandma's fault that Granddaddy hurt my mother. And the others. We had dinner and sat up talking up until after midnight; my mother drank coffee before bed like she always does and walked the floor all night while I slept. Debbie went home.

The next morning, I greeted my mother who was still in her bed. "How'd you sleep?"

"Not at all," she said. "I was in some pain, but it wasn't just that. I don't sleep at night, you know that."

"Well, I am sorry."

"How about you? You seemed to be asleep when I was up."

"Yeah, Mama, I slept well, but I did dream a lot. Nothing I can remember, and you know I like to record my dreams because I get guidance from them."

"Well, I must have slept some because I had a dream, too," Mama said. "Let me tell you about it and see if you can make some sense out of it because I can't." Mama had never told me her dreams before. I figured she was just trying to make conversation. She knew I valued dreams.

"I don't know what's going on inside of you well enough to really help, but I'll listen." I knew I was no dream analyst for others, but I was curious about her psyche and her soul's images. She talked. I listened.

"I saw Raeford, I think, but then I thought it wasn't Raeford, but someone else, another man who had a young girl less than two years old on his lap. Someone had gotten that baby pregnant! She sat there with her little round belly pooching out. I rubbed it and told her that it was a shame someone had done that to her, and if I ever found out who it was, I would burn his tail up! Now what do you think that means?" she asked me.

I was shocked. I knew what it meant to me. I heard her, and unconscious though she may have been of it herself, her rational mind boggled by the images, I knew I was hearing her confession. My question asked so long ago when I began this journey—*"How could a mother not know?"*—was answered. *This* was how a mother could *know* and *not* let her conscious mind know. I was amazed by the image of the pregnant two-year-old Sandra, for that it who the child was to me.

I was amazed that the man was Raeford and *not Raeford,* for my father, her first husband, looks like this last one. He is only 5' 2" tall like my daddy was, and he even has a walleye the way my daddy did. So, I knew I was the baby girl who was pregnant on, *not Raeford's lap,* but on my daddy's lap. I was pregnant with his abuse that my mother could not know, would not know, with her conscious mind because if she did, she would have to act: *She would have had to tear his tail up! And what would that have done to her?*

My daddy died before I was two years old, and since I have known that he abused me, I have wondered if he died because he, too, could not know what he had done and live. I mourned for him most of my life, believing my life would have been better if he had not died and if my family had not been pulverized.

Once I accepted that he abused me, I wondered if the cancer cells, which the body nurtures the way it nurtures embryonic cells, I wondered if those cancer cells received all the love, all the nurturing that should have come to me. And then I wondered, like I still do sometimes, if he were my father or if some other man were. I still hoped that someone else, someone other than the one who abused me, was my true father.

That hope no longer remained after my mother's confession. I turned to her and said calmly, "Mama, I don't know what your dream means, but I do know that a baby isn't able to nurture new life. So maybe some new part of you needs to be protected and nurtured and not required to do something it isn't ready to do yet."

"Well," she said, "I guess I am trying to move on with my life pretty fast. Getting married to Raeford after twenty years of living together brought me some peace and him some, too, I reckon." She had remained unmarried to him because she couldn't afford to lose the pension she received from the death of Edward, the husband who had suffered post-traumatic stress syndrome and had killed himself.

"Now we can be back in church," she continued, "and I have felt better than I have in a long time since we started going there. Just when I was about to spread my wings and go down to Florida and do some fishing, I fell. That trip's not going to happen."

I knew she feared riding in the big motor home she and Raeford owned. The last time she was in Florida was seven years earlier, and she had a stomach hemorrhage and then an operation that reduced her stomach and left her unable to gain weight. I knew she didn't want to go back, not really.

"You'll heal," I said. "The trip will happen when you're ready." I was still feeling the shock of her revelation, but I felt the need to nurture her, too. She seemed to settle.

"I think I'll nap a while," she said even though she had been awake for only an hour.

"Okay. I'm going for a walk."

I was out the door and down the lane when Debbie called a few minutes later. "Hey," I said.

"Hey, how are you?" she asked.

"Pretty good. I'm out walking."

"Wasn't that something last night when Mama was talking about her dad? I mean the words she chose were the words a person would use to talk about being sexually abused," Debbie said.

"Hm-m. I was so upset that she kept trying to blame Grandma and not Granddaddy for his misuse of her, I missed that she was characterizing it that way. But you're right. She asked how a father could treat his daughter 'that way,' as if it were different from the way he treated the others, including her sisters, and not just in degree.

"I knew that he made her take her pants off, and he beat her naked body when she was sixteen, but I didn't know she understood that was sexual abuse. I wonder what else he did to her.

"You know how we have wondered what happened when Granddaddy left the homestead and went to Florida to live with her? Grandma sure acted like Mama was more like the Redhead than like her own dutiful daughter. Still, I really didn't realize last night that she was categorizing his behavior as sexual abuse, but she was. She finally was."

"Yes, and it was as close as she has ever come to asking for forgiveness from us," Debbie said.

"You're right!" I knew Debbie was intuitive, but often I was the one doing the explaining. Her husband Paul had died two years earlier, and she had been in grief and recovery because of that loss and all the other losses she had suffered in her life. She had grown deeper in her understanding.

"You're right!" I said a second time. "She sat there, old and sick, the way he was old and sick when she forgave him for treating her 'that way' and told us that she had finally been able to forgive him. She was asking us to forgive her for treating us or letting us be treated 'that way'! Do you think it is possible that she knows what happened to me and knows that she endangered you when she had sex in the same motel room in which you were sleeping when you were in your teens?"

"I don't know if she knows it, so that she can say it, but she knows she needs forgiveness. And, Sandra, I have something else I want you to know. I've known it for a while, but I haven't been able to tell you. Paul knew. I told him before he died, several years before he died, and together we tried to make sense of it," she said.

She then told me a story of wounding, the details of which I will not divulge in these pages. It is her story, her life, not mine, and only of those places where her wounding intersects with my life, will I speak.

"Oh, my god, Debbie, I am so sorry!"

"It's okay," she said. "I have dealt with it—well, I mean I am dealing with it the way a person has to with a thing like that."

I remembered the Sunday before I married John when Debbie and I talked on the phone about Dolores's revelations to me about my father abusing her. I remembered Debbie's accusations, but I did not bring them up. I still had no memory of what had happened back then, except for the image of an angry girl-Sandra wagging her finger in her little sister's face and telling her not to tell. Tell what, I still didn't know.

"I am so sorry that you had to experience that," I said. "We were all so wounded, and we lived in a situation where the wounding seemed normal. How could we know differently until later in life? And knowing is just the beginning of healing."

"I know," she said. "I had forgotten about this for years, and then one day I remembered it. I was just walking along the beach, and I saw someone out of the corner of my eye, and I said to Paul that he reminded me of someone I hadn't seen in years. Then the rest came flooding back in. I'm glad I remembered while Paul was still alive. He was good about it. If I had remembered it after Paul died, I don't think I could have stood it," she said.

"It was good that you had him there to help. I wish I could have helped, but I've been so lost in my own wounding, I haven't had much to offer."

"Oh, you have always helped me. You've talked with me in ways that have helped me trust myself. You are good that way. And Paul was, in his own way, good that way, too. I know you never got to know him like that, but he was." Her voice cracked. It cracked a lot lately. She went back into her grief. "I'll talk with you later," she said. "I love you!"

"I love you, too," I said.

I walked down the lane and went back inside the house, grateful for all the New Year had already given me. I was sorry for Debbie. And then I had a moment of recognition that shocked me: For the first time in my quest to know what had happened to me, I was grateful that memory had failed me, and that instead, I had been guided by intuition and divine love and had been spared the undeniable, cruel, grisly, specific, human details that memory could have provided! My heart hurt for Debbie to whom memory had not been so kind, but I knew that she, too, would find her way.

Chapter 69

Why Don't You Just Get Over It?

I do. I have. I will. I may. Every single day.

For mine is a story about sexual abuse that is so ordinary that one in four young women will be abused before they are eighteen years old. Mine is a story about an ordinary wounding so profound that the fourth one who is abused, *who is me, who is my sister, who is my mother*, will feel the repercussions all her life. And for some of us, who were abused before consciousness had dawned fully enough to allow memory to record the act, the consequences will exist without a known cause and without proof, like the world demands, that the abuse ever occurred.

The repercussions of abuse vary from one woman to another in their particulars, but a destructive pattern emerges and ensnares and drives each abused one as it did me. For decades, I let the following pattern govern me:

- *I fell into my wounded consciousness.*
- *Though I thought myself a feminist, I acted as though I were fit only for service to a man.*
- *I projected all of my goodness onto another.*
- *I fell in love with the other.*
- *I mistook him for the god/goddess energies.*
- *Sex bound me to him for a season, so I did not recognize his abusing or using energies.*
- *I blamed myself for the problems I encountered in the relationship.*
- *To compensate and because I felt the pain so deeply, I went into a helping profession, thinking it was the pain of others I felt.*
- *The projection of my goodness onto the other started to slip.*
- *He was certainly no god.*
- *I began to feel his abuse or misuse of me—sometimes it was physical abuse, sometimes sexual, sometimes intellectual or emotional.*
- *I felt my own wound again, but I mistook its source.*

- *I always thought it was the particular partner I had chosen who had caused me the pain.*
- *I left. Him. Home. Jobs. Friends. Family.*
- *I repeated the cycle, leaving this man for that man and that one for still another. And none of them was the Goddess I was looking for, and surely, that is what I was doing even when I didn't know it. This was an imprint I picked up from my father's search for Her that ended in his abuse of me, and that caused me to seek Her in relationships, which abused me as he had.*
- *I would start a new life. I would discover it was the old life, maybe a little better in some ways, maybe a little worse. But it was the same pattern, and I would have to make life work all over again. New home. Sometimes an apartment. Sometimes a house. Sometimes a pauper. Sometimes a millionaire.*

After many repetitions of this pattern, finally, I brought it into the light. Then I let the wound itself preoccupy me, and I sought to find out and prove that I had been wounded. Those were stages I could not by-pass. I wonder if anyone can.

Still, the woman that I have become turns away from being consumed and goes inward, goes inward daily, because she knows that is where the Source is, where growth and safety lie, and where all that has been lost will be regained.

My healing has been life-long and my pattern of my healing is this:

Through dream guidance and psychotherapy, through visions, meditation, prayer, reflective reading, channeled guidance from Tamara and Mary Magdalene, Chi Gong, and through healing others, I attend to my holiness and remake my wholeness each day. When I abandon my daily rituals of healing, I become sick. I become ensnared in the dis-eased pattern again, and even my old second chakra bladder pain returns.

Though I long for it and may yet create it through my longing, so far for me, there has been no one moment of complete healing. Perhaps while I remain in the outer world that created my woundedness and more importantly, continues to wound me energetically through thought and deed with it patriarchal men's-locker-room consciousness, my healing must remain a continuous process, a continual "getting over it," full of falls and full of recoveries and full of openings to the Goddess within me, who it turns out, has traveled through the goddess-less years with me and endured the accumulated misogyny of the last four thousand years because I have, and you have, held her in our collective memories.

Now as she rises in me, as she comes because I call her name, and as she rises in others, she will come back to the world and heal it the way she heals me daily. Eventually, the pattern of energy, the matrix, will shift so that the wounding of the Goddess within each of us is no longer possible. And each day I "get over it," without denying or repressing the original wound, I am helping to call her forth.

In the meantime, without material proof, without recovering an ordinary human memory of the events I know happened, there will be those like my own mother, who will not be convinced that from the time I was born and left alone in the back of the service station in Greensboro until I was almost eighteen months old, my father, my personal father, abused me. He took advantage of my natural sucking instinct and committed *fellatio* with me, his infant daughter. Then, when I was nearing eighteen months old, he reached out for me and raped me anally. To those who doubt and to that part of myself that sometimes still doubts, I simply say that I cannot *prove* the abuse happened in this particular manner, but I *know* it happened, and these are the images my mind provides; this is the story my heart tells.

When my confidence in my knowledge fades, or when the memories of my divine confirming experiences seem far off, or when I have lost my way and do not feel connected to the divine, I fall again into that other mind, the demanding one. Then I simply take myself away from the world for a while, a few minutes, a day, or a few days.

I withdraw my energies from those of the abuser that, *in the guise of the rational mindset*, demands I give only one kind of proof, only the kind of proof accepted by the same mindset that allowed the abuse of my aunt, the abuse of me, the abuse of one in four women, in the first place. It is a sick mindset, and if I do not withdraw, I become sick in my mind, in my body, in my emotions, and in my spirit. I cannot afford to dally with these abusive energies—nor with people who do not believe my wounding happened.

I have stopped calling my brother Arthur. I don't care what he might have seen and understood when I was too young to see and understand in the world's way. He has had several decades to tell me what he might know, and at this point in my life, I don't need a human to tell me what happened. And I don't need a genetics test to confirm my knowing either. *My father—Daddy—*sexually abused me.

It doesn't matter that whoever he was, he may not have been my genetic father; for whoever he was, he held the place of father-love and father-trust in my life, and whoever he was, he violated it, and in violating that trust, he left me to violate myself and prepared me, like a coat cut for one wearer only, to feel the fit that was familiar, to feel that I had found my rightful partner, only when I was in the use of abusers or of unconscious "good men" who accepted, as if it were their right, my offer to put myself in their service and abandon my own talents and soul path. So, I do not care who he was—Bishop or Pope or some other. He was *Daddy*. He was *Father*.

In a culture in which the image of God is exclusively male, my father was my first experience of *God the Father*. No wonder then, that for me, God the Father and God the Son moved so far beyond the field of love that preachers in the pulpit said they inhabited, that for years, I could not feel love or approach the divine through them. Now the same world, the same collective consciousness that cut me off from God and wounded me almost unto death, and certainly unto self destruction for five decades, asks me for proof that will please it.

With Christ I say, such proof does not interest me, for I have learned to render unto Caesar what is Caesar's and unto God, what is God's. I have been allowed to venture into other dimensions, into those whole places where all that has ever happened is recorded vibrationally in the body's aura, in the body's electro-magnetic field. The light our bodies gives off remains and is visible to the inner eye, in the same way that the light of stars travels and allows us to see the stars, not as they are in present time, but as they were in the past.

The light energy that is woven together to make a human being retains the imprint of every moment, every experience, and every thought. Through human intervention, nothing can be removed and nothing added to this energy record. Sometimes in our quests to understand our lives, we get a glimpse of All That Is, and missing events can be seen by the inner eye in the same way amputated limbs can be felt long after they are physically removed.

Beyond these spiritual mysteries, this, too, I know: I am a *sensitive* by nature and by practice, and this means that I feel the collective energies and consciousness as well as personal experiences and events. In defense of my personal father, I have said that he acted out of the unconscious collective beliefs that gave him permission to do as he did.

He was a *man*, caught up in the archetype of the patriarchal god that had, in the minds and hearts of men, divorced itself from the divine feminine. Such a separation causes excruciating pain and longing and leads to the most heinous treatment of the personal female as the personal male *tries to take by force what it has lost through this divorce.* This does not excuse my personal father; rather, it exposes the shadow side of the patriarchal structure that empowered him.

This, too, I know: Within this archetypal drama, I put my Self into the service of the masculine because I had been groomed to do so, and that is the chief debilitating consequence of all sexual abuse. I feared the masculine and sought to appease it by serving it; and in this servitude, I have learned the dark ways of the one who would be master, the dark truth that the patriarchy tries to hide because this truth will galvanize huge resistance:

Growing up without knowing the Goddess causes the same dysfunctional pattern in the vibrational bodies of all women that being raped by the personal father caused in me.

As I separate my Self from servitude to the patriarchy, bit-by-bit and day-by-day, I risk exile, the new inquisition, the unraveling of my personal life. I am the proverbial messenger, risking death. Because growing up without knowing the Goddess caused me to be exiled from my true self, I risk all as I realign with the energies of the Divine Feminine and call her forth. She will heal human hearts and harmonize with the Divine Masculine to bring forth personal and collective wholeness.

Chapter 70

Epilogue: She Was Always Present

This writing has caught up with my life and gradually brought the light back.

It is the light of the Goddess, and it is She, in her myriad aspects, who has brought it back. She teaches my heart how, wounded and shut out in her dark phase and seemingly absent like the dark moon, she built my strength secretly by putting me in community with other women who had lessons to pass on to me. I absorbed what I could of those lessons as I lived in the dark with these women who—most often unconsciously, and however wrong-headedly, and in all kinds of degraded guises—passed on a spark of the Divine Feminine and kept one more girl child from growing up without the Goddess, after all.

I know now that I was never alone. *She* was always there, smoothing the way and trying to get my attention. So I offer my deep gratitude to all the manifestations of the Goddess thus far in my life, for it is their sparks which joined my own meager questing spark and brought me to Her, whom I call by the name of Tamara and by the name of her mother, The Mary Magdalene. In the following Women, in particular, the Goddess spark was present and finally ignited my own divinity, so that I have come to honor my Self. Because of them I feel the *Wouivre* flow through me, too.

• Through my daughter Ana and my daughter Dani, I have experienced the Goddess in her undegraded, purest form as the Goddess of Mercy and of Love, who saved me from the darkness spinning out of control in my soul. Dani and Ana present me daily with unconditional love and the opportunity to experience giving unconditional love. Through them, I have been privileged to witness the inevitable unfolding of the sweet, strong, innocent, and magnificent feminine, the *Goddess*, that inhabits the souls of these girls as She may when young girls are protected and guided. As Ana grew into her own individual Soul Beauty, and as Dani grew into her individual Soul Beauty, each called me back to my own soul, even knowing and reminding me of the *Mother*. They called out to Her presence in me and caused me to turn inward toward the Source, the pure love that they saw shine through the darkness of me, even when they were two years old, and I was so certain I was lost forever.

• From my mother, my human mother, I received the gift of wanderlust, an earthly expression of the Soul's passionate journey. Then Soul taught me to find the beautiful places of opening in Mother Nature and to return to those openings to seek the Divine Feminine. Also, from my mother, whose wounding led to voluntary and involuntary desertions and to my wounding and taught me all I needed to know of absence, I received the Goddess's gift of forgiveness and generational healing.

From my mother, who suffers in her body and her mind, I receive daily training in developing a compassionate heart.

• From Mrs. I. Smith, my first grade teacher, I received a glimpse of the Goddess of meditation and creation.

Mrs. I. Smith unchained and sacralized the dance of life in me, and she let Color come through me to express and create the ways of the material world. She allowed my mind to rest in color until it could gather itself to enter again the life of loss and suffering that others had created for me and where I would remain until I had the power to materialize my visions in the world.

• From my Grandmother Blair, whose sexuality, which she mistook for her power in the world, was eventually stripped away by drugs prescribed for schizophrenia, I received the Thirteenth Fairy Godmother/Goddess initiation.

Grandmother Blair dressed me early in the colors of the Pow-Wow, mistaken by the world for the colors of the harlot. She could not keep me safe as she took me forth into the world where men's eyes and rough voices touch and probe as surely as hungry hands do. In both its negative and its positive aspect, the Thirteenth Fairy Godmother holds empowerment, but in the wasteland of the patriarchy, this blessing of empowerment—also called the Poison Apple or the cruelty of the Stepmother who enforces the Time of the Cinders—must be taught in the dark corners, in the Other World away from the eyes of men.

Grandmother Blair forgot that the presence of power in women cannot be fully revealed or lived until, secretly, it has grown beyond the power of the patriarchy to do anything other than become receptive to it. For Grandmother Blair, the break between this world and the other one, where such things are known and taught, the space between the worlds, was no longer a passageway. It became a one-way street, a pit of darkness out of which she could not crawl, a room with bars on the windows and locks on the door at Butler Sanitarium.

She did what any Goddess would do. She stripped naked and left herself exposed in the doorway, not for the son who did see, but for me, the Grand daughter to see. This Dark Crone Goddess taught me fast that the world chained women like her and *like me* who wore the misunderstood garments of sacred dancers, of the Pow-Wow, and tried to walk in the light of day, without men in the world of men.

While she screamed and raged and found her nakedness thrust back inside that room with its barred door that shut out the light, she taught me how very powerful I was, that men would seek to chain me so, and she taught me to hide myself away and be silent until I could sneak past such henchmen. Here, certainly, was Ereshigal, and I was called to play Inanna and let my compassion for Grandmother Blair bring some new life into the world.

• From my Grandmother Morgan, the Troll, who guarded the bridges to the portals of Nature, and in doing so, marked them well for me, calling my attention to places I might not have entered— from her, I found my Mother the Earth.

Motherless no longer, I wandered alone among Gaia's many glories and felt her love and healing flow through me and felt the solitary sudden surprise of creation as it moved through me and brought into being that violet-strewn hillside that lifted me up to the sky, where I was no longer quarantined by fear of what violent men could, and would do, *and already had done* to me. I still return to Gaia for healing.

• From Grandmother Pope, who stooped by years of bearing babies and by work too hard for her small frame, still labored in the fields all day, cooked the meals, planted and cultivated the garden, and belled the cows home daily, I learned in the coming and the going, about indifference and about endurance. She lost her health, she used up her looks, she lost her teeth, she lost her uterus, she lost her husband, and before she lost her life, she showed me the Goddess reduced to powerlessness and still bound by devotion to the masculine.

She could do only what Granddaddy Pope required, for she was completely devoted to him. She died from stomach cancer we were told, but I know she was consumed by night grief that sought Granddaddy's Pope's big broad warm back, and never finding it after he died, save one time in dream so strong that it broke her heart to wake up to the world, she died and revealed that aspect of the Goddess that loves so hard it cannot live without its beloved.

The Goddess blessed me with the desire to be so loved and to love so well, and in seeking to find such love I, too, like Grandmother Pope went to the wrong source until slowly, through extreme sickness, I heard the Goddess calling, belling me home like Grandma did the cows, for there is no other source, save *Her*, from which to receive such love.

• From Aunt Dolores's troubled heart and mind and from her wounded body and spirit, I learned the lesson of ensnarement and disentanglement, for she was surely Arachne and Ariadne. Unconscious in those guises of the goddess, Dolores unknowingly prepared the way for me to understand the chakras and the energy bodies. For it was the invisible lines of energy that I perceived, with which she bound me, and out of which I had to find my way.

And again, unconscious in her prophetess aspect, in her Sybil aspect, when Dolores dreamed dreams and had visions and read "found" Bible verses for guidance from them, she drew me into the Goddess's realm of intuition. Dolores's divinations were meant to bind me to her worldview, and for a while they did. But divine guidance helps free me from all worldviews. Such is the power of the goddess even when she is suppressed, repressed, depressed, fragmented, or mutilated. Dolores's very dismemberment caused me eventually to constellate around my own center.

In this way and others, Dolores held and passed on the Goddess's Gift of Healing, which she practiced in the form of healing burns. In as natural a way as others put Band-Aids on small cuts, she placed her hands over burns of all sizes on my hands and arms, and on the bodies of those in our household. When she had stopped praying, the pain was gone, there was no blistering, and we were healed.

Even as she abused me emotionally, Dolores's Goddess aspect confirmed for me that I was a Healer, too, for when she turned to me, not knowing, but when she turned to me and took me into her home, it was to heal herself, to make herself conscious of what had been done to her, by living with someone who would always remind her of the presence of the abuser and onto whom she could project her hatred of him. Again and again, she did this until years later, months after my departure, years after the abuser himself had died, she sought emotional and psychological counseling. She saw. She called to ask for forgiveness.

Dolores also gave me the gift of disguise when she covered me with yards of fabric and tried to make a Goose Girl out of me. Lost in her own darkness, when she created darkness for me, she also activated my gift of discernment upon which I had to rely when she encouraged the Temple Dancer to emerge concurrently with the Goose Girl (and quickly marry!).

• My sister Debbie, my mother's blue-eyed beauty spot, gave me the gift of expectation, helping me through my envy of the Mother-love I imagined she received, to identify what it was I longed for, and to turn my envy into expectation, which guided me first to the personal mother for love and then to the Goddess. Later when Debbie's heart broke when her husband Paul died, I was given the gift of discernment to guide me as I learned to let go, get out of the way, and let the Goddess guide her.

• Nancy Drew, the worldly detective, guided me hunch-by-hunch into a secret realm where wise ones could re-establish the rightful heritage of cast-out Cinderella-type daughters like me. The Goddess in Nancy Drew's guise quietly tutored my intuition and prepared me for the Goddess of Literature to school me further.

• My spiritual mother, my other sister, my true friend, and my faithful guide, Joan, in her own expanded Goddess-self has radiated a vast field of love and acceptance for twenty-five years that has allowed me to awaken and experience my own expanded self and to realize that I, too, am a part of the divine; that I, too, am love; that I, too, am the Goddess.

Joan has guided me into the Otherworld of symbols and archetypes and to the portals of dream and vision and to the Holy Imagination. She has encouraged me to create my own openings, to bring my own gifts into the world, to love my wounded body, to respect its wisdom and to follow its guidance, for it, too, like Gaia, is the Goddess. Joan's presence has allowed me to experience the Mary Magdalene and participate as the Divine Feminine is re-born through earthly experience.

•And to Chartres cathedral and those who created her, I offer my gratitude, for she, too, has shown me the way to the Goddess. Within her walls, I felt the presence of the divine and recognized it as divine, as sweet, for the first time in my life.

Below her floors, I later learned that the *Wouivre* flows. The cathedral is a resonating chamber for Gaia's love that allowed it to attune me to the Divine Feminine within. I thank Chartes, which was designed intentionally to open our chakras, to sacralize the labyrinth of our lives, and to open the rose windows of our hearts as we journey into conscious connection with the Divine Feminine, and our bodies become her holy temples.

About the Author

Sandra Pope lives in Southeastern North Carolina where she writes and where she practices and teaches Healing Through Touch and Aromatherapy. Certified as a Healing Touch Practitioner, she works with groups and sees private clients in her healing studio. She is also available for distance healing as well as consultations on aromatherapy.

She can be contacted through her book website at www. GrowingUpWithoutTheGoddess.com or through her aromatherapy website at www.youngliving.org/sandrapope or through her social network, set up to assist survivors of abuse at http://www. thrivingnotjustsurviving.ning.com.

Resources

Here are some books that have helped me on my healing path.

The Mary Magdalene Within
Joan Norton.
www.themarymagdalenewithin.com
blog.marymagdalenewithin.com.

The Woman with the Alabaster Jar; Mary Magdalene, Bride in Exile;
Magdalene's Lost Legacy; The Goddess in the Gospels; and Tarot
Trumps and the Holy Grail
Margaret Starbird.
www.margaretstarbird.net

The Secret Teachings of Mary Magdalene
Claire Nahmad & Margaret Bailey.

Sacred Places of Goddess: 108 Destinations
Karen Tate.

The Sacred Embrace of Jesus and Mary; The Gospel of Mary
Magdalene
Jean-Yves LeLoup.

Montsegur and the Mystery of the Cathars; Cathedral of the Black
Madonna
Jean Markale.

The Holy Land of Scotland
Barry Dunford.
www.sacredconnection.ndo.co.uk

The Mysteries of Chartres Cathedral
Louis Charpentier.

Gaia's Sacred Chakras
Margaret Bertulli.

You Can Heal Your Life
Louise L. Hay.

Finding Angela Shelton
Angela Shelton.
www.findingangelashelton.com

Joy's Way
W. Brugh Joy, M.D.

Vibrational Medicine
Richard Gerber, M.D.

Mandala
Judith Cornell, Ph.D.

Hands of Light
Barbara Ann Brennan.

Wheels of Light
Rosalyn L. Bruyere.

Mudras: Yoga in Your Hands
Gertrud Hirschi.

Ogam: The Celtic Oracle of the Trees
Paul Rhys Mountfort.

Aromatherapy for Healing the Spirit
Gabriel Mojay.

Healing Oils of the Bible
David Steward, Ph.D.

Here are my favorite websites and groups:

http://groups.yahoo.com/group/goddesschristians/

http://groups.yahoo.com/group/magdalene-list/

www.blog.marymagdalenewithin.com

http://www.northernway.org/weblog/

www.moondance.org.

www.findingangelashelton.com

www.nortonacupuncture.com/

www.themarymagdalenewithin.com
blog.marymagdalenewithin.com.

www.margaretstarbird.net

www.liciaberry.com

2524751